AAUSC 2017 Volume—Issues in Language Program Direction

Engaging the World: Social Pedagogies and Language Learning

Sébastien Dubreil, Carnegie Mellon University

Steven L. Thorne, Portland State University—Rijksuniversiteit Groningen

Editors

Staccy Katz Bourns, Northeastern University

Series Editor

CENGAGE

Australia • Brazil • Mexico • Singapore • United Kingdom • United States

CENGAGE

AAUSC 2017 Volume - Issues in Language Program Direction: Social Pedagogies and Entwining Language with the World
Sébastien Dubreil, Steven L. Thorne, Stacey Katz Bourns

Sr. Product Team Manager: Heather Bradley Cole

Product Assistant: Catherine Bradley

Marketing Manager: Sean Ketchem

Production Management and Composition: Lumina Datamatics Inc.

Manufacturing Planner: Betsy Donaghey

© 2019, 2018 Cengage Learning, Inc.

Unless otherwise noted, all content is © Cengage

ALL RIGHTS RESERVED. No part of this work covered by the copyright herein may be reproduced or distributed in any form or by any means, except as permitted by U.S. copyright law, without the prior written permission of the copyright owner.

> For product information and technology assistance, contact us at **Cengage Customer & Sales Support, 1-800-354-9706.**
>
> For permission to use material from this text or product, submit all requests online at **www.cengage.com/permissions.**
> Further permissions questions can be emailed to **permissionrequest@cengage.com.**

Library of Congress Control Number: 2017954595

Student Edition:
ISBN: 978-1-337-55449-7

Cengage
20 Channel Center Street
Boston, MA 02210
USA

Cengage is a leading provider of customized learning solutions with employees residing in nearly 40 different countries and sales in more than 125 countries around the world. Find your local representative at **www.cengage.com.**

Cengage products are represented in Canada by Nelson Education, Ltd.

To learn more about Cengage platforms and services, visit **www.cengage.com.**

Purchase any of our products at your local college store or at our preferred online store **www.cengagebrain.com.**

Printed in the United States of America
Print Number: 01   Print Year: 2017

Contents

Acknowledgments — vii

AAUSC Editorial Board 2017 — ix

Annual Volumes of Issues in Language Program Direction — xi

Abstracts — xiii

Sébastien Dubreil (Carnegie Mellon University) & Steven L. Thorne (Portland State University and University of Groningen)	**Introduction** Social Pedagogies and Entwining Language with the World	1

PART 1: The Learner in the Environment: Inhabiting the City, Community Engagement, and Service Learning

Stéphane Charitos (Columbia University) & Nelleke Van Deusen-Scholl (Yale University)	**Chapter 1** Engaging the City: Language, Space, and Identity in Urban Environments	15
Alberto Bruzos (Princeton University)	**Chapter 2** *Encuentros con el Español*: A Case Study of Critical Service Learning in the Latino Community	37
Diana Ruggiero (University of Memphis)	**Chapter 3** Lessons from the CruCES Project: Community Service Learning and Intercultural Sensitivity in the Foreign Language Classroom	64
Vivan Brates, Citlalli Del Carpio, Alica A. Miano, Paitra Houts (Stanford Unviersity), Irene Carvajal (San Jose State University), & Misla Barco (East Palo Alto Academy)	**Chapter 4** *Abriendo Caminos*: Breaking New Ground in Community-Engaged Language Learning	87

PART 2: Literacy, Symbolic Representations, and the Learner as Social Actor

Stéphanie Pellet (Wake Forest University) & Lindsy Myers (University of Missouri-Kansas City)

Chapter 5
Social-Pedagogical Life Imitates Art: Scaffolding the Voices of L2 Fans and Critics   111

Kristen Michelson (Texas Tech University) & Elyse Petit (Vanderbilt University)

Chapter 6
Becoming Social Actors: Designing a Global Simulation for Situated Language and Culture Learning   138

Jessica Greenfield (Oberlin College), Vivian M. Finch & Stacey Margarita Johnson (Vanderbilt University)

Chapter 7
Networked Learning: Students as Producers, Curators, and Consumers of Authentic Resources on Campus and Abroad   168

Chantelle Warner (University of Arizona) & Diane F. Richardson (U.S. Military Academy)

Chapter 8
Beyond Participation: Symbolic Struggles with(in) Digital Social Media in the L2 Classroom   199

Cori Crane (Duke University), Matthias Fingerhuth (University of Vienna), David Huenlich (Institute für Deutsche Sprache)

Chapter 9
"What Makes This So Complicated?" On the Value of Disorienting Dilemmas in Language Instruction   227

PART 3: Social Pedagogical Interventions: A View from the Terrain

Isabelle Drewelow (University of Alabama)

Chapter 10
A Socio-Constructivist Approach to Developing Intercultural Empathy   255

Vincent L. VanderHeijden (University of Texas at Austin)

Chapter 11
Of Cookies and Saints: Deconstructing L2 Learners' Myths of the Target Culture   266

Lara Ducate & Lara Lomicka (University of South Carolina)

Chapter 12
Engaging Students in Intentional Cultural Learning during Study Abroad   276

Jeanne M. Johnson (El Dorado Middle School)

Chapter 13
L'Incubateur: Increasing Student Engagement through Global Simulation and Gaming Pedagogy in the L2 Classroom   294

Editors   306

Contributors   306

Acknowledgments

The 2017 volume of the annual AAUSC Issues in Language Program Direction series is the outcome of generous contributions from many individuals. We would first like to express our sincere appreciation to members of the AAUSC Editorial Board who provided us with incisive commentary, suggestions, and feedback during the planning stages of this volume. We are particularly indebted to Series Editor Stacey Katz Bourns for her generous assistance (and temporal encouragements) throughout the process.

We are grateful for the expertise and efforts of our referees and wish to thank the following individuals for acting as referees and manuscript readers. All quality publications depend on colleagues' willingness to help in this way, and we very much appreciate your careful reviews: Heather Willis Allen, Nike Arnold, Carl Blyth, Paula Garrett-Rucks, Millie Gimmel, Erin Kearney, Glenn Levine, Reyes Llopis-Garcia, Gillian Lord, David Malinowski, Hiram Maxim, Nicole Mills, Ana Oskoz, Kate Paesani, Jonathon Reinhardt, Andrew Ross, Colleen Ryan-Scheutz, Julie Sykes, Therese Tardio, and Anne Whiteside.

The volume contributors, of course, deserve special thanks for their willingness to engage in and explore a wide array of social pedagogies in diverse in- and out-of-class contexts.

Finally, we wish to acknowledge department chairs and heads, administrators, and language program directors who recognize and value experimental pedagogies that seek to enhance engagement with the broader world beyond university classroom settings. We hope that the social pedagogies reported in this volume will not only amplify conditions for language learning, but that they will also highlight the capacity of world language education to foster empathy and intercultural understanding at a time when such abilities are greatly needed.

Sébastien Dubreil and *Steven L. Thorne*
Editors

AAUSC Editorial Board 2017

Stacey Katz Bourns, Series Editor	Northeastern University
Heather Willis Allen	University of Wisconsin
Catherine Barrette	Wayne State University
Carl S. Blyth	University of Texas
Cori Crane	Duke University
Robert Davis	University of Oregon
Jane Hacking	University of Utah
Charles J. James	University of Wisconsin
Carol A. Klee	University of Minnesota
Beatriz Lado	Lehman College, CUNY
Glenn Levine	University of California, Irvine
Judith E. Liskin-Gasparro	University of Iowa
Lara Lomicka Anderson	University of South Carolina
Hiram H. Maxim	Emory University
Nicole Mills	Harvard University
Kate Paesani	University of Minnesota
Lisa Parkes	Harvard University
Fernando Rubio	University of Utah
Colleen Ryan	Indiana University
Joshua Thoms	Utah State University
Per Urlaub	Middlebury College
Johanna Watzinger-Tharp	University of Utah

Annual Volumes of *Issues in Language Program Direction*

2016   *The Interconnected Language Curriculum: Critical Transitions and Interfaces in Articulated K-16 Contexts*
Editors: Per Urlaub and Johanna Watzinger-Tharp

2015   *Integrating the Arts: Creative Thinking about Foreign Language Curricula and Language Program Direction.*
Editors: Lisa Parkes and Colleen M. Ryan

2014   *Innovation and Accountability in Language Program Evaluation*
Editors: Nicole Mills and John Norris

2013   *Individual Differences, L2 Development, and Language Program Administration: From Theory to Application*
Editors: Cristina Sanz and Beatriz Lado

2012   *Hybrid Language Teaching and Learning: Exploring Theoretical, Pedagogical and Curricular Issues*
Editors: Fernando Rubio and Joshua J. Thoms

2011   *Educating the Future Foreign Language Professorate for the 21st Century*
Editors: Heather Willis Allen and Hiram Maxim

2010   *Critical and Intercultural Theory and Language Pedagogy*
Editors: Glenn S. Levine and Alison Phipps

2009   *Principles and Practices of the Standards in College Foreign Language Education*
Editor: Virginia M. Scott

2008   *Conceptions of L2 Grammar: Theoretical Approaches and Their Application in the L2 Classroom*
Editors: Stacey Katz and Johanna Watzinger-Tharp

2007   *From Thought to Action: Exploring Beliefs and Outcomes in the Foreign Language Program*
Editor: H. Jay Siskin

2006   *Insights from Study Abroad for Language Programs*
Editor: Sharon Wilkinson

2005   *Internet-mediated Intercultural Foreign Language Education*
Editors: Julie A. Belz and Steven L. Thorne

2004 *Language Program Articulation: Developing a Theoretical Foundation*
Editors: Catherine Barrette and Kate Paesani

2003 *Advanced Foreign-Language Learning: A Challenge to College Programs*
Editors: Heidi Byrnes and Hiram Maxim

2002 *The Sociolinguistics of Foreign Language Classrooms: Contributions of the Native, the Near-native and the Non-native Speaker*
Editor: Carl S. Blyth

2001 *SLA and the Literature Classroom: Fostering Dialogues*
Editors: Virginia M. Scott and Holly Tucker

2000 *Mentoring Foreign Language Teaching Assistants, Lecturers, and Adjunct Faculty*
Editor: Benjamin Rifkin

1999 *Form and Meaning: Multiple Perspectives*
Editors: James F. Lee and Albert Valdman

1998 *Research Issues and Language Program Direction*
Edited by Kathy Heilenman

1997 *New Ways of Learning and Teaching: Focus on Technology and Foreign Language Education*
Editor: Judith Muyskens

1996 *Patterns and Policies: The Changing Demographics of Foreign Language Instruction*
Editor: Judith E. Liskin-Gasparro

1995 *Redefining the Boundaries of Language Study*
Editor: Claire Kramsch

1994 *Faces in a Crowd: The Individual Learner in Multisection Courses*
Editor: Carol Klee

1993 *The Dynamics of Language Program Direction*
Editor: David P. Benseler

1992 *Development and Supervision of Teaching Assistants in Foreign Languages*
Editor: Joel C. Walz

1991 *Assessing Foreign Language Proficiency of Undergraduates*
Editor: Richard V. Teschner

1990 *Challenges in the 1990s for College Foreign Language Programs*
Editor: Sally Sieloff Magnan

Abstracts

Part 1—The learner in the environment: Inhabiting the city, community engagement, and service learning

STÉPHANE CHARITOS AND NELLEKE VANDEUSEN-SCHOLL

Engaging the City: Language, Space, and Identity in Urban Environments

Cities bring together a great diversity of people and cultures and constitute the backdrop for many of the sociocultural processes shaping the new century. Yet urban spaces are not just the product of urban design and architectural concepts. They are also constructed, appropriated, and given meaning through the social and linguistic interactions of the people who inhabit them, in other words, at the confluence between language and space. The languages of the city are in a dynamic relationship with the urban spaces where they occur. In this chapter, we discuss current developments in language pedagogy and connect them with the recent literature on social pedagogies and spatial analysis. We first explore their potential to serve as a bridge between formal language classroom instruction and motivated, purposeful engagement with language usage beyond the classroom and then reflect on how place-based curricular offerings can help language programs connect with the other disciplines that also study and engage with the city. We end by highlighting opportunities for building communities of practice within and outside the classroom and offering suggestions for incorporating principles, tools, and techniques to help L2 learners connect with the evolving nature of the modern multilingual and multicultural global city.

ALBERTO BRUZOS

Encuentros con el Español: A Case Study of Critical Service Learning in the Latino Community

This chapter presents a pedagogical model that combines service learning with course materials on Spanish language in the United States to promote critical reflection on the social and political dimension of Spanish. In order to situate this model within larger debates, I examine the points of connection between social pedagogies and approaches to second language education that bring the social dimension of language to the foreground, blending language learning with the development of an understanding of the cultural, social, political, and ideological aspects of language; I also consider the intersection between critical approaches to second language education and service learning. I describe the course curriculum, organized around five thematic units that examined different aspects of Spanish language in the United States, and outline pedagogical tools and practices, including a sample lesson on the immigrant condition. Finally, I use qualitative data gathered through weekly service-learning journals to consider the impact of the course on the students' understanding of Spanish language and their own identities as learners.

Diana Ruggiero

Lessons from the CruCES Project: Community Service Learning and Intercultural Sensitivity in the Foreign Language classroom

The 2007 Modern Language Association (MLA) report called for a transformation in the governance, curricula, and aims of modern language programs. Specifically, it urged language educators and program directors to shift their curricular emphasis away from divisive disciplinary agendas to the shared goals of translingual and transcultural competence. The emergence of new course offerings, particularly in the area of community service learning (CSL), reflects these concerns. Yet while much of the language scholarship on translingual and transcultural competence focuses on the acquisition of linguistic skills, cultural knowledge, and critical thinking skills, less attention has been given to the development of cognitive orientations critical to the acquisition of intercultural competence. Drawing on developmental and process models of intercultural sensitivity, this chapter contributes to the existing literature in illuminating the role and value of CSL in developing attitudes and mindsets conducive to the acquisition and development of intercultural competence. This chapter presents the findings of a study of intercultural sensitivity development (ISD) in the context of a CSL project titled Creating Communities, Engaged Scholarship (CruCES). The study sought to assess how and to what extent service learning helps to foster the development of intercultural sensitivity among students in language courses. Implications for Language Program Directors (LPDs) to deploy this model on a programmatic scale are presented.

Vivan Brates, Citlalli Del Carpio, Alica A. Miano, Paitra Houts, Irene Carvajal, and Misla Barco

***Abriendo Caminos:* Breaking New Ground in Community-Engaged Language Learning**

This qualitative study of a critically conscious (Freire, 1970/1993) community-engaged learning (CEL) track in a second-year university Spanish program examines (1) students' evolving identities as speaker/actors (Kern & Liddicoat, 2008) of and in a language, (2) their increased appreciation of the cultural wealth (Yosso, 2005) evident in Spanish-speaking communities, and (3) students' enhanced abilities to reflect upon these phenomena and develop perceptions about various societal systems at play (Plann, 2002). The study describes three quarter-length courses, each engaged with a different Spanish-speaking community partner: an art class at a nearby Boys & Girls Club, a Spanish for heritage speakers class at a local high school, and a class of elderly adults studying for their U.S. citizenship test at a local institute. Through a line-by-line analysis of students' written texts, this chapter bears out Bettencourt's (2015) contention that a CEL approach combined with world language study expands student learning in nontraditional ways. In this study, students developed their identities linguistically, culturally, socially, and civically, gaining new solidarities with communities and community members. Gains were not unidirectional and also included setbacks such as persistent misperceptions and stereotypes, which, though sometimes discouraging, also provided opportunities for class discussion and ongoing course improvements.

Part 2—Literacy, symbolic representations, and the learner as social actor

STÉPHANIE PELLET AND LINDSY MYERS

Social-Pedagogical Life Imitates Art: Scaffolding the Voices of L2 Fans and Critics

This chapter describes a modular intermediate French course (Pellet & Myers, 2016) anchored by a constructivist approach to social L2 reading and writing. Connected by digital technologies fostering a community of shared readership, students encounter a metaphor of fan interaction and engagement in the contemporary French short story, *"Odette Toulemonde"* (Schmitt, 2006). The course incorporates multiple levels of readership and authorship by playing out the social themes of the narrative. This model redefines traditional roles by embracing continuums rather than dichotomies such as reader-writer, fiction-reality, classroom and real-world interaction. Such authentic transcultural encounters turn students into digital-footprint-making producers (Sharpe, Beetham, & de Freitas, 2010) rather than mere consumers. More specifically, social pedagogies transform potentially isolated readers and language learners into authors, fans, and critics in an extramural classroom through communal reading and textually inspired, real-life activities. Subsequently, this model dovetails current language program transformations favoring integrative curriculum design focused on cultural inquiry (MLA, 2007) that is socially inclusive, adaptive, encourages knowledge co-construction, and promotes process over product.

KRISTEN MICHELSON AND ELYSE PETIT

Becoming Social Actors: Designing a Global Simulation for Situated Language and Culture Learning

Recent developments in multiliteracies scholarship and pedagogies have highlighted the situated nature of language use and the diversity of ways that meanings are expressed, calling attention to creative, agentive processes of designing meanings using linguistic and semiotic resources for particular communication purposes within discourse communities. One way in which foreign language teaching can engage students in second language/culture discourse communities and social worlds is through a Global Simulation (GS) pedagogy. A GS consists in the creation of a fictitious, socioculturally realistic lifeworld where learners take on specific roles and interact within a particular community as they work collaboratively to advance a storyline or complete a project. By adopting a character, students become social actors who engage with cultural practices as they appropriate language and other symbolic resources in order to communicate particular meanings across different discourse contexts. We present a GS curriculum developed in fourth-semester French based on the *Immeuble* model (Debyser, 1980) and carried out through a Pedagogy of Multiliteracies (New London Group, 1996). We describe the overarching organization of curricular content, including tasks designed for students' interpretive and productive engagement with texts. We present one module—immigration—and students' textual responses and reflections on this module. Finally, we discuss the experience of designing a GS curriculum and include considerations for the development of simulations.

Jessica Greenfield, Vivian M. Finch, and Stacey Margarita Johnson

Networked Learning: Students as Producers, Curators, and Consumers of Authentic Resources on Campus and Abroad

This chapter examines the impact of a study abroad course design in which students are part of a network of learners who act as producers, curators, and consumers of authentic resources through an asynchronous collection, distribution, and usage cycle. This student-driven approach allows students from different semesters and locations to collaborate in the production of, augmentation of, and engagement with authentic resources. The chapter begins with a proposal for a pedagogical model for networked learning in study abroad courses based on recent disciplinary literature and outlines potential ways to involve on-campus students in the curation and use of the authentic resources. We present findings of one cohort of students on a short-term study abroad trip in Sicily to answer the questions: (1) What kinds of assignments will prove most beneficial to study abroad students while also providing useful resources for subsequent on-campus students? (2) How can this model be made more feasible, and therefore more sustainable, for instructors and students? The authors present conclusions about the viability of the model and suggestions for next steps.

Chantelle Warner and Diane F. Richardson

Beyond Participation: Symbolic Struggles with(in) Digital Social Media in the L2 Classroom

Integrating digital social media in foreign language curricula expands the space of the relatively stable world of the classroom to include more dynamic and complex social worlds. One of the struggles for scholars and practitioners of instructed foreign language environments is how to merge this complexity with the classroom, which is saturated with its own frames of reference and typical ways of communicating. This chapter looks at two instructional units implementing digital communications in a fifth-semester, intensive German course with a curriculum inspired by multiliteracies and genre-based curricular models (e.g., Byrnes & Sprang, 2004; Maxim, 2008). In both cases, sociable digital media—digital games and online discussion forums—were perceived by the instructors and the LPD as an opportunity to overcome the two-dimensionality of text-centric pedagogies (see Lotherington & Ronda, 2014). The focus of the analysis is two case studies—one student from each unit—one positioned as a "struggling" student and the other positioned as a "good" student at the start of the engagement with digital media. Through an analysis of the symbolic struggles that students face as they positioned themselves within the layered social spaces afforded by the integration of digital media into other classroom practices, the authors make a case that digital social pedagogies can enable students to imagine alternative positions for themselves beyond the typical participation frameworks of the classroom—even when their actions do not necessarily resemble the learning trajectories envisioned by LPDs.

CORI CRANE, MATTHIAS FINGERHUTH, AND DAVID HUENLICH

"What Makes This So Complicated": On the Value of Disorienting Dilemmas in Language Instruction

This contribution considers how challenging moments arising in social pedagogies can serve as powerful learning opportunities for learners and teachers. Drawing on transformative learning theory (Johnson, 2015; Mezirow, 1994, 1997), which sees "disorienting dilemmas" as catalysts for reflection and changes in viewpoint, the study chronicles the experiences of four participants (coordinator, pedagogical designer, teacher, and student) involved in a "Reacting to the Past" game (Carnes, 2014) on German–Comanche relationships in 1847 Texas, a game that was planned for—but ultimately not carried out in—a collegiate intermediate German course. Although the game was successfully played in previous semesters, in fall 2015, a formal complaint was issued shortly before it was to be performed in class. The game was cancelled; in its place teachers discussed the content material with students and problematized the activity itself. This chapter describes how the four participant groups responded to this crisis moment and discussed the multifaceted, interconnected learning opportunities that "disorienting dilemmas" in social pedagogies can result in.

Part 3—Social pedagogical interventions: A view from the terrain

Isabelle Drewelow

A Socio-Constructivist Approach to Developing Intercultural Empathy

The pedagogical intervention presented in this chapter uses a recent event that received global exposure (the 2015 terrorist attack on the satirical journal *Charlie Hebdo*) to engage learners' critical awareness of the subjective dimension of freedom, especially freedom of speech. To facilitate learners' encounter with and reflection on variation of cultural frames of reference, the intervention integrates geosemiotics theory (Scollon & Scollon, 2003) within a socio-constructivist approach to learning. A collaborative engagement inside and outside the classroom is enabled with LinoIt, a digital and interactive bulletin board. The chapter begins with curricular considerations to create a participatory and empathy-generating classroom-based learning environment. A detailed description of the sequence of project-based activities and assessments designed for a third-semester French course follows. The research and creative projects can be adapted to lower or higher level L2 courses and include other culturally organized constructs. I conclude with insights into how to use the design of the learning activities and the pedagogical sequence as a model for further curricular development and for the professional development of graduate students and instructors.

Vincent VanderHeijden

Of Cookies and Saints: Deconstructing L2 Learners' Myths of the Target Culture

Lessons on culturally integral products of winter holiday *speculaas* cookies and the holiday figures of St. Nicholas and his attendant, Black Pete—always portrayed in blackface—are presented to illustrate possibilities for prompting reflection on difficult topics such as colonial legacy and the cultural dynamics of exclusion and belonging in foreign language (FL) Dutch instruction. *Speculaas* is a product of Dutch colonial power and practices, which made tropical spices affordable in cold Northern Europe, while the feast of *Sinterklaas* has become a contested site in Dutch culture precisely for its racial dynamics at the heart of a fundamentally Dutch cultural practice. By didacticizing such examples, language instructors can help students develop transcultural abilities, specifically within the domain of "critical cultural awareness" (Byram, 1997). This chapter suggests that the development of nuanced understandings of the target language-culture is both a long-term process requiring explicit curricular design and constitutive of key skills with applications beyond the FL classroom. I conclude with thoughts on the challenge this approach can pose for the professional development of pre-service and in-service instructors.

Lara Ducate and Lara Lomicka

Engaging Students in Intentional Cultural Learning during Study Abroad

This action research project creates intercultural learning opportunities by engaging students with the culture of the target country. During their study abroad experiences, German intermediate language learners became engaged with their environment to negotiate intercultural, translingual, and transcultural contexts by the deliberate act of noticing. Assigned to a particular instructor-identified theme, such as transportation or public spaces, students analyzed and reflected on each picture to distinguish how it fit into the LESCANT (Victor, 1992) categories (language, environment, social organization, context, authority, non-verbal, and time). We investigated the following questions: (1) What do students notice as they intentionally pay attention to a particular theme in the host country? (2) How do students' understandings of German or their own cultures change over the five-week program? Data consist of study abroad students' pictures, captions, and final questionnaires. Our goal was to promote and illustrate a deeper engagement with the target culture beyond the typical study abroad classroom and host family experiences and to share ideas for successfully engaging students in critical thinking about their translingual and transcultural experiences through interpersonal and social means.

Jeanne M. Johnson

L'Incubateur: Increasing Student Engagement through Global Simulation and Gaming Pedagogy in the L2 Classroom

This research seeks to increase learner engagement in a third-year high school French class through GS, based on the principles of video game design and participatory culture. This virtual start-up incubator is set in the backdrop of La Halle Freyssinet, an actual incubator in the 13th *arrondissement* in Paris. As they developed their team's start-up companies, students became entrepreneurs and pursued their own interests, navigating their future selves, personally and professionally. They also completed instructor-led tasks that provided structure and communicative tools in the L2. Along with student choice, another motivating factor was a final competition for virtual investor funds. Results show that participants' engagement—as measured through surveys and reflective narratives as well as instructor observations—is increased when students are given a choice in their learning, are challenged to see themselves in the learning scenario, and compete with their peers for top position.

Introduction
Social Pedagogies and Entwining Language with the World

Sébastien Dubreil, Carnegie Mellon University
Steven L. Thorne, Portland State University and Rijksuniversiteit Groningen

Under current geopolitical conditions of social, environmental, and economic fragility and instability, the need for education to cultivate empathy, heighten attentiveness to the biosphere, and augment commitment to civic engagement imposes itself with urgency (Rifkin, 2012). As fundamentally social-relational phenomena, semiotic agility and critical language awareness serve as critical resources for ameliorating and transforming selves, communities, and societies. These points suggest that instructed language education would benefit from greater integration with a variety of lifeworld contexts and communities. In response to this need, contributions to this volume propose approaches to pedagogically mediated second language learning that link classroom activities with relevant social practices occurring outside of instructional settings. As Byrnes (2011) has suggested, "[T]he point to be made is this: Language learning is no longer to be primarily of and in the classroom alone but of, with, and for the 'community'" (p. 291). Indeed, the developmental and experiential affordances of engaging with, and in some cases contributing to, university-external communities are central to the content of this volume. In our use of the term, the conceptualization of community extends beyond a reference to ostensible *a priori* social groups and instead indexes identifiable repertoires of social practices that are themselves continually in formation and undergoing some degree of transformation across time.[1] Practically speaking, this volume focuses on two components in Byrnes's statement, namely that (1) foreign or world language (L2) learning is fundamentally a social and socially situated endeavor and (2) that it ought not to be limited to learning about

---

[1] The notion of community involves complex questions of who defines the community, issues of membership (including mechanisms of inclusion and exclusion), and its sociohistorical and cultural contexts of occurrence (Thorne, 2009, 2011). Moreover, a primary goal of instructed second language learning is to cultivate students' capacity to adapt to, and participate in, a variety of contexts in which the language is used, likely involving the navigation of multiple possibly overlapping communities arrayed across physical and digital environments.

language and culture *in the classroom*. Essentially, the overarching question guiding contributions to this volume asks, "How can we more dynamically integrate the vibrancy of linguistically mediated social engagement outside of classroom settings with the pedagogical efficacy of instructional activity in the classroom?"

To address this question, the 2017 volume of the AAUSC series draws inspiration from—and appropriates to the context of L2 studies—the framework of social pedagogies (Bass & Elmendorf, 2012) in which the learner is envisioned as a *locuteur/acteur* (speaker/social actor—Kern & Liddicoat, 2008). This emphasis on students as speakers/social actors acknowledges the relevance of conventional foci such as language forms and cultural facts, but it also more expansively builds upon the idea that students are social agents who mobilize symbolic and linguistic resources and competencies to successfully negotiate complex intercultural, transactional, and ideational dimensions of collective human interactivity. From this perspective on L2 learning, multilingualism and multiculturalism become *de facto* interpersonal—and thus social—phenomena. Consequently, the pedagogical approaches we deploy in the L2 classroom ought to take into account this social, community-oriented perspective on learning to more fully comprehend, and contribute to, a diversity of culturally organized systems of activity.

Social pedagogies, as defined by Bass and Elmendorf (2012), are articulated as four core elements. Social pedagogies:

- take into account the audience: "the representation of knowledge for an authentic audience is absolutely central to the construction of knowledge in a course" (p. 2);
- strive to build a sense of intellectual community through collaboration and engagement with multiple perspectives;
- help students "deepen their reflections, build links across courses and semesters, and bridge curricular and co-curricular learning" (p. 2); and
- cultivate self-reflection.

In the case of L2 education, this means expanding the scope of what learners do by couching the language learning experiences in contexts and communities outside of the academy. To give two small-scale examples, one could imagine having students write letters to Amnesty International or participate in a project similar to the Shared Studios "Portals" exhibit,[2] an installation that enables people in New York City to discuss their daily lives with people in Tehran, Iran (among other sites), crossing linguistic and cultural boundaries in immediate, experiential, and interpersonally grounded ways.

In the social pedagogy framework, "learning is not only distinctly a social activity, but the implementation of social learning—the act of constructing and

---

[2] Information on the Shared Studios Project, founded by Amar Bakshi, can be found here: http://www.sharedstudios.com/.

communicating understanding to an authentic audience" (Bass & Elmendorf, 2012, p. 2). Learners are encouraged to connect with a variety of community contexts, physical and semiotic environments, and/or political or social problems. In so doing, they cultivate a taste for working with a certain degree of unpredictability and ambiguity, develop an ability to adapt, and, through exercising agency and authorship in and out of the classroom, develop their own voice in the L2. As Thorne (2011) has argued, the superordinate goal of L2 education is to catalyze "the development of dispositions that enable complex, nuanced, recipient-aware, anticipatory, and improvisational communicative capacities" (p. 306).

The framework of social pedagogies aligns in striking ways with the critical pedagogies framework (i.e., Freire, 1970) applied to Second Language Acquisition (SLA) by Norton and Toohey (2004) in that it envisions language as "not simply a means of expression or communication" but rather as "a practice that constructs and is constructed by, the ways language learners understand themselves, their social surroundings, their histories, and their possibilities for the future" (Norton & Toohey, 2004, p. 1), a characterization akin to what Kramsch (2006) identifies as symbolic competence. Seen from this perspective, L2 teaching and learning is positioned as an agent for personal as well as societal transformation.

From an instructional point of view, this orientation endeavors to help students—and instructors—more powerfully integrate semiotic engagement and structured reflection as mutually beneficial activities. An explicit coupling of instructed L2 education with activity beyond the classroom also serves to enhance the ecological validity of L2 teaching and learning (Thorne, 2013a).

Despite earlier calls to address the bifurcated structure of foreign language (FL) departments and disciplinary boundaries to reflect the idea that language "is a complex multifunctional phenomenon that links an individual to other individuals, to communities, and to national cultures" (MLA, 2007, p. 2), practices in FL classrooms have been slow to evolve, though curricular innovation based in literacy-based teaching and multiple literacy approaches (Allen & Paesani, 2010; Byrnes, Maxim, & Norris, 2010) provides interesting advances in this direction. This volume aims to build upon suggestions in the Modern Language Association's (MLA) 2007 report by providing approaches and implemented examples of curricular innovation that seek to constructively disrupt conventionally oriented FL programs and to expand the conditions of possibility (Foucault, 1970/2002) of instructionally rooted L2 education. This has important implications for the way L2 educators structure FL programs, the way they design language-learning environments for their students, and even how they envision their students. By appropriating the framework of social pedagogies, we hope to foster fundamental innovation in L2 programs that generate transformative experiences for L2 students and that ultimately unite language education with activity in the world while also positioning L2 learning more centrally within both the academic and exogenous communities.

What does the notion of social pedagogies more specifically mean in the area of L2 education and what is its potential impact on program design and pedagogical practices? First, the use of social pedagogies can help L2 educators redesign learning environments that take into account multiple possibilities for L2 learning. In recent years, there has been a considerable research on multilingual and multicultural language experiences (e.g., Kramsch, 2009) as well as issues related to literacy, digital literacies, and multiliteracies (e.g., Kern, 2000, 2015; New London Group, 1996; Thorne, 2013b). The social turn in SLA research (Block, 2003) was notably driven by the perceived disconnect between approaches to SLA that narrowly address cognitive processes in isolation from situated uses of language for making meaning in work, public, and interpersonal life contexts. Additionally, the increased physical mobility of people (students, workers, immigrants, expatriates, etc.) as well as the availability of information and communication technologies afford access to a wide range of linguistic and cultural communities, resulting in multilingual and multicultural contact and the emergence of linguistic and cultural hybridities in both physical and digital spaces (Blommaert, 2010; Thorne & Ivković, 2015).

In short, contemporary communities are rapidly evolving in often connected physical and virtual spaces. These processes are sometimes catalyzed by technologies that create new contexts for new social practices such as affinity spaces, which Gee (2005) defines as "places where people affiliate with others based primarily on shared activities, interests, and goals, not shared race, class culture, ethnicity, or gender" (p. 67). Such cultural phenomena suggest that L2 learning ought to be porously integrated with opportunities for language use and learning as a part of meaningful social practice. Our view is that the L2 classroom has not in any way lost its relevance; rather, explicit instruction provides a setting within which curricular materials as well as imported experiences from the social wilds can be analyzed and practiced in controlled and fine-grained ways (Gee, 2004), forming a conducive learning space that is inclusive of experiential engagement in outside lifeworlds.

The idea of the community as a metaphor for the L2 classroom has been explored (e.g., Hall, 2002), as has the idea of extending learning tasks outside the classroom by bridging the instructed setting with various communities of relevance to students (e.g., see Holden & Sykes, 2011; Reinhardt & Thorne, 2011; Thorne & Reinhardt, 2008). In such learning communities, members leverage their individual knowledge, skills, and expertise to learn actively and collaboratively. Considerable research also continues to be carried out in the area of Computer-Assisted Language Learning (CALL) to explore the potential of social media to enhance L2 instruction and foster language and culture learning (e.g., Arnold & Ducate, 2011; Ducate & Arnold, 2006; Goodfellow & Lamy, 2011). These approaches underscore that a critical part of L2 learning is to be able to decipher and interpret what is happening when language is at work in discourse communities, in all of its complexity and ambiguity, and to be able to acquire the abilities necessary to participate in physical and online communities that bring the classroom together with tangible aspects of both historically stable as well as emergent-mutable discourse domains that are alive in the broader social world.

This social dimension of language learning becomes particularly salient when communicative events are contextualized and cultural context is shown to play a crucial role in the meaning-making process—that is, interpersonal interaction makes relevant issues of power, identity, social positioning, and so forth. The symbolic nature of language and its relation to social structure creates conditions under which the practical meaning of interpersonal interaction involves extra-linguistic factors such as history and subjective positioning in social structures (Bourdieu, 1972). L2 learning from this perspective is a problem-solving language game situated within and across communities than can be accessed and analyzed inside and outside the classroom. Contributions to this volume examine the ways in which social relationships structure L2 pedagogy as a community-building project in which learners hone a wide variety of abilities (linguistic, cultural, and related to problem solving and collaboration) that lead them to become more effective communicators and community builders. Reciprocally, the discomfort and unease sometimes reported by language learners in the social pedagogies-informed interventions in this volume suggest that encounters outside of the classroom are perceived as consequential and sometimes socially difficult (e.g., Crane, Fingerhuth, & Huenlich; Warner & Richardson, from this volume).

The learning experiences referred to by contributors to this volume exist on a continuum from fully face-to-face to largely online and from primarily institution-based to contexts outside of the traditionally conceived educational sphere. The principal idea is that the structured unpredictability of encounters and/or social relationship development out in the world require paying attention, adaptation to new and perhaps unexpected situations, and negotiation of pragmatically sensitive and culturally specific social practices. Consequently, framing L2 pedagogical practices as social pedagogies encourages language educators to seriously envision what it would mean to manage the interface between formal and informal learning contexts as a deliberate enterprise as they relate to instructed L2 course design. In other words, how do we integrate the typical content of the various courses that comprise a language program (at the elementary, intermediate, and advanced levels) with authentic communicative gestures that occur in students' lifeworlds in various textual genres? In this sense, social pedagogies aim to have a deep transformative effect on the L2 learner. In particular, when effectively designed, such learning environments can equip L2 learners to function in multilingual and multicultural societies by enabling them to realize that emerging as multilingual and multicultural subjects is a critical component to academic and professional success (see, e.g., Kramsch, 2009; Thorne, 2013b).

Envisioning and structuring L2 pedagogies along these aforementioned lines would mean seriously addressing, as FL educators, how we "reassemble the social" to paraphrase Latour (2005). That is to say, we need to consider how we can incorporate communities (in the making), which exist physically and/or virtually, and then utilize these linguistic and cultural processes that are at the core of the community-building project as a primary object of study in the confines of L2 classrooms: "Effective citizenship and productive work now require that we interact effectively using multiple languages, multiple Englishes, and communication patterns that more frequently cross cultural, community, and national boundaries" (New London Group, 1996, p. 64). By equipping our students to navigate increasingly linguistically diverse and culturally complex social environments, we give them the means to truly be the designers of social futures. In pedagogical terms, this means engaging students in high-investment social acts and then helping them to critically examine such engagements in order to understand how to more powerfully and responsively function linguistically, pragmatically, and culturally. At its core, we are proposing an adaptive pedagogy that would situate language and culture as lived practice as a central organizing principle of FL study. Cultivating social pedagogies help us to bridge between pedagogical amplification in classroom spaces and social action in the world, ultimately giving students the translingual and transcultural tools to participate effectively in complex and diverse communities in the future.

Individual Contributions to the Volume

This volume is divided into three parts. Contributions in Part 1 present ways in which L2 learners can inhabit and engage with cityscapes and communities in meaningful ways. In Engaging the City: Language, Space, and Identity in Urban Environments (Chapter 1), following an eloquent description of the central relevance of interfacing L2 learning with multicultural and multilingual cities, Stéphane Charitos and Nelleke Van Deusen-Scholl describe the development of a Spanish language curriculum that emphasizes interdisciplinary study and critical reflection on the city as a way for students to cultivate curiosity regarding the diversity, richness, and complexity of urban environments. Leveraging techniques of spatial analysis and place-based pedagogy, they highlight specific approaches that help L2 learners directly engage with issues of language, identity, and place in contemporary urban settings. Alberto Bruzos, in Encuentros con el *Español*: A Case Study of Critical Service Learning in the Latino Community (Chapter 2), makes a compelling case for designing courses with the local community in mind and explores the sociopolitical dimensions of the Spanish language, Latino identity, and instructed language learning and teaching on the one hand and service learning on the other. Working with community leaders, he aligned his course designs with the realities of the ideological position of Spanish in the local space; students are prompted to critically reflect on and engage with the complexities of language as a social semiotic practice. Similarly, Diana Ruggiero in Lessons from the CruCES Project: Community Service Learning and Intercultural Sensitivity in the Foreign Language Classroom (Chapter 3) worked closely with multiple local stakeholders to design service learning opportunities for her students in a manner that would serve real needs of the local Latino community. Through these service opportunities and self-reflective assignments, students' mindset and attitudes evolved, and their intercultural sensitivity increased. The last chapter in Part 1, *Abriendo Caminos*: Breaking New Ground in Community-Engaged Language Learning (Chapter 4), by Vivian Brates and her colleagues, also builds on the notion of mutual benefit in community-engaged learning and describes a critically conscious Freire-inspired (1970/1993) project that linked students with local Spanish-speaking communities through arts, literature, and civic involvement. They show how, after overcoming initial apprehensions, students gained new solidarities with local Latino communities that enhanced linguistic, cultural, social, and civic learning on the part of the various individuals and communities involved.

Part 2 consists of contributions that envision the L2 curriculum holistically so that innovation does not remain bounded to isolated courses. In proposing programmatic and curriculum-wide efforts to transform students into social actors in virtual and physical contexts, these projects endeavor to foster students' diversity of literacies and to engage with symbolic representations of language and culture, which includes engaging—and dealing with—difficult subjects and struggles. In Social-Pedagogical Life Imitates Art: Scaffolding the Voices of L2 Fans and Critics (Chapter 5), Stéphanie Pellet and Lindsy Myers share a constructivist multiliteracy-driven curriculum based on the novel *Odette Toulemonde* (Schmitt, 2006) in which students share an online space where they conduct collaborative reading and engage with each other and the text and potentially with French-speaking readers elsewhere. Students in this space are able to develop their sense of identity and voice in French, and this platform will remain available over time, creating a trace and a perennial community of readers, authors, and critics. Kristen Michelson and Elyse Petit in Becoming Social Actors: Designing a Global Simulation for Situated Language and Culture Learning (Chapter 6) also set up a learning space that combines a physical and virtual component in the form of a global simulation in which students each play a character and collaborate to advance the narrative, experimenting with culturally authentic discursive practices. As they explore social issues in contemporary France, students become actors within the community they are building. In Networked Learning: Students as Producers, Curators, and Consumers of Authentic Resources on Campus and Abroad (Chapter 7), Jessica Greenfield and her colleagues create a community of learners that spans multiple instructional settings and curricular levels. In their project, they leverage the participation of students in study abroad contexts to construct learning tasks that result in their creating and curating a collection of authentic resources that will be used as learning materials in domestic lower-level courses. Not only does this create a sense of responsibility for the students creating the content, this could also be motivating for domestic students to further pursue L2 studies. The last two contributions in Part 2 examine challenges and difficulties associated with social pedagogies as they introduce elements of uncertainty, especially as students are encouraged to confront delicate topics. In Beyond Participation: Symbolic Struggles with(in) Digital Social Media in the L2 Classroom (Chapter 8), Chantelle Warner and Diane Richardson examine students' experiences in a digital media unit within a multiliteracy-inspired curriculum, focusing on their participation and positionality in digital discourse spaces. They found that students embraced or resisted participation in various ways over the course of the semester, thus affording them more agency in their participatory choices. In what Makes This So Complicated?" On the Value of Disorienting Dilemmas in Language Instruction (Chapter 9), Cori Crane and her colleagues show how dealing with culturally sensitive topics can derail even a carefully planned instructional sequence (e.g., a role-play about the historical relationship between German settlers and the Comanche tribe). In turn, they also show that the strength of the preparation coupled with responsive and adaptive pedagogy can turn these difficult circumstances into a valuable teaching moment by helping students to process this disorienting dilemma by recognizing and reflecting on multiple perspectives and subjectivities.

The contributions that comprise Part 3 focus more specifically on social pedagogical interventions centered on offering students opportunities for motivated, purposeful communicative (social) interaction, with the goals of (1) enhancing opportunities for social action and community-based activities or other forms of civic engagement during university-level course work and (2) developing learners' critical thinking skills through participation in and analysis of social interactions. Starting from a survey of French people following the 2015 *Charlie Hebdo* attacks (to understand who identified/agreed with the "Je suis Charlie" statement), Isabelle Drewelow in A Socio-Constructivitist Approach to Developing Intercultural Empathy (Chapter 10) uses a multimodal discussion board to guide and engage her students with the multiperspectival nature of culture, including the symbolic dimension and issues of power differential around notions such as free speech. Through reflective and creative activities, students gain a sense of empathy and also reflect on their own culture. Vincent Vander Heijden, In Cookies and Saints: Deconstructing L2 Learners' Myths of the Target Culture (Chapter 11) attempts to reach similar goals and to foster his students' transcultural competence through the critical examination of two specifically Dutch holiday-related objects: *speculaas* (cookies) and the figure of Black Pete. Situating these objects at the confluence of a colonial past and contemporarily practiced traditions, his students acquire a more nuanced understanding of Dutch culture. In Engaging Students in Intentional Cultural Learning during Study Abroad (Chapter 12), Lara Lomicka and Lara Ducate show how the Lescant model (1992) can be adapted to German language and culture instruction in a study abroad context to focus students' attention to how language is used in public spaces to structure and inform the cultural practices that take place in these spaces. Finally, Jeanne Johnson in *L'Incubateur*: Increasing Student Engagement through Global Simulation and Gaming Pedagogy in the L2 Classroom (Chapter 13) shows how students' engagement can be enhanced when the curriculum is organized as a global simulation based on actual current events. Collaborating with a school in France, students in mixed groups (i.e., French and American) created virtual start-up companies as if they were housed in the up-and-coming Halle Freyssinet, an incubator that opened in summer 2017 under the name Station F in the 11th arrondissement of Paris. Each company had to have a name, a product, and a rationale for why it was likely to succeed. As importantly, these companies bore in them the imprint of two cultural systems.

Relevance to Language Program Directors and L2 Educators

Despite a growing body of research on the potential effectiveness of language learning outside traditional classroom settings, the means by which to developmentally amplify such experiences and elegantly interface them with instructed L2 programs has heretofore remained underaddressed or limited in scope. This volume on social pedagogies, broadly described, helps us to reimagine language education by providing pedagogical frameworks for the integration of instructional settings with community-engaged learning. Some of the contributions to this volume showcase a particular course, while others propose pedagogical initiatives that span language programs or curricula. All contributors include explicit suggestions for expanding curricula and language learning opportunities in ecologically embedded ways.

This volume promotes language learning as a social activity, both in its process and its purpose. Fundamentally, this volume seeks to support language educators who wish to design learning environments that take into account the contemporary realities and contexts of L2 use. Contributors offer suggestions and case study accounts addressing (1) how to reframe language study and design new curricula to prepare students for a multilingual, multicultural world; (2) how to expand the notion of classroom community, in particular its social elements; and (3) how to envision the interface of L2 instruction and opportunities for language learning in the wild. It is our hope that the diverse approaches to social pedagogies for L2 education included in this volume will be helpful specifically to Language Program Directors (LPDs).

By opening up the boundaries of language study, we hope to make language learning more central to university-level education and more aligned with life-long learning objectives that extend beyond classroom study and to foster the development of globally aware dispositions in our students. In sum, even though this volume is predicated on concepts that have been present in SLA for some time, it rearticulates them through the lens of implementable social pedagogies. The boundaries of L2 use have shifted, and it is incumbent upon L2 educators to make a case for the relevance of emerging communicative contexts in a world increasingly marked by the neoliberal ideology of productivity and consumerism at the expense of fostering empathy and building sustainable relationships in multicultural, multilingual societies. Although today's students, millennials and members of Gen Z, have been derided as being self-centered and disengaged, like all humans, they are also hungry for active participation in their own learning, making decisions of consequence, and having an effect on the world. As LPDs and L2 educators, it is critical that we channel and leverage these tendencies in order to equip our students with the critical thinking and interactional competencies they need in order to understand others and themselves and perhaps ultimately to make a positive impact on the world around them.

References

Allen, H., & Paesani, K. (2010). Exploring the feasibility of a pedagogy of multiliteracies in introductory foreign language courses. *L2 Journal, 2*, 119–142.

Arnold, N., & Ducate, L. (Eds.). (2011). *Present and future promises of CALL: From theory and research to new directions in language teaching*. San Marcos, TX: CALICO Publications.

Bass, R., & Elmendorf, H. (2012). Designing for difficulty: Social pedagogies as a framework for course design. Retrieved from https://blogs.commons.georgetown.edu/bassr/social-pedagogies/

Block, D. (2003). *The social turn in second language acquisition*. Washington, DC: Georgetown University Press.

Blommaert, J. (2010). *The sociolinguistics of globalization*. Cambridge, UK: Cambridge University Press.

Bourdieu, P. (1972). *Esquisse d'une théorie de la pratique*. Geneva, Switzerland: Droz.

Byrnes, H. (2011). Perspectives. *Modern Language Journal, 95*(2), 291–292.

Byrnes, H., Maxim, H. H., & Norris, J. M. (2010). Realizing advanced L2 writing development in a collegiate curriculum: Curricular design, pedagogy, assessment. *Modern Language Journal, 94*(supplement s1), monograph.

Ducate, L., & Arnold, N. (Eds.). (2006). *Calling on CALL: From theory and research to new directions in foreign language teaching*. San Marcos, TX: CALICO Publications.

Foucault, M. (1970/2002). *The order of things: An archaeology of the human sciences*. London, UK: Routledge.

Freire, P. (1970). *Pedagogy of the oppressed*. New York, NY: Continuum.

Gee, J. P. (2004). *Situated language and learning: A critique of traditional schooling*. New York, NY: Routledge.

Gee, J. P. (2005). Semiotic social spaces and affinity spaces: From the age of mythology to today's schools. In D. Barton & K. Tusting (Eds.), *Beyond communities of practice: Language, power and social context* (pp. 214–232). Cambridge, UK: Cambridge University Press.

Goodfellow, R., & Lamy, M.-N. (2011). *Learning cultures in online education*. New York, NY: Continuum.

Hall, J. K. (2002). *Methods for teaching foreign languages: Creating a community of learners in the classroom*. Columbus, OH: Prentice-Hall.

Holden, C. L., & Sykes, J. M. (2011). Leveraging mobile games for place-based language learning. *International Journal of Game-Based Learning, 1*(2), 1–18.

Kern, R. (2000). *Literacy and language teaching.* Oxford, UK: Oxford University Press.

Kern, R. (2015). *Language, literacy, and technology.* Cambridge, UK: Cambridge University Press.

Kern, R., & Liddicoat, A. J. (2008). De l'apprenant au locuteur/acteur. In G. Zarate, D. Lévy, & C. Kramsch (Eds.), *Précis du plurilinguisme et du pluriculturalisme* (pp. 25–33). Paris, France: Éditions des archives contemporaines.

Kramsch, C. (2006). From communicative competence to symbolic competence. *Modern Language Journal, 90*(2), 249–252.

Kramsch, C. (2009). *The multilingual subject.* Oxford, UK: Oxford University Press.

Latour, B. (2005). *Reassembling the social.* New York, NY: Oxford University Press.

MLA Ad Hoc Committee on Foreign Languages. (2007). Foreign languages and higher education: New structures for a changed world. Retrieved from https://www.mla.org/Resources/Research/Surveys-Reports-and-Other-Documents/Teaching-Enrollments-and-Programs/Foreign-Languages-and-Higher-Education-New-Structures-for-a-Changed-World.

New London Group. (1996). A pedagogy of multiliteracies: Designing social futures. *Harvard Educational Review, 66*(1), 60–92.

Norton, B., & Toohey, K. (2004). *Critical pedagogies and language learning.* Cambridge, UK: Cambridge University Press.

Reinhardt, J., & Thorne, S. (2011). Beyond comparisons: Frameworks for developing digital L2 literacies. In N. Arnold & L. Ducate (Eds.), *Present and future promises of CALL: From theory and research to new directions in language teaching* (pp. 257–280). San Marcos, TX: CALICO.

Rifkin, J. (2012). *Une nouvelle conscience pour un monde en crise.* Paris, France: Actes Sud.

Schmitt, E.-E. (2006). *Odette Toulemonde et autres histoires.* Paris, France: Albin Michel.

Thorne, S. L. (2009). "Community," semiotic flows, and mediated contribution to activity. *Language Teaching, 42*(1), 81–94.

Thorne, S. L. (2011). Community formation and the world as its own model. *Modern Language Journal, 95*(2), 304–307.

Thorne, S. L. (2013a). Language learning, ecological validity, and innovation under conditions of superdiversity. *Bellaterra Journal of Teaching & Learning Language and Literature, 6*(2): 1–27.

Thorne, S. L. (2013b). Digital literacies. In M. Hawkins (Ed.), *Framing languages and literacies: Socially situated views and perspectives* (pp. 192–218). New York, NY: Routledge.

Thorne, S. L., & Ivković, D. (2015). Multilingual Eurovision meets plurilingual YouTube: Linguascaping discursive ontologies. In D. Koike & C. Blyth (Eds.), *Dialogue in multilingual and multimodal communities* (pp. 167–192). Amsterdam: John Benjamins.

Thorne, S. L., & Reinhardt, J. (2008). "*Bridging activities,*" new media literacies and advanced foreign language proficiency. *CALICO Journal, 25*(3), 558–572.

Part 1
The Learner in the Environment: Inhabiting the City, Community Engagement, and Service Learning

Chapter 1
Engaging the City: Language, Space, and Identity in Urban Environments

Stéphane Charitos, Columbia University
Nelleke Van Deusen-Scholl, Yale University

Introduction

For many students, engaging with the world outside the classroom means connecting with an increasingly urban, multicultural, and multilingual environment. While in 1800, less than 2% of the world's population lived in citiesl, the United Nations is projecting that at the current rate of urbanization, two-thirds of all people on the planet will be living in urban centers or clusters by 2050 (United Nations, Department of Economic and Social Affairs, 2014). As a consequence, not only will cities become the principal prism through which one can achieve an understanding of modern life, but they could also potentially displace the nation-state as both the essential spatial unit for the organization of territory and the critical container of social processes (Sassen, 2006).

This fact notwithstanding, the city has always been, and will always be, one of the principal spaces where various groups, communities, and individuals negotiate and embed their identities. Consequently, investigating the history and patterns of cultural contact between the various populations living within a city's boundaries can prove to be an extraordinarily revealing lens for investigating social and cultural history in a broad range of urban contexts. By the same token, because urban spaces are also a place where culture and language coexist, the city can be the crucial arena for asking questions about language practices as well as the appropriate place where one can examine how the evolving types of interactions between space and language might fundamentally inflect a city's history. Unfortunately, and despite the fact that place and language are vital components, in any attempt to understand how city dwellers construct their identities, these two factors are often studied in isolation, if only because their interaction, especially within the context of modern urban cosmopolitanism, tends to be extremely complex and confusing to capture.

Cities have always been loci of heterogeneity. Already in his *Poetics*, Aristotle argued that cities could not be brought into existence by similar people. The city, as imagined by the Greek philosopher, could only be the creation of different kinds of people who come together to establish a community where they can live in common. And in fact, the profile of today's modern cities can best be described as one characterized by superdiversity and sociolinguistic complexity—that is, dense forms of social, cultural, and economic diversity that are found in multilingual and multicultural contexts (Blommaert, 2013a, 2013b; Blommaert & Rampton, 2011). Originally rooted in local specificities, cities have nowadays largely outgrown any purported one-to-one correlation between a people and a language. Instead, cities act as magnets that concentrate the diversity that results from increased factual and virtual mobility. The consequence of such intermingling of a multiplicity of ethnicities and cultures in a shared geographic space is that cities have become pivotal sites where one can readily encounter languages other than the local or official language(s). This in turn has led to a profound recasting of contemporary forms of cosmopolitan urbanism and irrevocably altered the profile of most modern urban landscapes in the process.

If the city has become the primary space where one can engage with multilingualism and the testing ground where one can study the shifting linguistic profile of modern urban landscapes, then asking relevant questions about the nature of the multilingual city can enhance our understanding of the ways language inhabits city spaces. Consequently, developing projects that directly engage with the multilingual richness of the city as a space of productive diversity can help us better understand how life in highly multilingual cities offers a broad choice of identities to those who live within their boundaries (cf. Block, 2008).

These developments have had profound implications for education in general and language education in particular. One of the driving forces impelling substantial changes in both pedagogical goals and instructional approaches (cf. Kramsch, 2017) is a heightened awareness of the current complex plurilingual and pluricultural contexts in which language learning takes place, since it affects both the ways in which learners construct relationships to each other inside and outside the classroom (e.g., in local communities, in study abroad programs, in the workplace) and influences the multiple ways by which they narrate and express these shifting relationships (cf. Norton, 2013).

If traditional language learning took place inside the classroom, new instructional models are emerging that encourage language learners to use their language resources for authentic communicative purposes outside the formal classroom through inquiry-based and collaborative projects in which they engage purposefully with the surrounding communities (cf. Benson & Reinders, 2011; Nunan & Richards, 2015). In this chapter, we focus specifically on the city as a rich resource for such intellectual engagement and cultural discovery.

Conceptual and Theoretical Framework

Over the past several decades, we have witnessed a pronounced shift in emphasis in language pedagogy away from a curriculum that, almost exclusively, stressed linguistic competencies toward one that includes transcultural competence and encourages learners to reflect critically while engaging creatively with their immediate environment. As a result, new pedagogical approaches have encouraged the use of more authentic language on the part of the L2 learner through the advocacy of real-world tasks. In this section, we briefly outline three major "turns" that have impacted this shift, and we discuss their implications for a more socially engaged pedagogy in an urban, multilingual environment: the social turn (cf. Block, 2003); the spatial turn (cf. Gunderson, 2014; Soja, 2003); and the bi/multi/plural turn (cf. Kramsch, 2017; Kubota, 2016; May, 2014a, 2014b; Ortega, 2010, 2011, 2013, 2014).

The Social Turn

In the mid-1990s, the so-called social turn in applied linguistics (cf. Block, 2003; Ortega, 2011) challenged the prevailing cognitivist and psycholinguistic orientations in Second Language Acquisition (SLA) theories and advocated for more socially oriented approaches to L2 learning. Social interaction and sociocultural context became central across a number of theoretical approaches, such as sociocultural theory based on Vygotsky's work in cultural historical psychology (e.g., Lantolf & Thorne, 2007; Ohta, 2017), research on identity (Norton, 2013), and recent work on language socialization (e.g., Duff, 2007; Duff & May, 2017). This, then, represents a fundamental shift that asserts that "the social environment is not the context for, but rather the source of, mental development" (Swain & Deters, 2007, p. 821). This reconceptualization of SLA has raised a number of significant implications for foreign and second language education (cf. Firth & Wagner, 1997, 2007) and has had a major impact on current pedagogical practices, which must now "take into consideration both the broader social and cultural context in which languages are learned and the multiple goals and purposes of language education within a plurilingual and pluricultural environment" (Kramsch, 2014, 2017).

The Spatial Turn

A second, more recent shift is the so-called spatial turn, a term introduced in the mid-1990s by the human geographer Edward W. Soja. Drawing largely upon the seminal work of Henri Lefebvre (1991), Soja (2003) challenged traditional notions of space across a range of disciplines, arguing that for too long, research had dealt exclusively with time while neglecting its link with spatiality. Since Soja's critical reevaluation, space can no longer be viewed as an empty container or as a static, inert backdrop to history. Rather, it must be regarded as a dynamic and relational arena that shapes, and is in turn shaped by, ideas, beliefs, principles, and values derived from every facet of social and cultural life.

While this new interest in issues of space and spatiality has mostly affected the social sciences and the field of cultural studies (Bodenhamer, 2007, 2010), it has not gone unnoticed in other disciplines. For instance, a number of studies and approaches in applied linguistics have explored the interrelationship between language and spatial practices from different perspectives (Johnstone, 2010). Scollon and Scollon (2003), for one, draw on both semiotic theory and multimodal discourse analysis, to conceptualize and introduce the notion of geosemiotics in order to explore how language is materially placed in the world. Pennycook (2010), for another, draws inspiration from Lefebvre to offer new ways of thinking about language as a complex and dynamic social practice that organizes space and gives meaning to it rather than considering it to be an entity that exists abstractly in particular spaces and at particular times.

The study of linguistic landscapes[1] (LL) is another relatively new addition to the recent field of studies within applied linguistic research that have an interest with issues of spatiality. LL studies attempt to shift the focus of sociolinguistics from speakers to spaces in general and to urban spaces in particular. LL—as the material manifestation of language—analyze language in public space in order to examine the context(s) in which language is found and used as a way of understanding "cultural, social, political and economic circumstances" (Ben-Rafael, Shohamy, & Barni, 2010, p. xi). In essence, LL endeavor to explain how linguistic signs in the built environment interweave with lived experiences to construct a sense of spatiality and produce social hierarchies (cf. Hélot, Barni, & Janssens, 2012; Hult, 2014). From this point of view, an in-depth understanding of how cities are fashioned necessitates a thorough analysis of how urban spaces are imbued with meaning as well as a rigorous examination of how they acquire symbolic meaning through the deployment of linguistic signs (e.g., Ben-Rafael, Shohamy, Hasan Amara, & Trumper-Hecht, 2006; Pennycook & Otsuji, 2015; Shohamy, Ben-Rafael, & Barni, 2010).

LL, as an integral element of urban landscapes, can therefore serve either as a lens to historically chart the various ways in which diversity organizes itself in rapidly

---

[1] The early and canonical definition of linguistic landscapes proposed by Landry and Bourhis (1997) states that "[t]he language of public road signs, advertising billboards, street names, place names, commercial shop signs, and public signs on government buildings combines to form the linguistic landscape of a given territory, region, or urban agglomeration" (p. 25). This has been updated and expanded by Cenoz and Gorter (2008) to more broadly define linguistic landscapes as language (spoken, written, visual) and other semiotic systems in public spaces—that is, "authentic, contextualized input which is part of the social context" (p. 274). The literature on the emerging field of linguistic landscapes as well as the related field of semiotic landscapes is rapidly becoming extensive (see also, for instance, Backhaus, 2007; Barni & Extra, 2008; Blackwood, Lanza, & Woldemariam, 2016; Blommaert, 2016; Gorter, 2006, 2013; Gorter & Cenoz, 2015; Hancock, 2012; Ivkovic & Lotherington, 2009; Jaworski & Thurlow, 2010a, 2010b; Nash, 2016; Rowland, 2013; Shohamy & Gorter, 2008; Stroud & Jegels, 2014).

globalizing urban environments or as a methodology that can help us better understand the linguistic dimension of contemporary globalization. As historical lenses documenting the complex histories of a particular place, LL can offer a compelling method of accounting for the complexity of superdiverse sociolinguistic environments from an ethnographic perspective (Blommaert, 2013). As a methodology, particularly within language education, LL can be productively explored as a conceptual framework and a pedagogical resource supporting language and literacy learning (cf. Cenoz & Gorter, 2008; Chesnut, Lee, & Schulte, 2013; Gorter & Cenoz, 2004; Hancock, 2012; Malinowski, 2009, 2010; Moore, 2008; Rowland, 2013; Sayer, 2009).

The Bi/Multi/Plural Turn

A final major shift in research emphasis in applied linguistics and sociolinguistics is the multilingual turn, a concept which was first introduced by Ortega (2010). This shift has run parallel to the growing interest in the phenomenon of linguistic superdiversity from across a variety of disciplines (see Blommaert, 2013; Blommaert & Rampton, 2011, discussed earlier). As May (2014b, p. 1) notes, ". . . the increasing focus on superdiverse linguistic contexts is welcome. It has usefully foregrounded multilingualism, rather than monolingualism, as the new norm of applied linguistic and sociolinguistic analysis." Ortega (2013) argues for a reframing of SLA to harness "the unique benefits of studying bi/multilingualism and late learning, all while making transdisciplinary connections of relevance" (p. 16). Kubota (2016), however, offers a critical perspective on what she terms the "multi/plural turn" in applied linguistics. She urges for a critical reflection on the broader discourses and ideologies of postcolonialism, poststructuralism, and neoliberalism within which the notion of plurilingualism is embedded and cautions that more attention should be paid "to the systems of power that produce racial, economic, and other inequalities related to plural and hybrid linguistic practices" (p. 491).

All three of these "turns" have opened new research perspectives, which have in turn influenced contemporary pedagogical practices in language education and have contributed to the introduction of more socially engaged and community-based learner activities that connect the classroom with the real world. In the next section, we will first discuss the broader move toward more social pedagogies across a variety of disciplines and then address the specific implications of social pedagogies for language education in an urban context.

Pedagogical Framework: Social Pedagogies and the Language Classroom

Over the past decade, rapid advances in communication and mobile technologies have permeated every aspect of our daily lives. These advances have also highlighted the social dimension of what it means to access and share knowledge in a highly networked culture and have focused our attention on how the "social life of information" (Brown & Duguid, 2000) can have significant implications on our appreciation of the social dimension of learning. Having reinforced our understanding of education as a socially situated collaborative process (Dewey, 1963; Vygotsky, 1978), they should also help us recast our understanding of how learning approaches based on social pedagogies can and should be designed and integrated in today's formal educational context.

Broadly speaking, social pedagogies are educational approaches that endeavor to establish a relationship between individual learning and the sociocultural context in which that learning takes place. Social pedagogies seek to make learning more visible and more effective by connecting authentic tasks to the overall learning processes and inscribing learning within the broader social context. They do so by striving to both establish and support communities of intellectual engagement within the classroom and connect students to communities outside the classroom.

Drawing insights from the work of Randy Bass and Heidi Elmendorf (2010, 2011), social pedagogies are design approaches that seek to provide students with the tools and the opportunities needed to engage and interact with authentic audiences (i.e., anyone other than the formal classroom instructor) in iterative cycles of engagement. As students move through a cycle of discovery, exploration, and engagement with a set of disciplinary concepts, they begin to establish a personal relation to knowledge in the context of audience and community. Social pedagogies thus allow students to position themselves as actors who experience how "acts of communication and representation connect authentic tasks to learning processes, learning process to adaptive practices, practices to learning environments and intellectual communities, and how the constellation of these elements help [them] integrate their learning by connecting to larger contexts for knowledge and action" (Bass & Elmendorf, 2011).

Within L2 education, there has been an increasing desire to incorporate social pedagogy into the formal language classroom, which, in turn, has led to a renewed interest on implementing pedagogical practices that better connect language learners with the broader community at large and with spatial concepts such as "place" and "location" in a multiplicity of ways.

Until recently, place was often an especially alien concept for language education. To the extent that place was conceptualized at all, it was conceived largely as an abstract concept. Classrooms and other formal learning environments physically separated the learner from the outside world in which the target language was actually spoken. Curricular material further reinforced this isolation by presenting content with little to no respect to the actual lived contexts of the communities, cultures, and places in which the language being taught and learned was spoken (cf. Holden & Sykes, 2011).

Increasingly though, social pedagogies have been used as the basis to connect language students with meaningful opportunities for interaction and engagement with location and with real audiences outside the classroom through a variety of instructional approaches (e.g., community-based learning, project- or inquiry-based learning, and service learning).

In this context, community-based learning refers to a wide variety of instructional methods and programs that educators use to connect what is being taught in schools to their surrounding communities, including local institutions, history, literature, cultural heritage, and natural environments. This approach is motivated by the belief that all communities have intrinsic educational assets and resources that educators can use to enhance learning experiences for students. Proponents generally argue that students will be more interested in the subjects and concepts being taught, and they will be more inspired to learn, if academic study is connected to concepts, issues, and contexts that are more familiar, understandable, accessible, or personally relevant to them. In this respect, Overfield (1997, p. 485) notes that "situating foreign language education within the literal and metaphorical spaces of our communities serves to emphasize the relevance of foreign languages in the contemporary world." The concept also plays an increasing role in the revitalization of indigenous and Native American languages (cf. May, 1999). McCarty and Watahomigie (1998, p. 311), for instance, argue that "[i]ndigenous community-based language education is more than an academic enterprise; it is both an act of self-determination and of resistance—a contestation of oppression and language restrictionism." By using the "community as a classroom," students do not simply have more opportunities to apply learning in practical, real-life settings but can in fact situate those experiences within a relevant sociocultural context.

Across a wide spectrum of disciplines, students are encouraged to learn and create together and harness their creativity in support of their learning in a collaborative context. Many programs are developing courses that explicitly call upon students to become more active and engaged learners while also making it easier for students to integrate content- and product-centered activities into their formal instruction to help them purposefully engage with the world outside their respective institution even while they are still students. This has led to a surge of interest in project- and inquiry-based learning opportunities, guided and unguided fieldwork, direct engagement with surrounding cultural institutions or communities, and it explains as well the thriving popularity of internships (cf. Justice et al., 2007).

In the context of study abroad programs, service learning projects integrated in the language curriculum are providing for a deeper and more authentic engagement with the L2 community (cf. Ducate, 2009; Kinginger, 2011). Finally, technology-mediated approaches are also increasingly employed to connect language learners more closely to and involve them more deeply in the local communities to better understand their histories, social contexts, and local customs. Mobile-assisted learning, place-based gaming, and augmented reality gaming are some examples of ways in which learners can connect virtually to local spaces (cf. Thorne, Black, & Sykes, 2009; Squire, 2009).

Having briefly defined social pedagogies, we now turn to some specific examples of projects that have sought to implement social pedagogies' design approaches, with a focus on making explicit connections between language practice and the notion of place within the specific context of urban landscape.

Implementation and Practice: Making the Connections

This section unpacks some of the key components that characterize a number of programmatic initiatives at Columbia and Yale that have begun to investigate the use of language in the public space insofar as this can make visible for language learners how discursive (and other) practices can shape a given geographical space into a series of specific, historical, and localized places. In particular, we will discuss their potential to serve as both a bridge between formal classroom instruction and motivated language usage opportunities beyond the classroom and as a support for design approaches inspired by social pedagogies. The concluding section will highlight some of the shortcomings of these initial projects and suggest ways in which they could be improved and how future cross-disciplinary and collaborative projects might be designed to further connect the language classroom with the evolving nature of the modern, multilingual, and multicultural global city.

Reading the City Symposium and Subsequent Initiatives

In spring 2015, Columbia University organized a symposium, "Reading the City," which aimed at bringing together scholars and students from different disciplines in a joint discussion about the complex interplay between language, space, and identity in urban areas. It laid the bases for creative ways to translate recent research activity and theoretical insights into cities and urban environments into practical opportunities that would more closely tie the classroom to the city and to the communities that live within its boundaries.

The symposium had three main goals: first, to foreground New York City (NYC) as a polyphonic and malleable space—and specifically situate the university within it; second, to open up a space of critical reflection to broaden and enrich the study of urban environments beyond narrowly circumscribed disciplinary boundaries and encourage conversation between social scientists, humanists, and language educators; and third, to find creative ways to translate research activity and theoretical insights into cities into opportunities for rich student engagement outside of the confines of the formal classroom.

The symposium led to a number of concrete initiatives and projects that have extended it in significant ways. Among these, we note the following:

- We have established a working group whose membership crosses both disciplinary and institutional boundaries. The group meets regularly and tries to identify opportunities for rich, collaborative engagement (both practical and theoretical) with the multilingual city around us.
- A number of faculty members in the social sciences and the language programs have begun to align their respective syllabi in an effort to enrich each other's classes and help their students better explore the complex interplay of language, space, and identity in urban settings.
- A number of language programs have begun reworking their curricula to include an active engagement with some aspect of the greater NYC urban environment.
- We have initiated a series of workshops to examine the role of language in urban environments in order to help refocus language learners' attention to the importance of the social contexts in which meaning and identities are constructed and to help them better understand the broad network of flexible positions and changing identities that characterizes the realities of multilingual and multicultural cities.
- We have built and launched a web-based tool, Cityscape (http://cityscape.lrc.columbia.edu), that allows users to connect topographical and linguistic information in order to document, map, and engage with linguistic phenomena according to their areal differentiation.

Brief Case Studies: Examples from the Classroom

While several courses at Yale and Columbia have begun to incorporate activities that aim to engage students with the urban landscapes of New York and New Haven, many of these activities often remain ancillary to a pedagogy that remains largely focused on formal classroom learning.[2] Even though instructors routinely make use of materials and resources, including newspaper articles, audio recordings of conversations, or videos of recent TV programs, in order to bring fragments of the outside world into the language classroom and construct "an associative bridge between the classroom and the world" (J. Heaton, cited in Smith, 1997), few have structured their class around a systematic exploration of the world outside the classroom and used student-driven research and fieldwork

---

[2] At Columbia, some of these initiatives include the incorporation of specific activities in the Hindi language program to allow students to explore the notion of Desi identity among the diaspora that makes up the various Indian communities of the greater NYC. Within its exploration of the possibilities that digital humanities open up for Yiddish Studies, the Yiddish language program at Columbia integrates activities enabling students to actively enrich its Mapping Yiddish New York initiative, which endeavors to document all aspects of Yiddish culture in New York. At Yale, the Translate New Haven project is a new initiative by the Center for Language Study that encourages students to imagine a more multilingual New Haven through translation of the English that is visible and audible in public spaces into other languages. In addition, a number of community-based projects have been launched in language classes in Korean, Chinese, Arabic, German, Hebrew, and Vietnamese.

as both an integral part of the course and as the basis for meaningful and authentic language use. Such exploration, however, could provide students with opportunities for language usage that are more interactive, social, and multimodal than the discourse of the language classroom.

The Spanish language program at Columbia is one program that has methodically exploited the potential of inquiry- and project-based learning to engage every student in a critical reflection on the urban landscapes of NYC. As outlined on the department's website (http://dh-laic.com/pdf/OH16small.pdf), the curriculum is conceived as an integrated program that requires students to connect with the broader Hispanic social and cultural context through a series of research projects that take language learning beyond the classroom.

Required at all levels of the program, this engagement becomes progressively more complex as students move up the language sequence. Starting with an initial focus on noticing the presence and usage of Spanish in the city, it gradually calls on the students to interact more fully with, and reflect upon, the various modes of expression of Spanish in the public realm and with the broader manifestation of Hispanic culture in the NYC area. This work can be either individual or collaborative, can take the form of ethnographic research that involves interacting with Spanish communities located in NYC or abroad, and is often mediated by technology and social media. We will examine two courses in particular as brief case studies of this approach.

The first, Spanish 1102, is a second-semester, elementary Spanish language course taught by Lee B. Abraham. As an integral part of the course, each student is required to analyze art in public space and then produce a course project that demonstrates their understanding of selected artistic manifestations of Hispanic culture in NYC. This project, which seeks to carefully scaffold student interactions throughout the semester (see Malinowski, 2015, p. 108), accounts for 15% of the final course grade. Students, using photographs, videos, and field notes, document guided visits to murals in East Harlem and Brooklyn, write two reflective essays, and produce a 10-minute video in Spanish about the role of public art in the evolving construction of Latino identities within the broader urban landscapes of these neighborhoods. Each student is also required to use the course blog site to provide feedback on their peers' essays and videos and, through a series of self-reflections, discuss the value of the evidence presented.

Students do all background reading about El Barrio in Spanish, and the video and the essays are completed in Spanish as well. Both of these assignments align well with the grammar and the vocabulary that are already a part of the course syllabus for Elementary Spanish II—namely, the two past "tenses" in Spanish (the preterit and the imperfect) and the vocabulary for describing art that is integrated into the chapters in the textbook focusing on the past tenses in which students examine important historical figures, including artists, in Spain and Latin America. As such, these tasks are congruent with the basic framework of an LL project.

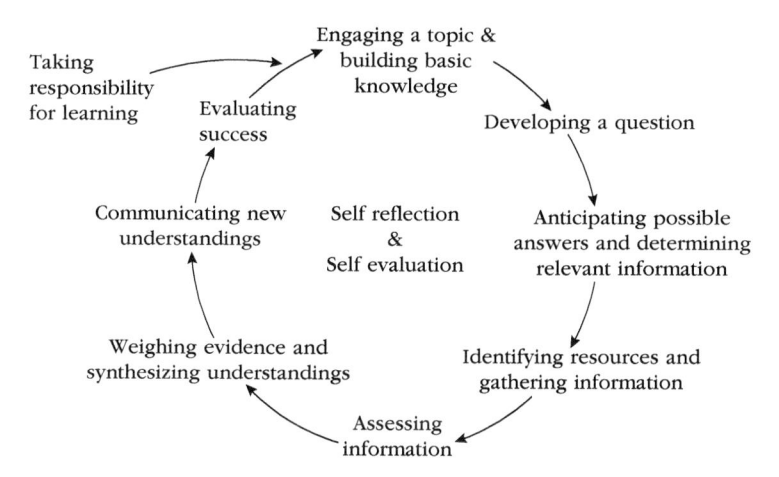

Figure 1.1. The inquiry process according to Justice et al. (2007), p. 203

The design parameters of each individual project are based upon the tenets of inquiry-based learning, which are introduced to the students during a class presentation by the instructor, following the process outlined in Justice et al. (2007, p. 203) as illustrated in Figure 1.1.

Following the presentation, students develop a research proposal on a topic in Latino(a)/Hispanic/Spanish art in public spaces in NYC that is of personal interest to them and generate a specific question (or set of questions) as the basis of their inquiry. The project is not about how to view public art per se but rather about understanding the historical and social setting in which the public art is created. Throughout the research and implementation phases of the project, the instructor serves both as an advisor providing students with ongoing feedback to help refine their research strategies and as a guide who steers them to appropriate information and resources. For example, as they work with the LL using inquiry-based learning throughout the semester, students use blogs not only to document their ongoing work with the LL—including their essays, their reflections, a storyboard, and a video—but also to receive feedback from the faculty member teaching the course and from a social science research librarian.

The second course, "Twitter and the City—ÑYC," is a third-semester language course taught by Reyes Llopis-Garcia. It makes use of social media as both a source of information about NYC in Spanish and as a tool students can use to (1) curate the linguistic and cultural resources they have identified in the public sphere and (2) broadcast their reflections about these resources and the broader cultural content of ÑYC.[3] This portion of the course, worth 15% of the final grade,

---

[3] The tilde over the iconic abbreviation "NYC" is a grapheme that serves to acknowledge the significant Hispanic presence in the city and the ubiquity of the city's Spanish speakers.

asks students to be attentive to the presence of Spanish in the city whether it be visually (announcements, advertisements, LL, etc.), aurally (conversations, recordings, other forms of oral interactions, etc.), or culturally (exhibits, lectures, cultural and social events, concerts, movies, etc.). Students capture and document these indicators of Hispanic presence in the city either by posting tweets categorized with an appropriate hashtag or by uploading and geotagging photographs to Cityscape (a tool described in the section earlier). The 140-character limit to each individual tweet forces students to focus on form and accuracy, while the usage of Cityscape encourages them to reflect upon the role of context, location, and juxtaposition of visual linguistic markers within a given landscape. Each student is also required to submit a critical essay and give an oral presentation in which they use both their own contributions and those of their classmates to reflect on how their perception of the Spanish identity of NYC and the role of Spanish within the boundaries of the city has developed and changed over the course of their involvement in the project.

These two courses illustrate how the systematic and structured exploration of urban landscapes can function as the focus for a series of activities and inquiry-driven questions about situated language that generate meaningful and authentic L2 usage inside and outside the classroom space. They also allow us to measure its value for students enrolled in them, identify specific challenges and difficulties they face in such environments, and evaluate the feasibility of extending such courses to other language programs. In both cases, students had multiple opportunities to think about, talk about, and process core concepts about the social presence of Spanish and Hispanic culture in the greater NYC area. Working with activities that required students to engage *in situ* with the target language and culture allowed them to experience aspects of Spanish and Hispanic life in New York that went beyond the textbook or course materials. Being exposed to the various ways by which a community sees itself and talks about itself in the public space introduced students to important concepts and increased their intercultural communicative competence. It also became the basis for perceptive self-reflection on how they—as language learners—situate themselves with respect to Spanish and Hispanic culture as well as to their own language and culture.

The students reported that the inquiry-driven questions and projects made them more aware of the reality of Hispanic presence in NYC, created a personal connection to the language, which in turn increased their motivation to learn it, and, in general, increased their overall satisfaction with the course. Students also noted that the collaborative activities and the group fieldwork increased student–student and instructor–student interactions and helped create a sense of intellectual community in the classroom that bonded over their shared exploration of the social presence of Spanish and Hispanic cultures in NYC. Finally, students repeatedly expressed satisfaction that the course design provided them with tools and skills that went beyond simply heightened cultural or linguistic competences.

Working in groups, presenting their findings, and defending their respective points of view increased their awareness of diverse perspectives; sharpened their interpersonal, interpretive, and presentational modes of communication; taught them to negotiate meaning across languages and cultures; honed their research skills; and prepared them for real-life social and employment situations.

We will next suggest ways by which these pioneering projects could be improved and how future cross-disciplinary and collaborative projects might be designed to more closely connect the language classroom with the modern multilingual and multicultural city. While formal learning environments isolate the learners from the outside world, working on projects that are connected to a specific urban landscape by way of a series of authentic tasks and real-life activities, learners are able to ground their learning in local phenomena and come to understand the local community on a deeper level.

Challenges, Implications, and Future Directions

While it is encouraging that a number of pedagogical initiatives are being developed to prepare L2 learners with the skills necessary for intercultural competence (cf. Bardovi-Harlig, 2001; Félix-Brasdefer, 2007; Modern Language Association, 2007) and to better situate L2 education within both the literal and the metaphorical spaces outside the formal confines of the classroom, it is also clear that a number of challenges remain to be addressed. In this section, we briefly address some of these challenges and outline some possible future directions for incorporating social pedagogies, promoting reflective practices, including the study of urban landscapes, and providing learners with meaningful opportunities to use the target language beyond the classroom.

The various linguistic explorations of urban landscapes undertaken at Columbia and elsewhere continue to be largely distinct, discreet, and unconnected across language programs. If we want to escape a pattern of linguistic insularity and truly explore the nature of urban landscapes in multilingual cities, there is a need for more comprehensive projects that analyze and describe not only the individual facets of a city's multilingual and multicultural diversity but also the richness of its aggregated entirety. After all, the essence of a multilingual city is bound to be more than the sum of each of its monolingual parts.

We need to help our students (and our faculty) break out of their local urban insularity and recognize the fact that cities, and in particular "global cities," are not isolated entities but rather nodes in an ever-growing global network of commercial, political, financial, and cultural transactions so that when they ask questions about their own city, they also need to take into account global linguistic and spatial dimensions and reframe their investigations accordingly. While location-sensitive projects can help reclaim the significance of the local in the global age and counterbalance pedagogical approaches in the L2 classroom that make little to no reference to the actual lived contexts in which the target language is spoken (Kramsch & Thorne, 2002; Thorne et al., 2009), we must also be sensitive to the dynamic nature of urban environments and the accelerating phenomena of real and virtual global mobility.

In the past two decades, research on the sociolinguistics of multilingualism has been transformed by a number of epistemological shifts, which have radically changed our understanding of the relationship between language and society (cf. García & Fishman, 2001; Gardner & Martin-Jones, 2012). Already, in the late 1990s, Michael Byram (e.g. Byram, 1997; Byram & Fleming, 1998) argued that linguistic competence was not enough to develop intercultural competence and that experiential learning could be more beneficial to language learners in that they could "experience situations which make demands upon their emotions and feelings and then reflect upon that experience and its meaning for them" (Byram, 1997, p. 13). Accordingly, students should be helped to recognize that the city is not a spectacle to be passively viewed but rather a space dynamically produced and shaped by a series of practices (linguistic, cultural, and otherwise) that intimately connect people to the places in which they live.

Language programs should assist students in making the vital change in stance from that of a passive spectator who superficially observes and records the imagery of the city to that of an active interpreter who produces urban descriptions that can be used to decipher the city. This may require in turn embracing an active pedagogy that adopts a more ethnographic approach to the study of the target language and culture. However, while recognizing the value of ethnography for studying specific aspects of social and cultural life in the field, it is also important to differentiate between ethnography as an established approach to social research and as a method in language education (Roberts, 2001). Our concern as language educators should not be to prepare students to become trained anthropologists. Our concern should be to familiarize our students with the main tenets of the ethnographic method in order to provide them with "an anthropological sensibility" (Pocock, 1975, pp. 1–29) that will enable them to carry out small-scale ethnographic research projects or studies as part of their language education.

As Damen (1987) has argued, ethnography is both germane and applicable to language and culture education because "it stimulates the process of exploring, describing and understanding an unknown culture by means of actual ethnographic enquiry, contrastive analysis of real cultural groups" (p. 54–56). Therefore, making use of practices and techniques adapted from ethnography in support of more traditional teaching practices deployed in the language classroom can be used to enhance learning and strengthen the overall language curriculum in several ways.

Broadly speaking, ethnography can help language learners deepen their understanding of cultural phenomena, of themselves, and of others and ultimately enhance their attitude toward the study of a foreign language as well as their understanding of their own culture and the culture of local speakers of the L2 (cf. Heath & Street, 2008). And, more generally, the incorporation of ethnography-inspired projects in the language classroom can help produce positive attitudes toward speakers of the target language in preparation for the subsequent execution of cross-cultural projects that can be integrated into the course curriculum and class requirements (cf. Egan-Robertson & Bloome, 1998).

In addition, ethnography can equip students with study and research skills that can easily be transferred to other aspects of their education or even to their future employment. By learning basic ethnographic concepts such as "making strange," "foreshadowed problems," "participant observer," and "thick description," students are introduced to notions that form part of the essential skills and techniques in the field when observing and recording the everyday. Students can then relate the habits of observation, reflexivity, challenging of stereotypes, and close analysis of data nurtured by these notions to other aspects of their language course.

Finally, as Heath and Street (2008) have also pointed out, "doing ethnography" cannot be separated out as an academic activity from engagement with public life, and it can therefore serve to link classroom activities with social action for improving both students' lives and the communities in which they live and study.

Language programs could also introduce and adopt techniques and concepts from oral history (adapted to the needs of language learners) to record and map the memories of urban residents so as to preserve individual and collective urban histories and promote vertical readings of the city. Introducing the concept of the city as a palimpsest would allow students to better understand how a particular geographic space has been shaped and reshaped over successive generations, thereby giving rise to different and successive "senses of place."

An in-depth investigation of urban landscapes and the communities that shape and are shaped by these spaces and under these conditions can not only help deepen the learners' awareness of cultural identity in the community under study but also increase their ability to uncover deeper sociopolitical changes. This could help them accept, interpret and communicate with others, develop a critical social awareness, and become involved in broader issues of social justice.

Students must also be required to reflect on the dynamic qualities of urban environments rather than simply gather static snapshots of a particular place at a particular time. According to Simmel (1903), dynamism is the essence of urban life, and many aspects of urban living involve movement. Thus, they should learn to interrogate movement as it occurs in the multicultural urban landscape rather than simply notice it without questioning it.

As L2 educators, we need to systematically make use of mapping and data visualization techniques and tools that go beyond the visual representation of who speaks what language where at a given point in time and try, instead, to capture and present the dynamic interplay of language and location that is central to city life. What are needed are maps that try to render sociolinguistic ethnographies of language in use in order to try to understand the ways in which linguistic resources, everyday tasks, and social space are intertwined and how the organization of the city—its economies, markets, movements, affiliations—might be linked to the organization of language: its values, mixtures, mobilities, and connections. Students might contribute to the creation of such maps by providing empirical findings and geo-coded statistics as well as information about a particular area with individuated observations, pictures, personal narratives, and other forms of "thick descriptions" that would allow for the visualization of sometimes invisible or overlooked communities. They could thus create multilayered maps that constitute a rich representation of a given space and index their possible geopolitical meanings as well as their sociocultural associations. We should also take into account the fact that the physical city now extends into the digital realm and should allow for the comparative mapping of "objective" representations of cities with their digital avatars.

We also need to devise innovative ways to make use of collaborative and user-driven crowd-based models, such as mobile crowdsourcing and other forms of geo-referenced User Generated Content, to collect linguistic data that would allow for a more precise analysis of the linguistic situation of superdiverse global cities, including the linguistic reformulation of social and ethnic identities that occurs as global populations flow together in such cities.

Finally, we need to explore how one can break free of a linguistic logocentrism that privileges the visual to the detriment of the other senses. Ideally, we should produce alternative maps of the city that call upon the other senses (smellscapes, soundscapes, gustatory and tactile maps, etc.) at least as much as those that record visual stimuli and consider how a given space might be sensorily organized in relation to broader social, linguistic, and cultural practices.

"Reading the Multilingual City: New York City, Urban Landscapes and Urban Multilingualism" is a course currently being developed at Columbia that tries to address these challenges. The course is intended to be part of the undergraduate global core requirement and seeks to bring the city and multilingualism into conversation in order to throw light on the history of New York as an urban space constantly shaped by the coexistence and interaction of multiple cultures and languages. The course explores urban multilingualism through a variety of critical, theoretical, and cultural lenses that interrogate the relationship between the spatial organization of a city and its linguistic profile.

The course promotes inquiry-based, immersive learning activities within a social pedagogy framework that require students to think about how languages exist(ed) in the city as embodied, situated practices. Students are asked to investigate research questions at the nexus of language and the urban environment; complete mapping exercises designed to help them reflect on the spatial dimension of multilingualism in an urban environment; and produce an original digital artifact that crystallizes their experience and illustrates a constitutive aspect of a particular language or of a particular set of discursive practice in the urban landscape.

While the course as designed is not a language course as such, it is an example of a type of course that can function as a bridge between language education and other parts of the curriculum; bring an interdisciplinary perspective to language education; and, in general, reinvigorate language and culture across the curriculum programs by promoting meaningful content-focused language usage outside the traditional language classroom. The course could, for instance, be taught in tandem with regular foreign language courses or include breakout or discussion sessions conducted in a variety of languages, facilitated by graduate or advanced undergraduate native speakers. Either way, such a course would offer numerous opportunities for students to extend their knowledge of a second language beyond L2 courses and apply their linguistic skills to course content, research, and projects in nonlanguage disciplines.

Conclusion

In this chapter, we have highlighted possible synergies between critical language education and place-aware pedagogies in order to emphasize how a synthesis of insights from theories of space and place and from social pedagogies can underpin the design of spatially informed language curricula. The examples provided illustrate how making urban landscapes the object of a sustained, critical analysis can enable language instructors to design rich pedagogical practices that extend formal classroom instruction and allow them to establish productive linkages between literacies in specific contexts and broader social practices.

Developing interdisciplinary research projects and pedagogical practices that more closely tie the classroom to the city and to the communities that live within its boundaries provides a new impetus toward a broader consideration of the value of place and location for language education. It reveals the potential of the complex, evolving nature of the modern multilingual and multicultural city for situated, critical language learning and, in particular, how the systematic study of and engagement with specific elements of situated language can be a powerful resource to promote student-driven learning. Specifically, it can make visible for students how discursive (and other) practices can shape a given geographical space into a series of defined, historical, and localized places.

Shifting the emphasis from language learning as an individual process to one that is more socially engaged, and moving away from a process in which learners only acquire language in a classroom setting in which language and content learning are carefully scaffolded through a structural syllabus focused on acquiring language forms, allows language educators to develop new curricula and new approaches to language teaching that both adopt learning methods suited to the needs of a diverse student population and maximize engagement for all students. These approaches can enable them to connect personal experiences across classrooms, curricula, and the broader community and provide opportunities for language learners to engage deeply with context-based learning materials and pursue authentic interactions in their local communities, which provide them with a dynamic and meaningful context for realistic language usage while also increasing their motivation to put into practice what they have learned.

Acknowledgments

We would like to express our sincere thanks to Lee Abraham and Reyes Llopis-Garcia for allowing us to include their innovative classroom projects to illustrate new ways of engaging language students with the city through project- and inquiry-based learning. We also wish to thank the editors and two anonymous reviewers for their helpful and constructive comments and feedback.

References

Backhaus, P. (Ed.). (2007). *Linguistic landscapes: A comparative study of urban multilingualism in Tokyo*. Bristol, UK: Multilingual Matters.

Bardovi-Harlig, K. (2001). Evaluating the empirical evidence: Grounds for instruction in pragmatics. In K. Rose & G. Kasper (Eds.), *Pragmatics and language teaching* (pp. 13–32). Cambridge, UK: Cambridge University Press.

Barni, M., & Extra, G. (Eds.). (2008). *Mapping linguistic diversity in multicultural contexts*. Berlin, Germany/New York, NY: Mouton de Gruyter.

Bass, R., & Elmendorf, H. (2010). What are social pedagogies? Retrieved from https://blogs.commons.georgetown.edu/bassr/social-pedagogies/

Bass, R., & Elmendorf, H. (2011). Designing for difficulty: Social pedagogies as a framework for course design. *Teagle Foundation White Paper*. Retrieved from https://blogs.commons.georgetown.edu/bassr/social-pedagogies/

Ben-Rafael, E., Shohamy, E., & Barni, M. (2010). Introduction: An approach to an "ordered disorder." In E. Shohamy, E. Ben-Rafael, & M. Barni (Eds.), *Linguistic landscape in the city* (pp. xi–xxviii). Bristol, UK: Multilingual Matters.

Ben-Rafael, E., Shohamy, E., Hasan Amara, M., & Trumper-Hecht, N. (2006). Linguistic landscape as symbolic construction of the public space: The case of Israel. *International Journal of Multilingualism, 3*(1), 7–30.

Benson, P., & Reinders, H. (Eds.). (2011). *Beyond the language classroom*. Basingstoke, UK: Palgrave Macmillan.

Blackwood, R., Lanza, E., & Woldemariam, H. (Eds.). (2016). *Negotiating and contesting identities in linguistic landscapes*. London: Bloomsbury Publishing.

Block, D. (2003). *The social turn in second language acquisition*. Washington, DC: Georgetown University Press.

Block, D. (2008). *Multilingual identities in a global city*. Basingstoke: Palgrave Macmillan.

Blommaert, J. (2013a). *Ethnography, superdiversity and linguistic landscapes: Chronicles of complexity*. Bristol, UK: Multilingual Matters.

Blommaert, J. (2013b). Language and the study of diversity. *Tilburg Papers in Culture Studies, 74*, 1–14.

Blommaert, J. (2016). The conservative turn in linguistic landscape studies. Retrieved from https://alternative-democracy-research.org/2016/01/05/the-conservative-turn-in-linguistic-landscape-studies/

Blommaert, J., & Rampton, B. (2011). Language and superdiversity. In K. Arnaud, J. Blommaert, B. Rampton, & M. Spotti (Eds.), *Language and superdiversity* (pp. 21–48). New York, NY: Routledge.

Bodenhamer, D. J. (2007). Creating a landscape of memory: The potential of humanities GIS. *International Journal of Humanities and Arts Computing, 1*, 97–110.

Bodenhamer, D. J. (2010). The potential of spatial humanities. In D. J. Bodenhamer, J. Corrigan, & T. M. Harris (Eds.), *The spatial humanities: GIS and the future of humanities scholarship* (pp. 14–30). Bloomington, IN: Indiana University Press.

Brown, J. S., & Duguid, P. (2000). *The social life of information*. Cambridge, MA: Harvard Business Press.

Byram, M. (Ed.). (1997). *Face to face: Learning "language-and-culture" through visits and exchanges*. London, UK: CILT.

Byram, M., & Fleming, M. (Eds.). (1998). *Language learning in intercultural perspective: Approaches through drama and ethnography*. Cambridge, UK: Cambridge University Press.

Cenoz, J., & Gorter, D. (2008). The linguistic landscape as an additional source of input in second language acquisition. *IRAL-International Review of Applied Linguistics in Language Teaching, 46*(3), 267–287.

Chesnut, M., Lee, V., & Schulte, J. (2013). The language lessons around us: Undergraduate English pedagogy and linguistic landscape research. *English Teaching, 12*(2), 102.

Damen, L. (1987). *Culture learning: The fifth dimension in the language classroom*. Reading, MA: Addison Wesley Publishing Company.

Dewey, J. (1963). *Experience and education*. New York, NY: Collier.

Ducate, L. (2009). Service learning in Germany: A four-week summer teaching program in Saxony-Anhall. *Die Unterrichtspraxis/Teaching German, 41*, 32–40.

Duff, P. (2007). Second language socialization as sociocultural theory: Insights and issues. *Language Teaching, 40*, 309–319.

Duff, P., & May, S. (Eds.). (2017). *Language socialization. The encyclopedia of language and education* (Vol. 8). Dordrecht, The Netherlands: Springer.

Egan-Robertson, A., & Bloome, D. (1998). *Students as researchers of culture and language in their own communities. Language & social processes [Series]*. Creskill, NJ: Hampton Press.

Félix-Brasdefer, J. C. (2007). Pragmatic development in the Spanish as a FL classroom: A cross-sectional study of learner requests. *Intercultural Pragmatics, 4*(2), 253–286.

Firth, A., & Wagner, J. (1997). On discourse, communication, and (some) fundamental concepts in SLA research. *Modern Language Journal, 81*, 285–300.

Firth, A., & Wagner, J. (2007). Second/foreign language learning as a social accomplishment: Elaborations on a reconceptualized SLA. *The Modern Language Journal, 91*(Focus Issue), 800–819.

García, O., & Fishman, J. A. (Eds.). (2001). *The multilingual apple: Languages in New York City*. New York, NY: Mouton de Gruyter.

Gardner, S., & Martin-Jones, M. (Eds.). (2012). *Multilingualism, discourse, and ethnography*. New York, NY: Routledge.

Gorter, D. (Ed.). (2006). *Linguistic landscape: A new approach to multilingualism*. Bristol, UK: Multilingual Matters.

Gorter, D. (2013). Linguistic landscapes in a multilingual world. *Annual Review of Applied Linguistics, 33*, 190–212.

Gorter, D., & Cenoz, J. (2004). Linguistic landscapes and L2 learners in multilingual contexts. *Paper at EUROSLA, 14*, 8–11.

Gorter, D., & Cenoz, J. (2015). Translanguaging and linguistic landscapes. *Linguistic Landscape: An International Journal, 1*(1–2), 54–74.

Gunderson, J. (2014). Introduction to spatial theory. Retrieved from https://sites.utexas.edu/religion-theory/bibliographical-resources/spatial-theory/overview/

Hancock, A. (2012). Capturing the linguistic landscape of Edinburgh: A pedagogical tool to investigate student teachers' understandings of cultural and linguistic diversity. In C. Hélot, M. Barni, & R. Janssens (Eds.), *Linguistic landscapes, multilingualism and social change* (pp. 249–266). Frankfurt, Germany: Peter Lang.

Heath, S. B., & Street, B. V. (2008). *On ethnography: Approaches to language and literacy research. Language & Literacy (NCRLL)*. New York, NY: Teachers College Press.

Hélot, C., Barni, M., & Janssens, R. (Eds.). (2012). *Linguistic landscapes, multilingualism and social change*. Frankfurt, Germany: Peter Lang.

Holden, C., & Sykes, J. (2011). Leveraging mobile games for place-based language learning. *International Journal of Game-Based Learning, 1*(2), 1–18.

Hult, F. M. (2014). Drive-thru linguistic landscaping: Constructing a linguistically dominant place in a bilingual space. *International Journal of Bilingualism, 18*(5), 507–523.

Ivkovic, D., & Lotherington, H. (2009). Multilingualism in cyberspace: Conceptualising the virtual linguistic landscape. *International Journal of Multilingualism, 6*(1), 17–36.

Jaworski, A., & Thurlow, C. (Eds.). (2010a). *Semiotic landscapes: Language, image, space*. London, UK: Continuum.

Jaworski, A., & Thurlow, C. (2010b). Introducing semiotic landscapes. In A. Jaworski & C. Thurlow (Eds.), *Semiotic landscapes: Language, image, space* (pp. 1–10). London, UK: Continuum.

Johnstone, B. (2010). Language and place. In R. Mesthrie (Ed.), *Cambridge handbook of sociolinguistics* (pp. 203–217). Cambridge, UK: Cambridge University Press.

Justice, C., Rice, J., Warry, W., Inglis, S., Miller, S., & Sammon, S. (2007). Inquiry in higher education: Reflections and directions on course design and teaching methods. *Innovative Higher Education, 31*, 201–214.

Kinginger, C. (2011). Enhancing language learning in study abroad. *Annual Review of Applied Linguistics, 31*, 58–73.

Kramsch, C. (2014). Teaching foreign languages in an era of globalization: An introduction. *Modern Language Journal, 98*(1), 296–311.

Kramsch, C. (2017). Applied linguistic theory and second/foreign language education. In N. Van Deusen-Scholl & S. May (Eds.), *Foreign and second language education. The encyclopedia of language and education* (Vol. 4). Dordrecht, The Netherlands: Springer.

Kramsch, C., & Thorne, S. (2002). Foreign language learning as global communicative practice. In D. Block & D. Cameron (Eds.), *Globalization and Language Teaching* (pp. 83–100). London, UK: Routledge.

Kubota, R. (2016). The multi/plural turn, postcolonial theory, and neoliberal multiculturalism: Complicities and implications for applied linguistics. *Applied Linguistics, 37*(4), 474–494.

Landry, R., & Bourhis, R. Y. (1997). Linguistic landscape and ethnolinguistic vitality: An empirical study. *Journal of Language and Social Psychology, 16*, 23–49.

Lantolf, J., & Thorne, S. L. (2007). Sociocultural theory and second language learning. In B. van Patten & J. Williams (Eds.), *Theories in second language acquisition* (pp. 201–224). Mahwah, NJ: Lawrence Erlbaum.

Lefebvre, H. (1991). *The production of space*. Oxford, UK: Blackwell.

Malinowski, D. (2009). Authorship in the linguistic landscape: A multimodal-performative view. In E. Shohamy & D. Gorter (Eds.), *Linguistic landscape: Expanding the scenery* (pp. 107–125). New York, NY: Routledge.

Malinowski, D. (2010). Showing seeing in the Korean linguistic cityscape. In E. G. Shohamy, E. Ben-Rafael, & M. Barni (Eds.), *Linguistic landscape in the city* (pp. 199–218). Bristol, UK: Multilingual Matters.

Malinowski, D. (2015). Opening spaces of learning in the linguistic landscape. *Linguistic Landscape: An International Journal, 1*, 95–113.

May, S. (Ed.). (1999). *Indigenous community-based education*. Clevedon, UK: Multilingual Matters.

May, S. (Ed.). (2014a). *The multilingual turn: Implications for SLA, TESOL, and bilingual education*. New York, NY: Routledge.

May, S. (2014b). Introducing the multilingual turn. In S. May (Ed.), *The multilingual turn: Implications for SLA, TESOL, and bilingual education* (pp. 1–6). New York, NY: Routledge.

McCarty, T., & Watahomigie, L. (1998). Indigenous community-based language education in the USA. *Language, Culture, and Curriculum, 11*(3), 309–324.

Modern Language Association Ad Hoc Committee on Foreign Languages. (2007). *Foreign languages and higher education: New structures for a changed world*. Retrieved from https://www.mla.org/Resources/Research/Surveys-Reports-and-Other-Documents/Teaching-Enrollments-and-Programs/Foreign-Languages-and-Higher-Education-New-Structures-for-a-Changed-World

Moore, D. (2008). Linguistic landscape and language awareness. In E. Shohamy & D. Gorter (Eds.), *Linguistic landscape: Expanding the scenery* (pp. 253–269). New York, NY: Routledge.

Nash, J. (2016). Is linguistic landscape necessary? *Landscape Research, 41*(3), 380–384.

Norton, B. (2013). *Identity and language learning: Extending the conversation*. Bristol, UK: Multilingual Matters.

Nunan, D., & Richards, J. C. (Eds.). (2015). *Language learning beyond the classroom*. New York, NY: Routledge.

Ohta, A. (2017). Sociocultural theory and second/foreign language education. In N. Van Deusen-Scholl & S. May (Eds.), *The encyclopedia of language and education. Foreign and second language education* (Vol. 4). Dordrecht, The Netherlands: Springer.

Ortega, L. (2010). *The bilingual turn in SLA*. Plenary speech delivered at the American Association for Applied Linguistics Conference, Atlanta, GA.

Ortega, L. (2011). SLA after the social turn: Where cognitivism and its alternatives stand. In D. Atkinson (Ed.), *Alternative approaches to second language acquisition* (pp. 167–180). New York, NY: Routledge.

Ortega, L. (2013). SLA for the 21st century: Disciplinary programs, transdisciplinary relevance, and the bi/multilingual turn. *Language Learning, 63*(S1), 1–24.

Ortega, L. (2014). Ways forward for a bi/multilingual turn in SLA. In S. May (Ed.), *The multilingual turn: Implications for SLA, TESOL, and bilingual education* (pp. 32–54). New York, NY: Routledge.

Overfield, D. (1997). From the margins to the mainstream: Foreign language education and community-based learning. *Foreign Language Annals, 30*(4), 485–491.

Pennycook, A. (2010). *Language as a local practice*. New York, NY: Routledge.

Pennycook, A., & Otsuji, E. (2015). *Metrolingualism: Language in the city*. New York, NY: Routledge.

Pocock, D. (1975). *Understanding social anthropology*. London, UK: Hodder and Stoughton

Roberts, C. (Ed.). (2001). *Language learners as ethnographers* (Vol. 16). Bristol, UK: Multilingual matters.

Rowland, L. (2013). The pedagogical benefits of a linguistic landscape project in Japan. *International Journal of Bilingual Education and Bilingualism, 16*(4), 494–505.

Sassen, S. (2006). The global city: Introducing a concept. *The Brown Journal of World Affairs*, *11*(2), 27–43.
Sayer, P. (2009). Using the linguistic landscape as a pedagogical resource. *ELT Journal*, *64*(2), 143–154.
Scollon, R., & Scollon, S. W. (2003). *Discourses in place: Language in the material world*. New York, NY: Routledge.
Shohamy, E. G., Ben-Rafael, E., & Barni, M. (Eds.). (2010). *Linguistic landscape in the city*. Bristol, UK: Multilingual Matters.
Shohamy, E., & Gorter, D. (Eds.). (2008). *Linguistic landscape: Expanding the scenery*. New York, NY: Routledge.
Simmel, G. (2013). The metropolis and mental life. In J. Lin & C. Mele (Eds.), *The urban sociology reader* (pp. 23–31). New York, NY: Routledge. (Original work published 1903)
Smith, B. (1997). Virtual realia. *Internet TESL Journal*, *3*(7). Retrieved from http://iteslj.org/Articles/Smith-Realia.html
Soja, E. (2003). Writing the city spatially. *City*, *7*(3), 269–280.
Squire, K. (2009). Mobile media learning: Multiplicities of place. *Horizon*, *17*(1), 70–80.
Stroud, C., & Jegels, D. (2014). Semiotic landscapes and mobile narrations of place: Performing the local. *International Journal of the Sociology of Language*, *2014*(228), 179–199.
Swain, M., & Deters, P. (2007). "New" mainstream SLA theory: Expanded and enriched. *Modern Language Journal*, *91*(S1), 820–836.
Thorne, S. L., Black, R., & Sykes, J. (2009). Second language use, socialization, and learning in internet interest communities and online gaming. *Modern Language Journal*, *93*(1), 802–821.
United Nations, Department of Economic and Social Affairs, Population Division. (2014). *World urbanization prospects: The 2014 revision, highlights (ST/ESA/SER.A/352)*. Retrieved from https://esa.un.org/unpd/wup/Publications/Files/WUP2014-Highlights.pdf
Vygotsky, L. S. (1978). *The mind in society: The development of higher psychological processes*. Cambridge, MA: Harvard University Press.

Chapter 2
Encuentros con el español: A Case Study of Critical Service Learning in the Latino Community

Alberto Bruzos, Princeton University

The Social and Critical Turn in Language Education

According to Bass & Elmendorf (2012), social pedagogies are "design approaches for teaching and learning that engage students with what we might call an 'authentic audience' (other than the teacher)." The notion of "community" is central in two different ways: "Ideally, social pedagogies strive to build a sense of intellectual community within the classroom and frequently connect students to communities outside the classroom." As applied to language education, social pedagogies are crucial to address the shortcomings of communicative language teaching (Magnan, 2008) by creating opportunities for students to go beyond the classroom and become members of communities of practice where the target language is spoken, thus leaving the role of "learners" and entering into the role of "speakers/social actors" (Kern & Liddicoat, 2008).

The notion of speaker/actor moves the focus from a conception of language as a system and toward "a conception of language as a dynamic, semiotic resource that the individual combines with other resources to act within the social world" (Kern & Liddicoat, 2008, p. 20). This social approach to language education echoes the increasing interest in social perspectives in the field of Second Language Acquisition (Block, 2003; Firth & Wagner, 1997; Thorne, 2005). It is also aligned with Halliday's (1978) social semiotics, Dell Hymes's (1996) critique of Chomskian linguistics, and more recent developments in applied linguistics and sociolinguistics, which have brought into focus such concepts as "investment," "imagined communities/imagined identities" (Norton, 2013; Norton & Toohey, 2011), "subjectivity" (Kramsch, 2010), and the idea of "language as a local practice" (Pennycook, 2010).

Moreover, the focus on the social dimension of language and the emphasis placed on particularity, intersubjectivity, and reflection is something that social pedagogies share with the type of critical competences increasingly demanded in language education, such as Claire Kramsch's "symbolic competence" (Kramsch, 2006, 2011; Kramsch & Whiteside, 2008), the Modern Language Association's

(MLA) "translingual and transcultural competence" (MLA, 2007), and Jennifer Leeman and Ellen Serafini's "critical translingual competence" (Leeman & Serafini, 2016).

Following the working definition proposed by Kimberly Vinall (2016, p. 5), symbolic competence is "the potential to become aware of and critically reflect on and act on the crossing of multiple borders between linguistic codes and cultural meanings, the self and others, various timescales and historical contexts, and power structures." In order to develop symbolic competence, it is necessary to abandon narrow structuralist approaches to language teaching and engage with language variation, style, discursive practices, and intertextuality (Kramsch, 2011).

The MLA's translingual and transcultural competence shares with symbolic competence a focus on intercultural communication[1] and the goal of developing "critical language awareness, interpretation and translation, historical and political consciousness, social sensibility, and aesthetic perception" (MLA, 2007). Whereas symbolic competence and translingual and transcultural competence focus on cultural meanings and discursive practices, critical translingual competence is more clearly informed by issues of social justice, critical language awareness, and language attitudes and ideologies (Leeman & Serafini, 2016). Despite the differences between these three competences,[2] they can be regarded as variations of a broader approach that brings the social dimension of language to the foreground, blending language learning with the development of an understanding of the cultural, social, political, and ideological aspects of language, linguistic variation, and discourse.

Engaging students in considering how a particular language or variety can be made the object of ideologies, social hierarchies, and political agendas is particularly relevant to the teaching of Spanish in the United States. On the one hand, Spanish is a pluricentric language with numerous regional and national linguistic norms, for the most part mutually intelligible but with different social meanings, levels of acceptability, and degrees of mobility.[3] On the other hand, in the United

---

[1] "The idea of translingual and transcultural competence . . . places value on the ability to operate between languages" (MLA, 2007).
[2] While symbolic competence, particularly as portrayed in Kramsch and Whiteside (2008), considers language contact phenomena such as code-switching and translanguaging, the MLA's definition of translingual and transcultural competence seems to reinforce the boundaries between languages and cultures, portraying students as monolingual English speakers and establishing the goal to acquire a delimitable "target language" (Kramsch, 2014; Leeman & Serafini, 2016). Leeman and Serafini (2016, pp. 64–65) are particularly at odds with this issue; in fact, they propose that the language curriculum must aim to develop the understanding that linguistic variation (including language contact and multilingual practices) is both "a resource for carrying out a wide array of social and political functions and communicating a wide range of symbolic meanings" (p. 65) and a source of language attitudes and ideologies.
[3] See Blommaert's (2010) discussion on the mobility of semiotic resources.

States, Spanish is a minoritized language with a complex social and political significance: it carries the double stigma of being the language of the colonized, the immigrant, the uneducated, and the poor (García & Mason, 2009) and of being an inferior variety of Spanish, deformed and polluted by the influence of English (del Valle, 2011; García, 2011). This is an issue that we should confront if we want our students to become speakers/social actors, to develop a personal voice, and, no less important, to be able to apprehend other voices, understanding *voice* here as a cultural and political notion (Kramsch, 2008)—that is, "the object of identity and community claims."[4]

A pedagogy that blends language learning and critical language awareness[5] should address painful but necessary questions[6] regarding the value of the target language in the life of our communities: Why is Spanish seen as a resource for foreign language learners and as a detriment to the social mobility of Latino students? What is behind the idea of Spanish as "a major potential threat to the country's cultural and political integrity" (Huntington, 2004, p. 33)? Do all Latinos speak Spanish? Do they speak "standard" or "proper" Spanish? What varieties of Spanish are promoted as proper or standard Spanish? What varieties are evaluated as inferior? Why? By whom? And how are these evaluations visible? When is it appropriate for a Spanish language learner to use Spanish with Latinos?

Such questions have been earlier raised by scholars like Ofelia García (2011, 2014), Jennifer Leeman (2004, 2014), José del Valle (2011, 2014), and Nelson Flores and Jonathan Rosa (2015), among others, thus far with little or no influence on the teaching of Spanish as a foreign language. On the contrary, the field is characterized by a lack of politically engaged approaches (Herman, 2007; Hortiguera, 2011; Leeman, 2014) as well as by optimistic discourses on the economic value of the Spanish language (see Muñoz-Basols, Muñoz-Calvo, & Suárez García, 2014).

In the following section, I outline a pedagogical model to promote critical reflection on the social and political dimensions of Spanish through a curriculum combining service learning with course materials on Spanish language in the United States. This model is based on the advanced Spanish course titled SPA 304: Spanish in the Community, offered at Princeton University in spring 2016. First, I discuss the course goals and context, focusing on the use of service learning in Spanish language education. Then, I describe the course curriculum and pedagogical practices, including a sample lesson. Finally, I present and discuss qualitative

---

[4] For a discussion on the role of student and community voices in heritage language education, see Martínez and Schwartz (2012).
[5] I use this term as a shorthand for the kind of critical competence discussed previously. For other uses of critical language awareness as an umbrella term, see Fairclough (1999) and Alim (2005).
[6] See Ennser–Kananen (2016) for a discussion on the role of pain, conflict, and discomfort in language education.

data gathered through service-learning journals, considering the impact of the course on the students' understanding of Spanish language and their own identities as learners.

Service Learning in Spanish Language Education

Although the proliferation of community-based service-learning programs in U.S. language teaching is relatively recent (Thompson, 2012), their historical origins have been traced to the early 20th century (Rabin, 2011, 2014). Service learning is particularly relevant for Spanish (Hellebrandt, 2006), the second most spoken language in the United States, with almost 38 million speakers (Ryan, 2013). However, as noted by Glenn Martínez and Adam Schwartz (2012), Spanish instruction in the United States has usually involved a Eurocentric academic focus: "The voices of even the most immediately local language communities have not been heard and have remained missing and thus are silenced" (p. 39). In contrast, partnering with Spanish-speaking communities in the United States offers an opportunity to deal with issues that are generally marginal to the Spanish language curriculum, if not totally absent from it. I am referring to social conditions like poverty, discrimination, immigration issues, educational barriers, as well as common multilingual practices like code-switching and translanguaging. Such issues and practices are carefully expunged from Spanish language textbooks (Cubillos, 2014; Herman, 2007). Moreover, they also tend to be avoided by Spanish departments, which generally focus on the dialects, literatures, and cultures of Spain and Latin America, and "both directly and indirectly . . . transmit ideologies of nationalism (one language, one nation), standardness (a commitment to linguistic purity and correctness), and monolingualism and bilingualism (assumptions about the superiority of monolingual native speakers)" (Valdés, González, López García, & Márquez, 2003). Inasmuch as textbooks and departments regard Spanish as a foreign language, rather than as a local one, one could argue that they reproduce and reinforce the very ideologies that hinder the legitimacy of Spanish in the United States (Bruzos, 2016).

Service learning, then, offers an opportunity to counteract the prevailing utilitarian and Eurocentric approach to Spanish language teaching (Carney, 2013).[7] Nonetheless, it can also be used to serve a more instrumental and institutional vision, "[commodifying] local communities as resources for language practice" (as criticized by Leeman, 2011), or as a testing ground where "future leaders and

---

[7] To be sure, the utilitarian approach to language teaching is not limited to Spanish. As Monica Heller (2003, 2010) has argued, in recent times there has been a shift from understanding language as being a marker of ethnic and national identity, to understanding language as a commodity that can be acquired, measured, marketed, and exploited. The tension between these two ways of conceiving language (as an objectively measurable skill, and as a constituent and a marker of identity and authenticity) is most evident in the field of language teaching (Heller, 2010).

Table 2.1. Instrumental versus Critical Service Learning (based on Leeman, 2014)

Instrumental Service Learning	Critical Service Learning
Frames students' activities as "charity."	Examines the structural, political, and ideological implications of the problems faced by local communities; questions the role of language in issues of discrimination and exclusion.
Constructs local communities as "resources" or "authentic sites" for language practice.	Establishes a bidirectional and mutually beneficial partnership between students and community members.

participants will reinforce the pleasure of giving and cooperating" (Weldon & Trautmann, 2003). In fact, the literature on Spanish service learning is characterized by a contrast between approaches that focus on measurable outcomes for language students (see Caldwell, 2007; Pellettieri, 2011; Weldon & Trautmann, 2003) and critically engaged approaches (see d'Arlach, Sánchez, & Feuer, 2009; Jorge, 2010; Leeman, Rabin, & Román–Mendoza, 2011; Martínez & Schwartz, 2012; Parra, 2013; Plann, 2002; Trujillo, 2009).[8]

The decision to offer SPA 304 was based on the desire to address the complexity inherent in the position of Spanish as both a local and a foreign language in the United States. As I developed the course, I had in mind the model of critical service learning proposed by Leeman and the social turn of language research and pedagogy discussed in the previous section. Finally, the course was also a response to the growing interest in "service and civic engagement" at Princeton[9] and many other universities.

Overview of Spanish 304: Spanish in the Community

SPA 304 was an advanced course for students with a minimum of five semesters of Spanish or an equivalent competence in the language. The course had an enrollment of 14 students and met twice a week for 90 minutes. Students also spent 60–90 minutes a week (a total of 15–18 hours over the course of the semester) on a service-learning activity that involved working with local programs that served

---

[8] Although Table 2.1 construes as a dichotomy the opposition between instrumental and critical approaches, perhaps we should see it as tension inherent to service learning. Raddon and Harrison (2015) consider this issue, examining contradictory evaluations of service learning in relation to different conceptualizations of neoliberalism.

[9] A report released by the Princeton University Service and Civic Engagement Self-Study Task Force on June 2015 (Service and Civic Engagement Self-Study Task Force, 2015) proposed that "service and civic engagement could be made an embedded and pervasive lens, generating a positive learning spiral throughout the arc of education at both the undergraduate and graduate levels."

Latino children. Some students acted as "big siblings" at Community House Big Sibs, a student-led mentorship project connecting Princeton University students with elementary school students. A second group of students were tutors at Princeton Young Achievers (PYA), an after-school program run by the local YMCA. A third group collaborated with a new dual language program, where they read in Spanish to kindergarten and first-grade students.

Course Content

Class materials included a variety of texts, documents, and videos in English and Spanish. The materials were interdisciplinary and organized around five thematic units that examined different aspects of Spanish language in the United States:

1. *Spanish: an American language* considered the past and present of Spanish language and Spanish-speaking communities in the United States. Drawing on Escobar and Potowski (2015) and Portes and Rumbaut (2001), we unpacked the concept of "immigrant generation" and discussed patterns of language maintenance and assimilation, connecting them to the conflict between the multilingualism characteristic of U.S. society and the language ideology that constructs English as the one and only language of American national identity (Pavlenko, 2002).

2. *Spanish: an immigrant language* examined the ideas of "citizenship" and "illegality" with regard to Latino immigrants in the United States. Given the complexity of these notions, we drew on materials from a variety of media representative of diverse genres and perspectives: film (Young, 1977), ethnographic research (Gomberg-Muñoz, 2010), photo-essay (Berger & Mohr, 2010), video testimonies (AFSC of Western Massachusetts, 2013), critical discourse analysis (Santa Ana, 2002), and cultural studies (Chavez, 2008).

3. *Spanish: a language of identity* tried to shed light on the relation between the Spanish language and Latino identity. Drawing on Leeman (2004), Flores (2000), Tienda and Mitchell (2006), and Mora (2014), we discussed the origins, meanings, and implications of panethnic categories like *Hispanic* or *Latino* as well as their ties to bureaucracy, mass media, and activism. To see how actual Latinos view Latino identity and the intersections with language and race, we used radio and video testimonies like Martínez and Rios (2015) and Brewster, Foster, and Stephenson (2016). Finally, we addressed bilingual identities through the writings of Chicano poet and activist Gloria Anzaldúa (1987) and the testimonies of Latino students compiled by Carreira and Beeman (2014).

4. Building on the previous units, *Spanish: a contested language* examined the language ideologies behind the subaltern status of the Spanish language in the United States. Working in pairs, the students read and summarized a selection of readings on the topic, including Aparicio (2000), Zentella (2007), Hill (2008), and excerpts from Lippi-Green (2011). From those readings, they extracted key notions like "language ideology," "linguistic capital," "linguistic insecurity," "prescriptivism," "linguistic dispossession," "differential bilingualism," "Mock Spanish," and "accented language," which were defined and discussed by the whole class. We then

scrutinized Huntington's (2004) "The Hispanic Challenge" to make the case that language prejudices are often rooted in anti-immigrant and antibilingual attitudes. Following Dávila (2001), Berg (2002), Fuller (2013), and Negrón-Muntaner, Abbas, Figueroa, and Robson (2014), we considered Latino representation in film and mainstream English-language media, looking at the stereotypes imposed on Latino artists and also at their strategies of resistance and subversion. This opened the way for a discussion on how the language use of Latinos is represented in mainstream films and TV, where Latino characters are usually identified by emblematic use of Spanish (*mi amor, señorita*) or by Spanish-accented English, even though most U.S.-born Latinos speak English without a marked accent (Fuller, 2013). To achieve a more nuanced understanding of the boundaries between English and Spanish and between different varieties of Spanish, we read and discussed Urciuoli's (1991) work on the relationship between language, class, and race in New York's Lower East Side as well as an excerpt from Genova and Ramos-Zayas's (2004) ethnography on Mexican and Puerto Rican communities in Chicago.

5. In the last unit, *Spanish: a language of opportunity*, we looked at Spanish as a form of economic and social capital. First, we opposed the different value that the Spanish language has for those who study Spanish as a foreign language and for bilingual Latinos (Pomerantz, 2002). Building on this contradiction, we saw that bilingualism can be constructed as a resource, a right, or a problem (Ricento, 2005; Ruiz, 1984). We then looked at studies that show the socioeconomic benefits of language maintenance (Agirdag, 2014; Portes & Fernández-Kelly, 2007; Portes & Rumbaut, 2014; Rumbaut, 2014) and examined models of bilingual education (García, 2008). To illustrate a model that nurtures *dynamic bilingualism*, we discussed Bartlett and García's (2011) study on Gregorio Luperón High School in New York. To conclude, we revisited notions and references from throughout the course to discuss and contrast José Ángel N.'s (2014) and Dan-el Padilla-Peralta's (2015) coming-of-age memoirs.

Assignments and Pedagogy

To contextualize the materials, a reading guide was circulated before each class (see an example in appendix). Reading guides were typically 4–10 pages long and included learning goals, key concepts, relevant examples, links to online resources and documents, and questions on the material. Before class, students wrote down their thoughts, feelings, and reactions in an online reading journal. They also had to keep a second journal to record their impressions of their work with the community.

All reading guides, discussions, and assignments were in Spanish. While reading journal entries were brief (typically around 100–150 words) and mostly undirected,[10] service-learning journal entries were longer (400–500 words) and

---

[10] Only the first few guides included succinct prompts that the students could follow in their reading journal entries. Very soon I realized that entries were more genuine and interesting when the students chose not to follow my prompts, so I stopped providing them altogether.

responded to an assignment sheet based on the DEAL Model for Critical Reflection (Ash & Clayton, 2009).[11] During class time, students engaged in discussions around the readings and other documents, making connections with what they had observed and experienced during their community service.

Class discussions were complemented by a project for which students had to write and present to the class a narrative about one of their ancestors who first arrived in America or about a friend or person who had immigrated to the United States; to complete their narrative, they conducted interviews and did research in historical documents and archives.[12] There was also a final research project that involved fieldwork and the use of academic sources to explore a topic related to Spanish language and Spanish speakers in the United States.

In order to provide students with tools to gather and interpret data for their final research project (see later in this chapter) and to be more observant during their work with the community, we used some of the readings as models to discuss qualitative research methods (in particular, participant observation and interviews) as well as issues of ethical research (power and positioning, privacy and confidentiality, etc.).[13]

Finding relevant content in Spanish was one of the main challenges in assembling the course syllabus. For most of the topics, there were many readings available in English and just a few in Spanish, most of which drew heavily on English sources. For this reason, around 70% of materials were in English. Although reading guides were instrumental to articulate in Spanish course topics, issues, and terminology, I was worried that students would resist reading in English for a Spanish course. However, when I asked about this in an anonymous survey administered at the end of the semester, they all indicated that they had valued the experience. In particular, they expressed their preference for "having interesting topics/conversations [rather] than simply practicing Spanish at the expense of those interesting subjects." Additionally, reading in English facilitated dealing with longer and more ambitious materials; as one student wrote, "I actually preferred to read in English, because when I read in English I can understand the text much better, and I then can discuss it in Spanish with more confidence."

In the next section, I describe a lesson plan around a reading in English. I detail how the lesson was organized to offer contextual support, facilitate interpretation and discussion, and elicit critical response to the material.

---

[11] I am grateful to Trisha Thorme for suggesting this model.
[12] I adapted this project from Fox (2009, p. 114).
[13] Discussions on methods and ethical issues were always incidental and grounded in particular examples encountered in course readings. For discussions on research methods, I drew on DeWalt and DeWalt (2002), Schostak (2006), Seidman (2015), and Gold and Nawyn (2013, part IX). For issues of ethical research, I followed Cameron, Harvey, Frazer, Rampton, and Richardson (1993) and Madison (2012).

Sample Lesson: Excerpts from *A Seventh Man*, by John Berger and Jean Mohr[14]

The reading guide for Berger and Mohr's (2010) photo-essay began with a text on the differences between "immigrant" and "refugee."[15] This brief text served the purpose of clarifying semantic oppositions (*inmigrante/refugiado; migrante/ emigrante/inmigrante*) and activating relevant vocabulary in Spanish (*persecución política, buscar refugio, establecerse en otro país, país en conflicto, desplazamiento*). It also served to establish a framework of expectations and previous knowledge. Thus, I opened the class by questioning the students about the distinction between immigrants and refugees:[16] What made this distinction so important? Was this just a semantic issue? What was at stake here for those "forced to leave their country because of wars, revolutions or political persecution"?

This first discussion served to introduce the idea that categories like "immigrant," "refugee," and "citizen," which are administrative tools with the power to shape people's destinies (Ngai, 2014), do not necessarily have the objective and unquestionable meaning that we tend to assume they have. As one student wrote in her reading journal:[17]

> *Por ejemplo, cada cubano que huye a los EE.UU. puede automáticamente ser elegible para recibir asilo político Pero los mexicanos que huyen de situaciones opresivas de manera similar en los territorios controlados por los cárteles no lo son. Esa es la parte que me perturba más: hay algún tipo de juicio arbitrario realizado sobre las calificaciones de un inmigrante vs. refugiado.*[18]
>
> For example, every Cuban who runs away to the U.S. can automatically receive political asylum. But Mexicans who similarly run away from oppressive situations in territories controlled by drug cartels do not receive asylum. This is the part that makes me the most uncomfortable: there is a type of arbitrary judgment made about the qualifications of an immigrant vs. a refugee.

---

[14] For the full reading guide, see appendix. An extract from *A Seventh Man* (different from the one included in SPA 304) is available online at *Race & Class*, *16*(3), 251–257. https://doi.org/10.1177/030639687501600303

[15] Retrieved from http://www.fundeu.es/recomendacion/refugiado-inmigrante/

[16] It is worth mentioning that this question was being debated by U.S. media in the context of the European refugee crisis. For instance, see Sengupta (2015).

[17] Reading and service journals received feedback on vocabulary and grammar as well as brief responses with comments and questions. Students used this feedback to correct their entries. This excerpt and the ones that follow include their corrections but have not been further edited for grammar and vocabulary.

[18] As a side note, in January 2017, the Obama administration put an end to the policy (so-called wet foot, dry foot policy) that granted those Cubans who had reached the U.S. shore the chance to remain, qualify for expedited "legal permanent resident" status, and eventually gain U.S. citizenship.

To take this question further, I asked students to work in pairs to write their own definitions of "immigrant," which we then compared and discussed. In contrast to the definition provided by Fundéu ("anyone who arrives in a country with the intention to establish residence there"), all the students coincided in connecting immigration to labor. This took us very close to Berger and Mohr's view of immigration, in which labor plays a central role:

> For capitalism migrant workers fill a labour shortage in a specially convenient way. They accept the wages offered and, in doing so, slow down wage-increases in general. . . . The migrant is in several ways an "ideal" worker. He is eager to work overtime. He is willing to do shift work at night. He arrives politically innocent. (2010, pp. 141–142)

The prereading section was followed by three paragraphs about the material's theme and origin. This part of the guide also gave some clues as to how to read the excerpts—a mix of narrative, poetry, immigration figures, Marxist theory, and photographs, *A Seventh Man* can be difficult to pin down otherwise. Finally, it introduced the issue of whether a document from the 1970s can still be relevant to understanding the predicament faced by today's immigrants.

Since the text was in English, the questions aimed at eliciting critical response rather than facilitating comprehension.[19] Specifically, the questions focused on the relevance and reception of the text, asking students to connect it to previous readings and to present immigration debates in the United States. They also considered the relation between form and subject matter, which in fact singularizes Berger and Mohr's take on the migrant condition (Becker, 2002).

The lesson concluded with a brief PBS documentary on immigrant farm workers in the San Joaquin Valley, California.[20] This documentary served to highlight the relevance of *A Seventh Man* for understanding today's migration. Moreover, it offered an ideal platform to consider issues of privilege and positioning within a service-learning project. Accordingly, the questions in the guide drew attention to the way the reporter dealt with the immigrant community, either directly (issues of communication) or indirectly (issues of representation and exploitation). In this case, there were many things that the students found problematic:[21]

- The reporter did not speak Spanish; he communicated with the immigrants through a translator.
- The documentary individualized and gave voice to employers and activists, whereas immigrant workers were represented as a silent and passive collective.

---

[19] For materials in Spanish, this section of the reading guide was typically longer and combined questions that focused on comprehension of details and general meaning with questions to elicit a critical response.
[20] Available online at http://www.pbs.org/frontlineworld/rough/2009/09/california_the.html
[21] The following issues come from my class notes and the students' reading journals.

- The reporter did nothing to gain the immigrants' trust; instead, he questioned them about their legal status and their intentions to return to Mexico in front of the camera.

Having discussed these problems as a group, we concluded that we should view this documentary as a cautionary tale, an opportunity to gain awareness of potential pitfalls that we ought to avoid in our relationship with the community.

Student Reflections on Language and Identity

In order to assess the impact of the course on the students' understanding of the Spanish language and their own identities as learners, I conducted a qualitative analysis of the service-learning journals. I looked for emergent themes related to issues central to the course syllabus (language and identity; language and citizenship; language and power; multilingualism; bilingual education; language discrimination and prejudice, etc.). Specifically, I looked for reflections connecting theory (course content) to practice (community service). I was interested in the extent to which the students had applied the issues and concepts discussed in the classroom to make sense of their actual service experiences and what issues and notions seemed to be more relevant to this endeavor. More generally, I also looked for mentions of incidents or circumstances related to language and to students' identities as learners and speakers of Spanish.

In total, the students wrote 113 journal entries. Around 60% of the entries engaged in some way with issues relevant to the course content. Nevertheless, there was considerable variability among students: while four favored a descriptive approach with little or no reflection, focusing instead on circumstances or events and the feelings and thoughts evoked by them, six other students seemed very sensitive to issues of language, identity, power, and discrimination, deploying either theoretical concepts or personal experiences (or a mix of both) to reflect on their service encounters. A third group of four students alternated between both approaches. This suggests that, at least for some students, the service component served as a site to engage in participant observation and conduct "fieldwork" in the sense in which Michael Byram (1997) uses this term.[22]

In the following section, I share some reactions and reflections on common themes that highlight the impact of the service learning experience on the students' understanding of Spanish language and their own identity as learners.

---

[22] For Byram (1997, pp. 68–69), *fieldwork* (as opposed to *independent experience)* involves a pedagogical structure, learning objectives determined by the teacher often in consultation with learners, and a prospective and retrospective relationship with the classroom.

English versus Spanish.

Although the students worked with Latino children who could communicate in both Spanish and English, our community partners mostly operated in English. The preference for English had to do with the program's goals and volunteers (not all of whom could speak Spanish) as well as with the diverse population they served.[23] For this reason, it was clear from the beginning that the main goal of the service component was not to serve as a context to practice Spanish. Instead, taking into consideration the needs of our community partners (Lear & Abbott, 2009) and the perils of otherwise commodifying service learning (Leeman, 2011), I envisioned this part of the course as an opportunity for the students to interact with the Spanish-speaking community residing in Princeton and to become aware of the challenges they confront: language barriers, discrimination, access to housing and education, and other issues that we also examined in our readings and discussions. Certainly, the students also found opportunities to communicate in Spanish, particularly those who volunteered to read at the dual language program. But instead of following the dictates of the teacher or the premises of a teaching method, they had to function in bilingual environments that demanded critical decisions (see EXCERPT 1) and interventions (see EXCERPT 2).

EXCERPT 1
R. *(la coordinadora de PYA) nos habló sobre el estatus bilingüe de los niños en PYA. Dijo que la mayoría de ellos hablan español, pero no les gusta hablar en español si no es necesario. Explicó que a veces habla con los estudiantes en español, pero siempre responden en inglés. Esta tendencia está relacionada con el tema de generación sociolingüística de que leímos y como los niños pierden su habilidad de hablar en español debido a la presión social. R. nos dijo que preguntaría a los niños si podían hablar en español con nosotros para que podamos aprender, pero J. y yo respondimos que queremos hacer lo que vaya a ayudarles más. Creo que la meta de este servicio es ayudar a los niños en vez de nosotros mismos. Es probable que aprendamos de la experiencia pero creo que el foco del servicio debe ser en los estudiantes.*

R. (the coordinator of PYA) spoke to us about the bilingual status of the PYA kids. She said that the majority speak Spanish, but don't like to speak Spanish if it isn't necessary. She explained to us that sometimes she speaks to the students in Spanish, but they always respond in English. This tendency is related to the idea of sociolinguistic generation that we read about, and how children lose their ability to speak Spanish because of social pressures. R. told us that she would ask them if they could speak Spanish

---

[23] Both Community House Big Sibs and PYA help children from low- and moderate-income neighborhoods, not exclusively Latinos. The population served by the dual language program was even more diverse in terms of both ethnicity and social class.

with us so we could learn, but J. and I responded that we want to do whatever would help them most. I believe that the goal of this service is to help the kids instead of ourselves. We will probably learn from the experience, but I believe that the focus of the service should be on the students.

EXCERPT 2
La madre de M. llegó a PYA para recoger a su hija, solo para ver que ella no estaba. . . . Ella no pudo hablar con los otros voluntarios sobre su hija, porque ellos no hablan español. . . . Entonces necesité traducir entre todos, y los chicos estaban muy orgullosos al ver que puedo hablar español. Y la madre de M. estaba tan agradecida de que yo podía hablar en su lengua, porque la ayudé mucho. Llamé a la escuela para ver si M. estaba allá (no estaba). Hablé con L. y M., los otros voluntarios, para saber si M. había venido a PYA los días pasados. La madre no podría haber obtenido esta información si nadie hubiera podido hablar español.

M.'s mother arrived at PYA to pick up her daughter, only to discover that she wasn't there. . . . She couldn't speak with the other volunteers about her daughter because they didn't speak Spanish. . . . So I needed to translate between everyone, and the kids were very proud to see that I can speak Spanish. And M.'s mother was very grateful that I could speak her language, because I helped her a great deal. I called the school to see if M. was there (she wasn't). I spoke with L. and M., the other volunteers, to see if M. had come to PYA on previous days. The mother couldn't have obtained this information if no one had been able to speak Spanish.

Spanish as a local language.

A common theme that emerged in the journals was the discovery of the local Latino community and, consequently, of Spanish as a local language. This was the case with a student who, after her weekly work at PYA, could not start her car and had to wait for two hours until a tow arrived.

EXCERPT 3
Durante ese tiempo, tenía la oportunidad de observar el barrio que rodea PYA y las personas en las calles. Fue interesante porque la mayoría eran latinos, y parecía que la gente en este barrio caminaban o montaban sus bicicletas en vez de conducir (quizás muchos de ellos no tienen automóviles). También me di cuenta de que este barrio es un mundo separado del resto de Princeton. Si mi carro estuviera en la calle Nassau, podría haber entrado en Starbucks, Panera, u otra tienda para esperar. Este barrio, donde está PYA, es muy diferente, y revela el aburguesamiento que ha ocurrido en Princeton.

During this time, I had the opportunity to observe the neighborhood that surrounds PYA and the people in the streets. It was interesting because the majority were Latinos, and it seemed like the people of this neighborhood walked or rode bikes instead of driving (perhaps many of them don't have cars). I also realized that this neighborhood is a separate world from the rest of Princeton. If my car were in Nassau street, I could have entered into Starbucks, Panera, or another store to wait. This neighborhood, where PYA is located, is very different, and reveals the gentrification that has occurred in Princeton.

This discovery is particularly striking if we consider that it takes less than five minutes to walk from the university campus to this Latino neighborhood. The close presence of a lively community of immigrants from Guatemala, Mexico, and Honduras, unbeknownst to many, is in stark contrast to the fact that our students generally experience Spanish as a local language only through expensive study abroad and internship programs in Spain and Latin America. Thus, the tendency to ignore U.S. Spanish is not only manifest in the dialects and cultural references that inform our curricula; as Gao and Park (2015, p. 80) have argued , "Different places can present themselves as more efficient sites for learning certain languages, based on factors such as prevalent multilingualism or (supposed) authenticity of local language varieties." Students showed a clear critical understanding of the socio-economic disparities behind spatial segregation. As another student wrote:

EXCERPT 4
La comunidad de Princeton tiene una profunda división con respecto a la diversidad económica y racial que algunas veces hace invisibles a los que vienen de poblaciones subrepresentadas. La parte de Princeton que todos los estudiantes conocen es bonita y tiene varias boutiques y siempre está llena de turistas. Si se camina sólo cinco minutos por la calle Witherspoon, se encuentra un mundo completamente diferente que caracteriza la segregación espacial que existe en Princeton.
The Princeton community has a profound division with respect to economic and racial diversity that sometimes makes invisible underrepresented populations. The part of Princeton that all the students are familiar with is pretty and has many boutiques and is always full of tourists. If one walks only five minutes on Witherspoon street, one finds oneself in a completely different world that characterizes the spatial segregation that exists in Princeton.

Language as a social practice.

Residential segregation organizes urban space around ethnicities and income levels, thus confining minoritized languages to certain neighborhoods and social interactions. This spatial order is only one of the many factors that regulate language in multilingual communities.[24] The awareness that language is governed

---

[24] The spatial order can be further examined through linguistic landscape projects; for guidance, see Shohamy and Gorter (2009); Martínez (2003); García, Espinet, and Hernández (2013).

by a complex web of spatial, contextual, and social circumstances is evident in the following comment:

EXCERPT 5
Lo más saliente es el uso dinámico del lenguaje y su capital cultural correspondiente en contextos diferentes. El primer día que fui al PYA, F. me dijo que prefería hablar en inglés en vez de español, y supuse que se comunicaría mejor en el idioma que había escogido, pero me di cuenta durante el semestre que mi conclusión no era verdad. Ni F. ni los demás hablaban con ninguno de los voluntarios en español aunque varios eran hablantes nativos del idioma. También hablaban en inglés entre ellos; sin embargo, casi todos los chicos hablaban español con sus padres cuando ellos llegaron para recogerlos. No entiendo totalmente las distintas esferas culturales que gobernaban la elección de cada lengua, pero es claro que usaban el inglés en el contexto académico mientras que el español era más familiar.

The most salient thing is the dynamic use of language and its corresponding cultural capital in various contexts. The first day I went to PYA, F. told me he preferred to speak in English instead of Spanish, and I supposed that he would communicate better in the language he had chosen, but I realized during the semester that my conclusion wasn't true. Neither F. nor any of the others spoke with any of the volunteers in Spanish, although many of them were native speakers of the language. They also spoke English among each other; nonetheless, almost all the kids spoke Spanish with their parents when they came to pick them up. I don't understand completely the different cultural spheres that govern the choice of each language, but it's clear that they used English in an academic context, whereas Spanish was more familiar.

The experience that students gained during their weekly community service made them reevaluate their assumptions and look afresh at the relationships between language and context. For instance, this student's comment suggests that his work and observation at PYA allowed him to understand that deciding which language to use, or whether one may mix languages, involves complex social codes that go beyond the set of forms and rules people commonly regard as English or Spanish. In fact, being in regular contact with monolingual English and Spanish speakers, children in immigrant neighborhoods from early on learn to switch from one language to the other and negotiate the linguistic diversity that surrounds them (Zentella, 1997). For them, English and Spanish are resources that can be used to express solidarity or mark ethnic boundaries, signal conformity to social rules, or exhibit a position of resistance (Urciuoli, 1991).

Language and identity.
As one student wrote, the community service component of the course "made everyone in the class feel closer to the Princeton community (the town, not the

campus)." However, this closeness compelled students to rethink their identities as learners and speakers of Spanish. Some comments that managed to establish a link between classroom discussions and personal observations were particularly sharp. For example, a student who for the first time had responded in Spanish to her "little sibling" returned to Urciuoli's (1991) work to comprehend her reaction:

EXCERPT 6
Era claro que mi respuesta en español le había sorprendido. Me dijo, "How did you know to say that?" Cuando le pregunté cómo se había sentido acerca de mi breve uso de español, me dijo "It's awkward." . . . Parece que para ella, tal como para los puertorriqueños en el artículo de Urciuoli, el español es suyo; pertenece a su comunidad y sus miembros (como D. y M., con quien habla en español). Pero cuando alguien ajena, como yo, lo habla es algo "awkward" e incómodo.

It was clear that my response in Spanish had surprised her. She told me, "How did you know how to say that?" When I asked her how my brief use of Spanish had felt, she said, "It's awkward." . . . It seems that for her, as for the Puerto Ricans in Urciuoli's article, Spanish is hers; it belongs to her community and its members (like D. and M., with whom she speaks in Spanish). But when someone from the outside, like me, speaks Spanish, it's "awkward" and uncomfortable.

It is important to note that the conception of Spanish in terms of belonging, which the student is developing here, puts into perspective the institutional discourses about the value of learning the Spanish language that permeate our universities and departments, making clear that issues of power are central to determine who is accepted as a legitimate member of a speech community. In fact, the non-Latino students enrolled in SPA 304 (and particularly those who were learning Spanish to work as doctors, lawyers, or social workers in Latino communities) were very impressed by Urciuoli's account of how some of her informants resented white Americans speaking in Spanish to them, something that they saw as threatening and even racist (Urciuoli, 1991, pp. 298–299).[25] As the same student went on to explain in a subsequent journal entry:

EXCERPT 7
El texto de Urciuoli demuestra que aunque el español puede ser necesario en algunos contextos para participar en la comunidad, no garantiza la aceptación de extranjeros. Las políticas de poder también son muy importantes en la percepción del uso de la lengua

---

[25] We find the same attitude in Sabino Arana, the father of Basque nationalism. Arana was horrified by the prospect of Spaniards learning Basque: "If our invaders were to learn Basque, we would have to abandon this language . . . and devote ourselves to speak Russian, Norwegian or any other language unknown to them as long as we were under their rule" (Sarrionandia, 2012, p. 523).

en varios contextos. Pensando de nuevo en una de mis experiencias tempranas con Big Sibs—cuando M. pensó que no era posible que podía hablar español—es posible que la percepción de poder también tuviera un papel en su reacción. Quizás desde su perspectiva, una persona 'mayor' que pertenece a una institución como Princeton estaba invadiendo una lengua que era suya, personal y familiar. . . . Mientras que para A. el español es una lengua vinculada a concepciones de pertenencia, conexiones y entendimiento cultural, para mí el español es más bien un recurso o habilidad. A. usó mi celular para grabar videos de L. y mirar las fotos que había tomado y me preguntó por qué mi celular estaba en español. Le contesté que lo había puesto así porque quería practicar español.

Urciuoli's text demonstrates that although Spanish can be necessary in certain contexts to participate in the community, it doesn't guarantee acceptance of strangers. The politics of power are also very important in the perception of language use in various contexts. Thinking again about my early experiences with Big Sibs when M. thought that I couldn't speak Spanish—it's possible that the perception of power had a role in her reaction. Perhaps from her perspective, an "older" person who comes from an institution like Princeton was invading a language that was hers, personal and familiar. . . . Whereas for A. Spanish is a language linked to conceptions of belonging, connections, and cultural understanding, for me, Spanish is more a resource or skill. A. used my cellphone to record videos of L. and to look at the photos I had taken and she asked me why my cellphone was in Spanish. I responded that I had put it like that in order to practice my Spanish.

In addition to questioning the idea that membership in a speech community is automatically available to those who have acquired certain linguistic resources (grammar rules, accents, repertoires, styles), this student seems to be keenly aware that power dynamics of age and status complicate her role as social actor/speaker of Spanish. This makes her see herself as someone who may be trespassing a personal and familiar language. Also noteworthy in this excerpt is the student's awareness that, because of the status of Spanish as a minoritized and contested language, there is an element of cultural appropriation in learning Spanish as a skill or professional resource. The deep impact of this realization on the student's identity as a learner and speaker of Spanish is patent in the following excerpt:

EXCERPT 8
En estos "encuentros con el español," M. y A, mostraron que para ellas, el español no es algo que puede ni debe entender una persona como yo, una negra "americana." Nunca había experimentado este tipo de respuesta al oírme hablar español; especialmente contradijo mi experiencia en Cuba donde mucha gente pensó que era cubana hasta que hablaba.

In these "encounters with Spanish," M. and A. demonstrated that for them, Spanish isn't something that someone like me, a black "American," could or should understand. I had never experienced this type of response from someone hearing me speak Spanish; it especially contradicted my experience in Cuba, where many people would think I was Cuban until I spoke.

Limitations and Issues of Implementation

The main limitation of this case study is the difficulty of generalizing from a singular experience and reproducing it in a different context. Nevertheless, there are some significant theoretical and practical issues that emerge from the pedagogical model described earlier with respect to its implementation in other institutions.

As I explained previously, dealing with English language materials in a Spanish class did not upset my students, nor was it detrimental to their ability to articulate the subject matter in Spanish. On the contrary, they found that reading in both English and Spanish made it easier for them to understand concepts and perspectives, which in turn improved their confidence to participate in class discussions. Nevertheless, Escobar and Potowski (2015) is a very complete and accessible resource for teachers who would rather include more readings in Spanish.

The use of Spanish with the community is a different issue. As a general rule, students should not expect to use Spanish all the time (Lear & Abbott, 2009). Teachers and program directors who would rather maximize the use of Spanish in the service experience should look for community partners and tasks that need Spanish language assistance (for models, see Leeman et al., 2011; Martínez & Schwartz, 2012). In any case, the use of Spanish should not be imposed on individuals who would rather use English with the students.

Reflection is an essential component of a successful service-learning experience. In particular, reflection prompts are necessary to serve as a bridge between coursework and community work (Eyler & Dwight, 1999). The variability of responses to the service experience in SPA 304 journals raises the question of whether to opt for a broad approach, hoping that students will make meaningful connections between class material and lived experiences, or to provide them with narrow and goal-oriented guidelines, even when this may predispose all learners to conceptualize their community partners and experiences in a similar fashion, or to offer precisely the type of feedback that they think will satisfy the teacher.[26] Although students need scaffolding, excessive scaffolding "turns learning into an abstraction, something that happens externally. The more scaffolding there is, the less embodied the learning will be" (Sample, 2012). This is an important issue to consider when designing and implementing a class with a service component.

---

[26] For a study that addresses the reliability of student feedback and reflection, see Barreneche (2011, p. 113).

Conclusion

Social approaches to language education call into question the idea that language acquisition is a process that can be "categorized, evaluated, tested and described from a quantitative point of view along a linear scale of development" (Kern & Liddicoat, 2008, p. 20). Instead of this abstract, objective, and often standardized conception of learning, social pedagogies propose a more personal and "embodied" relation to knowledge (Bass & Elmendorf, 2012). According to this point of view, social approaches to language education are designed to situate instruction in environments where communication can be authenticated (Magnan, 2008; Van Lier, 1996) and where learners can function as social actors (Kern & Liddicoat, 2008).

The focus on social action, engagement, and subjectivity makes social pedagogies particularly suited for the purpose of developing critical competences. Because of the pluricentricity of the Spanish language and the minoritized and troubled condition of Spanish in the United States, in the field of Spanish language education, there is a demand for critical approaches that explore "the principles and social meaning of variation, the sociolinguistic functions of translanguaging practices, language attitudes and ideologies, the relationship between language and identity, and the sociopolitics of language inside and outside the U.S." (Leeman & Serafini, 2016) and in which "the development of communication skills is not conceived as the acquisition of a purely technical ability but imagined as the acquisition of a greater capacity to engage in communicationally challenging and socio-politically loaded encounters" (del Valle, 2014, p. 370). In this chapter, I have presented a model of an advanced course that attempts to respond to these demands by combining community service and course materials on the social, cultural, and political dimensions of Spanish in the United States.

The observations that students recorded in their service-learning journals suggest that the cyclical combination of classroom discussion and fieldwork led them to reconsider their understanding of Spanish and their own identities as learners and speakers of this language. The impact was particularly powerful for those who managed to integrate their classroom and community experiences. Among other things, students became aware of issues of language and power; language and identity; monolingualism and multilingualism; language ideologies and prejudices; language variation, and U.S. language policy. They became aware of the implications that speaking Spanish may have for different people: for the colonizer and the colonized; for the privileged and the unprivileged; for the learned and the illiterate; for the monolingual and the multilingual. Their intense "encounters with Spanish," in and outside of the classroom, put into perspective their previous learning and experiences, making visible the gap between the image of Spanish projected by our curricula and the complexities of Spanish in actual speech communities.

Acknowledgments

I would like to thank the volume editors and the anonymous reviewers for their insightful suggestions to improve the manuscript. I am also thankful to Trisha Thorme and Maria Bohn for their support and guidance to develop SPA 304. Special gratitude goes to community program supervisors, Rosie Segovia, Sofía Gómez, and Tracey Goldberg, and to the extraordinary group of students who made this work possible.

References

AFSC of Western Massachusetts. (2013, September 25). Testimony project [Video file]. Retrieved from https://www.youtube.com/watch?v=jhCorZyXb6Y

Agirdag, O. (2014). The long-term effects of bilingualism on children of immigration: Student bilingualism and future earnings. *International Journal of Bilingual Education and Bilingualism, 17*(4), 449–464.

Alim, H. S. (2005). Critical language awareness in the United States: Revisiting issues and revising pedagogies in a resegregated society. *Educational Researcher, 34*(7), 24–31.

Anzaldúa, G. (1987). *Borderlands: The new mestiza*. San Francisco, CA: Aunt Lute Books.

Aparicio, F. (2000). Of Spanish dispossessed. In R. Dueñas González & I. Melis (Eds.), *Language ideologies: Critical perspectives on the Official English Movement* (Vol. 1, pp. 248–275). Mahwah, NJ: Lawrence Erlbaum Associates.

Ash, S. L., & Clayton, P. (2009). Generating, deepening, and documenting learning: The power of critical reflection in applied learning. *Journal of Applied Learning in Higher Education, 1*, 25–48.

Barreneche, G. I. (2011). Language learners as teachers: Integrating service-learning and the advanced language course. *Hispania, 94*(1), 103–120.

Bartlett, L., & Garcia, O. (2011). *Additive schooling in subtractive times: Bilingual education and Dominican immigrant youth in the Heights*. Nashville, TN: Vanderbilt University Press.

Bass, R., & Elmendorf, H. (2012). Social pedagogies: Designing for difficulty. Social pedagogies as a framework for course design. Retrieved from https://blogs.commons.georgetown.edu/bassr/social-pedagogies/

Becker, H. S. (2002). Visual evidence: *A seventh man*, the specified generalization, and the work of the reader. *Visual Studies, 17*(1), 3–11.

Berg, C. R. (2002). *Latino images in film: Stereotypes, subversion, and resistance*. Austin, TX: University of Texas Press.

Berger, J., & Mohr, J. (2010). *A seventh man: A book of images and words about the experience of migrant workers in Europe* (2nd ed.). London, UK: Verso.

Block, D. (2003). *The social turn in second language acquisition*. Washington, DC: Georgetown University Press.

Blommaert, J. (2010). *The sociolinguistics of globalization*. Cambridge, UK: Cambridge University Press.

Brewster, J., Foster, B., & Stephenson, M. (2016, February 29). A conversation with Latinos on race [Video file]. Retrieved from http://www.nytimes.com/2016/02/29/opinion/a-conversation-with-latinos-on-race.html

Bruzos, A. (2016). El capital cultural del español y su enseñanza como lengua extranjera en Estados Unidos. *Hispania, 99*(1), 5–16.

Byram, M. (1997). *Teaching and assessing intercultural communicative competence*. Clevedon, UK: Multilingual Matters.

Caldwell, W. (2007). Taking Spanish outside the box: A model for integrating service learning into foreign language study. *Foreign Language Annals, 40*(3), 463–471.

Cameron, D., Harvey, P., Frazer, E., Rampton, B., & Richardson, K. (1993). Ethics, advocacy, and empowerment: Issues of method in researching language. *Language and Communication, 13*(2), 81–94.

Carney, T. M. (2013). How service-learning in Spanish speaks to the crisis in the humanities. *Hispania, 96*(2), 229–237.

Carreira, M. M., & Beeman, T. (2014). *Voces: Latino students on life in the United States.* Santa Barbara, CA: ABC-CLIO.

Chavez, L. R. (2008). *The Latino threat: Constructing immigrants, citizens, and the nation.* Stanford, CA: Stanford University Press.

Cubillos, J. H. (2014). Spanish textbooks in the US: Enduring traditions and emerging trends. *Journal of Spanish Language Teaching, 1*(2), 205–225.

d'Arlach, L., Sánchez, B., & Feuer, R. (2009). Voices from the community: A case for reciprocity in service-learning. *Michigan Journal of Community Service Learning, 16*(1), 5–16.

Dávila, A. M. (2001). *Latinos, Inc: The marketing and making of a people.* Berkeley and Los Angeles, CA: University of California Press.

del Valle, J. (2011). Política del lenguaje y geopolítica: España, la RAE y la población latina de Estados Unidos. In S. Senz & M. Alberte (Eds.), *El dardo en la Academia* (pp. 551–590). Barcelona, Spain: Melusina.

del Valle, J. (2014). The politics of normativity and globalization: Which Spanish in the classroom? *The Modern Language Journal, 98*(1), 358–372.

DeWalt, K. M., & DeWalt, B. R. (2002). *Participant observation: A guide for fieldworkers.* Plymouth, UK: Altamira Press.

Ennser-Kananen, J. (2016). A pedagogy of pain: New directions for world language education. *The Modern Language Journal, 100*(2), 556–564.

Escobar, A. M., & Potowski, K. (2015). *El español de los Estados Unidos.* Cambridge, UK: Cambridge University Press.

Eyler, J., & Dwight E. G. (1999). *Where's the learning in service-learning?* San Francisco, CA: Jossey-Bass.

Fairclough, N. (1999). Global capitalism and critical awareness of language. *Language Awareness, 8*(2), 71–83.

Firth, A., & Wagner, J. (1997). On discourse, communication, and (some) fundamental concepts in SLA research. *The Modern Language Journal, 81*(3), 285–300.

Flores, J. (2000). *From bomba to hip-hop: Puerto Rican culture and Latino identity.* New York, NY: Columbia University Press.

Flores, N., & Rosa, J. (2015). Undoing appropriateness: Raciolinguistic ideologies and language diversity in education. *Harvard Educational Review, 85*(2), 149–171.

Fox, H. (2009). *"When race breaks out": Conversations about race and racism in college classrooms.* New York, NY: Peter Lang.

Fuller, J. M. (2013). *Spanish speakers in the USA.* Bristol, UK: Multilingual Matters.

Gao, S., & Park, J. S.-Y. (2015). Space and language learning under the neoliberal economy. *L2 Journal, 7*(3), 78–96.

García, O. (2008). *Bilingual education in the 21st century: A global perspective.* Malden, MA; Oxford, UK: Wiley-Blackwell.

García, O. (2011). Planning Spanish: Nationalizing, minoritizing and globalizing performances. In M. Díaz-Campos (Ed.), *Handbook of Hispanic sociolinguistics* (pp. 667–685). Malden, MA; Oxford, UK: Wiley-Blackwell.

García, O. (2014). U.S. Spanish and education: Global and local intersections. *Review of Research in Education, 38*(1), 58–80.

García, O., Espinet, I., & Hernández, L. (2013). Las paredes hablan en El Barrio: Mestizo signs and semiosis. *Revista Internacional de Lingüística Iberoamericana, 21*(1), 135–152.

García, O., & Mason, L. (2009). Where in the world is US Spanish? Creating a space of opportunity for US Latinos. In W. Harbert, S. McConnell-Ginet, A. Miller, & J. Whitman (Eds.), *Language and poverty* (pp. 78–101). Bristol, UK: Multilingual Matters.

Genova, N. D., & Ramos-Zayas, A. Y. (2004). *Latino crossings: Mexicans, Puerto Ricans, and the politics of race and citizenship*. New York, NY: Routledge.
Gold, S. J., & Nawyn, S. J. (Eds.) (2013). *Routledge international handbook of migration studies*. New York, NY: Routledge.
Gomberg-Muñoz, R. (2010). *Labor and legality: An ethnography of a Mexican immigrant network*. New York, NY: Oxford University Press.
Halliday, M. A. K. (1978). *Language as a social semiotic: The social interpretation of language and meaning*. London, UK: Edward Arnold.
Hellebrandt, J. (2006). Spanish service-learning research from 1999–2003: Effects on faculty, department, community and discipline. *Hispania, 89*(4), 919–926.
Heller, M. (2003). Globalization, the new economy, and the commodification of language and identity. *Journal of Sociolinguistics, 7*(4), 473–492.
Heller, M. (2010). The commodification of language. *Annual Review of Anthropology, 39*, 101–114.
Herman, D. M. (2007). It's a small world after all: From stereotypes to invented worlds in secondary school Spanish textbooks. *Critical Inquiry in Language Studies, 4*(2), 117–150.
Hill, J. H. (2008). *The everyday language of white racism*. Chichester, UK; Malden, MA: Wiley-Blackwell.
Hortiguera, H. (2011). "They are a very festive people!" El baile perpetuo: Comida, arte popular y baile en los vídeos de enseñanza de español como lengua extranjera. *Razón y palabra, 78*. Retrieved from http://dialnet.unirioja.es/servlet/articulo?codigo=3820948
Huntington, S. P. (2004). The Hispanic challenge. *Foreign Policy, 141*, 30–45.
Hymes, D. (1996). *Ethnography, linguistics, narrative inequality: Toward an understanding of voice*. London, UK: Taylor & Francis.
Jorge, E. (2010). Where's the community? *Hispania, 93*(1), 135–138.
Kern, R., & Liddicoat, A. J. (2008). Introduction: From the learner to the speaker/social actor. In G. Zarate, D. Lévy, & C. Kramsch (Eds.), *Handbook of multilingualism and multiculturalism* (pp. 17–23). Paris, France: Éditions des Archives Contemporaines.
Kramsch, C. (2006). From communicative competence to symbolic competence. *The Modern Language Journal, 90*(2), 249–252.
Kramsch, C. (2008). Voice in L2 acquisition: Speaking the self through the language of the other. In G. Zarate, D. Lévy, & C. Kramsch (Eds.), *Handbook of multilingualism and multiculturalism* (pp. 25–27). Paris, France: Éditions des Archives Contemporaines.
Kramsch, C. (2010). *The multilingual subject*. Oxford, UK; New York, NY: Oxford University Press.
Kramsch, C. (2011). The symbolic dimensions of the intercultural. *Language Teaching, 44*(3), 354–367.
Kramsch, C. (2014). Teaching foreign languages in an era of globalization: Introduction. *The Modern Language Journal, 98*(1), 296–311.
Kramsch, C., & Whiteside, A. (2008). Language ecology in multilingual settings: Towards a theory of symbolic competence. *Applied Linguistics, 29*(4), 645–671.
Lear, D., & Abbott, A. (2009). Aligning expectations for mutually beneficial community service-learning: The case of Spanish language proficiency, cultural knowledge, and professional skills. *Hispania, 92*(2), 312–323.
Leeman, J. (2004). Racializing language: A history of linguistic ideologies in the US Census. *Journal of Language and Politics, 3*(3), 507–534.
Leeman, J. (2011). Standards, commodification, and critical service learning in minority language communities. *The Modern Language Journal, 95*(2), 300–303.
Leeman, J. (2014). Critical approaches to the teaching of Spanish as a local-foreign language. In M. Laporte (Ed.), *The Routledge handbook of Hispanic applied linguistics* (pp. 275–292). London, UK: Routledge.

Leeman, J., Rabin, L., & Román–Mendoza, E. (2011). Identity and activism in heritage language education. *The Modern Language Journal, 95*(4), 481–495.

Leeman, J., & Serafini, E. J. (2016). Sociolinguistics for heritage language educators and students: A model for critical translingual competence. In M. Fairclough & S. Beaudrie (Eds.), *Innovative approaches in HL pedagogy: From research to practice* (pp. 56–79). Washington, DC: Georgetown University Press.

Lippi-Green, R. (2011). *English with an accent: Language, ideology and discrimination in the United States* (2nd ed.). London, UK; New York, NY: Routledge.

Madison, D. S. (2012). *Critical ethnography: Method, ethics, and performance* (2nd ed.). Thousand Oaks, CA: Sage Publications.

Magnan, S. S. (2008). The unfulfilled promise of teaching for communicative competence: Insights from sociocultural theory. In J. Lantolf & M. Poehner (Eds.), *Sociocultural theory and the teaching of second language* (pp. 351–379). London, UK: Equinox.

Martínez, A., & Rios, F. (2015, September 8). Are you "Latino enough"? How (not) speaking Spanish creates Latino identity questions [Radio broadcast episode]. Retrieved from http://www.scpr.org/programs/take-two/2015/09/08/44388/are-you-latino-enough-how-not-speaking-spanish-cre/

Martínez, G. (2003). Signs of the times: Globalization and the linguistic landscape along the US Mexico border. *Río Bravo: A Journal of Borderlands: New Series, 2*(1), 57–68.

Martínez, G., & Schwartz, A. (2012). Elevating "low" language for high stakes: A case for critical, community-based learning in a medical Spanish for heritage learners program. *Heritage Language Journal, 9*(2), 37–49.

Modern Language Association. (2007). *Foreign languages and higher education: New structures for a changed world*. Retrieved from https://www.mla.org/Resources/Research/Surveys-Reports-and-Other-Documents/Teaching-Enrollments-and-Programs/Foreign-Languages-and-Higher-Education-New-Structures-for-a-Changed-World

Mora, G. C. (2014). *Making Hispanics: How activists, bureaucrats, and media constructed a new American.* Chicago, IL: University of Chicago Press.

Muñoz-Basols, J., Muñoz-Calvo, M., & Suárez García, J. (2014). Hacia una internacionalización del discurso sobre la enseñanza del español como lengua extranjera. *Journal of Spanish Language Teaching, 1*(1), 1–14.

N., J. A. (2014). *Illegal: Reflections of an undocumented immigrant.* Urbana, Chicago, and Springfield, IL: University of Illinois Press.

Negrón-Muntaner, F., Abbas, C., Figueroa, L., & Robson, S. (2014). The Latino media gap: A report on the state of Latinos in US media. Retrieved from https://fusiondotnet.files.wordpress.com/2015/02/latino_media_gap_report.pdf

Ngai, M. M. (2014). *Impossible subjects: Illegal aliens and the making of modern America.* Princeton, NJ: Princeton University Press.

Norton, B. (2013). *Identity and language learning: Extending the conversation* (2nd ed.). Bristol, UK: Multilingual Matters.

Norton, B., & Toohey, K. (2011). Identity, language learning, and social change. *Language Teaching, 44*(04), 412–446.

Padilla Peralta, D. (2015). *Undocumented: A Dominican boy's odyssey from a homeless shelter to the Ivy League.* New York, NY: Penguin Press.

Parra, M. L. (2013). Expanding language and cultural competence in advanced heritage- and foreign-language learners through community engagement and work with the arts. *Heritage Language Journal, 10*(2), 253–280.

Pavlenko, A. (2002). "We have room for but one language here": Language and national identity in the US at the turn of the 20th Century. *Multilingua, 21*(2–3), 163.

Pellettieri, J. (2011). Measuring language-related outcomes of community-based learning in intermediate Spanish courses. *Hispania, 94*(2), 285–302.

Pennycook, A. (2010). *Language as a local practice.* New York, NY: Routledge.

Plann, S. J. (2002). Latinos and literacy: An upper-division Spanish course with service learning. *Hispania, 85*(2), 330–338.

Pomerantz, A. (2002). Language ideologies and the production of identities: Spanish as a resource for participation in a multilingual marketplace. *Multilingua, 21*(2/3), 275–302.

Portes, A., & Fernández-Kelly, P. (2007). Sin margen de error: Determinantes del éxito entre hijos de inmigrantes crecidos en circunstancias adversas. *Revista Migraciones, 22,* 47–78.

Portes, A., & Rumbaut, R. G. (2001). *Legacies: The story of the immigrant second generation.* Berkeley and Los Angeles, CA: University of California Press.

Portes, A., & Rumbaut, R. G. (2014). *Immigrant America: A portrait* (4th ed.). Berkeley and Los Angeles, CA: University of California Press.

Rabin, L. (2011). Community service and activism in heritage languages, New York City, 1915–1956. *Foreign Language Annals, 44*(2), 338–352.

Rabin, L. (2014). Service-learning/*Aprendizaje-servicio* as a global practice in Spanish. In M. Lacorte (Ed.), *The Routledge handbook of Hispanic applied linguistics* (pp. 168–183). New York, NY: Routledge.

Raddon, M.-B., & Harrison, B. (2015). Is service-learning the kind face of the neo-liberal university? *The Canadian Journal of Higher Education, 45*(2), 134–153.

Ricento, T. (2005). Problems with the "language-as-resource" discourse in the promotion of heritage languages in the U.S.A. *Journal of Sociolinguistics, 9*(3), 348–368.

Ruiz, R. (1984). Orientations in language planning. *NABE Journal, 8,* 15–34.

Rumbaut, R. G. (2014). English Plus: Exploring the socioeconomic benefits of bilingualism in Southern California. In R. M. Callahan & P. C. Gándara (Eds.), *The bilingual advantage: Language, literacy, and the labor market.* Clevedon, UK: Multilingual Matters.

Ryan, C. (2013). Language use in the United States: 2011. United States Census Bureau. Retrieved from https://www.census.gov/prod/2013pubs/acs-22.pdf

Sample, M. (2012, December 18). Intrusive scaffolding, obstructed learning (and MOOCs). Retrieved from http://www.samplereality.com/2012/12/18/intrusive-scaffolding-obstructed-learning-and-moocs/

Santa Ana, O. (2002). *Brown tide rising: Metaphors of Latinos in contemporary American public discourse.* Austin, TX: University of Texas Press.

Sarrionandia, J. (2012). *¿Somos como moros en la niebla?* (J. Rodríguez Hidalgo, trans.) Pamplona, Spain: Pamiela.

Schostak, J. (2006). *Interviewing and representation in qualitative research.* Maidenhead, UK: Open University Press.

Seidman, I. (2015). *Interviewing as qualitative research: A guide for researchers in education and the social sciences.* New York, NY: Teachers College Press.

Sengupta, S. (2015, August 27). Migrant or refugee? There is a difference, with legal implications. *The New York Times.* Retrieved from https://www.nytimes.com/2015/08/28/world/migrants-refugees-europe-syria.html

Service and Civic Engagement Self-Study Task Force. (2015). Final report. Princeton University. Retrieved from http://www.princeton.edu/strategicplan/taskforces/sce/

Shohamy, E. G., & Gorter, D. (Eds.). (2009). *Linguistic landscape: Expanding the scenery.* New York, NY: Routledge.

Thompson, G. (2012). *Intersection of service and learning: Research and practice in the second language classroom.* Charlotte, NC: Information Age Publishing.

Thorne, S. L. (2005). Epistemology, politics, and ethics in sociocultural theory. *The Modern Language Journal, 89*(3), 393–409.

Tienda, M., & Mitchell, F. (Eds.). (2006). *Multiple origins, uncertain destinies: Hispanics and the American future.* Washington, DC: National Academy Press.

Trujillo, J. A. (2009). *Con todos:* Using learning communities to promote intellectual and social engagement in the Spanish curriculum. In M. Lacorte & J. Leeman

(Eds.), *Español en Estados Unidos y otros contextos de contacto: Sociolingüística, ideología y pedagogía* (pp. 369–395). Madrid, Spain: Iberoamericana.

Urciuoli, B. (1991). The political topography of Spanish and English: The view from a New York Puerto Rican neighborhood. *American Ethnologist, 18*(2), 295–310.

Valdés, G., González, S. V., López García, D., & Márquez, P. (2003). Language ideology: The case of Spanish in departments of foreign languages. *Anthropology & Education Quarterly, 34*(1), 3–26.

Van Lier, L. (1996). *Interaction in the language curriculum: Awareness, autonomy, and authenticity.* New York, NY: Longman.

Vinall, K. (2016). "Got Llorona?" Teaching for the development of symbolic competence. *L2 Journal, 8*(1), 1–16.

Weldon, A., & Trautmann, G. (2003). Spanish and service-learning: Pedagogy and praxis. *Hispania, 86*(3), 574–585.

Young, R. M. (1977). *Alambrista!* [Motion picture]. United States: Filmhaus.

Zentella, A. C. (1997). *Growing up bilingual: Puerto Rican children in New York.* Malden, MA: Wiley-Blackwell.

Zentella, A. C. (2007). "Dime con quién hablas y te diré quién eres": Linguistic (in)security and Latin@ unity. In J. Flores & R. Rosaldo (Eds.), *The Blackwell companion to Latino studies* (pp. 25–39). Malden, MA: Blackwell.

Appendix

ANTES DE VER LOS MATERIALES

FUNDEU.ES: *Refugiado* no es lo mismo que *inmigrante*[1]

El término *refugiado* se aplica al que huye por un conflicto o por persecución política, por lo que no equivale a *inmigrante*, que es cualquier persona que llega a un país para fijar su residencia en él.

En las noticias sobre la crisis que vive Europa con relación a la llegada masiva de personas procedentes de África y de Asia se encuentran ejemplos como los siguientes: «La Guardia Costera griega rescata a más de 700 inmigrantes en 48 horas», «Una crisis de inmigrantes sin precedentes obliga a la UE a buscar respuestas» y «Merkel y Rajoy preparan juntos la cumbre de los refugiados».

Como criterio general y según las definiciones del Diccionario académico, *inmigrante* es un término que incluye a todos aquellos que inmigran, es decir, que llegan a un país para establecerse en él; también puede hablarse de *emigrante*, si el punto de vista es el del país de salida, o *migrante*, que incluye a ambos y es más frecuente en el español de América.

Desde un punto de vista lingüístico, y con independencia de la definición precisa establecida en derecho internacional, un *refugiado* es aquel que 'se ve obligado a buscar refugio fuera de su país a consecuencia de guerra, revoluciones o persecuciones políticas'.

---

[1] Fuente: http://www.fundeu.es/recomendacion/refugiado-inmigrante/

Dado que no todos los refugiados buscan establecerse en otro país, sino que solo huyen por su propia seguridad —a menudo de modo temporal, como se aprecia en los casos donde la protección la han encontrado en un campamento fronterizo con el país en conflicto—, es impropio llamarlos *inmigrantes*.

En la actual crisis de la Unión Europea hay claros indicios de que este desplazamiento de masas obedece a una guerra y a la persecución política, por lo que lo preciso en todos los ejemplos anteriores habría sido optar por *refugiados*.

John Berger & Jean Mohr – *A Seventh Man*. Extractos

Este libro, con texto de John Berger y fotografías de Jean Mohr, fue escrito en 1973-1974 y es un retrato de la vida migrante en Europa occidental.

De acuerdo con el análisis del sociólogo Howard Becker, el libro es un collage de "poesía; historia de «Él», un trabajador migrante arquetípico, explicando este estatus con lujo de detalles, todo lo que eso significa y, lo más acertado de todo esto, de forma tanto específica como genérica; estadísticas sobre los trabajadores migrantes: demografía, orígenes, accidentes en el trabajo, y otra serie de elementos relevantes; algunas generalizaciones de la teoría marxista sobre el desarrollo capitalista, las relaciones entre países desarrollados y subdesarrollados, y la explotación de los trabajadores migrantes; y fotografías que no están referenciadas, ni explicadas, ni analizadas en el texto, sino que, antes bien, se presentan de tal manera que desarrollan su propia forma de comunicar".[2]

John Berger declara en el prefacio que el libro se ha quedado anticuado en algunos aspectos. Sin embargo, recientemente ha sido traducido y editado en México por el sello independiente oaxaqueño sur+ (2011) y por la editorial española Captain Swing (2015). El editor mexicano Pablo Rojas, de hecho, opina que el libro es "más actual que nunca". "Cuando lo lees o relés", dice, "esas historias que le contaron a Berger hace 35 o 40 años son las mismas que puedes encontrar en el tren de Tapachula, en el camino a Tijuana, en una Casa del Migrante o en una estación de Lechería".[3]

1. En Estados Unidos, en 2016, el libro se lee con una doble distancia espacial y temporal. ¿Cómo le llega a un lector americano contemporáneo el mensaje del libro? ¿Es este mensaje todavía actual?
2. ¿Cuáles son las ideas centrales de este documento? Intenta resumirlas en 3-4 puntos.
3. ¿Qué convergencias y divergencias hay entre el mensaje de Berger y Mohr y lo que hemos venido leyendo y discutiendo en clase?

---

[2] Ver http://www.antropologia.cat/files/Quaderns-e16(1-2)_Becker.pdf
[3] Ver http://archivo.eluniversal.com.mx/cultura/64944.html

4. ¿Qué ideas y citas te parecen más relevantes pensando en la situación actual de los inmigrantes y la inmigración en Estados Unidos?
5. En tu opinión, ¿cómo funciona el montaje de texto y fotografías para retratar la condición migrante?

http://1.bp.blogspot.com/_6BfXcmq8vyk/TK_EbVVWZtI/AAAAAAAAB7U/h1mMI7kiNqs/s1600/56276.jpg

California: The Immigration Dilemma

http://www.pbs.org/frontlineworld/rough/2009/09/california_the.html

En 2009, el reportero Jason Margolis viajó por el *Valle de San Joaquín* (California) para ver cómo había influido la crisis económica de 2008 en las condiciones de trabajo de los inmigrantes. El documental incluye testimonios de trabajadores inmigrantes y también de algunos propietarios agrícolas [*farmers*].

Lee el texto de presentación y después haz clic en **WATCH VIDEO** para ver el documental (11:25 minutos).[4]

1. ¿Qué relación hay entre lo que cuenta el reportaje y otros materiales del curso (especialmente Berger y Mohr, Gomberg-Muñoz y el documental "Testimonio Project")?
2. ¿Qué ideas sobre la inmigración mexicana y el trabajo inmigrante aparecen en el documental? ¿Quién tiene las distintas ideas o puntos de vista? ¿Es el documental objetivo, o se alinea con una de esas ideas o puntos de vista?
3. Observa con atención la escena en la que Margolis entrevista a un grupo de trabajadores. ¿Qué piensas sobre esta escena?
4. ¿Por qué crees que el primer propietario agrícola al que entrevista Margolis [1:45] se resiste a hablar del estatus de sus trabajadores delante de la cámara? ¿Cómo responde el propietario al que entrevista dentro del auto [3:05]?
5. ¿Por qué crees que la chica a la que Margolis entrevista en la manifestación [*demonstration*] miente en primera instancia sobre su estatus [9:50]? ¿Por qué cambia de opinión? ¿Qué harías tú en su lugar?
6. El estatus de los trabajadores parece ser tabú tanto para los empleadores como para los empleados. ¿Qué diferencias hay entre el silencio de las dos partes? ¿Qué consecuencias tiene este tabú?
7. ¿Qué piensas sobre la manera en que Margolis aborda el tema y los sujetos [la gente] del reportaje? Si tú fueras un reportero o una reportera, ¿habrías hecho algo diferente? ¿Qué?

---

[4] Si no puedes ver el vídeo, usa el siguiente enlace: https://www.youtube.com/watch?v=C0ACLhxrc1U

Chapter 3
Lessons from the CruCES Project: Community Service Learning and Intercultural Sensitivity in the Foreign Language Classroom

Diana Ruggiero, University of Memphis

Introduction

In a 2007 report on the state of foreign language (FL) programs in higher education, the Modern Language Association (MLA) issued a call for change in the governance structure, curricula, and agenda of language programs in order to meet the current and future educational and professional needs and challenges of students in the 21st century. Specifically, the report advocated for a diversification and integration of the curriculum beyond disciplinary boundaries through an emphasis on shared objectives: the development of translingual and transcultural competence.

Although the impact of the MLA's call for transformation has yet to be fully assessed, it nonetheless resonates with the increasing diversification of language program course offerings and degree programs as well as with the emergence of scholarship in the areas of Languages for Specific Purposes (LSP) and Community Service Learning (CSL), which are particularly well suited to advance the aims of the MLA report. To contribute to a growing body of scholarship (see, e.g., McBride, 2010; Rodriguez-Sabater, 2015) and further illuminate the role and value of CSL in fostering translingual and transcultural competence, this study focuses on intercultural sensitivity development (ISD) within the context of a CSL project.

In fall 2015, students enrolled in SPAN 4703, an upper-division course on Spanish for the professions and the community, participated in a grant-funded collaborative community service-learning project involving two local nonprofit organizations, Caritas Village and El Centro Cultural Latino de Memphis, and community members from the diverse West Binghampton neighborhood of Memphis, Tennessee. The Creating Communities, Engaged Scholarship (CruCES) project sought to build community and capacity in West Binghampton through the combination of entrepreneurship and the arts. Throughout the semester, students worked together with designated community leaders to develop and market sustainable, arts-based microeconomy projects that would later be taught to others within the community. In the process, students also engaged in a study on intercultural sensitivity.

Using mixed methods to assess the impact of the CruCES project, the purpose of this study was to address the following research questions: (1) Does CSL promote ISD among students? If so, how and to what extent? (2) What factors may or may not contribute to the development of intercultural sensitivity in this particular case as well as in a service-learning context in general? (3) How might service-learning experiences be improved so as to provide an environment conducive to the development of intercultural sensitivity? (4) Lastly, what insights does this particular study pose for our understanding of intercultural sensitivity (what it is and how it is developed) and for the assessment of intercultural sensitivity?

The connection between intercultural sensitivity and translingual and transcultural competence is implicit though made complicated by the proliferation of distinct yet related terminology across a spectrum of disciplines addressing intercultural competence. Translingual and transcultural competence connote the ability to move between multiple languages, communication modalities, cultures, and cultural contexts with a degree of ease and fluidity (MLA, 2007). This adaptability, in turn, is part and parcel of what language, behavioral, cognitive, and other scholars refer to as intercultural competence or one's ability to effectively and appropriately interact with others in an intercultural context (Deardorff & Edwards, 2013). Intercultural competence is therefore characterized in terms of skills, behaviors, and attitudes, including linguistic competence. To date, language scholars addressing intercultural competence focus predominantly on the acquisition and development of language skills and cultural knowledge necessary for enacting effective and appropriate intercultural communication and enhancing global citizenship (e.g., Byram, 1997, 2009; Liddicoat & Scarino, 2013; Timpe, 2013). Yet much remains in the way of exploring how language study can enhance or help foster the underlying attitudes conducive to the acquisition and further development of intercultural competence. This study concerns itself therefore not with the linguistic aspects of intercultural competence but with the related concept of intercultural sensitivity or the underlying attitudes conditioning the acquisition, demonstration, and development of intercultural and, by extension, translingual and transcultural competence.

Literature Review

The benefits of CSL for language learning are well documented in the existing literature on LSP and CSL. In addition to fulfilling the communities goal area of the American Council on the Teaching of Foreign Languages' (ACTFL) world-readiness standards (Abbott & Lear, 2010), CSL has the potential to motivate student learning, strengthen linguistic skills, develop professional language skills, and foster translingual and transcultural competence (Barreneche, 2011; Ebacher, 2013; Hellebrandt, Arries, & Varona, 2003; Hellebrandt & Jorge, 2013; Pérez-Llantada & Watson, 2011). In the process, it empowers students and local communities in bridging the needs and aspirations of students, language programs, and institutions of higher learning with those of local, or even global, communities and community partners (Carracelas-Juncal, 2013; Lear & Abbott, 2009; Lear & Sanchez, 2013; Magaña, 2015; Petrov, 2013). Though not without its challenges, the increasing interest in and integration of CSL into the language curricula, as evident in the growing scholarship on CSL (Hellebrandt & Jorge, 2013), speaks to its relevance to LSP and by extension to the greater goals and aims of modern language programs in promoting community engagement.

As noted earlier, the terms "translingual" and "transcultural competence" connote the skills, behaviors, and attitudes exemplified in the concepts of intercultural competence and intercultural sensitivity. The interdisciplinary and diverse literature on intercultural competence employs often overlapping definitions of intercultural competence, intercultural sensitivity, and other related terms that have recently been critically examined (Deardorff, 2006). According to Deardorff (2006), a consensus definition of the term "intercultural competence" emphasizes effective and appropriate interaction within intercultural contexts. This definition is reinforced by that of Spitzberg and Changnon (2009), who similarly assert that intercultural competence connotes "the appropriate and effective management of interaction between people, who, to some degree or another, represent different or divergent affective, cognitive, and behavioral orientations to the world" (p. 7). As with translingual and transcultural competence, intercultural competence is therefore often discussed in the academic literature in terms of its demonstrative skills, behaviors, and attitudes (Spitzberg & Changnon, 2009).

In comparison, the term "intercultural sensitivity" is often used interchangeably with intercultural competence. Its use in discussions of developmental and process-oriented models of intercultural competence, however, suggests a more nuanced definition of intercultural sensitivity that directs attention to cognitive orientations rather than behavioral skills and traits. Specifically, Bennett (1993) and Deardorff (2009) define "intercultural sensitivity" in terms of one's attitudes or mindset regarding difference (e.g., cultural, racial, ethnic, socioeconomic). Intercultural sensitivity thus refers specifically to attitudes or mindsets indicative of one's ability to develop and demonstrate intercultural competence. Following Bennett and Deardorff, this study uses the term "intercultural sensitivity" to refer to one's underlying attitudes regarding difference (i.e., cultural, racial, ethnic, socioeconomic) conditioning the ability to acquire and demonstrate intercultural competence.

As a lifelong process (Deardorff & Edwards, 2013), ISD occurs over time and through contact with others of different backgrounds (e.g., cultural, racial, ethnic, socioeconomic). Bennett (1993) suggests that the development of intercultural sensitivity occurs in predictable stages, which he outlines in his Developmental Model of Intercultural Sensitivity (DMIS). Consisting of six stages (denial, defense, minimization, acceptance, adaptation, and integration), Bennett's DMIS posits that continued exposure to difference positively impacts the development of intercultural sensitivity. In short, intercultural contact allows for the adaptation of cognitive orientations. Bennett's model ultimately suggests that these stages progress from an ethnocentric to an ethnorelative mindset, meaning that one will not only become more tolerant of difference with continued intercultural contact but will eventually identify with, or more specifically integrate oneself within, the mindset of the "other."

Similarly, Deardorff's (2009, Deardorff & Edwards, 2013) Process Model of Intercultural Sensitivity (PMIS) emphasizes process over specific behaviors in the acquisition of intercultural competence. Envisioned as a circular process, Deardorff's model posits that the acquisition, demonstration, and continued development of intercultural competence and sensitivity begin and end with one's underlying attitudes and mindset. Envisioned as a circular feedback loop, her model moves from internal to external outcomes and back, beginning with attitudes and moving through newly acquired knowledge and comprehension and critical thinking skills to desired external outcomes (i.e., behaviors) and back to attitudes. Both Bennett's and Deardorff's models illuminate the need for attending to not only the acquisition of communicative skills, cultural knowledge, and critical thinking skills in the development of intercultural competence but also cognitive orientations. For language educators and program directors, this means providing opportunities for engaging in intercultural contact beyond the classroom.

Despite the significance of CSL for ISD, to date, only two studies (McBride, 2010; Rodriguez-Sabater, 2015) specifically examine the relationship between CSL and ISD and focus on CSL and intercultural sensitivity among students in FL classrooms. They both suggest a positive correlation between CSL and ISD. McBride (2010) examined student intercultural competence over the course of a tutoring or teaching assignment with second language learners. She found that the students most engaged in the Second Language Acquisition process of their respective tutorees provided greater depth of reflection in their journals and therefore demonstrated a higher degree of intercultural competence after a semester-long program. McBride argued that successful student engagement with CSL requires a frame of reference (a concept borrowed from a previous study of new teacher cognition—Levin, Hammer, & Coffrey, 2009) focused on the needs of the community in question rather than on the needs of the self. McBride also contended that though student training in reflective writing might produce more instances of intercultural competence, such explicit instruction misses the larger point of refocusing student attention on the CSL experience and needs of the community.

Similarly, Rodriguez-Sabater (2015) examined student end-of-course reflection papers in an L2 Spanish course for evidence of intercultural competence.

Using Bennett's (2008) intercultural competencies framework (i.e., mindset, skillset, and heartset) to assess journal entries, she found that students demonstrated the highest number of intercultural competence skills in the area of mindset, which refers to statements reflecting student attitudes and beliefs. Similarly to McBride, Sabater suggested that lack of experience or training with reflective writing among the students might account for the low demonstration of intercultural competence in the other two competency areas.

Service learning has also been found to be beneficial for heritage learners (see Carracelas-Juncal, 2013; Magaña, 2015; Petrov, 2013; Thompson, 2012). Taken collectively, these studies support the notion that CSL has an impact on student attitudes and beliefs regarding CSL, community service, and difference (e.g., cultural, racial, ethnic, socioeconomic). For example, Thompson (2012) found that the CSL experience fostered reflection on cultural and socioeconomic differences among heritage learners, despite the fact that they share a common language with the community they serve, a finding echoed in studies by Petrov (2013), Magaña (2015), and Carracelas-Juncal (2013). As a result, the service-learning experience proved to be personally transformative for the heritage learners, who benefited from their newfound awareness in terms of increased self-esteem and motivation to continue learning Spanish to serve the community (see Carracelas-Juncal, 2013). Though focused on the identity process of heritage learners and not on the question of intercultural sensitivity *per se*, these findings are nonetheless significant in that they foreground the transformative potential of the CSL experience as expressed in student reflections. Indeed, reflection on difference as a result of intercultural contact necessitates a reflexive and critical encounter with the self, which then potentially leads to modification of one's fundamental attitudes regarding others (Deardorff & Edwards, 2013).

Method

Inscribing itself in this line of inquiry, this study critically approaches the design of the CruCES project and specifically addresses the challenges in the assessment of intercultural competence and sensitivity encountered in McBride's (2010) and Rodriguez-Sabater's (2015) studies by refining the assessment tools. Specifically, this study uses quantitative and qualitative methods in the assessment of ISD and examines how student reflection journals can be enhanced by incorporating digital photographs and critical reflection questions in addition to written reflections. Both Bennett's DMIS and Deardorff's PMIS are used to analyze and assess the development of student intercultural sensitivity. Lastly, this study design draws on Deardorff and Edwards's (2013) contention, building on Gordon Allport's (1954) contact hypothesis that intercultural contact alone is insufficient to engender intercultural sensitivity. Rather, a successful CSL project must be inclusive, equitable, cooperative/collaborative, and mutually supportive for all stakeholders involved. The CruCES project was designed so that all stakeholders, including students, would have a voice in and agree upon the design and goals of the project.

Course/Project Design

SPAN 4703 is an upper-division Spanish course focused on Spanish for the professions and the community. Offered as an elective, this course integrates service learning as a core pedagogical method. Class time is evenly divided between traditional classroom learning and CSL. During the CruCES project, for example, class convened on campus on Tuesdays and off campus at Caritas Village on Thursdays. On campus, classroom time was devoted to the presentation and discussion of theories, concepts, and issues related to Spanish for the professions and CSL, such as intercultural competence models, LSP pedagogy, CSL project design, and community partnerships. Off campus meetings, in contrast, were devoted to the project and related activities within the community itself. This meant engaging with locals, participating in workshops, and collaborating with community project leaders toward the development of the arts-based projects while at Caritas Village. In addition, students were required to complete an additional 14 hours of community service beyond the hours spent toward the project during designated class/CSL times. These hours could include additional hours devoted to the project or to some other related service opportunities. Many students, for example, chose to engage in translating and interpreting activities for local organizations such as Caritas Village, a major partner in the CruCES project.

The CruCES project partnered SPAN 4703 with Caritas Village and El Centro Cultural Latino de Memphis (housed in Caritas Village). Both organizations are located in the heart of West Binghampton, a culturally and linguistically diverse and historically troubled neighborhood that has recently experienced a surge in new immigrants. The greater Binghampton area encompasses approximately two square miles located between Midtown and East Memphis. According to 2010 census data, the population of Binghampton numbers over 12,000 individuals, the majority of whom self-identify as African Americans. Approximately 14% of the population are immigrants, the majority of whom hail from Latin American, African, and Asian countries, including Mexico, El Salvador, Kenya, Sudan, Ethiopia, China, Nepal, Vietnam, Cambodia, and India. According to information compiled by the Community Leveraging Investments for Transformation (LIFT) organization, many of these immigrants are refugees who come to Binghampton specifically as a result of the area's social services and affordable housing. Indeed, while the area has historically suffered from unemployment, urban blight, low educational achievement, and poverty-related crime, Binghampton residents today benefit from the presence and work of numerous organizations offering a variety of social services to the community and working to better living conditions in the area, including Caritas Village and El Centro in addition to the Binghampton Development Corporation, Planned Parenthood, and the Christ Community Health Center, to name a few.

Founded by Onie Johns, who also served as director until January 2017, Caritas Village is a community center that provides a broad range of services for the people of West Binghampton and Memphis in general. A single, two-story brick building on the corner of Harvard Avenue and North Merton Street, Caritas Village consists of a restaurant, a spacious dining and meeting area (which also serves as an art gallery), a large, multipurpose room on the second floor, and an outside community garden. Caritas Village provides free meals for those in need, free health screening, educational and cultural resources, and artisan and artwork. Most significantly, it provides a space for people and organizations to gather, share, and serve the community. Thus, in addition to local community members, Caritas hosts a broad spectrum of the surrounding population, including college professors and students, business people, politicians, and community organizations such as El Centro Cultural de Memphis.

Founded by Richard Lou, also chair of the art department at the University of Memphis, El Centro similarly provides needed social and educational services as well as cultural resources to and for the Memphis Latino population, such as English language classes; workshops and informational programs related to professional, social, and legal matters of local concern; and cultural and educational workshops for families and children (e.g., art and theater classes, karate lessons, and information sessions on higher education preparation and funding for children of first-generation immigrants). They also engage the greater Memphis population through cultural festivals and events such as the annual Tamale festival, which features a tamale cooking competition, live music and dance by local Latino artists, information tables on local Latino and Latino-serving organizations, local food vendors, and activities for children. Both Caritas Village and El Centro were crucial in providing the physical space and means for CSL and engagement during the CruCES project.

Collaborative by design, the CruCES project partnered students in groups with community leaders toward the completion, marketing, and sale of sustainable arts-based projects. Community leaders were solicited and chosen with the help of Caritas Village and El Centro Cultural Latino de Memphis. The primary criteria for inclusion in the project were residence within the neighborhood of Binghampton and knowledge of a unique cultural tradition or skill in the area of the arts that could be developed during the project. In all, four community leaders participated in the project, each possessing a diverse range of artistic knowledge and skills, mainly in the areas of artisan work. Through dialogue, community leaders and the student groups chose a project that could eventually be shared with others in the community as a viable and sustainable entrepreneurial activity. Students and community leaders devoted the remainder of the semester to further developing and marketing the project and product. Student engagement with community leaders and others within the neighborhood of West Binghampton occurred primarily at Caritas Village during the designated time for the Thursday afternoon meeting of SPAN 4703. Student engagement with the community, however, extended beyond class time as per project needs and course requirements.

In addition to the group projects, students and community leaders, along with other interested individuals of the West Binghampton neighborhood, jointly participated in workshops, lectures, and discussions related to the project and to CSL. Guest speakers from the university and local organizations, for example, presented and gave workshops on teamwork and leadership, photography, microeconomics, marketing, entrepreneurship, and Latin American music and culture. Team leaders likewise presented their respective artistic skills and cultural traditions. Students facilitated a World Café–style discussion addressing the concerns and needs of the West Binghampton neighborhood and the issues of community and community service. Lastly, many students volunteered additional hours interpreting for the free health clinic operated out of Caritas Village. In sum, students devoted a total of 28 hours during which they engaged with the community, in the form of collaborative service learning, volunteer work, or jointly participating in workshops. Though significant, the number of hours was not as crucial to the outcome of the project as was the design and attitude of the students.

Participants

In total, 15 undergraduate students (4 males, 11 females), enrolled in SPAN 4703, participated in this study. As an upper-division Spanish course with a prerequisite requirement for enrollment, the students, not all Spanish majors, exhibited a range of command in their Spanish speaking and writing abilities from intermediate to advanced. Indeed, a little over half of the participating students were heritage learners (total eight) who likewise demonstrated a range of speaking and writing abilities from the intermediate to advanced level. In the initial survey, of the 15 participants, 3 students reported having had some experience with service learning from a previous class, while total 9 reported having had experience in the community volunteering in some capacity, either through school, church, or some other organization.

Study Design

The CruCES project involved a mixed-methods study design to assess student ISD over the course of the project. The quantitative portion of the study involved the use of pre- and post-project surveys. The pre-project survey questions related to student experience with CSL and community engagement and perceptions of intercultural sensitivity and of how they thought the CSL project might impact their intercultural sensitivity. The post-project survey questions similarly addressed student perceptions of how their experience with CSL during the course of the semester impacted their thoughts on community, community service and engagement, and intercultural sensitivity. The post-project survey questions thus differed from those of the pre-project survey in that the post-project survey specifically sought to gauge student perceptions of their ISD as a result of participation in the CruCES project. As such, the surveys do not necessarily conform to a standard pre-posttest design.

The qualitative portion of the study consisted of a three-part digital reflection journal involving digital pictures, a written reflection, and critical reflection questions. Though reflection journals are frequently used in CSL assessments (Deardorff, 2009), they nonetheless pose a challenge in that students often fail to engage the assignment with sufficient depth of reflection. McBride (2010) and Rodriguez-Sabater (2015) recognize that this may be due to a lack of experience with reflective writing. They also note that when provided with training and models in reflective writing, students tend to overcompensate in seeking to conform to the expectations of the teacher, thus further exacerbating the problem of assessment. So as to not influence student reflections and journal results, no formal instruction on reflective writing or models were given to the students. Students were asked only to reflect on their experience with the CruCES project and individual group efforts, whether observations, insights, frustrations, or other comments. Given that the focus of the study was on cognitive orientations, or attitudes, students were given the option to write their journal entries in the language in which they felt most comfortable reflecting.

The problem of student reflective writing abilities was mediated, in part, through the use of digital photographs and critical questions. Though digital media is increasingly integrated in language instruction and in service-learning projects to help facilitate the learning process and make more evident the project process and outcomes (e.g., Paesani, Allen, & Dupuy, 2016), the value of digital photography in specifically assessing student ISD is yet to be considered. Following anthropological assertions that visual representations convey subjective experiences and perceptions of reality rather than an objective truth (Pink, 2013; Ruby, 1982), digital photographs provide a unique means of observing shifting student experiences and perspectives. Specifically, digital photographs have the potential to reveal one's evolving relationship to place and others. In the context of this study, therefore, digital photographs served to reinforce student journal entries and provide greater depth of clarity and perspective on student perceptions of Caritas, the community, and the CruCES project. Students were thus instructed to take digital photographs of any aspect of the project that they deemed personally meaningful or relevant. This included, but was not limited to, pictures of Caritas; of the project process, materials, and products; of the project groups and community leaders; of other community members not directly engaged in the group projects; and of the workshops and guest speakers.

Lastly, students were asked to complete each entry with a series of self-generated critical questions stemming from their experience with the project and that could be used as points of discussion and/or reflection. These questions were likewise used to gauge the shifting subjective experiences and perspectives of the students over the course of the project. Taken together, the journal entries, digital photographs, and the self-generated critical questions provided a richer perspective of the students' experience with the CruCES project and their developing attitudes regarding difference and CSL that could be used to more accurately assess ISD. As per the syllabus and project design, students completed one journal entry every two weeks, submitting a total of 8 journal entries per student. In total, this study surveyed 120 journal entries.

At the conclusion of the semester, survey results and journal entries were coded, analyzed, and assessed for intercultural sensitivity using Bennett's (1986, 1993, 2004) DMIS stages. The respective parts of the journal entries were examined individually as well as in relation to one another across the codes identified. Each journal entry was then assigned a number, from one to six, corresponding to each one of Bennett's six stages of intercultural sensitivity. In all instances, journal entries were examined for statements reflecting attitudes and mindsets indicative of Bennett's respective stages of ISD. Given that progress along the stages is nonlinear and that individuals may demonstrate both ethnocentric and ethnorelative positions on different topics within the same journal entry, half numbers were used to indicate journals wavering between two respective stages of Bennett's model. An example of a contradictory set of statements would include the following: "My group has become fast friends; I've never had such a good experience working in groups. It makes me believe that collaboration between strangers is possible" (stage four of Bennett's scale); "Rosa, one of the cooks, has been in the United States for eight years. I know this is a Spanish class, but I don't understand how you can live someplace for so long and not speak the language" (stage three of Bennett's scale). In an instance such as this, a rating of 3.5 would be assigned to the journal entry. In the final analysis, student ISD was triangulated using survey data, journal results, and teacher observation.

It is important to note that although Bennett's model provides a useful framework for quantifying and plotting student ISD over the course of the semester, it is the overall transformation of student attitudes and perceptions regarding difference that is most significant for this study. Deardorff's PMIS (2006, 2009) in particular is useful in underscoring the transformative potential of intercultural contact as one's attitudes regarding difference serve as the basis for the acquisition, demonstration, and continued development of intercultural sensitivity. This serves as a reminder that no matter where and how far individuals enter and progress along Bennett's scale, they will inevitably emerge from such positive intercultural experiences with transformed attitudes and mindsets.

Results

For the purposes of this volume, the following sections present the final and overall findings of the CruCES project study and discuss the finding's implications and relevance for the integration of CSL in FL programs and curricula.

Surveys

The pre-project survey (see Appendix for survey questions) showed that, despite varying levels of experience with CSL and community service, students perceived themselves as possessing a high degree of intercultural sensitivity from the outset of the project. At the same time, the majority of participants indicated that they anticipated benefiting from participating in a CSL project in terms of their ISD and competence. This perception is corroborated in the post-project survey, which likewise showed that students maintained a high perception of their respective intercultural sensitivity while maintaining the belief that they benefited from participating in the CSL project. Only two participants consistently disagreed with survey statements correlating CSL with ISD in both pre- and post-project surveys. Overall, however, pre- and post-project surveys showed no significant differences in student self-reports of intercultural sensitivity before and after the CruCES project. Survey results also showed that the majority of the students nonetheless perceived a positive relationship between CSL and their intercultural sensitivity. Table 3.1 shows the results for the post-project survey.

Table 3.1 Post-Project Survey Results

Survey Questions Correlating CSL and Intercultural Sensitivity (on a scale of 1–5)	Column A (mean)	Column B (standard deviation)
Made me more willing to engage in dialogue with others	4.29	1.27
Helped me better understand people of different ages, abilities, cultures, or economic backgrounds	4.29	1.44
Encouraged me to consider perspectives other than my own	4.07	1.27
Helped me to gain more knowledge about the community with which I worked and the issues that community faces	4.14	1.23
Helped me to develop my intercultural communication skills	4.07	1.33

Journals

Journals revealed a gradual shift over the course of the CruCES project in students' attitudes regarding difference and CSL. This was evident across the reflective writing comments, digital photographs, and self-generated critical questions.

In general, the narrative arc for the majority of the journals progressed from skepticism and caution at the beginning of the project to curiosity and understanding in the middle to acceptance and belonging by the end. For example, in the first journal, one student noted her initial reluctance in undertaking the service-learning project due to the amount of work, time, and dedication it would require. She also noted that while not overly enthusiastic about the project, she recognized the significance of helping others less fortunate than herself. These sentiments were reinforced by her critical questions: "How much will the project leaders expect of us? What if I do not have the time to devote to this project? Will I be safe there [at Caritas Village]?" Similarly, the student's photographs for the first journal likewise reflected her attitudes regarding service learning and difference in that they consisted of a series of long-range, wide-angle shots of objects at Caritas Village, such as paintings, decorations, and furniture, chosen seemingly at random.

The student's attitude had changed by the fourth journal. Invested in the project, she had begun to develop relationships with her fellow group members, the community project leader, and community members frequenting Caritas Village. The student's written reflections during this time reveal an appreciation for the project as a vehicle for breaking down barriers between people of different backgrounds and for developing relationships, as shown in the following three comments:

> . . . The most interesting thing about this activity [group project] is that the group has become very close; we have gotten to know one another much more than what we normally would have in a class. We are constantly in communication so that the project turns out to be a success.
> . . . Our project leader ingeniously sees the opportunity and potential to change it [recycled materials] into something different. What I liked most about her is that she said you do not always need money to make money, you can use your creativity to produce money. This way of thinking only emerges when one has experienced need [poverty] and has learned to value even the simplest of things.
> . . . The children at Caritas are very interested in what we are doing. The other day these two little girls and their mothers watched us work. We made room at the table for them and soon they were helping us!

These attitudes were likewise reflected in the student's questions and photographs. By the fourth journal, her self-generated questions focused on the needs and outcomes of the individual group efforts and on whether or not the group would be able to help the project leader in fulfilling the broader goals of the CruCES project. Similarly, the photographs for the fourth journal present a series of close-range pictures of the group project product and materials, fellow group members at work on the project product, and the team leader showing the group how to make the product.

By the final journal, this particular student demonstrated a complete transformation in her attitude regarding service learning and difference that she herself acknowledged in the written reflection portion of the journal entry. In the final journal, she writes:

> I have become more open to the idea that this class is different from other classes and that service learning goes beyond volunteer work. I now understand why we are spending 50% of our class time at Caritas rather than at the University. There is a reason for it beyond the fact that our teacher likes it here [Caritas]. If we only talked about community and community service in our classrooms without experiencing being in the community and working alongside the community, it would not have had the same impact. This experience has transformed me in ways that I am sure I cannot yet explain.

As in the previous journals, these sentiments are likewise reflected in the critical questions and digital photographs. Thinking beyond the CruCES project, the questions in the final journal addressed the role of community engagement in the student's life beyond the university and a concern for the future well-being of the community project leaders:

> How can I continue the work we started in CruCES? Will the project leaders continue? Will we remain in contact? How can I use what I learned in CruCES about community building in my own career and community?

The digital photographs for the final journal, in turn, consist of a series of close-range pictures of people, including fellow project members, project leaders, community members, and the student herself. These photographs differed from previous photographs in that they were deliberately posed and framed as group pictures, as opposed to action pictures, and included selfie-style photographs taken with the student herself.

Though not all participant journals exhibited as strong a transformation or as linear a progression as that of the aforementioned example, the general narrative arc held true for all but one of the students. In the case of the outlying student, her journal entries throughout the semester consistently revealed a high degree of intercultural sensitivity in terms of attitudes regarding difference and CSL while at the same time a reluctance to fully commit to and engage with the project. Written reflections and critical questions, for example, revealed an understanding of and sensitivity toward the value of CSL and of the impact of cultural and socioeconomic differences on the formation of distinct worldviews. Yet the digital photographs for all of the student's journal entries are of an impersonal nature: long-range, wide-angle, and seemingly indiscriminate pictures of objects or of people participating in daily routines at Caritas.

As suggested in the narrative arc of the journals, final analysis using Bennett's DMIS stages corroborates the notion that participation in CSL fosters ISD. The initial journal entries show that student intercultural sensitivity at the outset of the project varied between stage two and four, with the majority of journals rated between two and three (toward the ethnocentric side of Bennett's spectrum). This stands in contrast to student self-reported perceptions of high intercultural sensitivity in the pre-project survey. Over the course of the semester, journal entries show gradual progress along Bennett's DMIS stages though not necessarily unidirectional. The majority of students progressed by one or one and a half stages, many moving from the ethnocentric to ethnorelative side of Bennett's spectrum, while two participants experienced uneven progress. Additionally, two participants' DMIS ratings seemed to show no overall progress, though they revealed a high level of intercultural sensitivity from the initial journal entry through the last. Overall, however, analysis of the student journals confirms that the majority of students did, in fact, experience an increase in their ISD over the course of the CruCES project. Table 3.2 shows student journal entries rated along the categories of Bennett's stages of ISD. In addition to the mean for each student, journal entry, and for all journal entries, the table also shows the gain, or overall progression along Bennett's stages, between journal one and journal eight for each student and for the class as a whole.

Discussion

The results of the survey and journals support the argument that CSL fosters ISD. Perhaps more importantly, however, they further illuminate the relationship between the two and underscore the notion that participation in CSL has the potential to transform one's attitudes and ideas concerning difference. All participating students, regardless of their initial start and end point along Bennett's DMIS stages, demonstrated through their reflection journals a shift in attitudes concerning difference and CSL. This implies that CSL is a pedagogical method well suited to foster and develop student intercultural sensitivity by virtue of its ability to structure positive and meaningful intercultural contact alone.

Surveys

The survey results pointed to potential challenges in self-reporting of intercultural sensitivity. As noted earlier, students reported having a high degree of

Table 3.2 Journal DMIS Ratings

Student	Journal 1	Journal 2	Journal 3	Journal 4	Journal 5	Journal 6	Journal 7	Journal 8	Mean	Gain
A	3.5	3.5	4	4	4	3	3.5	3.5	3.63	0.00
B	4	4	5	5	5	5	5	5	4.75	1.00
C	3.5	3.5	4.5	4.5	4.5	4.5	5	5	4.38	1.50
D	4	4.5	5	5	5	5.5	5.5	5.5	5.00	1.50
E	4.5	4.5	4.5	4.5	4.5	4.5	4.5	4.5	4.50	0.00
F	3.5	3.5	4	4	4	4.5	4.5	4.5	4.06	1.00
G	4	4.5	4.5	4.5	5	5	5	5	4.69	1.00
H	2.5	2.5	3	3	3	3.5	3.5	3.5	3.06	1.00
I	3	3	3.5	3.5	3.5	4	4	4	3.56	1.00
J	2	2	2.5	3	3	2.5	2.5	3	2.56	1.00
K	3	3	3	3	3.5	3.5	3.5	4	3.31	1.00
L	3.5	3.5	4	4	4	4	4.5	4.5	4.00	1.00
M	3	3	3.5	3.5	3.5	3.5	4	4	3.50	1.00
N	2.5	2.5	3	3	3.5	3.5	4	4	3.25	1.50
O	3.5	3.5	4	4	4.5	4.5	5	5	4.25	1.50
Mean	3.33	3.40	3.87	3.90	4.03	4.07	4.27	4.33	3.90	1.00

intercultural sensitivity in both the pre- and post-project surveys, indicating no overall gains in student ISD. This result is somewhat misleading, however, when viewed in relation to the reflection journals and student survey results regarding perceptions of the benefits of CSL for the development of intercultural sensitivity and competence. Though the survey instrument itself could have been problematic (i.e., question type and wording), it is more likely that students are unaware of or unwilling to admit their own limitations and biases concerning intercultural sensitivity. Similarly, negative perceptions of CSL's benefits for intercultural sensitivity recorded in the surveys may inaccurately reflect the motivations behind participant responses. For example, the journal entries of several students revealed that, though they recognized the value of CSL for intercultural sensitivity, their previous exposure to difference as a result of CSL, community service, or cultural background and upbringing made them uncertain as to how or whether the CruCES project would impact their own ISD. Student perceptions of their own intercultural sensitivity in relation to past experiences therefore had an impact on how they responded to questions concerning CSL and intercultural sensitivity.

Journals

The reflection journals illuminate challenges in the assessment of intercultural sensitivity as well as nuances in the nature of ISD. As noted in previous studies of CSL and intercultural sensitivity/competence, the use of reflection journals as a form of assessment presupposes that students possess the ability to effectively and appropriately engage in reflective writing. Many students, however, lack explicit training and/or experience in reflective and reflexive writing, and though explicit instruction may lead to better journaling, it does not necessarily lead to more accurate assessment of student intercultural sensitivity as a result of student desires to please and to excel in classroom assignments simply for the sake of doing so. Indeed, the design of the reflection journal was such that student perceptions of their CSL experience would be documented from at least one if not three angles (i.e., student observation, reflection, and questions). The design of the journals was therefore helpful in assessing student intercultural sensitivity and in understanding student progress along the DMIS stages.

As noted earlier, student ISD tended toward three types: gradual linear progression, nonlinear progression, and seemingly static evolution, the latter two being of particular interest. Though ethnocentric comments increased for participants who experienced a regression along the DMIS stages, those perceptions were not necessarily recorded in the digital photographs. Reasons for the abrupt change in the tone of student reflections may potentially be attributed to personal circumstances unrelated to the project, such as stressors in family, work, school, and other areas. Indeed, frustrations over balancing the demands of the project with those of work, school, and family were noted in many of the self-generated questions in the initial journal entries. As such, the evident regression may be no more than a reflection of fluctuations in attitude and personality informed by external circumstances. That these circumstances inform student engagement with and perceptions of the CSL project is unavoidable, however, and may need to be factored into teacher, community partner, and program expectations and assessment of CSL project goals relating to student outcomes. The regression may also be indicative of the complexity of human nature as related to the demonstration of intercultural sensitivity. This is to say that, unlike the homogeneity of perspectives implied in Bennett's respective developmental stages, an individual may simultaneously hold contradictory attitudes and viewpoints. Considering this possibility, assessment of intercultural sensitivity could potentially benefit from research in psychology and cognitive science.

In comparison, the sole participant revealing no progress along the DMIS categories revealed a high degree of intercultural sensitivity across the journal entries but failed to appropriately engage in the project and thus maintained a distance between herself and the community constituted by the CruCES project participants and the patrons of Caritas Village. This distance was effectively captured in the impersonal nature of the accompanying digital photographs. In this particular instance, the distance was explicitly acknowledged by the participant and justified in terms of external circumstances (i.e., work, school, and family). Despite the regression and seeming lack of progress, however, these outliers as well as all of the other journal entries revealed a substantial change in student attitudes concerning CSL, community service, and difference between the first and final journal entry. This suggests that participation in CSL has the potential to positively impact intercultural sensitivity in students regardless of where they start, how far they progress, and how, specifically, they move along Bennett's DMIS stages.

Digital Photographs

Perhaps most revealing of student transformation in attitudes were the digital photographs, which captured the students' personal transformation from outsider to insider within the community and project over the course of the semester. The final analysis confirms this to be the case for all but one of the project participants.

Photographs from the first journal represented the students' initial encounter with Caritas Village and therefore included pictures primarily of objects, such as artwork, that conveyed the uniqueness of the place. Those few initial photographs of people at Caritas Village employed a wide-angle frame and were taken indiscriminately and at a distance. These may be interpreted as being reflective of student feelings of unfamiliarity, reticence, and curiosity at the same time, themes likewise conveyed in the written portion of the journal entries. As the project progressed, however, many of the photographs became more intimate, so much so that by the last journal, many of the photographs were framed as "selfies" containing the individual student along with group leaders, project members, and Caritas Village patrons. This transition may be interpreted as the students' integration within group, project, and Caritas Village.

The sole exception to this narrative of integration came from one student whose photographs reflected a general distance self-imposed by the student in question throughout the journal entries. As previously noted, the evident distance was explicitly addressed by the student, who chose to abstain from full integration within the project/group because of personal reasons entirely unrelated to the project itself. Of interest, however, is the fact that this particular participant's reticence to fully engage was likewise documented in the choice of subject and framing of the digital photographs. This suggests that digital photography or other means of visual documentation may be an apt tool to document and assess student ISD in the context of CSL.

Conclusion and Implications

The CruCES project study confirmed that CSL positively informed ISD among participating students. Analysis of the data showed that the extent to which the CSL experience had an impact on student intercultural sensitivity depended on a number of factors, including the relative degree of student intercultural sensitivity at the outset of the project (i.e., their initial mindset); their overall investment and engagement with the project; and student backgrounds and external circumstances (e.g., previous experience with CSL, exposure to cultural and socioeconomic differences, work, family life, school). The data also showed that students' trajectories along Bennett's DMIS stages range from seemingly no progress to steady progress and various occurrences of uneven progress in-between. As made evident in the journal entries and especially in the digital photographs over the course of the project, however, all students demonstrated a shift or transformation in attitudes regarding CSL, community service, and difference. This suggests that regardless of the initial mindset of the students and their differing trajectories along Bennett's DMIS stages, student intercultural sensitivity will inevitably benefit from participation in a CSL project.

As Deardorff and Edwards (2013) noted, the relative efficacy of CSL in engendering student intercultural sensitivity is dependent upon the degree to which collaboration and equity is built into the design of the project itself, a result confirmed by this study, highlighting the collaborative nature of the CruCES project. From the outset of the project, Caritas Village and El Centro Cultural Latino de Memphis were invested in the overall design of CruCES and in the grant writing process as partners with an equal voice and stake in the outcomes of the project. Within the broad parameters outlined by the stakeholders, students and community members (i.e., leaders and other participants) were equally allowed to collaboratively develop the arts-based projects pursued within each respective group. In so doing, each group collectively negotiated their own specific goals, objectives, and operational procedures. A certain amount of autonomy was therefore conferred to the respective groups, which led to greater motivation and investment on the part of students and community leaders. The CruCES project design allowed students specifically to play an active role in collaboratively shaping the project. At the same time, it provided a space for constant and constructive interaction, collaboration, and dialogue. Furthermore, students, community partners, and community members continually dialogued about CSL, community service, the specific needs of the West Binghampton community, and culture through various workshops and discursive spaces of shared experiences throughout the project.

These study findings affirm the value of CSL in furthering FL program goals to develop intercultural competence as well as suggest the need for more critical engagement with—and training in—CSL design and implementation. Given the value of intercultural competence for today's and tomorrow's global economy, FL program supervisors would greatly benefit from investing in and encouraging the integration of CSL within existing curricula. Beyond the development of intercultural communicative competence, CSL is perhaps most valuable because of its ability to engender transformative results in student attitudes concerning difference and community service. Acquiring these skills could potentially greatly help the development of intercultural competence (including communicative competence). It could also help prepare students for subsequent intercultural encounters well beyond the classroom. Indeed, ISD is understood to be a lifelong process, as each encounter builds on, informs, and transforms an individual's foundational attitudes and beliefs. CSL is therefore well suited to prepare students for critically processing and reflecting on their own ISD, thereby maximizing the potential benefits of intercultural encounters. Regardless of the specific steps taken, support for the implementation of CSL can only benefit and further FL program goals and objectives related to fostering and developing translingual and transcultural competence.

References

Abbott, A., & Lear, D. (2010). The connections goal area in Spanish community service learning: Possibilities and limitations. *Foreign Language Annals, 43*, 231–245.

Allport, G. (1954). *The nature of prejudice*. Cambridge, MA: Addison-Wesley.

Barreneche, G. (2011). Language learners as teachers: Integrating service learning and the advanced language course. *Hispania, 94*(1), 103–120.

Bennett, M. J. (1986). A developmental approach to training for intercultural sensitivity. *International Journal of Intercultural Relations, 10*(2), 179–196.

Bennett, M. J. (1993). Towards ethnorelativism: A developmental model of intercultural sensitivity. In R. M. Paige (Ed.), *Education for the intercultural experience* (2nd ed., pp. 21–71). Yarmouth, ME: Intercultural Press.

Bennett, M. J. (2004). Becoming interculturally competent. In J. S. Wurzel (Ed.), *Toward multiculturalism: A reader in multicultural education* (2nd ed., pp. 62–77). Newton, MA: Intercultural Resource Corporation.

Bennett, M. J. (2008, October 10–11). *On becoming global souls: Building intercultural competence.* Paper presented at the first international conference on the development and assessment of intercultural competence, Tucson, AZ.

Byram, M. (1997). *Teaching and assessing intercultural communication competence.* New York, NY: Multilingual Matters.

Byram, M. (2009). Intercultural competence in foreign languages: The intercultural speaker and the pedagogy of foreign language education. In D. K. Deardorff (Ed.), *The Sage handbook of intercultural competence* (pp. 321–332). Thousand Oaks, CA: Sage Publications.

Carracelas-Juncal, C. (2013). When service-learning is not a "border-crossing" experience: Outcomes of a graduate Spanish online course. *Hispania, 96*(2), 295–309.

Deardorff, D. K. (2006). Identification and assessment of intercultural competence as a student outcome of internationalization. *Journal Studies in International Education, 10*(3), 241–266.

Deardorff, D. K. (2009). Implementing intercultural competence assessment. In D. K. Deardorff (Ed.), *The Sage handbook of intercultural competence* (pp. 477–491). Thousand Oaks, CA: Sage Publications.

Deardorff, D., & Edwards, K. (2013). Framing and assessing students' intercultural competence in service learning. In P. Clayton, R. Bringle, & J. Hatcher (Eds.), *Research on service learning: Conceptual frameworks and assessment: Communities, institutions, and partnerships* (pp. 157–183). Sterling, VA: Stylus Publishing.

Ebacher, C. (2013). Taking Spanish into the community: A novice's guide to service-learning. *Hispania, 96*(2), 397–408.

Hellebrandt, J., Arries, J., & Varona, L. (2003). *Juntos: Community partnerships in Spanish and Portuguese.* Boston, MA: Thomas/Heinle.

Hellebrandt, J., & Jorge, E. (2013). The scholarship of community engagement: Advancing partnerships in Spanish and Portuguese. *Hispania, 96*(2), 203–214.

Lear, D., & Abbott, A. (2009). Aligning expectations for mutually beneficial community service-learning: The case of Spanish language proficiency, cultural knowledge, and professional skills. *Hispania, 92*(2), 312–323.

Lear, D., & Sanchez, A. (2013). Sustained engagement with a single community partner. *Hispania, 96*(2), 238–251.

Levin, D. M., Hammer, D., & Coffrey, J. E. (2009). Novice teacher's attention to student thinking. *Journal of Teacher Education, 60*(2), 142–154.

Liddicoat, A., & Scarino, A. (2013). *Intercultural language teaching and learning.* Malden, MA: Wiley-Blackwell.

Magaña, D. (2015). From pedagogy to communities: Issues within and beyond the Spanish heritage language classroom. *Studies in Hispanic and Lusophone Linguistics, 8*(2), 375–388.

McBride, K. (2010). Reciprocity in service learning: Intercultural competence through SLA studies. *Proceedings of Intercultural Competence Conference, 1,* 235–261.

MLA Ad Hoc Committee on Foreign Languages. (2007). Foreign languages and higher education: New structures for a changed world. *Profession, 12,* 234–245.

Paesani, K., Allen, H. W., & Dupuy, B. (2016). *A multiliteracies framework for collegiate foreign language teaching.* Boston, MA: Pearson.

Pérez-Llantada, C., & Watson, M. (Eds.). (2011). *Specialized languages in the global village: A multi-perspective approach.* Newcastle upon Tyne, UK: Cambridge Scholars Publishing.

Petrov, L. A. (2013). A pilot study of service-learning in a Spanish heritage speaker course: Community engagement, identity, and language in the Chicago area. *Hispania, 96*(2), 310–327.

Pink, S. (2013). *Doing visual ethnography*. Los Angeles, CA: Sage.
Rodriguez-Sabater, S. (2015). Service learning and intercultural competence in the Spanish as a second language classroom. *Southern Journal of Linguistics, 39*(1), 1–23.
Ruby, J. (1982). *A crack in the mirror: Reflexive perspectives in anthropology*. Philadelphia, PA: University of Philadelphia Press.
Spitzberg, B. H., & Changnon, G. (2009). Conceptualizing intercultural competence. In D. K. Deardorff (Ed.), *The Sage handbook of intercultural competence* (pp. 2–52). Thousand Oaks, CA: Sage Publications.
Thompson, G. L. (2012). *Intersection of service and learning: Research and practice in the second language classroom*. Charlotte, NC: Information Age Publishing.
Timpe, V. (2013). *Assessing intercultural language learning: The dependence of receptive sociopragmatic competence and discourse competence on learning opportunities and input*. Frankfurt am Main, Germany: Peter Lang AG.

Appendix

Pre-project survey questions

DEMOGRAPHIC QUESTIONS (OPTIONAL)

Gender: M   F

Race:

Ethnicity:

Age:

BACKGROUND AND PAST EXPERIENCE WITH SERVICE LEARNING

Did you or your family speak another language other than English at home?	Y N
Do you have previous experience with community service learning in the past?	Y N
Do you have previous experience with community service?	Y N
If you answered yes to the previous questions, was your community service experience related to your faith or linked to a religious organization?	Y N

INTERCULTURAL SENSITIVITY

On a scale of 1–5, rate your degree of intercultural sensitivity (i.e., your awareness and sensitivity to cultural and other differences such as racial, ethnic, and socio-economic):

1	2	3	4	5
very low	below average	average	high	very high

INTERCULTURAL SENSITIVITY AND COMMUNITY SERVICE LEARNING

On a scale of 1–5, with 1 being strongly disagree to 5 being strongly agree, please rate the following statements:

Participation in community service learning will make me more willing to engage in dialogue with others.

    1   2   3   4   5

Participation in community service learning will help me better understand people of different ages, abilities, cultures, or economic backgrounds.

    1   2   3   4   5

Participation in community service learning will encourage me to consider perspectives other than my own.

    1   2   3   4   5

Participation in community service learning will help me to gain more knowledge about the community with which I will work and the issues that community faces.

    1   2   3   4   5

Participation in community service learning will help me to develop my intercultural communication skills.

    1   2   3   4   5

Post-project survey questions

DEMOGRAPHIC QUESTIONS (OPTIONAL)

Gender: M F

Race:

Ethnicity:

Age:

BACKGROUND AND PAST EXPERIENCE WITH SERVICE LEARNING

Did you or your family speak another language other than English at home?   Y N

Do you have previous experience with community service learning in the past?   Y N

Do you have previous experience with community service?   Y N

If you answered yes to the previous questions, was your community service experience related to your faith or linked to a religious organization?   Y N

INTERCULTURAL SENSITIVITY

On a scale of 1–5, rate your degree of intercultural sensitivity (i.e., your awareness and sensitivity to cultural and other differences such as racial, ethnic, and socio-economic):

1	2	3	4	5
very low	below average	average	high	very high

INTERCULTURAL SENSITIVITY AND COMMUNITY SERVICE LEARNING

On a scale of 1–5, with 1 being strongly disagree to 5 being strongly agree, please rate the following statements:

Participation in community service learning made me more willing to engage in dialogue with others.

1   2   3   4   5

Participation in community service learning helped me better understand people of different ages, abilities, cultures, or economic backgrounds.

1   2   3   4   5

Participation in community service learning encouraged me to consider perspectives other than my own.

1   2   3   4   5

Participation in community service learning helped me to gain more knowledge about the community with which I will work and the issues that community faces.

1   2   3   4   5

Participation in community service learning helped me to develop my intercultural communication skills.

1   2   3   4   5

Chapter 4
Abriendo caminos: Breaking New Ground in Community-Engaged Language Learning

Vivian Brates, Citlalli Del Carpio, Alice A. Miano,
Paitra Houts, Stanford University

Irene Carvajal, San Jose State University

Misla Barco, East Palo Alto Academy

Introduction

It has been argued that the Communities Standard (National Standards Collaborative Board, 2015) may be the most critical for language learning, yet world language programs and curricula only sporadically emphasize community engagement (Magnan, Murphy, Sahakyan, & Kim, 2012). Specifically, the "School and Global Communities" Standard states, "Learners use the language both within and beyond the classroom to interact and collaborate in their community and the globalized world" (National Standards Collaborative Board, 2015, p. 102). With respect to this Standard vis-à-vis Spanish and other languages, we argue that a critical consciousness approach (Freire, 1970/1993) is essential for program effectiveness in community-engaged curricula. More broadly within world language teaching and learning, a critically conscious, social justice stance is increasingly seen as important (Glynn, Wesely, & Wassell, 2014). Particularly relevant in the U.S. context, where roughly 35 million Latinxs (note that "Latinx" is used as a gender-neutral term throughout) speak Spanish (Krogstad, Stepler, & Lopez, 2015), it seems obvious that postsecondary Spanish programs would want their students to be involved in Spanish-speaking communities. What is less obvious is how to articulate programs that cultivate an awareness of the complex social and cultural dynamics that entwine local environments with broader societal and global forces.

In seeking this critical awareness vis-à-vis the world language curriculum, we therefore prefer the term "community-engaged learning" (CEL) to the more commonly used "service learning." This serves as a first step toward emphasizing principles of ethical and effective engagement such as reciprocity, commitment, and cultural humility (Haas Center, 2016). Speaking of CEL versus "service learning" underscores solidarity and does not assume that language learners are necessarily endowed with the skills or training to provide an essential "service" to community partners (see Campus Compact, 2016).

Kern and Liddicoat (2008) similarly eschew the term "language learner" as static and instead reframe students as actively engaged "speaker/actors." Indeed, their theory, based in the kinesis of linguistic pluralism and open communicative interaction, ponders the question of how speaker/actors dynamically "conceptualize new perspectives about themselves (and thereby redefine themselves), based on the linguistic and cultural resources available to them" (p. 27, translation). That is, how does the social interaction between speaker/actors in a language, or multiple languages, influence one's negotiation of identity? Their approach provides a sharpened lens through which to examine activity, agency, and community among speaker/actors within dynamic social settings.

Guided by this aforementioned work, this chapter examines one university's efforts to establish a critically conscious CEL program in Spanish and asks:

1. Do CEL students in a critically conscious language-learning program evolve in their identities as speaker/actors of a language and within a language community?
2. Do CEL students of Spanish grow in critical intercultural awareness of and appreciation for the community cultural wealth (Yosso, 2005) of Spanish-speaking communities, both local and global?
3. Do CEL students grow in their ability to critically assess "institutions, social systems, and their own contribution to and effect on a given community" (Plann, 2002, p. 331)?

In short, beyond expected language proficiency gains, how do CEL students develop as critically aware speaker/actors as they step into language communities beyond the classroom, using CEL as a framework for social learning (Bass & Elmendorf, n.d.)?

Literature Review

CEL as a curricular practice finds its roots in the pedagogies of John Dewey and Paulo Freire (Barreneche & Ramos-Flores, 2013). Dewey (1942) emphasized community and valued not only formal education but also learning from direct experience. Freire (1970/1993) rejected traditional pedagogies, which generally view learners as passive receptacles, and viewed formal schooling as an institutional apparatus that reproduces existing social orders. Freire advocated for a critical pedagogy of human self-actualization that would reveal and challenge societal inequities. In these values, we find community engagement's foundation for its speaker/actor participants, which we may term the "four R's": reciprocity, reflection, responsibility, and respect. Jacoby (1996), for instance, emphasized that CEL must address goals as defined by the community partner and that student learning arises from this symbiotic relationship built on reciprocity. As noted by Zlotkowski (1999), "service learning deliberately seeks to reverse the long-established academic practice of using the community for the academy's own end" (p. 82). For learning to manifest, however, reflection is key (Eyler, 2002; Jacoby, 1996; Zlotkowski, 1999). For Eyler, the quality of community-engagement programs is directly linked to the quantity and quality of opportunities for reflection.

Responsibility evokes the democratic goal of preparing students to be civically engaged in their communities and society (Plann, 2002). Note that Sigmon (1979) named "relevance" in lieu of our "responsibility" in his four R's of service learning. While we appreciate the fundamental importance of delineating academic coursework objectives that relate to the engagement experience (Burgo, 2016, following Duncan & Kopperud, 2008), the four R's stressed here center on speaker/actor agency. Finally, respect for diversity and the humility to recognize perspectives, practices, and community cultural wealth other than one's own are likewise essential in CEL (Haas Center, 2016).

With respect to the Spanish language curriculum, a growing body of research has emerged on the subject of CEL. Hellebrandt and Varona's (1999) edited volume, endorsed by the American Association of Teachers of Spanish & Portuguese (AATSP), has been foundational to CEL projects. Subsequent publications include the AATSP handbook on CEL (Hellebrandt, Arries, Varona, & Klein, 2003), a special issue of *Hispania* (Long, 2013), and scholarship that extends beyond Spanish to include French, German, and Japanese (Hellebrandt & Jorge, 2013).

Research on CEL in instructed Spanish curricula documents increased motivation to use the target language, self-confidence and positive attitudes toward the target language and cultures, and a desire to continue studying the language (Burgo, 2016; Nelson & Scott, 2008; Pak, 2007; Pellettieri, 2011; Zapata, 2011). As Hartfield-Méndez (2013) noted, "Spanish is the second language of the United States, and departments of Spanish are being called upon to facilitate and articulate a nuanced understanding of this reality" (p. 356). CEL, she argued, can serve as a core component of this "nuanced understanding." Additionally, Bettencourt (2015) found that community engagement provides opportunities for learning that are otherwise unavailable in the Spanish classroom. For instance, CEL can stimulate vocabulary development to meet the needs of interaction *in situ*, and synergistically, opportunities for oral and written reflection on the CEL experience in classroom activities encourage students to elevate their language usage to express increasingly complex ideas (Bettencourt, 2015).

It is important to note that other research points to challenges surrounding community engagement in a second language. Lear and Abbott (2009) wrote of unfulfilled expectations on the part of students and community partners, while Barreneche and Ramos-Flores (2013) noted Coles's (1999) finding that university students who hailed from the same community as the engaged partner felt diminished by the presence of such partnerships. However, a CEL model emphasizing solidarity and reciprocity may help disrupt traditional notions that students are being called on "to serve the underserved," instead fostering a critical awareness of community cultural wealth, such as familial, linguistic, and resistant capital (Yosso, 2005), as well as societal mechanisms that reinforce disparate opportunity structures.

We propose (see Figure 4.1) that community-engaged language learning may foster developing identities as viable speaker/actors with a greater recognition of and respect for community cultural wealth. When language learning takes place within a critically conscious CEL program based in the four R's, speaker/actor participants may grow into new or expanding identities as they develop critical awareness of various forms of the community's cultural wealth. Such growth may be due in large part to the very challenges that CEL implicates. As noted by Pak (2007):

> The "counter-normative" nature of service-learning pedagogy (Clayton & Ash, 2004; Howard, 1998) is known to create some discomfort for both the faculty and students as they learn to move away from individualism, instructor control, predictability of traditional classrooms to self-critical analysis, shared responsibility, civic engagement, and active learning of "messy" service-learning classrooms involving community partners. (Pak, 2007, pp. 32–33)

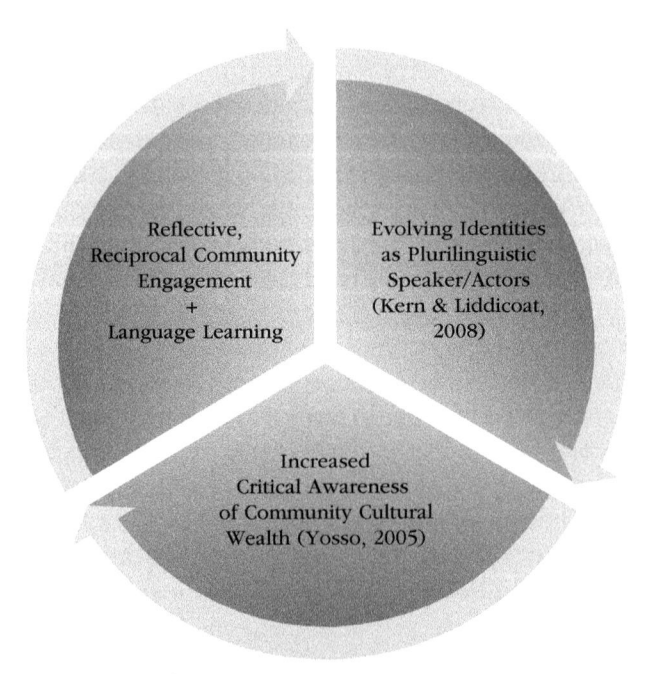

Figure 4.1. Development of CEL speaker/actor identities and critical awareness

If the "discomfort and dissonance" (Pak, 2007, p. 36) arising from the "'real-world' messiness and unpredictability" (Clayton & Ash, 2004, p. 59) of CEL courses have at times discouraged faculty involvement, it may be that second language researchers, too, have avoided some of this messiness. Much of the literature examining language learning together with CEL has downplayed the significance of critical awareness, often placing emphasis on language acquisition benefits, with limited consideration of participant roles, program effects within communities, or personal and social growth. Indeed, our own analytic focus here centers on Stanford students and not on their community partners. While we acknowledge the overwhelming importance of examining reciprocal effects among community partners, such an endeavor is largely beyond the scope of this chapter. As the field of CEL in language learning continues to develop, we hope further studies will help fill the void surrounding reciprocity.

Methods

Program Description

A central purpose of the CEL program within the Spanish Language Program ("Spanlang") is to provide students with opportunities to engage with and learn from local Spanish-speaking communities through the arts, literature, and civic involvement. The program arose from a partnership between the Stanford Language Center, Haas Center for Public Service, and the Vice Provost for Teaching and Learning (VPTL) to enhance Stanford students' understanding both of the Spanish language and local Latinx cultures while also supporting local organizations' missions. Through this partnership Stanford students and faculty are provided with additional resources, such as VPTL and Cardinal Course Grants, to invite key speakers, support transportation, provide needed materials, and generally enhance program delivery. In addition, the Haas Center connected Spanlang with two of its community partners, the Boys & Girls Club of the Peninsula (BGCP) and a local high school, East Palo Alto Academy (EPAA). The connection with Spanlang's original community partner, the International Institute of the Bay Area (IIBA), was forged by Brates, a regular volunteer there.

Since the inception of the Language Center in 1995, Stanford has had a one-year language requirement. Beyond the first year, Spanlang has offered three second-year tracks: one for heritage speakers and two others that focus on culture and international relations, respectively. In addition, two tracks, one in biological sciences and another in feminist studies, were offered in the 1990s but phased out due to declining enrollment.

Based on a pilot offered in Stanford's Sophomore College Spanish Immersion program in 2012 (Miano, Bernhardt, & Brates, 2016), as of this writing, Brates has taught Spanlang 13SL continuously for four years. Following Del Carpio's pilots of Spanlang 11SL and 12SL in 2015–2016, a three-quarter CEL track across the second year of Spanish study was established in 2016–2017 for students wanting to develop language skills while forging cultural connections with native speakers. In Spanlang 11SL, Stanford students study art and paint murals with BGCP middle schoolers; in 12SL, they create and engage in a community project with EPAA students; and in 13SL, they study the 100 questions of the U.S. citizenship exam together with Spanish-speaking adults at IIBA.

The planning and execution of these programs have involved significant and consistent ongoing communication between community partners, instructors, and administrators.

In all courses, Stanford students' oral and writing proficiencies place them within the Intermediate level on the proficiency scale of the American Council on the Teaching of Foreign Languages (ACTFL). In Spanlang, 11SL students tend to fall within the Intermediate Mid (IM) sublevel, while Spanlang 13SL students are typically at Intermediate High (IH) and working toward the Advanced level. Spanlang 12SL students tend to range between IM and IH. Other than instructors, the names of individuals mentioned in this chapter have been replaced with pseudonyms.

Each course begins with the FACE method of reflection, used in many CEL courses, in which students write about and reflect upon what they deem to be Facts, Assumptions, Challenges, and Expectations (FACE) regarding the engagement encounter. Before the first interaction with the community partner, students are asked to blog and then reflect together in class upon what they know about local Latinx communities as well as their expectations for the community engagement program, assumptions they may have (e.g., about community partners), and challenges they expect to face. The students also participate in a series of interpersonal language activities to help them prepare for successful communication in their respective engagement contexts.

Course Descriptions and Participants

Students in Spanlang 11SL (Second-Year Spanish, First Quarter, Community Engaged Learning Emphasis) engage with middle school students, all heritage speakers of Spanish, at the Redwood City, California, branch of BGCP. Artist and art instructor Irene Carvajal created a course for BGCP to explore themes around art and youth identity. Under her direction, art classes take place at the Redwood City site two afternoons weekly for one hour each. Stanford students from Spanlang 11SL attend sessions one to two times per week alongside BGCP students. Adolescence can be a challenging time. Providing a venue for youths to explore their identity is one way to assist them in connecting with the world and themselves and to help them gain a foothold as they mature. As such, the art course explores cultural roots relevant to many of the students, examining the Mexican and Chicanx muralist movements alongside the Chicanx Movement of the 1960s. Each program culminates with students creating a mural (or set of murals) together.

Stanford students begin Spanlang 11SL by reading selected articles in English and Spanish and watching documentaries in Spanish. These include critical race theorist Tara Yosso's (2005) article "Whose Culture Has Capital? A Critical Race Theory Discussion of Community Cultural Wealth" and a film by sociologist Manuel Ortiz Escámez on migrants from Michoacán, México, in Redwood City. Stanford students share ideas in class, reflect together through an online discussion forum, and write essays about issues surrounding art and migration. This chapter examines written texts of students who participated in the pilot in the Spring Quarter, 2016: six females and one male, one first-year student, four sophomores, and two juniors. It should be noted that although Spanlang courses accept up to 16 students per class, the average enrollment in our second-year classes over the past three years (2013–2014 to 2015–2016) was 7.5 students, more than 70% of whom were female.

Students in Spanlang 12SL (Second-Year Spanish, Second Quarter, Community Engaged Learning Emphasis) engage with heritage language students of Spanish at EPAA, a local high school. Del Carpio and her EPAA counterpart, Barco, organize a series of joint activities between their respective classes to explore, in Spanish, themes of community and identity through areas such as art, poetry, and environmental issues. In the pilot version described in this chapter, offered in the Winter Quarter, 2016, students from both schools attended a total of five functions together, a series of workshops followed by a gallery showing. International and local artists, poets, and environmentalists, via Skype or in person per their availability, led the various workshops.

Many of her EPAA students, says Barco, rarely see the world beyond their immediate community. This opportunity for engagement allows EPAA students to connect with the Stanford community and, via Skype, other Spanish-speaking communities outside the vicinity. Both groups of students, as part of their course content, study Spanish language works and articles that coincide with that quarter's theme. Connecting this content to their community engagement activities, students from both schools work together on a project and dialogue about how to visually and artistically display their work based on the workshops and their mutual experiences.

The participants were six female students: three first-year students, one sophomore, and two juniors. The theme for the quarter analyzed here focused on Latin American poetry. As a culminating project, students created their own "artistic poetry," writing poems and painting them on large canvases that they shared visually and orally at a quarter-end evening gala in EPAA's cafetorium.

In Spanlang 13SL (Second-Year Spanish, Third Quarter, Community Engaged Learning Emphasis), the main themes are immigration and citizenship. The course incorporates academic articles, newspapers, literary works, documentaries, and films surrounding topics of history, international relations, legislation, women and domestic work, media, cultural identity, public art, health, and human trafficking, all as they relate to immigration. At the same time, students spend two hours per week at the IIBA in Redwood City, where they work with adults preparing the 100 history and civics questions comprising the U.S. citizenship exam in Spanish. Due to their age and years of U.S. residence, the adults qualify to take the exam in Spanish. Stanford students use flashcards to help their partners prepare. There are also opportunities to learn about the lives of their partners through sharing life stories.

The course encourages students to engage, observe, inquire, and reflect on the impact of race, gender, ethnicity, social class, and other societal categories. Students research a topic of relevance to the community, such as human migration, public art, print literacy, or domestic work, and interview community partners regarding possible related experiences. In addition to completing a research paper on the subject, students share their findings through written and oral class reflections, returning to previous assumptions about societal categories. This process is designed to foster new insights that extend beyond students' original experiences, beliefs, behaviors, and assumptions.

The participants included in the analyses here took Spanlang 13SL in the fall of 2015. They included 12 students: 9 female and 3 male, 4 first-year students, 4 sophomores, 3 juniors, and 1 senior, including one Spanish and one Portuguese heritage speaker.

In sum, the Spanlang CEL program emphasizes:

- engagement in a respectful, collaborative relationship with community partners;
- interaction within multilingual, Latinx communities;
- direct knowledge and understanding of other cultures;
- connections of lived experiences within the broader context of local issues;
- learning about differences in backgrounds, worldviews, and social contexts within local communities;
- combining knowledge accumulated from both classroom and community;
- connections with other disciplines; and
- comparisons of students' experiences with those of members of other communities.

The syllabus and calendar for each course, as well as photos of engagement sessions, testimonials, and other materials, can be found at http://spanlang.stanford.edu.

Data

In the interest of time and resources, we limited our data to digitized documentation, mostly class blog posts and course evaluations (see Table 4.1 below). This admittedly excluded other valuable forms of documentation, such as

Table 4.1. Summary of Types of Data Collected

Spanlang Course	Online Blogs	Other Reflections	Course Evaluations	Word Count Totals
11SL	12 blogs 17,371 words	Final project: essay format 9,523	Four responses (comments only) 355 words	27,249
12SL	2 blogs 2,775 words	Final project: poetry format (written jointly with EPAA students) 521 words One 12-minute podcast	Six responses (comments only) 453 words	3,749 + podcast
13SL	6 blogs 17,316 words	None	Nine responses (comments only) 1,251 words	18,567

handwritten reflections. An additional limitation was the absence of uniformity from class to class with respect to data gathering. This was attributable, perhaps in part, to the aforementioned "messy" nature of CEL and to the competing demands of establishing a CEL program while at the same time conducting research about it. For instance, the pilot of Spanlang 12SL required especially intensive and frequent interinstitutional planning, which may have trumped consideration for more extensive data collection. There were also differences in terms of assignments. Spanlang 11SL and 12SL, but not 13SL, included final projects in the data, while 11SL required twice as many blogs as 13SL and considerably more than 12SL. Yet a Spanlang 12SL student, when tasked in a separate course with creating a podcast about her "most impactful experience" at Stanford, chose to showcase her 12SL CEL experience. We included her podcast in our data as well.

Procedures and Analysis

Ours was a qualitative inquiry, undergirded by the assertion of discourse analysts that speaker/actors use language both to construct their reality and be constructed by it, mutually shaping their own and others' identities (e.g., Fairclough, 1992). This overarching notion guided our thinking as we sought to understand students' writings.

Our specific procedures began with gathering the data outlined previously. These documents were coded using HyperResearch software, with procedures drawn from grounded theory (Charmaz, 2005; Corbin, 2015; Strauss, 1987). Grounded theory provides systematic yet flexible tools for analyzing language content, with categories and theory developed emergently from the data. This methodology involved multiple levels of coding accompanied by memo writing that highlighted recurring themes and points of interest. A multistage, iterative coding process was executed roughly in the following order:

1. *Open coding*: line-by-line analyses and "questioning" of the data and comparing different data to one another to determine potential major and minor categories of meaning
2. *Axial coding*: developing categories with increasing elaboration and conjecturing about their interrelatedness to one another and to social contexts
3. *Selective coding*: to hone in on a central message

Importantly, lines of thinking within both grounded theory and discourse analysis value researcher intuition (Corbin, 2015; Johnstone, 2008). This was critical, given our data, which, with the exception of course evaluations, were written in a second (or sometimes a third) language. In analyzing our speaker/actors' texts in Spanish, we at times invoked "teacher intuitions" about meaning in addition to other social-contextual intuitions linked to our identities not only as instructors and researchers but also as participants in varying social contexts within our respective classrooms and community partnerships with BGCP, EPAA, or IIBA.

Findings

In all the classes under analysis, students grew into expanding speaker/actor identities, both in a linguistic sense (research question 1) and from a sociocultural standpoint (research question 2). In relation to question (2), more specifically, they began to recognize stereotypes they had held and to appreciate the resilience, linguistic capital, familial capital, and other forms of community cultural wealth (Yosso, 2005) within the communities where they interacted. To be sure, their gains did not completely expunge old stereotypes and insensitivities, but inroads were forged through connections with people and communities with whom the students would otherwise probably not have interacted. In terms of question (3), students did appear to develop in their ability to critically assess societal opportunity structures as well as the value—and limits—of their own contributions. At the same time, moving up the scale of our research questions from (1) to (3) seemed to implicate increasingly mixed results. As noted, there were many gains as well as setbacks. To summarize, Spanlang CEL students tended to advance along three channels vis-à-vis speaker/actor identities. The students grew:

a. linguistically, seeing themselves as increasingly viable Spanish speakers among native speakers;
b. culturally, seeing people who had previously been invisible to them and appreciating their community cultural wealth; and

    c. socially, developing a sense of solidarity with other speaker/actors within these newly available social milieux.

The sections that follow elaborate upon these findings.

Apprehensions Overcome

In each course, before beginning their community-engagement activities, students consistently expressed concerns that their second language abilities were insufficient to interact with native speakers. In Spanlang 11SL, all six female students expressed such concerns, but only the lone male did not; in 12SL (an all-female class), four students, or two-thirds of the class, expressed them; and in 13SL, six students (both male and female), or half the class, did so. Interestingly, Spanlang 12SL and 13SL students typically overcame these fears following the first meeting with their native speaker counterparts, while some Spanlang 11SL students took a second week or more to overcome their apprehensions.

Indeed, 11SL students appeared to face the toughest challenge: by and large, they had the lowest oral proficiency across the second-year track, and yet they worked with arguably the toughest crowd, middle schoolers. In fact, Willie, an 11SL student, reflected on the challenge of working with youths of that age. But by the end of the quarter, students appeared to view linguistic misunderstandings and challenges as learning opportunities in a continuum of ups and downs that, on the whole, led to a fruitful linguistic and cultural learning experience.

To a lesser degree, students also expressed trepidation about relating to people from lower socioeconomic backgrounds. One former 13SL student, now a 13SL course assistant, wrote: "Most [13SL students] have not really interacted, on a routine basis, with people who live through daily hardships. Thus, to ask about home, family, and work is awkward" (Gomez, 2016, sec. 2, para. 1). Students in other SL courses reflected similar sentiments. Before meeting her BGCP counterparts, Carrie (11SL) addressed two challenges she expected to face, commenting first on communication and second on family background: "no se las situaciones de las casas de los estudiantes, y por eso no estoy segura de que debo suponer"[1] ("I'm not familiar with the home situations of the students, and so I'm not sure what I should think"). Similarly, Vanessa (12SL), after noting that East Palo Alto is a diverse, low-income community, reflected on an initial concern: "Me dio miedo un poco porque no estaba segura si nos llevaríamos bien por causa de la circunstancias diferentes entre EPA [East Palo Alto] & Stanford" ("It scared me a bit because I wasn't sure if we'd get along due to the different circumstances between East Palo Alto and Stanford"). So, while students typically recognized the importance of stepping outside the famed (or perhaps, infamous) "Stanford

---

[1] Students' texts are not edited except for bracketed notes to aid comprehension.

bubble," some likewise expressed the discomfort that aforementioned researchers Clayton and Ash (2004) and Pak (2007) described.

Making Communities Visible

Many students wrote of newly gained perspectives. Spanlang 11SL student Andrea commented on how her vision had expanded to include a nearby but previously unknown community:

> *Me siento más interesada en la cultura y las vidas de inmigrantes de los estados unidos. Le tengo respeto grande a los estudiantes y los padres. . . . Antes de la clase, no sabía de la comunidad de chicanos/inmigrantes que viven en Redwood City. Siempre pienso que el área de la bahía solo tiene personas muy ricas de Silicon Valley. Pero otras personas viven aquí. Ahora, realize [viz. me doy cuenta] que hay un hermoso lugar con cultura y comida muy buena. También cuando yo veo una historia sobre inmigración en los noticias, yo escucho la historia.*
>
> I feel more interested in the culture and lives of immigrants in the United States. I have great respect for the students and their parents. . . . Before this class, I didn't know of the community of Chicanos [and] immigrants who live in Redwood City. I always thought that the Bay Area was made up only of very rich people in the Silicon Valley. But other people live here. I realize that there is a beautiful place with culture and good food. Also, when I see a story about immigration in the news, I listen to the story.

Andrea became aware of nearby Redwood City's Latinx community for the first time. Though perhaps stereotypically pointing to the "rich people" of Silicon Valley and an appreciation of "good food" in Redwood City, she also began to appreciate familial capital alongside diverse immigrant perspectives and the importance of seeking out and understanding them. Although she herself hailed from an Asian immigrant family, this realization came to light only through her interaction with a separate immigrant community. Indeed, in another post, she described her surprise at learning that some of the middle schoolers' patterns of English and Spanish use at home paralleled her own practice of responding in English to her parents' native Vietnamese.

Along similar lines, 12SL student Vanessa (see earlier), after expressing her initial apprehension over differences in socioeconomic background, likewise reflected on insights she had gained following her first three weeks in the class:

> *Después de la primera clase sobre [en] EPA [East Palo Alto], aprendí que la comunidad de EPA es muy diverso y tiene poco dinero. Me dio miedo un poco porque no estaba segura si nos llevaríamos bien por causa de la circunstancias diferentes entre EPA & Stanford. Las clases cambiaron mi perspectiva un poco porque aprendí que*

hay similitudes y vínculos entre yo y los estudiantes [de EPAA] que puedo usar para romper el hielo. Aunque no pude hablar mucho con los estudiantes, me parecen simpáticos, amables, y un poco tímidos.

After the first class about [in] EPA [East Palo Alto], I learned that the community of EPA is diverse and has little money. It scared me a bit because I wasn't sure if we'd get along due to the different circumstances between East Palo Alto and Stanford. The classes changed my perspective a little, because I learned that there are similarities and links between myself and the [EPAA] students that I can use to break the ice. Although I couldn't speak much with the students, they seem to me to be nice, friendly, and a little shy.

Besides seeing others and gaining exposure to their perspectives for the first time, considering others in new ways was also an important gain. Various 13SL students spoke about recognizing elements that both differentiate and unite Latinxs from different ethnic backgrounds. Two such students commented on their discoveries surrounding language varieties, and one, Ellen, noted:

Lorenzo es de Nicaragua y Raúl de Perú, y aunque no puedo diferenciar los matices de sus acentos diferentes, ellos me dijeron que es algo muy obvio. A mí me encanta la idea de "acentos" y palabras diferentes en la misma lengua para representar la misma cosa. La psicología alrededor de la difusión de lengua y acentos es una de las mayores razones porque estudio español.

Lorenzo is from Nicaragua and Raúl from Peru, and although I can't differentiate the nuances of their different accents, they tell me that it's something very obvious. I love the idea of "accents" and different words in the same language to represent the same thing. The psychology surrounding the diffusion of language and accents is one of the biggest reasons why I study Spanish.

Although she cannot yet hear the different varieties of Spanish she is encountering, Ellen gained an appreciation for the richness of language diversity and for linguistic capital inherent in Latinx communities.

Another 13SL student, Elise, was awed by the progress of her IIBA partner. The partner had had very little access to schooling and did not read or write but was quickly learning the answers to the citizenship exam:

. . . me impresiona muchísimo el progreso que ha hecho Alicia en unas pocas semanas de asistir a la clase. ¡Ha aprendido casi la mitad de las respuestas del examen! Ahora, está aprendiendo mucho más rápidamente que antes y ya no parece nerviosa.

. . . I'm impressed with the progress Alicia has made in just a few weeks of attending class. She learned almost half of the answers to the exam! Now she's learning much more quickly than before and she no longer seems nervous.

Another 13SL student similarly commented that her nonprint literate partner appeared to learn in "unusual" ways and was quite "intelligent." These students thus came to appreciate that formal schooling is not a prerequisite for learning and intelligence.

New Solidarities

The third and perhaps most important way that CEL students' speaker-actor identities evolved came from a heightened sense of solidarity. In Spanlang 12SL, for example, this emerged from their shared project surrounding poetry. Inspired by a series of workshops with Carvajal, Guatemalan poet/journalist Vania Vargas, and Argentinean actor/activist Fernando Ríos Kissner, the students used the theme "Nosotras/Nosotros somos de" ("We are from . . .") to compose, paint, and orally deliver their poems. Working in small groups that included at least one Stanford student and three to four EPAA students, this activity encouraged each group to concentrate on traits that united them. For instance, their poems made associations such as "Somos . . . del 101" referring to the freeway that divides affluent Palo Alto from low-income East Palo Alto but in a unifying way. They also made the connection, "Somos de . . . Stanford Hospital," referring to the birthplace of many in that group. Sometimes they pointed to their bilingualism, either directly or through code-switching: "Ser bilingüe es ser más poderoso y entendido" ("To be bilingual is to be more powerful and understood") and "Somos . . . de palabras y words" ("We are from words [Spanish] and words [English]"). At times their differences, such as traditional foods, seemed also to unite them, as in "somos . . . /De tamales y sauerkraut" ("We are . . . /From tamales and sauerkraut"). Sometimes they pointed directly to the Spanish language and its literature as what united them, referring to "el español que nos conecta" ("the Spanish that connects us") and saying "Nosotros somos . . . de poetas de América Latina" ("We are . . . from poets of Latin America"). Thus, although 12SL students routinely lamented that they didn't have more opportunities to meet and connect with their EPAA counterparts, their poetry demonstrated efforts by both groups to forge connections with and through each other and through Spanish language and literature.

Such reciprocity was a key feature of these new solidarities. Mary (13SL) wrote about an instance where two IIBA students, a married couple, had learned the answers to all 100 questions on the U.S. citizenship test. As such, the husband, Roberto, suggested that he and his wife, Ana, now use the flashcards provided to turn the tables and quiz their Stanford partners:

> [Roberto y Ana] [s]on muy dedicados . . . y no hay duda que ellos van a pasar sus exámenes de ciudadanía. Después de Ana y yo practicaron [viz. practicamos] todos de las tarjetas dos veces, Roberto tuvo una idea divertido. Roberto leyó las tarjetas a Ike [su compañero de Stanford] y él [Ike] tenía que responder y en la

misma vez, Ana me preguntó [me hizo las preguntas] también. Fue una competición muy divertido.

[Roberto and Ana] [a]re very dedicated . . . and there's no doubt that they'll pass their citizenship exams. After Ana and I practiced all the questions two times, Roberto had a fun idea. Roberto read the cards to Ike [his Stanford partner] and he [Ike] had to respond, and at the same time, Ana asked [me the questions] too. It was a very fun competition.

Mary went on to note that, differently from Ana and Roberto's solid command of U.S. government and history, she herself was unable to answer many questions about Mexican history during an in-class activity. Like her aforementioned classmates, Mary appreciated her partners' knowledge, and she additionally enjoyed the reciprocity of reversing roles with the flashcards.

Two Steps Forward, One Step Back. . .

But if gains were made, some stereotypes and other negativities persisted. Despite readings and class discussions surrounding CEL, for instance, many students continued to believe that they were performing a "service." At times, they referred to "helping" their partners without taking note of reciprocal benefits, such as learning life lessons, language, and culture straight from the source. At the same time, Spanlang 11SL students frequently assumed that their role was, in their words, to "control" the middle schoolers. The 11SL students, in fact, seemed preoccupied at times with the middle schoolers' behavior, as if a main goal of their shared art course was merely to gain the BGCP students' cooperation, rather than to invite them to explore the Chicanx Movement and participate in a community-based mural project. A few 13SL students, meanwhile, described their IIBA counterparts as socially "isolated" and even appeared to blame this presumed isolation on the immigrants themselves, without noting societal structures that may impede interaction among immigrants and the U.S.-born. One student, Gretchen, commented:

. . . conocí a una estudiante [de IIBA] que, a pesar de vivir en los Estados Unidos por cincuenta años, todavía no habla inglés. La comunidad de inmigrantes de Latino America es tan aislada que es posible no aprender el idioma del EEUU. Eso me parece increíble. Sin duda, es importantísimo los hispanohablantes guardar y mantener su cultura rica. Sin embargo, pienso que un nivel de aprendizaje de las costumbres Americanos [viz. estadounidenses], incluyendo el idioma, es necesario para relaciones positivas entre los inmigrantes y Americanos nativos [viz. estadounidenses nacidos en EE.UU.].

. . . I met an IIBA student who, despite living in the United States for 50 years, still doesn't speak English. The Latin American immigrant community is so isolated that it's possible not to learn the language of the U.S. This is incredible to me. Without doubt, it's very important for Spanish speakers to maintain their rich culture. However, I think that a level of learning about American [viz. U.S.] customs, including language, is necessary for positive relations between immigrants and native [U.S. born] Americans.

Gretchen was incredulous that someone could remain in the United States for 50 years without learning English, apparently neglecting important circumstantial and societal factors as follows:

- The IIBA student may have arrived at an older age, after the "critical period" beyond which, many linguists argue, it is difficult to learn a new language.
- The IIBA student may speak some English (perhaps at the Novice or Intermediate level on the ACTFL scale) but may be self-conscious about using the language with native speakers, just as many Stanford students felt about their Spanish when they began their community partnerships.
- One could similarly argue that the mostly white, wealthy communities that border largely Latinx areas like Redwood City's North Fair Oaks district, where IIBA is located, are likewise isolated and interact very little within neighboring Latinx communities.

Gretchen also referred to U.S. citizens as "Americanos," apparently not realizing that in Spanish, "americana" and "americano" are terms that refer to anyone from the American continent, seen as a single land mass stretching from Argentina to Canada. Her own choice in terminology thus reinforced the very isolation she decried. Finally, she seemed not to notice that her own activity at IIBA was an attempt to break down this isolation.

Analysis: Lessons Learned and Lasting Effects

As instructors in the CEL track, we learned through necessity that uncovering, acknowledging, and discussing misconceptions and stereotypes such as Gretchen's, not only within our classes but also with our community partners and with each other, is an essential component of the reflexivity that is key to CEL (Eyler, 2002). In the classroom, expressed stereotypes made for fruitful topics of debate, which enabled students to develop cognitive strategies to critically question and counter arguments, a process that likewise encouraged linguistic development. With community partners, acknowledging such negativities allowed us to better prepare for future encounters. In Spanlang 11SL, for instance, we wondered if the students' idea that they needed to monitor their BGCP counterparts' behavior might have stemmed from misinterpreting initial presentations given by BGCP leaders. In subsequent quarters, we thus communicated very clearly to Stanford students that they were to act as companions, not disciplinarians, for BGCP students. Finally, with each other, sharing the inevitable frustrations of this "messy" work, along with the achievements, provided immense mutual moral support for highly challenging, yet highly rewarding, work.

Another lesson learned involved listening to student feedback. After the pilot course, in response to student comments that they wanted more interaction with their EPAA counterparts, Del Carpio, now teaching 12SL year-round, restructured her class so as to join in with Barco's Spanish for heritage speakers twice weekly, increasing visits from 5 in the pilot to 20 per quarter.

Culminating Moments and Lasting Effects

Through it all, as CEL encounters progressed, students appeared to harbor fewer stereotypes and to engage in increased critical thinking, both as they advanced through the course and as they participated in more advanced courses across the spectrum of the second year. No matter their language level, however, in their final reflections, students, usually at their instructor's request, frequently pointed to culminating moments, usually a single unforgettable event within the course of the quarter. These moments appeared to create a lasting impact and to encapsulate an important lesson or takeaway from the engagement experience.

For Willie, that moment came when Laura, a BGCP student, shared a picture of herself taken in her native Guatemala:

> *Es la sexta semana de nuestra clase y otra hora ha pasado muy rápido. Estoy coleccionando mis cosas y ayudando limpiar el cuarto cuando Laura sacó una foto de su bolsillo. Muy entusiasta, ella nos mostró la foto a mí y las otras estudiantes de Stanford. Nos pidió [viz. preguntó] si podemos adivinar cuál de las personas en la foto es ella. En la foto hay tres chicas jóvenes [que] están de pie debajo del techo de un edificio y al lado de una pared verde. Me parece que es una escuela pobre . . . y ella nos contó que está en Guatemala. Reveló que es la más pequeña en el grupo, y por supuesto la más preciosa. Durante la clase ella me describió su pueblo guatemalteco y un pocito [viz. poquito] de su historia pero es difícil para mi imaginarla en esta situación y los eventos que la empujaron [viz. impulsaron a migrar] a los Estados Unidos. Creo que ella no tenía exactamente la misma situación de los hermanos en la película El Norte, pero es un recordatorio de las circunstancias de que mi privilegio me ha protegido. Es un momento sencillo, pero es profundo para mi y no lo olvidaré.*
>
> It is the sixth week of our class and another week has passed by very quickly. I'm gathering my things and helping to clean the room when Laura took a photo out of her pocket. Very enthusiastically, she showed the photo to me and the other Stanford students. She asked if we can guess which of the people in the photo is she. In the photo are three young girls standing below the roof of a

> building and next to a green wall. It seems like a poor school . . . and she told us it's in Guatemala. She revealed that she's the smallest one in the group, and of course the cutest. During the class, she described to me her Guatemalan town and a little of her story, and the events that forced her [to immigrate] to the U.S. I don't think she had exactly the same situation as the brother and sister in the film El Norte, but it's a reminder of the circumstances that my privilege has shielded from me. It's a simple moment, but it is profound for me and I won't forget it.

Willie thus contrasted his own privileged background to Laura's life experiences and the ways that certain advantages, such as schooling, are unevenly distributed in society.

Returning to Andrea (11SL), she commented on her growing political consciousness when a different BGCP student expressed fears about the rise of then presidential candidate Donald Trump:

> . . . *puedo resumir mi lección principal con una historia con los estudiantes de B&GC. . . . Durante la visita de la semana cuatro, una estudiante dijo que asusta de Donald Trump y sus opiniones sobre los inmigrantes Mexicanos durante su campaña por la presidencia. Me sorprendió porque los niños son muy jóvenes y en el pasado, [yo] no pensaba sobre los opiniones de los inmigrantes en las noticias. Por este razón, pienso que es muy importante de estudiar español para retar los estereotipos y comprender los perspectivos de otros personas. . . .*
>
> . . . I can summarize my main lesson with a story about the students from the Boys & Girls Club. . . . During the visit of week four, a student said that she was afraid of Donald Trump and his opinions about Mexican immigrants in his presidential campaign. It surprised me, because children are very young and in the past, [I] didn't think about the opinions of immigrants in the news. For this reason, I think it's very important to study Spanish to challenge the stereotypes and understand the perspectives of other people. . . .

A middle schooler's expressed fears, then, alerted Andrea to the harmful effects of Trump's attacks on U.S. Latinxs, noting that children, too, pay attention to the news. Further, this student related her finding to the importance of studying Spanish itself.

Another culminating moment was provided by an EPAA student, Manuel, and cited by Sandra, a 12SL student in her final project, a podcast, produced for another class. At first uninterested in the topic of poetry and seemingly disengaged, Manuel experienced an about-face when Carvajal mentioned that rap, an art form of great interest to him, is likewise a form of poetry. Manuel pulled the earbuds out of his ears and began to participate in class a great deal more. On his own, he crafted and later performed a series of raps. At the gala/gallery event, he performed his latest rap, which spoke of the emotional journey of leaving his mother in his native El Salvador to immigrate to the United States. Manuel brought down the house. Many in this standing-room-only audience of students, parents, teachers, and community members were brought to tears by his powerful performance, and Manuel was rewarded with a standing ovation.

Assigned in a separate class to recount the experience of her most impactful experience at Stanford to date, Sandra enlisted some of those classmates to help her create a podcast about her experience in 12SL with EPAA. The recording emphasized the solidarity realized between two seemingly disparate student groups. The podcast's finale featured another of Manuel's raps, followed by a quote from Del Carpio: "More and more, I discover that art is what creates unity, the element of . . . of creating something together." (Both the podcast and rap are available at http://spanlang.stanford.edu/second_year/spanlang12SL.html.)

In Spanlang 13SL, an anonymous student summed up the experience in a course evaluation, saying:

> The service learning component of this class was one of the absolute best experiences I've had at Stanford. For one thing, it really helped my language skills—the first time I went to volunteer at the International Institute I had a really hard time following what native speakers were talking about when they would speak naturally, but by the end of the quarter I was used to it and understood almost everything. Having the goal of communicating as effectively as possible with the people we were working with was the absolute best motivation for me to improve my Spanish. Even beyond the language component, though, interacting with the people at the Institute week after week and getting to know them personally was such an incredible experience. I think it's safe to say it gave me and my classmates a totally new perspective on immigration. Of course I have read a lot about the immigration debate in the news, but hearing the stories of people who have personally undergone huge struggles as immigrants to the U.S., you really start to look at these issues differently. Besides, you get to know people who are usually very different from yourself, which is always a good thing. I was sorry to say goodbye to all the wonderful people I met at the Institute! Overall, the service learning component of this class gave me not only greater language proficiency and a greater understanding and awareness of Latino and Latin American cultures, but also the confidence to interact with Spanish speakers in the U.S. in various contexts.

This student was visibly in the process of thinking critically about and finding her own path through these complex issues and linking them, and thereby herself, to the community around her.

Conclusion

This chapter studied our CEL program as it sought to expand from a single course into a second-year track. The evidence here suggests that CEL students in a critically conscious world language program can improve not only in language proficiency but also sociocultural and civic proficiency. Through careful course planning and frequent reflection, students increased their understanding of the cultural wealth inherent in and disparate opportunity structures faced by their community partners. Beyond this study, we suspect that many other insights are in the offing, and we encourage work that likewise emphasizes the reciprocal effects for community partners.

The opportunities for CEL to encourage speaker/actors to engage in a language, provided the CEL program is grounded in the four R's and committed to recognizing community cultural wealth (Yosso, 2005), seem boundless. CEL provided a channel through which the students described here overcame initial apprehensions about communicative abilities, created new solidarities, and came to see themselves and their community partners in a new light. As a Spanlang 11SL student, Pamela, summed it up, ". . . hay un mundo con vidas completamente afuera de exámenes, tareas y clases" (". . . there is a world with lives completely apart from exams, homework, and classes").

Further, our framework (Figure 4.1) encourages both student progress and programmatic cohesion. Forging inroads, *abriendo caminos*, the framework has provided a lens through which to experience communities beyond the university's borders and to do so in a socially responsible way: sharing companionship, reciprocity, and respect as well as curricular resources with community partners. It was and is a "messy" process, involving ups and downs for faculty, students, and partners. Yet that messiness provided novel avenues of social interaction and led to new forms of self-discovery through others. The Spanlang CEL program will continue to face and embrace these challenges as we likewise continue *abriendo caminos* with our students and community partners.

References

Barreneche, G., & Ramos-Flores, H. (2013). Integrated or isolated experiences? Considering the role of service-learning in the Spanish language curriculum. *Hispania*, 96(2), 215–228.

Bass, R., & Elmendorf, H. (n.d.) Social pedagogies white paper. Excerpt from "Designing for Difficulty: Social Pedagogies as a Framework for Course Design in Undergraduate Education." Retrieved from https://blogs.commons.georgetown.edu/bassr/social-pedagogies/

Bettencourt, M. (2015). Supporting student learning outcomes through service learning. *Foreign Language Annals*, 48(3), 473–490.

Burgo, C. (2016). Service-learning for students of Spanish: Promoting civic engagement and social justice through an exchange tutoring service. *Revista de Lingüística y Lenguas Aplicadas*, 11, 11–18.

Campus Compact. (2016). Catalyze campus engagement. Retrieved on July 5, 2016, from http://compact.org/what-we-do

Charmaz, K. (2005). Grounded theory in the 21st century: Applications for advancing social justice studies. In N. Denzin & Y. Lincoln (Eds.), *The Sage handbook of qualitative research* (3rd ed.). Thousand Oaks, CA: Sage Publications.

Clayton, P., & Ash, S. (2004). Shifts in perspective: Capitalizing on the counternormative nature of service-learning. *Michigan Journal of Community Service-Learning, 11*(1), 59–70.

Coles, R. (1999). Race-focused service-learning courses: Issues and recommendations. *Michigan Journal of Community Service Learning, 6*(1), 97–105.

Corbin, J. (2015). *Basics of qualitative research: Techniques and procedures for developing grounded theory* (4th ed.). Los Angeles, CA: Sage Publications.

Dewey, J. (1942). *Democracy and education*. New York, NY: Macmillan.

Duncan, D., & Kopperud, J. (2008). *Service-learning companion*. Boston, MA: Houghton Mifflin.

Eyler, J. (2002). Reflection: Linking service and learning—linking students and communities. *Journal of Social Issues, 58*(3), 517–534.

Fairclough, N. (1992). *Discourse and social change*. Cambridge, UK: Polity Press.

Freire, P. (1970/1993). *Pedagogy of the oppressed*. New York, NY: Continuum International Publishing Group.

Glynn, C., Wesely, P., & Wassell, B. (2014). *Words and actions: Teaching languages through the lens of social justice*. Alexandria, VA: American Council on the Teaching of Foreign Languages.

Gomez, K. (2016). What's it like to work with adults at the Institute? Retrieved August 30, 2016, from http://spanlang.stanford.edu/second_year/spanlang13SL.html

Haas Center for Public Service. (2016). Stanford University student affairs. Principles of ethical and effective service. Retrieved June 20, 2016, from https://haas.stanford.edu/about/about-haas-center/principles-ethical-and-effective-service

Hartfield-Méndez, V. (2013). Community-based learning, internationalization of the curriculum, and university engagement with Latino communities. *Hispania, 96*(2), 355–368.

Hellebrandt, J., Arries, J, Varona, L., & Klein, C. (Eds.). (2003). *Juntos: Community partnerships in Spanish and Portuguese: AATSP professional development series handbook*, Vol. 5. Boston, MA: Heinle.

Hellebrandt, J., & Jorge, E. (2013). The scholarship of community engagement: Advancing partnerships in Spanish and Portuguese. *Hispania, 96*(2), 203–214.

Hellebrandt, J., & Varona, L. (Eds.). (1999). *Construyendo puentes (Building bridges): Concepts and models for service-learning in Spanish*. Washington, DC: American Association for Higher Education.

Howard, J. P. (1998). Academic service learning: A counternormative pedagogy. In R. Rhoads & J. Howard (Eds.), *Academic service-learning: A pedagogy of action and reflection* (pp. 21–30). San Francisco, CA: Jossey-Bass.

Jacoby, B. (1996). Service-learning in today's higher education. In B. Jacoby et al. (Eds.), *Service-learning in higher education: Concepts and practices* (pp. 3–25). San Francisco, CA: Jossey-Bass.

Johnstone, B. (2008) *Discourse analysis* (2nd ed.). Malden, MA: Blackwell Publishers.

Kern, R., & Liddicoat, A. (2008). Introduction: De l'apprenant au locuteur/acteur. In G. Zarate, D. Levy, & C. Kramsch (Eds.), *Précis du plurilinguïsme et du pluriculturalisme* (pp. 27–33). Paris, France: Éditions des archives contemporaines.

Krogstad, J. M., Stepler, R., & Lopez, M. H. (2015). English proficiency on the rise among Latinos. PEW Research Center. *Hispanic Trends*. Retrieved August 30, 2016, from http://www.pewhispanic.org/2015/05/12/english-proficiency-on-the-rise-among-latinos/

Lear, D., & Abbott, A. (2009). Aligning expectations for mutually beneficial community service-learning: The case of Spanish language proficiency, cultural knowledge, and professional skills. *Hispania, 92*(2), 312–323.

Long, S. S. (Ed.). (2013). Focusing on the scholarship of community engagement *Hispania, 96*(2), 201–202.

Magnan, S., Murphy, D., Sahakyan, N., & Kim, S. (2012). Student goals, expectations, and the Standards for Foreign Language Learning. *Foreign Language Annals, 45*(2), 170–192.

Miano, A., Bernhardt, B., & Brates, V. (2016). Exploring the effect of a short-term Spanish immersion program in a postsecondary setting. *Foreign Language Annals, 49*(2), 287–301.

National Standards Collaborative Board. (2015). *World-readiness standards for learning languages* (4th ed). Alexandria, VA: Author.

Nelson, A., & Scott, J. (2008). Applied Spanish in the university curriculum: A successful model for community-based service-learning. *Hispania, 91*(2), 446–460.

Pak, C.-S. (2007). The service-learning classroom and motivational strategies for learning Spanish: Discoveries from two interdisciplinary community-centered seminars. In A. Wurr & J. Hellebrandt (Eds.), *Learning the language of global citizenship: Service learning in applied linguistics*. Boston, MA: Anker Publishing Company, Inc.

Pellettieri, J. (2011). Measuring language-related outcomes of community-based learning in intermediate Spanish courses. *Hispania, 94*(2), 285–302.

Plann, S. (2002). Latinos and literacy: An upper-division Spanish course with service learning. *Hispania, 85*(2), 330–338.

Sigmon, R. (1979). Service learning: Three principles. *ACTION, 8*(1), 9–11.

Strauss, A. (1987). *Qualitative analysis for social scientists*. Cambridge, UK: Cambridge University Press.

Yosso, T. (2005). Whose culture has capital? A critical race theory discussion of community cultural wealth. *Race Ethnicity and Education, 8*(1), 69–91.

Zapata, G. (2011). The effects of community service learning projects on L2 learners' cultural understanding. *Hispania, 94*, 86–102.

Zlotkowski, E. (1999). Pedagogy and engagement. In R. Bringle, R. Games, & E. Malloy (Eds.), *Colleges and universities as citizens*. Boston, MA: Allyn & Bacon.

Part 2
Literacy, Symbolic Representations, and the Learner as Social Actor

Chapter 5
Social-Pedagogical Life Imitates Art: Scaffolding the Voices of L2 Fans and Critics

Stéphanie Pellet, Wake Forest University
Lindsy Myers, University of Missouri-Kansas City

Introduction

This chapter describes a modular, open-access, intermediate French course (Pellet & Myers, 2016) anchored in a constructivist approach to social second language (L2) reading and writing. With the support of digital librarians at Wake Forest University (WFU), a website, Tout le monde: A Collaborative Intermediate French Program (http://cloud.lib.wfu.edu/blog/toutlemonde/), henceforth TLM, was first piloted during the fall 2016 to support language learning within a social pedagogy framework. It built upon a literacy-based textbook, *Littéralement Parlant* (Pellet, 2016), meshing two distinct but complementary solutions for addressing the challenge of teaching L2 literacy. While *Littéralement Parlant* represents an attempt to design an Intermediate-level curriculum centered around reading, the website encapsulates "modules," a series of interconnected tools, including a blog (both written and audio), a social reading platform, and opportunities for extra mural fan expression. All aspects of the course are thematically linked to the short story and eponymous film *Odette Toulemonde* by Éric-Emmanuel Schmitt (2006). In this chapter, we provide a blueprint for conceptualization and implementation of social pedagogies in an intermediate-level language class and reflections on best practices and hurdles in doing so. After situating our approach within literacy, sociocultural, and social pedagogy frameworks, we describe the course, the development of the program, and the digital tools selected to support student learning and present an analysis of student production and reaction. We close with a discussion on the scalability and adoptability of this approach.

Social Approaches to L2 literacy

L2 literacy elaborates on the traditional L1 model (development of textual understanding and writing skills) stemming from a new awareness of the complex social interactions linked to a global society (hence, the concept of multiliteracy).

Kern (2000), in particular, articulated L2 literacy in response to common teaching practices that did little for fostering cultural awareness and discourse competence. In contrast with a traditional conception, his definition of L2 literacy focuses on "the use of socially-, historically-, and culturally-situated practices of creating and interpreting meaning through texts. It entails at least a tacit awareness of the relationships between textual conventions and their contexts of use and, ideally, the ability to reflect critically on those relationships" (p. 16). Grounded in a sociocognitive perspective, Kern's (2000) definition is articulated around seven key principles: interpretation, collaboration (writing for an audience), cultural conventions, cultural knowledge ("reading and writing function within particular systems of attitudes, beliefs, customs, ideals, and values," p. 17), problem solving, (self-)reflection, and language use. Taken together, they correspond to a "macro-principle: literacy involves communication" (p. 17). In continuity with the work of the New London Group (1996), he adapted the following four components as the pedagogical basis of a literacy approach to foreign language teaching: situated practice (relevancy to students' experiences), overt instruction (including metalanguage), critical framing (situating communication within social contexts), and transformed practice (manipulating existing texts with explicit awareness of the communicative and social contexts).

A key part of literacy is the integration of language skills. For instance, Barré-De Miniac, Brissaud, and Rispail (2004) stated that "it is no longer a simple matter of learning to read or to write, but also of reading and writing to learn" (p. 12); literacy as defined here encompasses speaking and listening as well since it extends the notion of text to include written and spoken boundaries, indeed including visual documents (e.g., advertisements), and across mediums (traditional vs. digital). Similarly, Kern (2003b) noted that "in literacy-based teaching the relation between reading, writing and talking is not linear but overlapping" (p. 52). In Center for Open Educational Resources and Language Learning's (COERLL) online reading module, Swaffar and Arens (2010) view reading in terms of a holistic curriculum that "emphasizes how the parts of a whole relate to each other to form the whole. From this perspective, reading relates to speaking, writing, listening comprehension, and culture" (A Holistic Approach to Reading section, para. 2). The third of their series of reading tasks, rereading, is particularly relevant to our project, which involves "active L2 production such as verbal or written analysis and argumentation" (A Holistic Approach to Reading section, para. 6) and longer, more complex discourse. This involves critical thinking so that "cultural context and the individual foreign language learner's own identity emerge as central to all acts of production" (A Holistic Approach to Reading section, para. 6). Essentially, this perspective on rereading as a set of tasks promoting skill integration goes hand in hand with cultural literacy.

The lack of a coherent and integrated programmatic approach within language departments negatively influences the development of advanced learners' competences (Byrnes, Maxim, & Magnan, 2003; Kern, 2000). To remedy this situation, Kern (2011) proposes that "a general goal of literacy-based language teaching is to reconcile communicative language teaching, with its emphasis on face-to-face verbal interaction, with the development of learners' ability to read, discuss, think, and write critically about texts. Accordingly, literacy-based teaching focuses on language use in social contexts, but integrates critical reflection about how discourse is constructed, how it is used toward various ends, and how it relates to the culture(s) that gave rise to it" (p. 4). L2 literacy, consequently, is seen as a necessary programmatic response to a complex, multicultural society.

The tenets of a constructivist, student-centered pedagogy naturally support this approach. Particularly significant for our project, which seeks to empower students as readers becoming authors, "[s]ociocultural theory, like interactionist SLA emphasizes the importance of learner interaction, but it is interested less in negotiation-evoked adjustments in input than in the social and cultural situatedness of learner activity, learners' agency in co-constructing meanings (as well as their own roles), and the importance of mediation by tools and signs" (Kern, 2006, p. 187). In parallel with learner's autonomy (Little, 2007; Savignon, 2007) and the construction of a learner's identity not modeled strictly after the native speaker's (Kramsch, 1997), sociolinguistic approaches to literacy view reading and writing in their cultural and social contexts.

At the center of transformational discussions on student engagement lies a framework harnessing the social aspects of learning. In other words, "[s]ocial pedagogies provide a way to tap into a set of intrinsic motivations that we often overlook: people's desire to be part of a community and to share what they know with that community" (Bruff, 2011). Social pedagogies capitalize on the contemporary "participatory culture" (Jenkins, Purushotma, Weigel, Clinton, & Robison, 2006), which features "strong support for creating and sharing creations with others" and "members who feel some degree of social connection with one another" (pp. 5–6). Similarly, undergraduate students noted that courses that had a profound impact on them included writing for their fellow learners because such writing "requires a different approach and a different authorial voice" and by "seeing different styles of writing and presentation, they become able to distinguish different levels of excellence" (Light, 2001, p. 65). Bass and Elmendorf (2012) promote social pedagogies that involve opportunities to interact with an "authentic audience," which means—and this is a critical aspect of their approach—someone other than the instructor. The three key areas they outline for course design and implementation—design (of effective social pedagogies), scaffolding (by supporting student work in stages), and assessment (that takes into consideration the connections between intermediate processes, formative assessments, and final products)—serve as a guide for the organization of this chapter.

Web 2.0 has proved to be a transformative, constructivist platform for self-regulated language learning (Thomas, 2009; Sharpe, Beetham, & de Freitas,

2010), allowing for knowledge co-construction (active learning; Schank, 1994), including metacognition, peer-to-peer writing and editing, intercultural communication (Thorne, 2003; Ware & Kramsch, 2005), and intercultural exploration (Arnold, Ducate, & Kost, 2009; Furstenberg, Levet, English, & Maillet, 2001; Hanna & de Nooy, 2003; Lee, 1998). Combining a redefined conception of L2 literacy and social approaches, TLM takes advantage of online social tools to create channels of expression across asynchronous modes (written, oral), allowing students to negotiate meaning together and communicate with each other not just for authentic interactions but to build knowledge together (e.g., social reading for enhancing textual understanding). In proposing a collaborative virtual space to the students, designed to become an aggregate but cohesive set of digital tools, we find Kern's (2015) three key processes of technology particularly productive: design, transformation, and mediation. "[D]esign is the creative process (and product) of transforming existing resources into new ones, in relation to particular needs, purposes, and contexts" (p. 7), with a focus on transformations as "reworkings, reframings, and recontextualizations of symbolic resources having to do with language, communication, and identity" (p. 7). Mediation recognizes the impact of not only the medium being used but also "the ways that physical environments, cultural contexts, social role relations, and activity frames affect how people communicate" (p. 8). From the outset, the social L2 literacy project discussed here was conceived as process oriented, one where the media adopted would foster transformative "reframings and recontextualizations," empowering students not only as readers but also collectively as knowledge producers.

Collaborative Program Development

In the intermediate-level program at WFU, we implement a literacy approach to learning French, inviting students to read a complete short story as a segue to reading-intensive, upper-level courses (at least with regard to length and level of difficulty). It enacts Kern's proposal that "literacy can be used as an organizing principle to design language curricula that problematize the linguistic, cognitive, and social relationships that link readers, writers, texts, and culture" (Kern, 2003a, p. 2). The two overarching course objectives lend themselves to an organic integration: the first objective was to get students to engage with the text through close, in-depth reading, and the second was to foster (a degree of) learner empowerment via "the implementation of a methodology for language learning that focuses on authenticity in contents, context, and task" (Rüschoff, 2009, p. 43). In the case we describe, integration was achieved at multiple levels.

The textbook *Littéralement Parlant* (Pellet, 2016) was developed by the instructor specifically around the short story "Odette Toulemonde" to support an integrated approach, complemented by an online, open-education French grammar resource, *Tex's French Grammar* (http://www.laits.utexas.edu/tex/;

Blyth & Kelton, 2000). The objective of the textbook is to promote both learning to read and reading to learn. The curriculum, like the short story, is divided into seven learning units or chapters centered around the reading process, each explicitly named for its link to the story.

Developing students' reading ability guided the choice of the short story "Odette Toulemonde"—at the intermediate level, students are not doing literary analysis but developing their L2 literacy skills as previously defined. Shorter than a novel yet an authentic text originally written for native speakers of French, it allows students to read a whole text, from beginning to end. Set mostly in Belgium, it tells the story of a young widow, struggling to make ends meet, who lives for the books written by her favorite author, Balthazar. When the latter, well-to-do and successful, is shaken by a merciless critique of his latest novel, he somehow lands in the small apartment where Odette lives with her two children. There, he discovers a much simpler but potentially more meaningful way of living. Balthazar is at risk of losing his identity as a talented author, and Odette, a simple fan, unexpectedly gains a voice by being acknowledged by Balthazar, in what is normally a one-way relationship. The story provides opportunities for exploring important questions regarding relationships between author and reader and/or fan and the potentiality of entering into a two-way dialogue (as opposed to a one-way, author-controlled communication). Such questions echo issues raised in L2 education: L2 learners' identity, their ability to gain a voice to express their ideas, teacher-controlled communication, and the lack of authentic readership students experience when they write solely for the teacher.

The short story is brief and uses contemporary vocabulary and structures that are adequate for a course focused on everyday language skills, and its storyline echoes relatable, universal themes (e.g., relationships, parenthood). The limited number of characters (two main characters and six secondary characters) helps students keep the storyline straight. Before Eric-Emmanuel Schmitt published the story, he directed the eponymous movie, which offers an opportunity for comparisons between the cinematic and literary texts and enhances the students' reading experience. This juxtaposition of media is supported by our "read-talk-watch-reread" course design in which corresponding film clips are selected for in-class viewing after initial reading and comprehension checks. "Odette Toulemonde" provides the foundation for creating a learning community with the common goal of reading a short story (supporting each other in the process), turning language learners into authors with their own voice, writing for each other and potentially for the francophone community at large, and co-constructing knowledge via story-inspired, authentic, process-oriented assignments.

The conception and implementation of such a large multicomponent project require careful handling of legal and copyright issues (for the short story and the movie). The TLM website, which hosts the course social tools, was designed under a Creative Commons Attribution-NonCommercial 4.0 International (CC BY-NC

4.0), which enables reuse, including remixing and derivative creation, by other educators and scholars but prohibits use for commercial gain without further permission from its authors. The TLM title is geared first toward the students themselves: inviting them to take part and ownership in the making of the website. It was also conceived as an open resource for other French instructors.

No e-book is currently available for the short story itself; students purchased a paper copy of Eric-Emmanuel Schmitt's story "Odette Toulemonde," which allowed the instructor to make available to them a teacher-annotated version of the text (glosses and grammar aids) via the learning management system. For the same reason, the social reading component of the course remains access-restricted on the TLM website. While an e-book would present obvious advantages, the hybridity of multichannel reading and reacting is not without potential benefits, including the anecdotal feedback from students who enjoy holding, reading, and finishing a book.

In the first iteration of the TLM program, 18 students, mostly freshmen, enrolled in the intermediate-level course (FR 153), which meets five times per week for 15 weeks. Students reported having taken between three and four years of high school French prior to taking this first college-level course. At the beginning of the semester, all students signed author agreements, whereby they gave their consent to participate in and to publish online graded assignments in various media formats as part of the course requirements. On the TLM website, students' production sits alongside instructor-prepared materials on the program website and by design becomes part of the input for others, which MacKinnon and Pasfield-Neofitou (2016) label Open Educational Resources (OER) "produsage" and in particular small-scale "little OER."

Scaffolding Modular Social Pedagogies

In the subsections that follow, we describe the tools and approaches that together form the social pedagogies of the TLM program: blogs, social reading, and extramural fan and critic activity.

Blogs.

Blogs are now well integrated in L2 learning, and their effectiveness is also well documented (see Thorne & Black, 2007). They provide an authentic context for students to expand L2 writing skills in various areas, including academic writing (Bloch, 2007), L2 fluency and accuracy (Armstrong & Retterer, 2008), metacognition (Yang, 2009) or self-reflection (Alm, 2009), to support exploration of L2 reading (Raith, 2009) and L2 culture learning (Ducate & Lomicka, 2005; Lee, 2011), or even as a medium supporting the development of oral skills (Pinkman, 2005). Their most salient feature, viewability, highlights the sharing affordance of blogs (Carney, 2009) expanding readership beyond the teacher (Thorne & Payne, 2005).

Carney (2009) identifies four areas where blogs can support language education: motivation, authenticity, collaboration, and literacy. Fernheimer and Nelson (2005) discuss the importance of understanding the blog genre as a discourse type with the potential to establish "classroom community norms that embrace engagement with others" (sec. 18); to cultivate this community, they required reading and responding to others' work: "interleaved written responses mitigate against the tendency to see one's writing as a lone 'voice in the wilderness'" (sec. 18). Thorne (2009) observed that "blog use formed an interstitial communication space where both academic and nonacademic discursive features were articulated through personally relevant expression, in essence that students were writing both to fulfill a class requirement while also writing to and for one another" (p. 87). Blogs have the potential to increase students' sense of autonomy and agency (empowerment), expanding on the concept of student-centered teaching. Franklin-Matkowski (2007) similarly observed that blogging seemed to have several positive attitudinal and language outcomes:

1. Students' fluency increased.
2. Students wrote with voice.
3. Students' confidence in their writing increased.
4. Students valued feedback from their peers which helps them learn about audience.
5. Students felt open and willing to express and share their writing, thereby creating a community.
6. Students developed and defined blogging as a genre appropriate for their class blog. (p. 119)

Nevertheless, this individualistic or highly personal space is not collaborative per se and requires careful articulation of expectations of contributions (see Krause, 2004). Carney (2009) also highlights the critical role played by teachers, citing Kern (2006): "Teachers must be prepared for new ways of structuring tasks, establishing exchanges, guiding and monitoring interaction, and evaluating performance, not to mention mastering the relevant computer applications" (p. 201).

In our context, a blog seemed particularly appropriate to support students' moving from sentential expression to connected discourse at the intermediate level. The overall objective highlighted in the syllabus was "to share your experience with your classmates." The blogging guidelines included a rationale for the blog called "Tout le monde en parle" ("Everyone's talking about it"), which stressed its communal character (blogging together, sharing with each other), and promoted a supportive environment (sharing victories and difficulties) and an expanded and authentic readership (students vs. professors only), hence turning students into authors. Students' weekly blog posts started on the second week of class and continued throughout the semester, with students posting every Monday and responding to two other posts every Thursday. To magnify authentic readership, the visiting French Assistant was invited to act as a respondent to students' comments every week, in an attempt to create a sense of dialogue and validation for students. Two additional key aspects of the rationale have to do with a common quality of blogs: they are centrally about communication and cross between an oral and a written genre. Consequently students' attention was drawn to the fact that with a blog, they are able to focus both on content as well as form, encouraging them to pay attention to language accuracy. Hence, students were encouraged to approach blogging as an open exchange of ideas as opposed to a formal academic essay. In the case of an L2 blog, spontaneity was valued to create an environment where students felt comfortable expressing themselves (fairly) freely. The blog was presented as a "sandbox" where they could try out linguistic forms without fear of failing or of receiving a negative evaluation (grade). Rather, communicating an idea (message) in a paragraph, engaging peers and community at large, and displaying a positive attitude were emphasized. Hence, the blog was conceptualized as an informal peer-to-peer, conversational-like mode of expression, while this written medium offered students the possibility to think through linguistic forms.

Thematically, the blog is deliberately connected to the story "Odette Toulemonde" and to the literacy-centered curriculum. For instance, the initial two topics centered around the reading process. The other topics explicitly connected to the storyline, taking an element of the story and turning it into personal perspectives. By allowing students to choose from a pair of topics, it creates a sense of ownership, and an authentic response seemed more likely. The following are sample prompts that invite students to recount their own experiences similar to Odette's experience with either wanting to meet Balthazar or reading his book in a single sitting:

> *Odette souhaitait rencontrer Balthazar. Qui voudrais-tu rencontrer? Pourquoi cette personne est-elle importante pour toi?*
> Odette wished to meet Balthazar. Who would you like to meet? Why is this person important to you? What book have you read without being able to put it down?
>
> *Quel livre as-tu lu sans pouvoir t'arrêter? Pourquoi ce livre t'a-t-il plu? Est-ce que tu as lu ce livre plusieurs fois? Est-ce que tu lis un livre passionnant, en ce moment? Lequel?*
> Why did you like this book? Did you read this book several times? Are you reading a fascinating book right now? Which one?

The audio blog, *Tout le monde écoute*, offers another means of expression directly linking the two communicative skills: speaking and writing. Like the written blog prompts, they are tied thematically to the narrative arc of Odette yet are purposefully designed to be logical tasks associated with speaking. Once again, students had the choice between two topics:

- "You are a friend of Balthazar, and watched Olaf Pim's deadly review of his latest novel. Call Balthazar and leave him a message on his answering machine... Maybe you want to check on him, or perk him up, or tell him how mean and wrong Olaf is . . . It's up to you. Attention: if you are a close friend of Balthazar, you probably use 'tu' to address him!"
- "You are a fan of Balthazar, and you are very angry after watching Olaf's terrible review of your favorite author's latest novel. Call Pims and leave him an angry message about how nasty he was to Balthazar. Attention: Since you don't know Olaf Pims personally, you need to use 'vous' when talking to him!"

While there are fewer audio blog assignments, they alternate with the written posts and together foster multiple literacies—employing different types of media, genres, levels of formality—embracing multiple channels of communication, all pointing toward a shared goal of textual interpretation, engagement (both as a creator and consumer), and communication.

Social reading.

Macaro (2003) posits that the lack of relative attention afforded to the L2 reading by researchers is partially due to the "relative invisibility of reading as a skill..." (p. 118) since production skills are more readily apparent and assessed. He argues for more substantive dialogue about the reading process since "true/false, multiple choice and other similar task types are all very well for keeping the students busy but they do not get at the processes involved in their reading" (p. 151). Academic reading presents teaching challenges for L1 texts just as much as L2 texts. Hayles (2007) calls attention to a generational shift in cognitive styles, contrasting the traditional deep attention cognitive mode to a rapidly emerging hyper attention mode that is becoming a defining feature of current student generations. During visits at other institutions, she reports faculty members complaining "I can't get my students to read whole novels anymore" (p. 188). She argues that this shift calls for creative and innovative educational strategies. If there is a sense that students are not able to engage (in-depth) with an L1 text, certainly the challenge to do so with an L2 text can only be more serious. If students approach (L1) reading simply as a task to be completed, how could they approach L2 reading differently and quite possibly with less confidence and more anxiety? Social reading in an L2 environment lets students notice, question, and decipher a text together. It breaks reading as an isolated experience, allows students to gain better understanding of the text by putting individual readings into a "communal pot," and promotes close reading.

Using digital social reading enables readers to become empowered in a way that is not comparable to book clubs in that readers leave a digital footprint, creating a two-way relationship with the author that could not exist prior to Web 2.0. Hypothes.is (https://hypothes.is), an open-source platform for annotating digital documents, was adopted to support the social reading component of the course. Students received pedagogical and technology-related guidelines. As with the blog, the rationale behind using social reading was shared with students, emphasizing co-construction of knowledge (as opposed to solitary reading) and close reading by commenting on specific parts of the text. Students also received guidance on the content of annotations, with the aim of generating topically broad comments. They were instructed to use annotations to signal lack of understanding, including asking classmates questions; to share personal reactions to the storyline; and to identify key words, themes, and cultural elements. Because social reading is aimed at enhancing textual understanding, students were given the choice to annotate in French or in English. Flexibility on how much to annotate seemed important for two reasons. First, allowing students to write a fragment, a sentence, or more in turn allowed them to focus on meaningful content. Second, social reading constituted an additional assignment for students, and previous research on computer-based communication (Hawisher & Pemberton, 1998; Pena-Shaff, Altman, & Stephenson, 2005) showed that there is a risk for communicative online assignments to be perceived as a burden, losing meaningfulness in the students' eyes, especially when these assignments become "too much," or when the grade reward is not commensurate with the time required. As with the written and audio blogs, students had to post two comments for each reading segment (matching the chapter) and, two days later, address one comment made by another classmate. Suggestions for responding to a comment were meant to help students frame responses. They could offer an answer to a question, mark their agreement/disagreement, and add information or alternative explanations. The grading system (both for initial annotations and for the ensuing response) was defined broadly (highly meaningful/somewhat meaningful/no comment) and shared with students. Since the social reading assignment sought to scaffold the reading process, assessment of correct L2 usage was not relevant. Finally, students were instructed to associate an instructor-defined tag with their comments.

Extramural fans and critics.

Another social approach to teaching and learning involves tapping into the practice of reading, watching, and writing as both students and fans or critics, which relates directly to L2 literacy. Black (2009) defines fan fiction as "a unique form of writing in which fans base their stories on the characters and plotlines of existing media and popular culture" in which fans as authors "extend storylines, create new narrative threads, develop romantic relationships between characters, and focus on the lives of undeveloped characters . . ." (p. 398). She found that English-language learners via their nonclassroom-based fan fiction texts "offered a challenge to conventional notions of 'good' writing as individualistic, author-centric, monolingual, and rigidly adherent to standard genres and conventions" (p. 422). Sauro and Sundmark (2016) in turn observed how fan fiction activities when used as a pedagogical tool in university foreign language classes "support literacy and language learning" (p. 422). Reading and writing fan fiction in English as foreign language can also be a motivation for improvement (Rossetti, 2014). The Odette story, movie, and creator, with their own significant digital footprints, offer avenues of exploration and comparisons and an opportunity to mirror fan reactions on our own site. The social tools and approaches described thus far in this chapter are either closed to the outside community, as in the case of the social reading, or, in the case of the blogs, are public yet not highly trafficked. In contrast, the extramural components are currently of two types. A *Cher Monsieur Schmitt* module scaffolds students-as-fans and critics of the living author. In this space, students are able to explore Schmitt's footprint and then send him a letter as final meta-reflection on reading the book and the course. The *Fans d'Odette* module (under construction at press time) is in reality a fan page that promotes bookmarking and reacting to the movie and the book. One aspect of it mimics the Rotten Tomatoes genre, in our case called *Oeufs à la neige* as a nod to a scene in the short story, with links to external web pages with relevant information on actors, authors, and critics. At the end of the semester, students rate both the film and short story on the *Oeufs à la neige* module. In further iterations of this produsage module, students will make their own fan-inspired materials, such as fan fiction for the written version and fansubs for the film. While we chose to label these particular social pedagogies as most closely relevant to fans and critics, in many ways, the blog assignments themselves could be viewed as a type of fan fiction since students are essentially rewriting many of the themes of the story with their own stories and perspectives.

Results: Student Data

This section is divided into two types of sample results: student production (examples from blogs, social reading, and the *Cher Monsieur Schmitt* module) and assessment results (surveys, test questions, and overall course performance).

Student-Written Blog

The following blog entries give a snapshot of students' posts throughout the semester. The posts selected here seek to capture the interaction that it facilitated at two points in the semester.

In her initial post (see Figure 5.1), the student makes effective use of the prompt to elaborate her answer. Her positive outlook is clear while also acknowledging the challenge of the task ahead. The classmate reply connects to the stated anxiety and asserts her viewpoint that while possibly difficult, the act of reading in French may support the overall objective of learning the language. The French Assistant likewise strikes a positive, encouraging tone in her reply.

2 SEPTEMBER 2016 / / 2 COMMENTS / EDIT

Je suis un peu anxieuse de commencer à lire Odette parce que je n'ai pas eu beaucoup d'experience en ce qui concerne la lecture des nouvelles. J'ai également parfois des difficultés à comprendre le sens des text. J'ai eu un experience similaire quand j'ai lu le Petit Prince; pendant ma lecture j'ai eu quelques difficultés mais avec l'aide de ma professeur c'etait un très bonne experience pour moi. Je doute de ma capacité de comprendre de longue phrases et comprendre le voix du narrateur. Je me sens préparé pour cette experience car je pense que ça va beaucoup m'aider en ce qui concerne ma grammaire et mon vocabulaire.

Replies (second reply is from French Assistant):

4 SETPEMBER 2016 AT 1:34 PM

‹je suis en peu anxieuse de lire Odette aussi. Je ne lis pas en français come ça. Quand j'etudie dans lycée j'ai lu en per, mais jamais lire un historie totalment. Je pense quand je lis Odette, j'aime lire parce qui c'est bonne pour etudie les français.

EDIT   REPLAY

7 SETPEMBER 2016 AT 6:01 PM

‹je suis certaine que le travail en classe t'aidera à comprendre plus facilement la nouvelle "Odette Toulemonde". Cela sera une expérience intéressante dans ton apprentissage du français, j'en suis sûre! Je te souhaite une bonne lecture!

Figure 5.1. Sample initial post (week two) and replies

In a later post (see Figure 5.2), students wrote a letter to their favorite author, just like Odette does in the story. In this open testimony to the works of Brian Jacques, the student's personal perspective clearly comes across. The reply shows that the classmate has picked up on the highly personal response, in addition to praising the quality of expression (meta-awareness).

Cher Brian Jacques,

J'écris à vous parce que vous êtes une de le plus grands raisons que j'aime lire. En grandissement, quand j'étais très jeune je lisais toutes des votre livres. Ils m'ont inspiré, Ils m'ont captivé, Ils m'ont transporté, Ils m'enseigné aimer lire et beaucoup d'autre chers leçons. Quand je les ai lu, je m'ai senti que j'ai été sur les aventures et dans le monde de Redwall. Aujourd'hui, je n'ai pas lu un autre auteur qui veut décrire les aliments avec votre talent (j'ai devenu très faim quand j'ai lu votre écriture sur aliments). J'aimais assez votre livres qu'ils m'ont inspiré à essayer et écrire quand j'étais un garçon (mais, je n'ai pas le talent pour écrire vous avez). Alors, vraiment, merci pure une vie avec plein des livres et imagination. Je partagerai votre livres avec mes enfants.

Merci,

Student reply:

14 OCTOBER 2016 AT 12:20 PM

Bonjour,   ! J'aime lire ton blog parce que ta langue est belle et ton français est très bon! Par exemple, je peux voir ton émotion quand tu dis "ils… ils… ils…". Je les adore!

EDIT   REPLY

Figure 5.2. Sample midterm post (week seven) and reply

Student Audio Blog

Toward the end of the semester, students were given the option to call in to a radio show to explain, as Balthazar's literary agent, why Balthazar had dropped out of the public scene. The transcription seeks to adhere to the student expression (content and grammar) as much as possible; hence, audible errors are marked.

> **AUDIO BLOG TRANSCRIPT**
>
> «Bonjour. Premièrement, merci pour permetter-moi faire une déclaration pour mon client Balthazar. Donc tout le monde sait que

Balthazar a disparu mais je sais qu'il est sûr. Je connais mon client : il est très créatif et spontané. Il est probable que Balthazar a voulu une vacation et le temps seul. Il a été très occupé le mois dernier et il a fait face à la critique d'Olaf Pims. Donc il avait besoin de temps pour penser et relaxer. C'est possible qu'il ait une idée pour un nouvelle livre. Et il est parti pour écrire sans les distractions. Chaque auteur a les méthodes différents quand ils vont écrire un roman. Je sais qu'il se sent bien pour tout en ce moment.»

Voicemail conventions are well respected in this student audio blog, which is effective communicatively even if imperfect in terms of language accuracy. The audio blog is also striking in the clear attempt students make in using, successfully or not, new grammar structures and vocabulary. In student replies (e.g., Figure 5.3), the common first sentence signals both the desire to be supportive and possibly the simplest form of positive feedback; message elaboration includes marking agreement, show of support (effectiveness of voicemail), and compliment on oral expression.

Students produced audio blogs that varied in length from about 30 seconds to more than a minute. That range, however, does not necessarily reflect students' ability to communicate orally, given individual differences in words per minute. Variation in length also reflects open-ended directions, which suggested to follow general social conventions for appropriate voicemails. Oral expression, especially on an open platform, is likely perceived as an intimidating activity. Short audio segments are therefore preferable at many levels.

A striking element in listening to audio blogs is that they feel real: it seems as if students were really talking to existing people, as opposed to fictive characters, and replies by classmates echo that sentiment as well. This form of *jeu de role* has students playing the game, as the typical markers of the voicemail genre attest (opening, closing; self-introduction either by name or by role/function). In their production, students are able to express attitudes and show empathy, via the voice of another character. We would argue that such interpersonal expression, encoding third-person empathy, is not often enabled in the typical intermediate-level classroom. The voicemail activity was conceptualized to promote oral expression with consideration for the students' level. Yet, it strikes us how it captures an

---

29 NOVEMBER 2016 AT 1:59 PM

Je pense tu es un vraiment fan de Balthazar. Vous le soutenez et le comprenez.

EDIT   REPLY

Figure 5.3. Student reply to audio blog sample

essential interpersonal genre, one that we all enact daily, but is likely rarely practiced by students.

Social Reading

The social reading annotations offer insight into how students interpret the text in early and later passes. Just like the other social aspects of this course, social reading, to be successful, requires clear expectations, modeling, and guides for interaction. In the first round of annotations, students often explain characters' reactions, make (clever) commentary, point out plot development, or react to the development. In the responses, they most often agree by adding a nuanced take on the original comment or by making further predictions. Annotations make constructive use of both English and French with some responses code-switching from the original. There is some evidence of vocabulary building and even of explicit links made with new vocabulary items presented in chapter units, as, for instance, when students call attention to a particular expression (e.g., *confiance en soi*) even within a comment written in English. This double-coding of words or expression indicates meta-awareness within textual interpretation.

In the following representative example of a student annotation and responses (see Figure 5.4), students make interpretative comments, explain motivations and effects of previous plot developments, and make predictions for what will follow:

Oct 16, 2016

Si mon éditeur passe plusieurs jours avec moi, c'est que ça va très mal, se disait-il.

Balthazar is now thinking the worst about himself and his writing. I agree wth the annotation above, this shows how much Olaf's comments affected him.

A.Namur

Hide replies (2)

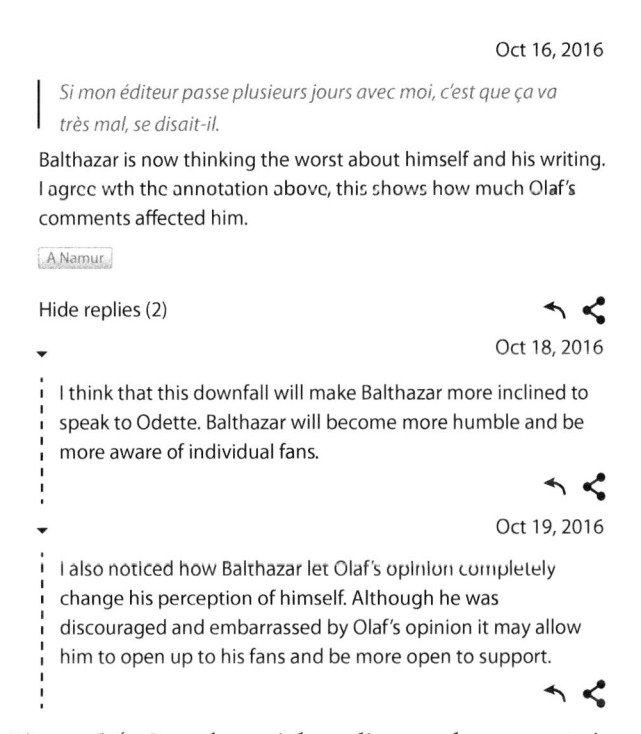

Oct 18, 2016

I think that this downfall will make Balthazar more inclined to speak to Odette. Balthazar will become more humble and be more aware of individual fans.

Oct 19, 2016

I also noticed how Balthazar let Olaf's opinion completely change his perception of himself. Although he was discouraged and embarrassed by Olaf's opinion it may allow him to open up to his fans and be more open to support.

Figure 5.4. Sample social reading student annotation with student replies

Oct 16, 2016

| *Bonjour, vous me reconnaissez ?*

Cette phrase est tres important. C'est tres interessant voir comment ils ont l'occassion rencontrer encore. Cette monte comment leur recontre va etre tres signficant maintenant. Le monde est un place peu.

Hide replies (1)

Oct 17, 2016

I agree that it is very important. It is interesting that she says that they haven't met. That way she gets a fresh start!

Figure 5.5. Sample social reading student annotation with student reply

They also make explicit acknowledgments about other student annotations, most often supporting the original post (see Figure 5.5). On the whole, we observe interpretive and presentational language in the original annotations intermingled with interpersonal in the replies.

Cher Monsieur Schmitt letter.

The *Cher Monsieur Schmitt* letter could be considered the capstone blog assignment for the course. In Figure 5.6, the student reflects on her reading experience and shares her opinions with the author.

Cher Monsieur Schmitt...

9 DECEMBER 2016 /   / 1 COMMENT / EDIT

Cher Monsieur Schmitt,

Bonjour! Je suis une étudiante Américaine qui étudie français, et cette semestre, nous avons lu votre nouvelle dans le cours. Ce qui était une expérience incroyablement intimidante, mais avec le temps, j'ai appris apprécier le défi. J'aime Odette, parce qu'elle est une protagoniste très sympathique et compatissante, mais je ne suis pas certaine que j'aie aimé les autres personnages. Cependant, ce qui ne m'a pas arrêté d'appréciament l'histoire. J'espère que tu continuera écrire les romans!

Figure 5.6. Sample *Cher Monsieur Schmitt* letter

The student follows genre conventions (greeting, self-introduction and topic sentence, closing sentence) while efficiently assessing her reading experience. The presentation of viewpoint is again evident with attention to interlocutor's face (appreciation of Odette yet nuanced criticism of the other characters).

Survey

The social pedagogy aspects of the course were evaluated via an anonymous survey to provide a more quantitative assessment of its success. The numerical results of this small-scale survey are presented in Appendix A. Overall, students report that the blog supports various aspects of their engagement in the class. In particular, at least half of the students find that the blog supports them "a lot" or "quite a bit," and there are very few cases (2%) that an outcome was "not at all" supported by the blog. The highly favorable response to the blog's success at both supporting focusing on communicating an idea and trying out new vocabulary and grammar indicates that students embraced the tone of the blog instructions, which primarily encouraged risk taking and communication. The more mixed response to tokens about understanding either the text or grammar/vocabulary served as a reminder that the relationships between these facets need to be more explicit both in the blog prompts and the in-class discussions. Moreover, the positive response to the query about motivation was a welcome result in light of the amount of work that the course requires on the part of all involved.

Answers from Test 1

Connections between the social assignments and the coursework were explicitly reinforced by questions on the exam: one asking (in French) about what they do and don't like about the blog and the other (in English) about what they find they have in common with their peers from reading the posts. Although we cannot dismiss the possibility that students were telling the instructor what they thought she wanted to hear on this graded section of the test, overall student comments were very positive and showed remarkable similarity in content (see Table 5.1).

These responses demonstrate community building and solidarity as well as a certain level of meta-awareness concerning strengths and weaknesses and a clear articulation that it is okay to make mistakes. Students agree that everyone is in the same place and shares nervousness about progress, which could be otherwise prohibitive, especially in Second Language Acquisition (SLA) with high affective filters. While they acknowledge that the blogs are a lot of work and some dislike being forced to make comments, they generally agree that reading their peers' work is not just informative but enjoyable too.

Correlations

What interaction, if any, exists between the students' course performance and their participation in virtual assignments? A quick way to gauge such potential

Table 5.1. Sample Exam 1 Responses Linked to Social Pedagogies

Q1. Ce semestre, vous participez à un blog. Qu'est-ce que vous aimez ou n'aimez pas à ce sujet?

- *Un blog donne un opportunitie pour utilise nouveux vocabulaire et temps [sic]*
- *J'aime lire ce que l'autres ont écrit [sic]*
- *J'aime comment le blog est informel. Alors nous pouvons parler nos idées vraiment. [sic]*
- *Je l'aime parce qu'il est interactif et différent.*
- *C'est beaucoup de travail.*

Q2. What have you found in common with your classmates when posting/responding on the blog?

- *I feel more comfortable with making mistakes because I know everyone is just as nervous as me.*
- *Nous sommes plus bons d'écrire le français que parler le. [sic]*
- *I found that when reading their work they have a lot of subject/verb agreement errors and them when i [sic] go back to my blog I notice I make the same type of mistakes.*
- *. . . we can help each other if someone doesn't understand the story, or just need help in French in general. . .*

Table 5.2. Blog Production and Course Performance Comparison: High versus Low Performers

Student	Blogs (average # of words)	Blog Grade (%)	Course Grade	Final Exam Grade
S1	106	97.5	A–	93
S2	105	97.5	A	83
S3	127	97.5	A–	90
S4	105	97.5	B	67
S5	95	87.5	C+	66
S6	99	87.5	C	67

interaction is to contrast blog production of students who had the best overall course performance with those with a low performance.

A cursory glance at Table 5.2 suggests that high performers showed a greater degree of sustained effort and/or engagement on the written blogs than low performers. Anecdotally, students' regular textual production (traditional homework assignments) suggests that they reaped benefit from the weekly blog postings (and blog responses); students' writing appeared to evolve toward paragraph-length, connected discourse, marking an appreciable difference from what students seemed able to produce when the semester started.

Discussion

How social is the student production? While the limited samples in a nascent project such as TLM prevented us from making any broad or definitive claims, we evaluated students' work qualitatively, by examining the content, the types of shared information, the range of topics discussed, the lexical and grammatical choices made, and the comprehensibility. The production varied according to the task, ranging from speech acts and specific genres (such as letters or reviews) to inviting the student into the fictional world. The high degree of comprehensibility is evidenced by reasonable, supportive, and thoughtful peer-to-peer feedback as seen in the student samples earlier. In their comments, students often used the blogger's first name and then empathized or shared a similar story. In other types of responses, students validated the blogger's feelings or offered a different way of seeing a situation in a respectful manner. They often made specific references to the post itself demonstrating they had carefully read the original post. These attributes distinguish this type of online commentary from the real world where the comment section is notorious for decaying into negative discourse. We attribute this high degree of accountability and positivity to visibility. Digital communication proves to be an equalizer for all students, even those who are shy since all are allocated the same space, font, and metaphorical volume; everyone raises their hand on the blog and has the same handwriting and the same accent. "The students saw the blog as a space in which they presented and represented aspects of themselves within a performative context. In this they were taking part in the cultural practices of representation which exist both inside and outside the formal structures of the course" (Potter & Banaji, 2012, p. 88). In the blog posts, student performance naturally oscillated between presentational, interpretive, and interpersonal. The original post is primarily presentational. However, interpersonal elements are arguably visible since the students are aware that they are going to be read by their peers; the responses engage the interpretive and interpersonal modes. The interpersonal mode is incomplete or one-sided since most attempts at clarification on the part of the responder were not often addressed by the original poster. This is of course a facet of social media interaction and course design. We seek to address this imbalance in future iterations of the course with more specific references to blog content in the classroom, to foster follow-up and closure on these topics.

Students' responses indicated that highly personal topics felt inviting to students (ethos) but were also inherently communicative: these were topics about which they had something to say. The interpersonal nature of the blog seemingly created a format in which students felt comfortable sharing (personal) ideas and stories. We posit that how these assignments are described and eventually assessed increases community building and interactive components of communication. For instance, nearly half of the students readily shared embarrassing moments as early as their second post. In connection to the main character's sudden inability to talk, students were invited to recount a similar experience and how they now felt about this embarrassing moment. It suggests that students felt they were interacting in a protected, supportive environment. If the blogging instructions (be positive) and the first blog topic (do you feel anxious/ready to read a short story in French?) likely played a role in establishing a positive climate, the nature of blogging cannot be ignored. The invitation to talk about personal experiences succeeded because the virtual medium allows for disinhibition and for the expression of true selves (or alternatively the trying out of new identities and personalities). These observations are in line with Gackenback and von Stackelberg (2011, p. 55) who highlighted that the lack of visual clues and judgments of their physical presence accounts for this greater freedom.

The virtual presence/physical absence became particularly evident when the course instructor attempted to play examples of the first audio blog submissions in class after students had commented on each other's audio blog, much in the same way they did for the written blogs, with supportive messages displaying agreement. When the instructor asked who was willing to have their message played, no one volunteered, and the audible silence in the classroom made it clear that the request was received as a face-threatening act. This observation is consistent with Kern's (2015) accounts of the advantages of online writing such as the lack of awkward pauses. It highlights the role of face and affective dimensions and how they play out differently online and in face-to-face interactions.

Despite the clear license to avoid complex or new grammatical structures, many students took advantage of this sandbox to utilize the relevant new concepts being covered in class and in the *Littéralement Parlant* course book. Grammatical and structural risk taking abounded. Students made their own self-directed links between grammar and vocabulary and the communicative goal. For example, many posts included structurally complex and not-yet-mastered grammatical features such as subjunctive, pluperfect, object pronouns, and past tenses. These types of observations are consistent with the changes observed by Yuldashev, Fernandez, and Thorne (2013) in L2 high school Spanish-language production on blog entries.

Nevertheless, from the mundane to the more significant, developing and coordinating the collaborative elements of this program has met significant challenges. While there were very few issues with student compliance as far as submitting the assignments (perhaps thanks to public accountability), getting students to use tags and putting assignments in the right place on the website were challenging. Although the majority of the student population could be considered digital natives, those native skills do not necessarily translate to consistent problem solving or rule abiding in the academic environment. Lack of appropriate tags makes it tedious to find and assess blogs, and it certainly affects how and to what degree students commented on each other's posts. In other words, anecdotal observations suggest that students often comment on the easiest blogs to find (i.e., the ones at the top of the page). While we pleaded repeatedly for tags on each blog assignment and appealed to students with "if the blog isn't searchable then it probably isn't gradable," there was still relatively low compliance. In addition to finding the blog entries, keeping tabs on multistep assignments (original post and then follow-up comment) in a space that is constantly expanding thanks to student production is no small feat. Along a similar line, we are constantly aware of the risk for student fatigue in this environment. To that end, we abide by our internal checklists: Is this explicitly relevant and integrated? How will the timing of the assignment affect its outcome and the outcome of concurrent assignments? With so many moving and evolving parts in this collaborative program, we remind ourselves that each module, as a dynamic and fully functioning subset, must be considered in light of the course as a whole and the users who are involved.

Expandability, Modularity, and Applicability to Other Language Program Directors

The social pedagogical approaches associated with this particular French course offer anywhere from a blueprint for social pedagogy integration, adaptation, or adoption of certain modules to potential full adoption. At the core of this project lies careful selection of a work that embraces cultural literacy, which in turn increases social pedagogy opportunities. In particular, the story of Odette exemplifies universal emotions packaged in a francophone setting. Our blog tag *je lis Odette* expands beyond the classroom; (francophone) readers throughout the world are discovering this story or have already done so. This situation increases opportunities for potential interaction with native speakers on topics broached in the short story since they are part of the discourse. While social pedagogies are adaptable to all levels of language learning, we find that the approach here is particularly fitting, owing to its pairing with Intermediate Low to Intermediate Mid learners and beyond. It fosters a satisfying capstone experience for lower division language requirement and offers a bridge to reading longer and more complicated texts and doing literary analysis.

The modular nature of the social pedagogy aspects of the course, including blog assignments, social reading, and movie reviews, allow for integration in pieces to a course in need of revitalization. Indeed, this method parallels the approach taken in building the course described in this chapter. The expandable nature of social pedagogies enables a program to be highly functional even when it is a work in progress.

As with any innovative courses, questions arise as to its fit within the program and sequence. The pilot course described in this study is, using the Common European Framework of Reference for Languages (CEFR) denotation, a bridge course situated at the B1/B2 level (Intermediate). Programmatic fit also means that the pilot semesters (Fall 2016 and Spring 2017) were adapted to preexisting parameters for the course, for instance, adjusting to the grade breakdown rather than creating a new one. The new grade breakdown had to make space for the social assignments, as the following table illustrates.

Table 5.3. Grade Breakdown before and with Social Pedagogy Implementation

Grade Breakdown (Fall 2015–pre-social pedagogy)		Grade Breakdown (Fall 2016–social pedagogy)	
Examens (four)	30%	Examens (four)	30%
Examen oral	5%	Examen oral	5%
Examen final	15%	Examen final	15%
Devoirs, participation	15%	Devoirs, participation	15%
Compositions	**25%**	Compositions	**15%**
Travaux Pratiques	**10%**	Blog	**20%**

Table 5.3 demonstrates the attempt to allocate significant weight to the social component of the course (critical in justifying students' efforts) while maintaining departmental guidelines, a concern that many Language Program Directors may have experienced when making curriculum decisions. It reveals how innovating in (L2) curriculum development may seem easier when adoption standards fit the preexisting curriculum.

We examined whether students' course performance was affected by the pedagogy used by comparing results for the same course before TLM with those obtained with our pilot course. The results (see Table 5.4) are strikingly similar, which is good news: the social pedagogy does not seem to negatively affect students' quantified course performance. In particular, the stability of grades across the final exams is noteworthy because the tests are similar in format and content.

Table 5.4. Course Grades in the Traditional Course and Social Pedagogy Course

	Fall 2015 (14 students)	Fall 2016 (18 students)
Average course grade	84	84
Final exam grade	79	78

We can reasonably hope that the social pedagogy may have increased students' confidence in reading in French and in expressing personal viewpoints while maintaining other domains of language mastery (e.g., accuracy) at overall similar levels.

As the title of the program implies, we propose that instructors at other institutions adopt (the concept of) this course, or some of its components, either in its entirety or in conjunction with an existing curriculum. In this scenario, students would be able to read content generated by students in their section and in other sections (which is the case in the second iteration of this course)—even across universities. While the public is currently able to read content, we seek ways to invite others—whether students of French or not—to comment and contribute. Additionally, a growing twitter presence (@TLMFrench) will increase traffic and visibility.

We conclude this section with a call to extend the social pedagogical approach to instructors who could benefit from its advantages. To this end, we propose an adaptive, semiprivate space "La Salle des Profs" on the TLM site for instructors who look to share strategies and materials. As previously mentioned, Schmitt's success as an author and the success of this short story in particular offer a media-rich, authentic toolkit upon which to expand. Odette Toulemonde realia—movie critiques, fan discourse, interviews with actors, interviews with Schmitt—abounds and can further enrich the reading, writing, and collaborative experience. For example, social reading could be easily expanded to include tags and links. The fan fiction components of the *Fans d'Odette* module are currently blank slates, which could be integrated by an instructor looking for creative assignments. We also foresee discussions on the creation and implementation of Integrated Performance Assessments. This forum is open to guide the transformation of teaching from an isolated or isolating practice to a communal, co-constructed opportunity.

Conclusion

We have presented a working model-in-progress of social pedagogies aiding the development of multiple literacies "through multiple experiences, in multiple contexts, with multiple text genres (both oral and written) for multiple purposes" (Kern, 2000, p. 37). The hybrid nature of the intermediate French-language program allowed for incremental and adaptive adoption. The early success of the program is apparent in reported and observed student engagement and student production. The digital formats that were often selected for ease of adoption allowed the students to become ready producers of content that sits side by side with instructor-generated content. While Potter and Banaji (2012) offer the possibility that their "blogs [. . .] were revelatory not in the sense that they were fostering inherently new processes so much as rendering them newly visible" (p. 89), we counter that blogs are a great equalizer of meaning-focused written voice, which isn't possible in face-to-face classroom interactions. Although highly regulated and required, the blogs and the social reading annotations scaffolded authentic, contextually rich encounters. While modular and adaptable, each element involved close attention to design and integration in the course as a whole.

This deliberate approach distinguishes full-functioning modules from haphazard addendums that risk disregarding the goodwill of the student population.

In short, this intermediate French program transforms potentially isolated readers and language learners into authors, fans, and critics in an extramural classroom through scaffolded and mediated reading and textually inspired, real-life activities. A cultural inquiry that is socially inclusive and adaptive, encourages knowledge co-construction, and promotes process over product may be a response to what Hayles (1999) hopes for: a posthuman that "embraces the possibilities of information technologies" and "understands human life is embedded in a material world of great complexity" (p. 5) as students find the humanity in the text and in each other.

Acknowledgments

We would like to acknowledge the tireless contributions of the Digital Initiatives & Scholarly Communication and Technology teams at Wake Forest University, especially Chelcie Rowell, digital initiatives librarian, Carrie Johnston, digital humanities research designer, and Ben Ellentuck, digital scholarship developer, for launching, supporting, and troubleshooting our online platform.

References

Alm, A. (2009). Blogging for self-determination with L2 journals. In M. Thomas (Ed.), *Handbook of research on web 2.0 and language learning* (pp. 202–220). Hershey, PA: Information Science Reference.

Armstrong, K., & Retterer, O. (2008). Blogging as L2 writing: A case study. *AACE Journal, 16*, 233–251.

Arnold, N., Ducate, L., & Kost, C. (2009). Collaborative learning in wikis: Insights from culture projects in German classes. In L. Lomicka and G. Lord (Eds.), *The next generation: Social networking and online collaboration in foreign language learning* (pp. 115–144). San Marcos, TX: CALICO.

Barré-De Miniac, C., Brissaud, C., & Rispail, M. (Eds.). (2004). *La littéracie. Conceptions théoriques et pratiques d'enseignement de la lecture-écriture*. Paris, France: L'Harmattan.

Bass, R., & Elmendorf, H. (2012). Designing for difficulty: Social pedagogies as a framework for course design. *Teagle Foundation White Paper.* Retrieved from https://blogs.commons.georgetown.edu/bassr/social-pedagogies/

Black, R. (2009). Online fan fiction, global identities, and imagination. *Research in the Teaching of English, 43*(4), 397–425.

Bloch, J. (2007). Abdullah's blogging: A generation 1.5 student enters the blogosphere. *Language Learning & Technology, 11*, 128–141.

Blyth, C., & Kelton, K. (Eds). (2000). *Tex's French Grammar: Grammaire de l'absurde*. Retrieved from http://www.laits.utexas.edu/tex/

Bruff, D. (2011). A social network can be a learning network. *The Chronicle of Higher Education*. Retrieved from http://chronicle.com/article/A-Social-Network-Can-Be-a/129609

Byrnes, H., Maxim, H., & Magnan, S. (Eds.). (2003). *Advanced foreign language learning: A challenge to college programs*. Boston, MA: Heinle.

One pedagogical approach to engaging students in second language/culture (LC2) discourse communities is a Global Simulation (GS), where learners adopt the role of a fictitious character and interact with each other in a simulated, yet realistic lifeworld. Such a curriculum can bring to light the social and cultural situatedness of language choices based on identity and sociocultural contexts and foster students' understanding of culture as webs of dynamic and variable social practices and ideologies constitutive of and constituted by discourse communities.

This chapter describes a GS curriculum developed for fourth-semester collegiate French informed by principles and frameworks from a *Pedagogy of Multiliteracies* (New London Group [NLG], 1996). First, we describe the foundational perspectives and pedagogical models underlying the curriculum. Next, we present a sample module, discuss examples of students' responses to tasks, and share several students' reflections on learning within this curriculum. Finally, we share recommendations with respect to curriculum design and include practical considerations for the development of similar curricula.

Global Simulation through a *Pedagogy of Multiliteracies*

Global Simulation

The origins of the GS model can be traced to the mid-1970s in France where it was initially used in French language arts settings (see Caré, 1995; Dupuy, 2006a). GS is an experiential learning framework that involves students taking on clearly identifiable character roles in a well-defined sociocultural setting, collaborating toward the elaboration of a story or completion of a project. While contexts may vary, a GS generally includes a balance of strategically placed incidents and room for emergent happenings and resources for familiarizing learners with the social and communication conventions of the community. A GS is "global" in that it is comprehensive, and tasks and activities are fully integrated within the broader project (Caré, 1995).

GS projects have been carried out around the world from various theoretical perspectives using a range of simulated settings and models, including the Apartment Building (*L'immeuble*; Debyser, 1980), the Village (Caré, 1993), and many so-called functional simulations. For example, Magnin (2002) presents GS as an interdisciplinary project, where a simulated hotel provides the framework for a FL class and a marketing class, each class carrying out tasks associated with their respective disciplines. Levine (2004) describes three GS models designed for German L2 learners: an Internet-based retail company, a museum of German culture, and a German film festival. These curricular projects integrate contemporary

Second Language Acquisition (SLA) theory with classroom instruction, drawing upon theories of interaction and negotiation of meaning, as well as peer scaffolding from a sociocultural theoretical perspective. Levine, Eppelsheimer, Kuzay, Moti, and Wilby (2004) expand the description of the 10-week long museum simulation, describing how students negotiated the most important cultural objects for their exhibit while also reflecting critically on the role of the museum and on conceptions and representations of culture.

Based upon the *Immeuble* framework wherein learners take on the roles of residents living together in an apartment building in the chosen setting, Dupuy's (2006b) GS offers a context for socializing students into LC2 discourses through engagement with authentic texts and a way to integrate at-home university coursework with study-abroad experiences. Dupuy (2006a) reports students' reflections from a similar course, where students overwhelmingly described the benefits of the GS in terms of fostering creativity, autonomy, and collaboration as they worked together to invent their community's story. Around the world, GS has been implemented from an action-oriented approach[1] for programs teaching French as a FL in Puerto Rico (Bosch Irizarry & Malaret, 2009) and in Latvia (Svilpe, 2014).

Although the GS literature largely reports on curricular models, several empirical studies have been undertaken. Mills and Péron (2009) designed a GS around the *Immeuble* in a third-semester L2 French writing course, investigating the impact of the GS on students' self-efficacy beliefs about writing across multiple domains. Findings included significantly improved self-efficacy beliefs among students, which the authors attributed, in part, to the way in which the GS and its associated writing and discussion tasks empowered students through the development of a collective class identity. Additionally, they noted that the GS afforded more choice and agency in completely writing tasks and that a depersonalized—yet coherent—character identity afforded space for more open expression of feelings, thoughts, and beliefs.

Péron (2010) also used the *Immeuble* framework in her advanced French course centered on the Vichy regime as a context within which students could situate historical facts and empathize with historical actors. A 1939 Parisian apartment building served as the setting in which students wrote their characters into being: a communist activist, a young Jewish student at the Sorbonne, a wealthy banker, and so forth. The project culminated in the elaboration of characters' written memoirs; student reflections from the course demonstrated the potential for GS to foster empathy. Drawing upon situated learning theory, Mills's (2011) *Immeuble*, elaborated through Facebook, demonstrated the affordances of a social

---

[1] An action-oriented approach is similar to early iterations of communicative language teaching that emphasize learner-centeredness and extralinguistic competencies such as information synthesis, analysis, teamwork, and creativity.

Carney, N. (2009). Blogging in foreign language education. In M. Thomas (Ed.), *Handbook of research on web 2.0 and second language learning* (pp. 292–312). Hershey, PA: Information Science Reference.

De Chavagnac, G. (Producer), & Schmitt, E.-E. (Director). (2006). *Odette Toulemonde* [Motion Picture]. France: Bel'Ombre Films.

Ducate, L., & Lomicka, L. (2005). Exploring the blogosphere: Use of web logs in the foreign language classroom. *Foreign Language Annals, 38*(3), 410–421.

Fernheimer, J., & Nelson, T. (2005, Fall). Bridging the composition divide: Blog pedagogy and the potential for agonistic classrooms. *Currents in Electronic Literacy* (9). Retrieved from https://currents.dwrl.utexas.edu/fall05/fernheimernelson.html

Franklin-Matkowski, K. (2007). *Blogging about books: Writing, reading & thinking in a twenty-first century classroom* (Unpublished doctoral dissertation). University of Missouri, Columbia, MO.

Furstenberg, G., Levet, S., English, K., & Maillet, K. (2001). Giving a virtual voice to the silent language of culture. *Language Learning and Technology, 5*(1), 55–102. Retrieved from http://llt.msu.edu/vol5num1/furstenberg/

Gackenback, J., & von Stackelberg, H. (2011). Self-online: Personality and demographic implications. In J. Gackenback (Ed.), *Psychology and the internet: Interpersonal, intrapersonal and transpersonal* (pp. 55–73). Burlington, MA: Academic Press.

Hanna, B., & de Nooy, J. (2003). A funny thing happened on the way to the forum: Electronic discussion and foreign language learning. *Language Learning and Technology, 7*(1), 71–85.

Hawisher, G., & Pemberton, M. (1998). Writing across the curriculum encounters asynchronous learning networks. In D. Reiss, D. Selfe, & A. Young (Eds.), *Electronic communication across the curriculum* (pp. 17–39). Urbana, IL: NCTE.

Hayles, N. K. (1999). *How we became posthuman: Virtual bodies in cybernetics, literature and informatics.* Chicago, IL: University Press.

Hayles, N. K. (2007). Hyper and deep attention: The generational divide in cognitive modes. *Profession, 13*, 187–199.

Jenkins, H., Purushotma, R., Weigel, M., Clinton, K., & Robison, A. J. (2006). *Confronting the challenges of participatory cultures: Media education for the 21st century.* Cambridge, MA: MIT Press.

Kern, R. G. (2000). *Literacy and language teaching.* Oxford, UK: Oxford University Press.

Kern, R. G. (2003a). Literacy and Advanced Foreign Language Learning: Rethinking the Curriculum. In H. Byrnes, H. Maxim, H., & S. Magnan (Eds.), *Advanced foreign language learning: A challenge to college programs* (pp. 2–18). Boston, MA: Heinle.

Kern, R. G. (2003b). Literacy as new organizing principle for foreign language education. In P. Patrikis (Ed.), *Reading between the lines: Perspectives on foreign language literacy* (pp. 40–59). New Haven, CT: Yale University Press.

Kern, R. G. (2006). Perspectives on technology in learning and teaching languages. *TESOL Quarterly, 40*, 183–210.

Kern, R. G. (2011). Teaching language and culture in a global age: New goals for teacher education. In H. W. Allen & H. Maxim (Eds.), *Educating the future foreign language professoriate for the 21st century* (pp. 3–16). Boston, MA: Heinle & Heinle.

Kern, R. G. (2015). *Language, literacy, and technology.* Cambridge, UK: Cambridge University Press.

Kramsch, C. (1997). The privilege of the non-native speaker. *PMLA, 112*(3), 359–369.

Krause, S. (2004). When blogging goes bad: A cautionary tale [Web log]. Retrieved from http://english.ttu.edu/kairos/9.1/binder.html?praxis/krause/index.html

Lee, L. (1998). Going beyond classroom learning: Acquiring cultural knowledge via on-line newspapers and intercultural exchanges via on-line chat rooms. *CALICO Journal, 16*(2), 101–120. Retrieved from calico.org/journalTOC.php

Lee, L. (2011). Blogging: Promoting learner autonomy and intercultural competence through study abroad. *Language Learning & Technology, 15*, 87–109. Retrieved from http://llt.msu.edu/issues/october2011/lee.pdf

Light, R. (2001). *Making the most of college: Students speak their minds*. Cambridge, MA: Harvard University Press.

Little, D. (2007). Language learner autonomy: Some fundamental considerations revisited. *Innovation in Language Learning and Teaching, 1*(1), 14–29.

Macaro, E. (2003). *Teaching and learning a second language: A guide to recent research and its applications*. New York, NY: Bloomsbury.

MacKinnon, T., & Pasfield-Neofitou, S. (2016). OER "produsage" as a model to support language teaching and learning. *Education Policy Analysis Archives, 24*(40), 40. Retrieved from http://wrap.warwick.ac.uk/78240

New London Group. (1996). A pedagogy of multiliteracies: designing social futures. *Harvard Educational Review, 66*(1), 60–92.

Pellet, S. (2016). *Littéralement Parlant*. Unpublished manuscript, Department of French Studies, Wake Forest University, Winston-Salem, NC.

Pellet, S., & Myers, L. (2016). *Tout Le Monde: A collaborative intermediate French program*. Wake Forest University. Retrieved from cloud.lib.wfu.edu/blog/toutlemonde/

Pena-Shaff, J., Altman, W., & Stephenson, H. (2005). Asynchronous online discussions as a tool for learning: Students' attitudes, expectations, and perceptions. *Journal of Interactive Learning Research, 16*(4), 409–430.

Pinkman, K. (2005). Using blogs in the foreign language classroom: Encouraging learner independence. *JALT Call Journal, 1*(1), 12–24.

Potter, J., & Banaji, S. (2012). Social media and self-curatorship: Reflections on identity and pedagogy through blogging on a masters module. *Comunicar, 19*(38), 83–91.

Raith, T. (2009). The use of weblogs in language education. In M. Thomas (Ed.), *Handbook of research on web 2.0 and language learning* (pp. 274–291). Hershey, PA: Information Science Reference.

Rossetti, E. (2014). *Reading and writing fan fiction in English as a foreign language: A survey study* (Unpublished dissertation). Università Ca'Foscari, Venezia.

Rüschoff, B. (2009). Output-oriented language learning with digital media. In M. Thomas (Ed.), *Handbook of research on web 2.0 and second language learning* (pp. 42–59). Hershey, PA: Information Science Reference.

Sauro, S., & Sundmark, B. (2016). Report from Middle-Earth: Fan fiction tasks in the EFL classroom. *ELT Journal, 70*(4), 414–422.

Savignon, S. J. (2007). Beyond communicative language teaching: What's ahead? *Journal of Pragmatics, 39*(1), 207–220.

Schank, R. C. (1994). Active learning through multimedia. *IEEE Multimedia, 1*(1), 69–78.

Schmitt, E.-E. (2006). *Odette Toulemonde et autres histoires*. Paris, France: Albin Michel.

Sharpe, R., Beetham, H., & de Freitas, S. (Eds.). (2010). *Rethinking learning for a digital age: How learners are shaping their own experiences*. New York, NY: Routledge.

Swaffar, J., & Arens, K. (2010). Reading. In Carl Blyth (Ed.), *Foreign language teaching methods*. COERLL, The University of Texas at Austin. Retrieved from coerll.utexas.edu/methods/modules/reading/01/holistic.php

Thomas, M. (2009). *Handbook of research on web 2.0 and second language learning*. Hershey, PA: IGI Global.

Thorne, S. L. (2003). Artifacts and cultures-in-use in intercultural communication. *Language Learning and Technology, 7*(2), 38–67.
Thorne, S. L. (2009). "Community," semiotic flows, and mediated contribution to activity. *Language Teaching, 42*(1), 81–94.
Thorne, S. L., & Black, R. (2007). Language and literacy development in computer-mediated contexts and communities. *Annual Review of Applied Linguistics, 27*, 133–160.
Thorne, S. L., & Payne, J. S. (2005). Evolutionary trajectories, internet-mediated expression, and language education. *CALICO, 22*(3), 370–397.
Ware, P., & Kramsch, C. (2005). Toward an intercultural stance: Teaching German and English through telecollaboration. *The Modern Language Journal, 89*, 190–205.
Yang, S.-H. (2009). Using blogs to enhance critical reflection and community of practice. *Educational Technology & Society, 12*(2), 11–21.
Yuldashev, A., Fernandez, J., & Thorne, S. L. (2013). Second language learners' contiguous and discontiguous multi-word unit use over time. *The Modern Language Journal, 97*(1), 31–45.

Appendix A: Survey and *tallied results

How much has the course blog, *Tout le monde en parle/écoute*, supported:

	A lot	Quite a bit	Some	Little	Not at all
1. Your understanding of the short story "Odette Toulemonde"	(3)	(8)	(4)	(1)	(2)
2. Making personal connections (identifying) with the events of the story	(4)	(8)	(5)	(1)	–
3. Your understanding of the course grammar/vocabulary	(3)	(6)	(9)	–	–
4. An opportunity for trying out course grammar/vocabulary	(6)	(9)	(3)	–	–
5. Your sense of who your classmates are and what they like	(4)	(6)	(7)	(1)	–
6. Your sense of what a good blog post looks like	(3)	(8)	(4)	(2)	(1)
7. Your in-class discussions	(4)	(5)	(7)	(2)	–
8. Your focus on *communicating an idea (or sharing a message)* when writing	(7)	(10)	(1)	–	–
9. Your motivation to improve your French	(5)	(10)	(1)	(2)	–

*The number in parentheses is the raw score.

Chapter 6
Becoming Social Actors: Designing a Global Simulation for Situated Language and Culture Learning

Kristen Michelson, Texas Tech University
Elyse Petit, Vanderbilt University

Introduction

Recent scholarship in new and multiliteracies has foregrounded the situated nature of language use and the diversity of ways that meanings are expressed. Language use, from new and Multiliteracies perspectives, is about the creative, agentive process of designing meanings using language and other signs as resources for particular communication purposes, where social identities and relationships and personal histories and perspectives are revealed in discourse. Implied in this view is an inextricable link between language and culture, where language is made meaningful in and through particular identities and their interactions within cultural contexts. However, lower-level foreign language (FL) teaching continues to feature instructional practices that promote decontextualized, transactional language usage with attention skewed toward oral communication (Byrnes, Maxim, & Norris, 2010; Kern & Schultz, 2005; Schulz, 2006) through materials that locate conversations in students' own lifeworlds rather than in target language discourse contexts (Liddicoat, 2000; Magnan, 2008). Further, widespread belief exists among FL learners and teachers that culture should be taught separately from language (see Chavez, 2002; Drewelow, 2012), either because students' second language (L2) proficiency is presumed insufficient to address complex topics (Sercu, 2002) or for the belief that allowing students to use their first languages (L1) detracts from the goals of language study (Byram & Kramsch, 2008; Knutson, 2006).

The notion of discourse offers a way to link language and culture, where discourse is understood as "ways of behaving, interacting, valuing, thinking, believing, speaking, and often reading and writing, that are accepted as instantiations of particular identities by specific groups . . ." (Gee, 2012, p. 3). By extension, cultural groups can be understood as discourse *communities*, where membership in a particular community is linguistically mediated (Kramsch, 1995).

network-based GS to foster a community of practice. Specifically, students used the virtual spaces of Facebook to assert their characters' identities and to develop a shared repertoire of authentic digital texts and narratives that were interwoven between the virtual community and students' individual textual productions. Finally, inspired by the original *Immeuble* framework and its subsequent iterations, Michelson and Dupuy (2014) carried out a GS through a *Pedagogy of Multiliteracies* (NLG, 1996) and investigated its impact on students' awareness of the interrelationship between social identities and genre and discourse choices as well as students' beliefs about language and language learning. Through data drawn from analysis of student artifacts and their reflections on their artifacts in semi-structured interviews, authors found that many students appropriated linguistic and visual *Available Designs* that aligned with their situated identities and the particular genre context, and importantly, students were able to articulate reasons for these choices. Additionally, using the Beliefs about Language Learning Inventory (BALLI) (Horwitz, 1988), Michelson and Dupuy compared beliefs about language, the object of language learning, and the importance of culture held by students enrolled in the GS versus a traditional format course at the same level. They found that while students across both formats had similar views on the role of vocabulary, memorization, practice, and culture, GS students tended to de-emphasize the importance of grammar as code by the end of the course, instead articulating its importance as a meaning-making resource.

In short, GS is an established pedagogical model with various instantiations and theoretical frameworks that demonstrate, each from slightly varying epistemological positions, the ability of a GS to integrate language and culture teaching, foregrounding learners as actors who use language to interact in realistic sociocultural contexts.

Designing the Multiliteracies Global Simulation Curriculum

The curriculum described in this chapter builds from Michelson and Dupuy's (2014) Multiliteracies GS. From a Multiliteracies perspective, a GS can make salient social roles and identities: the character role mediates language choice for the individual student; different characters illuminate the diversity of ways in which meanings can be made around a particular issue or text. As an organizing principle, we drew upon the notion of a primary-secondary discourse continuum (Gee, 1998; Maxim, 2004, 2009). Primary discourses are those learned at home in one's initial socialization context (Gee, 1998) and tend to be primarily oral in nature (Byrnes, 2006), while secondary discourses are the discourses of public life and institutions and are primarily learned in school (Gee, 1998). Linguistically, these discourse continua align with specific forms of expression. For example, the narrative style of primary discourses tends to focus on experience and is expressed in congruent forms of semiosis (i.e., things are nouns, actions are verbs, time is adverbs; Byrnes, 2006, p. 50). Meanings associated with secondary discourses are expressed through more synoptic forms such as nominalizations (Maxim, 2009). The benefit of structuring course content along these discourse continua is that this progression naturally mirrors developmental trajectories of L2 learners from beginning to more advanced stages, a process "characterized by . . . the cognitive move of restructuring the iconic, interactively-driven, experiential expression into a metaphorical and objective one" (Byrnes, Crane, Maxim, & Sprang, 2006, p. 90). With these discourse continua in mind, we prepared a spreadsheet with an overview of the curriculum, including a progression of themes, corresponding cultural topics, language functions, and lexicogrammatical foci. (See Appendix A.) Having this overview allowed us to set specific objectives for each module and to select textual genres we thought would best align with these foci. We subsequently engaged in a long process of text collection and generative discussions about how these texts and text types could be used to carry out our goals.

Within a Multiliteracies framework, texts are understood as cultural genres that contain an ensemble of semiotic resources that combine in patterned ways for a particular social purpose. Understanding the way that textual design choices (*form*) construe certain meanings and not others (*function*) can be achieved through analysis of contrasts between textual genres. To that end, we selected texts such as videos (from YouTube, Vimeo, online news reports), social media commentaries, blogs (i.e., for recipe sharing), literary texts, online news articles, feature stories, and so forth, organizing these along the aforementioned discourse continua. Figure 6.1 presents the units and modules.

Following two foundation modules, students progressed from defining and describing themselves to designing their immediate private spheres and communities (their apartments, their building, and other residents) before stepping out to explore their neighborhood, establish their work-life identities and practices, and ultimately, engage in discussions of public life. Each theme was approached through a specific cultural practice or controversial issue of contemporary and historical importance in France. For example, in Module 5: The Building Caretakers: The *concierge* and the *gardien d'immeuble*, texts included a website describing the technical responsibilities of the profession of a building caretaker, a video documentary of one videographer's own concierge, and excerpts from a contemporary novel and its filmic adaptation. Discussions centered on the evolution of responsibilities and stereotypes related to this figure and the implications of the terminological shift from *concierge* to *gardien d'immeuble*. In Module 6: Work Life and Leisure Time, texts included pie charts describing France's employment sectors, infographics depicting popular leisure activities, a video clip of a news segment reporting on how people spend their additional days off from the *Reduction du Temps de Travail* (RTT; laws aimed at reducing the workweek from 39 to 35 hours), and online testimonials of various individuals on the 35-hour workweek.

> **Unit I: Foundations**
> - Module 1: Language and Communication
> - Module 2: Stereotypes and Identities
>
> **Unit II: The Self at Home**
> - Module 3: The Portrait and the Self-Portrait
> - Module 4: The Building and Its Apartments
> - Module 5: The Building Caretakers: The *concierge* and the *gardien d'immeuble*
>
> **Unit III: The Self with Others**
> - Module 6: Work Life and Leisure Time
> - Module 7: Daily Life in the Building
> - Module 8: Family Life, Routines, and Meals
>
> **Unit IV: The Self in the World**
> - Module 10: Political Parties and the Media
> - Module 11: Immigration
> - Module 12: Secularism in France (*La laïcité*)
> - Module 13: The Environment

Figure 6.1. Overview of units and modules in the Multiliteracies GS

Multiliteracies and Textual Engagement through the Four Curricular Components

A potential carry-over from traditional views of language and literacy is to view texts as vehicles for delivering static, factual knowledge and interactions with texts as a way to practice language forms. Engagement with texts from a Multiliteracies perspective, however, is not about interacting through the linguistic mode alone as a way to access imagined "truths" but instead involves bringing in sociocultural knowledge and cognitive skills to interpret linguistic and other semiotic modes. In the NLG's (1996) proposal, meanings are exchanged through a process involving drawing upon *Available Design* resources (knowledge, experiences, material resources of language, and other semiotic modes) in the active and dynamic process of selecting, repurposing, and interpreting material forms of communication in order to create specific meanings (*Designing*) in both interpretive and productive communication contexts, ultimately affording the capacity to create new signs and meanings (the *Redesigned*). As Kern (2003) describes it:

> The point [of texts] is not simply to give (students) something to talk about (content for the sake of practicing language) but to engage them in the thoughtful and creative act of making connections between grammar, discourse, meaning, between language and content, between language and culture, between another culture and their own—in short, making them aware of the webs, rather than strands, of meaning in human communication (p. 42).

In keeping with these principles, the paradigm of the Four Curricular Components of the NLG's *Pedagogy of Multiliteracies* informed instructional tasks around texts. The four components (Situated Practice, Overt Instruction, Critical Framing, and Transformed Practice) offer a heuristic for teachers to be mindful of incorporating different ways of knowing into instructional activities and can be interwoven in a nonlinear, recursive sequence as students work with texts. An extension of this framework with similar pedagogical moves is the *Learning by Design* framework (Cope & Kalantzis, 2015), which invites students to learn language through scaffolded activities of experiencing, conceptualizing, analyzing, and applying as they reflect on the use and selection of various modes of expression and semiotic elements. Ultimately, the goal is to enhance understanding of how texts are embodied in social and cultural practices (Kern, 2015). Sample forms of textual engagement guided by the Four Curricular Components are outlined in Table 6.1.

It is important to note that all forms of textual engagement involve interpretive, interpersonal, and presentational communication, which can be foregrounded or backgrounded by choosing to carry out the activity orally, in writing, or through an integration of modes. For example, predicting content from subheadings (SP) can be carried out through instructional conversations, thus prioritizing oral interpersonal communication. Story retelling (TP) can be an interpersonal speaking task, such as having a phone conversation with a friend or family member, or a presentational writing task, such as a personal diary entry.

Daily lesson plans were designed around these Four Curricular Components. The use of a common template for lesson plans facilitated coherence and

Table 6.1. Sample Forms of Textual Engagement

Curricular Component	Focus	Sample Instructional Activities
Situated Practice (SP)	Immersion in the text with focus on textual patterns	Identify author, publication venue; predict content from subheadings; match subheadings with appropriate sections; identify keywords to match content; summary writing
Overt Instruction (OI)	Attention to form-meaning connections	Stylistic reformulations, for example, from formal to informal language
Critical Framing (CF)	Critical analyses of how and why meanings are made, that is, author purpose, ideologies in texts	Critical focus questions; textual comparisons
Transformed Practice (TP)	Application; discourse and language repurposed	Story retelling across different modes

consistency across multiple sections while still allowing for individual variation based on the dynamics of each class and their respective communities that emerged from the personas and stories created by students and their interactions. Technology was an integral component of the course: various Web 2.0 platforms (Moodle, Facebook, VoiceThread, eComma, and Google Docs) afforded different kinds of *character–character* and *character–text* interactions. Moodle 2.3 was used as the course management site for the collection and delivery of digital texts and assignments. Facebook Pages allowed for the development and enactment of characters' identities and day-to-day interactions with neighbors. VoiceThread, through its multiple modes of communication (oral recordings, written comments, visual, and audiovisual messages), provided a space for TP tasks related to character identity formation and interaction, such as creating and showing their apartment, inviting neighbors to visit, and leaving voicemail messages for each other. eComma, a digital social reading tool (see Blyth, 2014), was used to facilitate weekly book clubs between characters. Google Docs allowed students to collaborate with each other to complete online SP or OI activities. Although the course was offered in a traditional face-to-face format, the use of Web 2.0 tools afforded multiple and sustained possibilities for student participation and ongoing development of the community throughout the week.

Before distributing characters, we introduced two modules to help students understand the Multiliteracies approach to GS beyond a superficial role-play game. Module 1 focused on language registers, while Module 2 addressed stereotypes and nuances between one's ethnic, national, and cultural identities. Students chose their characters at the end of week two in anticipation of subsequent modules during which they would develop their personas. Character selection varied between semesters and instructors with the common goals of specifying a combination of roles that would most realistically represent current demographics in France. Instructor 1 based the building resident's roles on the country's population and created persona cards that specified gender, age, employment sector, marital status, and family relationships (e.g., some characters lived alone while others were part of a family unit). Cards were distributed to students at random; students had several minutes following distribution to compare cards and trade with one another. Instructor 2 based the personas on demographics of the 17th district where the simulation was based and created five sets of cards specifying gender, marital status, age ranges, employment sectors, and birthplaces (e.g., France, North Africa, Europe, French Overseas Territories (DOM-TOM), other international origins). Students then selected one card from each pile and handed the envelope of cards to their instructor, who later checked for any unrealistic combinations (e.g., divorced 13–17-year-olds or retired high school students) and listed the profiles on a Google Sheet. Students chose their specific ages and birthplace based on these general criteria. In both scenarios, students chose their own name and profile picture corresponding to their persona based on resources such as websites listing most common names by birth year (Doctissimo, n.d.). Instructors verified photos to make sure that popular celebrities or public figures with prior cultural associations had not been selected.

Beginning with week three, topics helped students get into the roles they would develop throughout the semester. For example, in Module 3, The Portrait and the Self-Portrait, texts included written self-portraits from literature (e.g., *L'élegance du hérisson*; Barbery, 2012) and engaged students in identification and reflection on direct and indirect characterizations (oral interpersonal, SP/OI). Students were given a rich set of descriptive vocabulary for conveying physical and character traits in preparation for writing their own self-portrait (written presentational, TP). In Module 4, The Building and Its Apartments, students explored French apartment buildings by comparing and contrasting styles and conventions with those of their own culture. Students brought sample photos of their characters' kitchens, living rooms, and so forth, which would reflect their visions of their characters' tastes and styles. Instructional conversations around these photos (oral interpersonal, OI/CF) exposed conventional differences in interior space between France and the United States in terms of style, size, use of space, and norms of interaction within private homes. With a renewed understanding of realistic representations, students narrated a tour of their apartments using VoiceThread (oral and visual presentational, TP). Activities in this module also drew students' attention to architectural features of Haussmannian buildings and their representations of social stratification within urban spaces. Module 5, The Building Caretakers: The *concierge* and the *gardien d'immeuble*, gave students the opportunity to step out of their apartments to connect with their neighbors and begin to engage in social life within the building. Each topic was designed to encourage students to consider the design resources (language, images, gestures, voice, intonation, etc.) indispensable for the construction and presentation of a realistic character that would fit into the simulated discourse context of contemporary French society and that would be clearly developed enough to engage within the global community through the sociocultural practices and discourses encountered in the course.

An additional component of our curriculum design involved deciding when tasks would be completed by students-as-themselves versus students-as-characters. Because class time was used primarily for activities in which students engaged with texts in the interpretive mode (reading, listening, viewing) through a combination of SP, OI, and CF tasks, we decided that while in class, learners would primarily participate as themselves, except for occasional role-play activities. For TP tasks (e.g., presentational writing: self-portrait, private journals, letters; interpersonal/presentational speaking: answering machine messages, phone conversations, video project; and interpersonal writing: social media interactions), students were asked to speak and write as their characters. For example, in the module on the *concierge* and the *gardien d'immeuble*, students wrote a journal entry from the voice of their character in which they imagined they were looking over the balcony of their apartment to the courtyard below, where they caught a glimpse of the concierge. Within the module on work life and leisure time, students wrote their character's opinion on French laws relating to the 35-hour workweek in social media posts. In the following section, we detail the objectives, texts, and tasks of Module 11: Immigration.

Sample Module from the Multiliteracies GS: Module 11—Immigration

This module introduces the theme of immigration by engaging students with the controversial deportation of Leonarda Dibrani, a 15-year-old Roma student in France who was arrested while on a school field trip. The very public, highly mediatized, political controversy around Leonarda's arrest offered an effective link to previous modules—Module 10: Political Parties and Module 2: Stereotypes and Identities—in which students had discussed France's multiethnic population through a collection of portraits of immigrants (*Histoire singulières*) on the History of Immigration Museum's website (Musée, 2013). Because this case involved a young girl of Eastern European origins, this allowed us to explore immigration from a perspective different from the typical discourses of immigration in France. Focusing our module on the Leonarda case was initially motivated by a desire to use the most current of events as an entry point into broader social issues. However, we decided to keep these texts in the curriculum for two more semesters due to the profound engagement of our students with Leonarda's case and the ongoing political turmoil portrayed in the French media well after the initial events. Table 6.2 displays the module's cultural and linguistic goals and objectives and accompanying texts.

Texts

For each module, we selected an ensemble of texts that would include many voices and opinions and, where relevant, expose controversies. In this module, we included an online news article (Rasplus, 2013) that appeared after the initial event summarizing the highly polemical reactions in four acts, in which different audio and video clips (our secondary texts) were embedded. The article is composed of a large image of Leonarda holding a doll, followed by four short paragraphs called "acts," narrating the events as a play (specifically, a tragedy) in which space, time, and protagonists play a role in the evolution of the unfolding drama. The first embedded video presents groups of high schoolers protesting in the streets in different cities, fighting for the rights of recently arrested teenagers. The second embedded video features French president François Hollande's public address in which he justifies the arrest and tries to calm the

Table 6.2. Module 11: Immigration

Focus	Example
GS module	Immigration
Cultural goals	• Reflect on similarities and differences between salient issues regarding immigration in France and the United States • Understand how activism is conventionally expressed and practiced in France
Communication functions	• Expressing and supporting opinions • Asking clarifying questions • Comparing and contrasting viewpoints • Expressing cause and effect • Drawing conclusions
Lexicogrammatical forms	• Discourse markers (*Connecteurs logiques*) • Spatiotemporal expressions
Primary genre	• Newspaper article summarizing the Dibrani case in four acts
Secondary genres	• Photograph of Leonarda Dibrani • Video of high school students protesting • Video of President Hollande's public address • Images of protests

controversy by inviting Leonarda to return to France, noting that "un accueil lui sera réservé" ("a welcome will be reserved for her"). Together the videos represent youth voices on one hand and official governmental positions on the other hand. Not only do these texts represent various voices and their reactions to the events, they exemplify different situation- and identity-dependent ways of speaking about these events, carried out through different modes of communication and design choices.

Tasks

It is important to note that we are using *tasks* in line with Byrnes (2002) and the nuances of Multiliteracies approaches wherein tasks are seen as a way to focus on—and engage in—situated language use, rather than as a way to practice language for transactional, "skill-using" communicative purposes (see Schulz, 2006, for discussion). Our approach thus differs from task-based language teaching (TBLT) in that the latter focuses on designing classroom tasks used to simulate primarily instrumental, real-world encounters or informational exchanges. As indicated earlier, each module began and ended with common tasks. For example, premodule CF tasks asked students to reflect on the week's topics from their first language/culture (LC1) perspective, while postmodule reflections invited comparisons between their first and second languages/cultures (LC1 and LC2). These reflections served to frame the module with both schema-activation and cultural reflection activities. The prompt for this module's prereflection read:

> Reflect on immigration in the US. What are the primary issues that surface when "immigration" is discussed in the US? (Note that you are not being asked to take a stand, but simply to present the primary concerns that are discussed around this topic in the US.)

The first class of each module typically began with students debriefing their reflections in pairs and discussing their familiarity with French perspectives on that theme through instructor-led conversations. At the end of each module, weekly quizzes included a CF question—asked and answered in English—about the themes addressed in the module. This module's question read:

> Discuss the reaction to Leonarda being removed from school and deported from France. Who has reacted and in what ways? In what ways would the public reaction be similar or different if this took place in the US?

Individual instructors varied daily lessons based on their classroom dynamics and their individual teaching styles, keeping the common objectives and tasks in mind. Table 6.3 next presents two lesson-sequence variations used to engage students with the texts described.

In both variations previously, the same texts were used with common objectives: to expose students to the issues and discourses surrounding the Leonarda controversy, to have students reflect on design choices (linguistic, visual, etc.) in media representations of those events, and to foster students' development and expansion of their own *Available Designs*. In Variation I, activities centered around the principles of critical media literacy, which "involves cultivating skills in analyzing media codes and conventions, abilities to criticize stereotypes, dominant values, and ideologies, and competencies to interpret the multiple meanings and messages generated by media texts" (Kellner & Share, 2007, p. 6). Class began with students examining the visual representation made of the "case," that is, visual designs used, potential target audiences, and its relationship to discourses of immigration. Instructional activities guided students in discussing authorial message and intent through these media and discoursal features. Variation II also began with the image of Leonarda, inviting students to connect affectively with the girl they saw. Activities recalled those in Module 3: The Portrait and the Self-Portrait, drawing upon notions of direct and indirect characterizations. In both cases, students engaged with visual designs (including the framing of Leonarda and her doll); however, Variation I foregrounded metacognitive reflections around media literacy, while Variation II foregrounded affective responses to those media designs. In working with the written text (four acts),

Table 6.3. Lesson-Sequence Variations for Module 11: Immigration

Texts	Instructional Activities	Curricular Components	Communication Modes
	• Students summarize their responses from the premodule reflection • Instructional conversations about immigration in France	OI, CF*	Interpersonal speaking
Photograph portraying Leonarda holding her doll	**Variation I:** 1. The image only is projected on board. Students describe visual components and interpret features (i.e., colors, layout, posture) and their relationship to the topic of immigration. • What draws your attention first? • What is placed at the center of the picture? • What colors are used? • Do you think they convey a particular meaning? • Who do you think the person is? How old is she? What do you notice about her position/posture? • What kind of emotions does she display? • What messages is the photograph trying to convey? • In what way could this picture be related to the theme of immigration? 2. Caption is revealed; students reflect on language choice and the impact on contextualizing the image. • Based on your first predictions, do the captions reinforce or contradict your predictions? In what ways? • What specific expressions from the caption help enhance or reinforce your understanding of the situation?	SP, CF	Interpersonal speaking Interpretative viewing
	Variation II: 1. Image is projected on board. Students-as-characters engage in an in-class presentational writing activity in which they imagine they have just met the girl in the picture. They describe her identity, origins, age, interests, how and where they met, what her name is, and what they think about her. 2. Several examples are presented and compared in a whole class discussion about media portrayals of individuals and effects on interpretation of viewers/readers. 3. Caption of photo is displayed; instructor gives brief overview of the context of the case.	SP, OI, CF	Presentational writing Interpretive reading (visual mode)

(Continued)

150

Texts	Instructional Activities	Curricular Components	Communication Modes
Written text of article— four acts	**Variation I:** 1. Through scaffolding activities, students focus on genre and then predict paragraph content from headings. Students reformulate paragraph titles with synonyms, making sure to respect the syntax used in the article (nominalization/verbalization). 2. Students, divided in groups, are assigned to one of the acts for which they determine and list discourse markers and spatiotemporal expressions. 3. Each group orally reports the events in chronological order, noting places and people involved. 4. As a whole class, students discuss the event and its impacts within French society.	SP, CF	Interpretive reading Interpersonal speaking/writing Presentational speaking

	Variation II:
	1. Instructor shows titles of each act; students predict content from titles.
	2. Students match headers to each paragraph/act.
	3. Students read one paragraph at a time with guided tasks (looking for cognates; circling discourse markers; noting features of formal language, verb tenses, passive/active constructions, specific examples of formal language register).
	4. As a whole class, students reformulate extracted sentences using subject-verb-object expressions with the modal verb *devoir* (must; to have to):
	  • For example, "Leonarda . . . est contrainte de quitter le car scolaire . . . " and "l'adolescente est . . . soumise à une obligation de quitter le territoire français." (Leonarda is forced to exit the school bus . . . the adolescent is under obligation to leave the premises of France.)
	  • *Leonarda doit sortir du bus.* (Leonarda has to get off the bus.)
	  • *Leonarda doit partir de la France.* (Leonarda has to leave France.)
	5. Instructor guides students in discussion of language choice in text (complex sentence structures) versus simple reformulations.
	6. Instructor guides students in summarizing Act I in three sentences. Students work in small groups, each summarizing one of the three subsequent acts; summaries are shared with the class.
	7. Story retelling: students-as-characters phone a neighbor and retell what happened and what they think about it.
		SP, OI, TP	Interpretive reading (written mode) Presentational writing Interpersonal speaking

(Continued)

151

Texts	Instructional Activities	Curricular Components	Communication Modes
Videos	**Variations I and II:** 1. In small groups students work on a different videotext using a worksheet to guide reflection on modes and meanings. 2. Students discuss importance of different texts and perspectives in the representation and reception of events.	SP, OI, CF	Interpretive reading/viewing Interpersonal speaking
TP based on all texts	1. Students-as-characters make a FB post with their opinion on the French government's deportation of Leonarda. (During module) 2. Students-as-characters write a personal journal entry in which they describe their feelings and opinions about the case. (One week later) Prompt: "Thinking about the different perspectives and conversations we have read about this week concerning the Leonarda affair, imagine your character is writing his/her personal reaction to the situation. How does he/she feel about this particular situation, including all relevant public events, the media treatment of the events? What does he/she think about immigration in general? In this journal pay attention to using expressions for giving an opinion." 3. Students-as-characters record an imagined phone conversation in which they describe to a friend or family member the protests, the events of the case, and their opinions about the events. (Three weeks later, final exam task) Prompt: "High-school students from the neighborhood are protesting Leonarda's case—blocking streets, making noise, littering, hanging around with friends and so on. In a one- to two-minute recording and from the voice of your character, imagine you are having a phone conversation with a friend, neighbor, or family member about the situation. In your recording address the following: Tell the person on the other line what is happening. Explain your character's reaction to the protests (annoyed? excited? wants to take part? etc.). Explain your character's opinion about the entire controversy. Be sure to make it clear who are you talking to on the other line. Be sure to also convey (through language, intonation, facial expressions, etc.) the extent to which your character is personally affected by the situation."	TP	Presentational writing Interpersonal speaking

* Note: The Four Curricular Components include SP, OI, CF, and TP.

both variations led students in OI activities that would call their attention to linguistic designs in the text and to possible alternatives through reformulations. Finally, because the two videos presented different perspectives expressed through different language registers, this gave students the opportunity to consider various viewpoints and discourses in order to find their characters' voices as residents in France.

In the following section, we turn to the voices of our students—as their characters and as themselves—in order to present examples of the way they responded to texts and topics within this module of the Multiliteracies GS curriculum.

Becoming Social Actors

Throughout the semester, interacting with topics, texts, and designs metacognitively and affectively through their characters and as themselves, students made conscious decisions about positions they would take up in response to the situations that arose during the simulation and how they would represent these through language and other semiotic designs. In this section, we demonstrate how the Multiliteracies GS served to engage students as participants within a contextualized cultural setting as well as agents of their own learning process.

TP tasks related to the Leonarda affair included Facebook posts, a personal journal about the controversy, and a speaking task for the final exam in which students called a friend to talk about the situation (see Table 6.3). In her initial recounting of the events, Character 1, a 25-year-old divorced woman from Brussels who worked at a nongovernmental organization (NGO), stated, "les jeunes se sont mobilisés" ("youth have mobilized"). Her choice of the word *jeunes* ("youth") positions her apart from this group, as someone who is older, who looks at the youth protesters with some distance, and who does not intend to join them. Later, she recounts the events to a friend over the phone explaining that she must hang up, because she is about to join the protests. She moves beyond the idea that the protests only involve youth as she takes up a new position of solidarity and decides to get involved, similar to how the case escalated among the French population as they gradually took more active positions. Protesting thus shifts from something other people do (i.e., youth) to something she feels compelled to do. Solidarity with the youth protests was adopted at the outset by Character 2, a 15-year-old male high school student. Recounting with energy in a string of sentences beginning with "and," he exclaims:

> Il y a beaucoup de controverse parce que ça. Et les lycéens sont très fâchés au cours de ça. Il y a les lycéens qui protestent en les rues. Et il y a les lycéens qui barricadent les écoles . . . Je suis d'accord avec tous ces personnes. Puis je joindrai la protestation à mon lycée!

There is so much controversy because of that. And the students are really mad about it. Students are protesting in the streets. And there are students barricading the schools . . . I agree with all of these people. So I'll be joining the protest at my school!

As a *lycéen* himself, he feels connected to the protests, ready to jump into the middle of the action. Contrary to Character 1, whose position of solidarity is delayed, Character 2's identity as a high schooler draws him in immediately. In his mind, it is his and his classmates' responsibility to demonstrate their support for Leonarda, who they see as one of them.

By contrast, Character 3, a 55-year-old, married, female painter and gallery owner, wanted nothing to do with the Leonarda affair. Throughout the simulation, she portrayed herself as belonging to an elite class, separate and apart from the masses. Recounting the events in a social media post, she said, "Les rues sont bloquées par citoyens, travailleurs et policiers" ("The streets are blocked by citizens, workers, and policemen"). She positions herself outside the fray by choosing words *citoyens* ("citizens") rather than *concitoyens* ("fellow citizens"), blaming the very people responsible for maintaining a productive and safe civil society for disturbing her life and causing disorder in the streets. "Je ne peux pas sortir mon immeuble parce que c'est un désordre, un désordre partout" ("I can't leave my building because it's a mess, a mess everywhere"). In her journal, albeit amidst token expressions of sympathy for Leonarda, she also admits, "Ainsi, je ne suis pas la personne la mieux placée pour parler de ce sujet, parce que mes opinions sont plus différentes à le gouvernement Français" ("Thus, I am not in the best position to discuss this subject, because my opinion [on the matter] is different from that of the French government"). She justifies her distanced stance through her disagreement with the government but appears to use this disagreement to mask her indifference.

For Character 4, a 43-year-old widowed male who works in fashion merchandising, his own involvement is not mentioned; however, he is implicated because his daughter is Leonarda's age and presumably feels compelled to join in the protests. He makes clear his full disapproval of her involvement in their imagined phone conversation during which he summons her home quickly because the streets are becoming dangerous: "Non!, tu peux pas . . . c'est trop dangereux" ("No! You can't . . . It's too dangerous"). Although he shows concern for his daughter, he does not necessarily position himself *against* the youth supporting Leonarda but instead invokes the danger of a minor being in the streets. Not only does he present himself as an overprotective father, he also demonstrates an understanding that the protests could quickly escalate.

A parental stance is also evident with Character 5, a 62-year-old female, married perfume-shop owner. In her case, she is not speaking directly to one of her own children, but her maternal stance is evidenced in her impassioned social media post: "Léonarda est seulement quinze ans! Quinze ans! Comment peut un enfant quitte le pays seul. Où est la justice? Où est l'amour?" ("Leonarda is only 15! 15! How can a child leave the country alone. Where is justice? Where is love?"). Rather than summarizing or describing the events, her reaction comes in the form of an appeal to her community to consider the injustice in this situation, playing to compassion by questioning the appropriateness of letting a child walk alone in the world and implying that supporting that child is a moral imperative. She uses "justice" not from a legal standpoint (since the government's reinforcement of immigration policy could be understood as having been done in the name of justice) but rather in a moral sense. As if anticipating that her interlocutors will stumble on this ambiguity of terms, she quickly adds, "Où est l'amour?" She seems to be anticipating the need to clarify that her own understanding of justice is as a form of compassion and that she is not interested in the legality of the government's response.

Character 6, a 38-year-old, male, divorced, father, unemployed former math teacher, makes a similar appeal to justice for Leonarda in his journal, invoking education and the right to remain with one's family as basic human rights. Throughout this journal, he references specific political parties (le Parti Socialiste [PS], le Front National [FN]) and their presumed stances, scolds Hollande, and concludes with "Honte au PS ! Honte au Valls ! Honte au Hollande !" ("Shame on the Socialist Party! Shame on Valls! Shame on Hollande!"). His passion is palpable in these punctuated reprimands to political leaders; his entire journal entry indexes this character as an engaged, informed citizen who participates regularly in the discourse of contemporary politics, as he invokes all the relevant players in his litany of shaming.

The diversity of these performances, made in response to the same texts, reveals the way students' design choices were motivated, in part, by their character's identities, their relationships with other characters, and their vision of their characters' involvement in social life, which were inevitably interwoven with their own identities and backgrounds. This is reflected in the linguistic and other semiotic resources they chose—punctuation, syntactic structure, colloquial formulaic expressions (e.g., *Honte à*)—as well as in the message content that brought their characters to life across multiple discourses. Moreover, as seen in their final portfolios, students realized that being engaged with these texts and tasks fostered their understanding of French society, enhanced their reflection about forms of discourse, and affected their personal awareness and perspectives on political and social issues. For example, Student 1 remarked, "The course also encompassed political controversies, such as secularism, immigration and deportation and the right to protest. As well, [it] highlighted the system of values that is unique of the French culture such as the importance of collectivism and solidarity." Student 4 also appreciated the dimension of seeing anew through her character:

> By adopting a character we were allowed to explore different aspects of French culture and investigate into these aspects we never thought of before! I believe that my character . . . was very different from myself and my general opinions but by creating a character that contradicts your values or opinions you are challenged to find the background knowledge to support these views.

However, not all students found taking on a character to facilitate their learning. Student 3, for example, demonstrated passive resistance in the construction of her character and did not substantively immerse herself in the GS community of practice. She remarked:

> Personally, I think the incorporation of having a character role did not help any more than if it was just regular assignments from my own personal point of view. Since I want to be able to build my own French language identity and practice it in the ways I personally would utilize the language, I believe having a character was not necessary.

Although she was an active student who took initiative in completing assignments and participating in class, her disposition toward the GS was indifferent. Like herself, the character she created was indifferent to problems in society and more interested in the creation and maintenance of her image as a bourgeois woman with disposable wealth and leisure time.

Regardless of the level of engagement of the students in developing and animating their characters through their design choices, these examples nevertheless demonstrate how the characters became mediating tools for contextualizing and catalyzing language use for students. Each student made unique choices about how they would position their characters—some keeping their distance and others demonstrating more profound engagement—and they drew upon a variety of *Available Design* resources in order to convey these positions.

Considerations for the Development of a Multiliteracies GS

In this final section, we offer several reflections and recommendations from our experiences developing and teaching this curriculum over four semesters with respect to student expectations, characters, texts, tasks, and tools. (See also additional guiding questions for developing a global simulation in Appendix B.)

Student Expectations

Many students came to the course expecting explicit grammar instruction, anticipating learning and practicing forms through mechanical exercises, and with a view of language learning that led some students to see the purpose of TP activities as practicing language forms. Instead, these activities aimed to allow students to redesign meanings for their own—or their characters'—purposes. Grammar review activities were assigned for homework through *Contextualized French Grammar* (Katz, 2013), and grammar was addressed in class through OI discussions about form and meaning as construed by identities, genres, and communication contexts. Additionally, some students came with preconceived ideas that the GS was a space for acting or drama and were initially intimidated by this idea. While drama approaches can also be interesting in FL classrooms, our intent was rather to create a context for conscious choices of forms of discourse, mediated by character identities and their positions within the simulation.

Because a Multiliteracies GS is an innovative and challenging pedagogical approach for L2 learners, we encourage instructors to implement brief in-class conversations during which students are reminded about—and perhaps asked to articulate—the purpose and objectives of activities both in and out of class. We also encourage instructors to invite students to contribute ideas to the continuing modification and development of the GS.

Characters

In order to both develop the community of residents and foster students' awareness of language choice, we alternated between spontaneous in-class interactions and slower, planned tasks that allowed for more conscious redesigning. Instructor 1 relied on role-play activities in class to help students identify the diverse personas of their classmates and to create connections that could be used on the social media platform. For example, at the beginning of the semester, while students were slowly developing their characters, students greeted their neighbors from the same floor, or their same-aged peers, and exchanged tips on decorating their apartments. These brief and spontaneous oral role-play activities took place at the beginning or end of the class period and allowed students-as-characters to bridge their interactions from the classroom into the virtual spaces. When the community was more strongly established on the social media platform, in-class role-play activities disappeared. Instructor 2 relied less on spontaneous in-class role-plays with students-as-characters and instead brought students' textual creations into the classroom and discussed design choices based on identities and contexts (OI). This helped students get to know the other fictional residents in the building. Finally, although students carried out their character roles throughout the semester, at times students reflected upon or responded to a text or topic as themselves. The resulting dichotomy encouraged us to constantly reflect on and develop a balanced set of activities and demanded constant cross-checks for clarity and precision in task prompts.

During the first two modules on stereotypes and language registers, we held in-class discussions about the importance of these concepts in the construction of the character and the community and invited students to reflect on which language register their characters might use in different settings based on their ages, professions, and so forth. The lesson on stereotypes and identities aimed to foster students' critical awareness of developing a culturally relevant character that went beyond superficial ideas about who French people are. Although we provided students with many supplemental resources (e.g. movies to watch, personal blogs to explore, suggested French social media sites), only the most motivated students followed up with these resources. Indeed, we realized across the semesters that students tended to choose professions that reflected popular discourses about France, such as fashion merchandiser, philosopher, chef, gallery owner, rather than construction worker, real estate agent, public transport driver, or bank teller. In subsequent semesters, students were assigned specific professions in order to avoid these stereotypes. A future iteration of this course might more intentionally build in a grading rubric for students' guided out-of-class character research in the development of realistic characters that expand beyond stereotypes.

Text Selection and Tasks

Obtaining meaningful texts that matched our intended goals and objectives was a formidable challenge involving many hours over weeks and months. This included iterative discussions about the appropriateness of language level, content, and how a particular text could be used for our purposes. Over time, the richness of many texts called our attention to the fact that it was more interesting to reuse the same texts for different topics rather than accumulating a range of new texts for each topic. Not only did this create cohesion within the curriculum by bridging topics across different modules, but it also allowed students to become familiar with the genre and the texts in more profound and meaningful ways, which increased their confidence. This reflects Paesani's (2005) assertion that "[i]n rereading the same text with a different purpose, students derive a sense of accomplishment from their progressively greater comprehension and more extended use of the text" (p. 19). Finally, in order to facilitate task familiarity and coherence and consistency in carrying out instructions, we reused the same types of questions for particular genres in SP and CF activities.

Upon review of students' performances on some TP tasks (notably journals), we noticed occasional mismatches between the task prompt and the genre. For example, in one journal, students were asked to describe a day in the life of their characters. This resulted in students' reappropriating formulaic language for daily routines and drawing on *Available Designs* from prior learning experiences with textbooks rather than producing accounts more personal to their characters. In retrospect, a more apt task prompt might be to have characters recount their day to a family member, friend, or neighbor through an oral speaking task. In this case, the audience would be clear and distinct, implicating members of the community, rather than the presumed audience of the instructor, and students' language choices might evidence greater expansion of their *Available Designs*.

Web 2.0 Tools

Integrating various technology tools was challenging despite the routines developed to support students, including devoting an entire class at the beginning of each semester in order to allow students to create their accounts, to explain the tools and their affordances, and to practice using the tools. Although each Web 2.0 tool used was recruited for its specific affordances and in service of very different goals—for example, annotating and chatting about texts (eComma) and communicating through multiple modes (VoiceThread)—we ultimately decided to limit the number of tools and platforms used in order to prevent students from feeling overwhelmed, a recurring theme in their course evaluations.

Suggestions for future instructors are summarized as follows:

Student Expectations:

- Implement periodic learning discussions in which students reflect on the purpose of the class lesson.
- Remind students and demonstrate that grammar is a resource for making meaning. Set clear expectations for which genres conventionally prioritize formal linguistic accuracy (e.g., a formal letter to the mayor) and which ones can be more flexibly and contingently vernacular in style (e.g., social media posts), and assess students according to these priorities.

Characters:

- Reflect on and develop activities and assignments that allow students to easily switch between student and character roles.
- Provide ample resources for students to familiarize themselves with culturally realistic professions and private life activities of LC2 discourse communities.
- Build in graded assignments for students' independent research about their characters' contexts (backgrounds, professions, etc.).

Text Selection and Tasks:

- Obtain texts of a variety of genres that differ in language register and other designs, and provide multiple points of entry into the text through tasks that draw on different ways of knowing.
- Integrate the same text within different modules in order to enhance cohesion, and foster students' confidence and motivation.

- Attend to the nature of task prompts such that TP activities engage students in realistic literacy practices with clearly identifiable audiences and communication contexts.

Web 2.0 Tools:
- Create a familiar and consistent weekly routine whereby certain tasks are completed on certain days of the week (e.g., premodule reflection every Sunday, book club discussions Monday and Tuesday, quizzes every Thursday).
- Create a road map in which homework, technology tools, and online platforms are outlined, including which assignments use which tools.
- Limit the number of technological tools and platforms. Integrate these tools as much as possible into one learning management system. Provide detailed instructions and in-class training on how to use the tools.

Final Reflections

As a way of creating spaces for meaningful interaction through language and other symbolic resources that take identity, culture, and discourse into account, we designed a GS utilizing a *Pedagogy of Multiliteracies* (New London Group, 1996) for Intermediate L2 French. In the simulation, the story world emerged out of a dialogic collaboration between students' conceptions of contemporary France and the discourses they encountered through extensive engagement with everyday texts of various genres.

Although a Multiliteracies GS curriculum can be daunting, since it demands, among other things, careful scaffolding of students' expectations about language learning, exposing students to culture and language through participation in realistic discourses is a worthwhile endeavor in giving students a new sense of what it means to learn a FL. In developing a character that was in many cases very different from themselves, what they believed, and how they behaved, students were given an opportunity to perceive and understand L2 discourse worlds in a more immersive way and to react to and connect with language in a way that became personal to them. Not only did they become part of a simulated LC2 community through their characters, but they also become part of a different kind of community of language learners: one that did not evaluate them from the standpoint of deficiencies in linguistic proficiency or target culture knowledge but rather one that supported their development as social participants involved in private and public life through personal expression.

As designers and instructors of a Multiliteracies GS, we were also challenged to consistently consider our own perspectives about language, culture, and FL teaching and learning, and to what extent our curriculum design and implementation effectively reflected these perspectives, as well as the role of our own situated identities in guiding our students to reflect on and participate in discourses. We wholeheartedly encourage future exploration and implementation of different GS contexts, infused with Multiliteracies pedagogies, for the benefits to both instructors and students who collectively co-construct discourse worlds in which both personal and global concerns emerge.

References

Barbery, M. (2012). *L'élégance du hérisson*. Paris, France: Gallimard.
Blyth, C. (2014). Exploring the affordances of digital social reading for L2 literacy: The case of eComma. In J. P. Guikema & L. Williams (Eds.), *Digital literacies in foreign and second language education* (Vol. 12, pp. 201–226). San Marcos, TX: CALICO.
Bosch Irizarry, A. M., & Malaret, L. (2009). Des îles et des langues: la simulation globale comme moyen d'échapper à l'isolement en milieu exolingue. *UPR Working Papers in Linguistics*, *2*(2), 40–54.
Byram, K., & Kramsch, C. (2008). Why is it so difficult to teach language as culture? *The German Quarterly*, *81*(1), 20–34.
Byrnes, H. (2002). The role of task and task-based assessment in a content-oriented collegiate foreign language curriculum. *Language Testing*, *19*(4), 419–437.
Byrnes, H. (2006). A semiotic perspective on culture and foreign language teaching: Implications for collegiate materials development. In V. Galloway & B. Cothran (Eds.), *Language and culture out of bounds: Discipline-blurred perspectives on the foreign language classroom* (pp. 37–66). Boston, MA: Thomson Heinle.
Byrnes, H., Crane, C., Maxim, H. H., & Sprang, K. A. (2006). Taking text to task: Issues and choices in curriculum construction. *ITL: International Journal of Applied Linguistics*, *152*, 85–110.
Byrnes, H., Maxim, H. H., & Norris, J. M. (2010). Realizing advanced foreign language writing development in collegiate education: Curricular design, pedagogy, assessment. *The Modern Language Journal*, *94*(Supplement), 1–235.
Caré, J.-M. (1993). Le village: une simulation globale pour débutants. *Le Français dans le monde*, *34*(261), 48–57.
Caré, J.-M. (1995). Inviter pour apprendre—les simulations globales. *Die Neueren Sprachen*, *94*(1), 69–87.
Chavez, M. (2002). We say "culture" and students ask "What?": University students' definitions of foreign language culture. *Die Unterrichtspraxis/Teaching German*, *35*(2), 129–140.
Cope, B., & Kalantzis, M. (Eds.). (2015). *A pedagogy of multiliteracies: Learning by design*. New York, NY: Palgrave Macmillan.
Debyser, F. (1980). *L'immeuble, roman-simulation en 66 exercices*. Paris, France: BELC.
Doctissimo. (n.d.). *Le guide des prénoms: Le top 20 des prénoms par année*. Retrieved from http://prenoms.doctissimo.fr/top-prenoms-annee.html
Drewelow, I. (2012). Learners' perceptions of culture in a first-semester foreign language course. *L2 Journal*, *4*(2), 283–302.
Dupuy, B. (2006a). Global Simulation: Experiential learning and preparing students at home for study abroad. In S. Wilkinson (Ed.), *AAUSC 2006: Insights from study abroad for language programs* (pp. 134–156). Boston, MA: Thomson Heinle.
Dupuy, B. (2006b). *L'Immeuble*: French language and culture teaching and learning through projects in a global simulation. In J. Hammadou-Sullivan (Eds.), *Project-based learning in second language education: Past, present and future*,

research in second language learning (pp. 195–214). Charlotte, NC: Information Age Publishing.

Dupuy, B., Michelson, K., & Petit, E. (2013). Fostering multiliteracies through a global simulation approach in intermediate French: A curricular project. In The Language Resource, a monthly publication of the National Capital Language Resource Center, 17(1). http://nclrc.org/teaching_materials/french/Feature-Dupuy-FosteringMultiliteracies.pdf

Gee, J. P. (1998). What is literacy. In V. Zamel & R. Spack (Eds.), *Negotiating academic literacies: Teaching and learning across languages and cultures* (pp. 51–59). Mahwah, NJ: Lawrence Erlbaum.

Gee, J. P. (2012). *Social linguistics and literacies: Ideology in discourses* (4th ed.). New York, NY: Routledge.

Horwitz, E. K. (1988). The beliefs about language learning of beginning university foreign language students. *The Modern Language Journal, 72*, 283–294.

Katz, S. (2013). *Contextualized French grammar: A handbook*. Boston, MA: Heinle Cengage Learning.

Kellner, D., & Share, J. (2007). Critical media literacy, democracy, and the reconstruction of education. In D. Macedo & S. R. Steinberg (Eds.), *Media literacy: A reader* (pp. 3–23). New York, NY: Peter Lang Publishing.

Kern, R. (2003). Literacy as a new organizing principle for foreign language education. In *Reading between the lines: Perspectives on foreign language literacy* (pp. 40–59). New Haven, CT: Yale University Press.

Kern, R. (2015). *Language, literacy, and technology*. Cambridge, UK: Cambridge University Press.

Kern, R., & Schultz, J. M. (2005). Beyond orality: Investigating literacy and the literary in second and foreign language instruction. *The Modern Language Journal, 89*(3), 381–392.

Knutson, E. M. (2006). Cross-cultural awareness for second/foreign language learners. *Canadian Modern Language Review/La revue canadienne des langues vivantes, 62*(4), 591–610.

Kramsch, C. (1995). The cultural component of language teaching. *Language, Culture and Curriculum, 8*(2), 83–92.

Levine, G. S. (2004). Global Simulation: A student-centered, task-based format for intermediate foreign language courses. *Foreign Language Annals, 37*(1), 26–36.

Levine, G. S., Eppelsheimer, N., Kuzay, F., Moti, S., & Wilby, J. (2004). Global simulation at the intersection of theory and practice in the intermediate-level German classroom. *Die Unterrichtspraxis/Teaching German, 37*(2), 99–116.

Liddicoat, A. (2000). Everyday speech as culture: Implications for language teaching. In C. Crozet & A. Liddicoat (Eds.), *Teaching languages, teaching cultures* (pp. 51–63). Melbourne, Victoria: Applied Linguistics Association.

Magnan, S. S. (2008). Reexamining the priorities of the *National Standards for Foreign Language Education*. *Language Teaching, 41*(3), 349–366.

Magnin, M. C. (2002). An interdisciplinary approach to teaching foreign languages with global and functional simulations. *Simulation & Gaming, 33*(3), 395–399.

Maxim, H. H. (2004). Expanding visions for collegiate advanced foreign language learning. In H. Byrnes & H. H. Maxim (Eds.), *Advanced foreign language learning: A challenge to college programs* (pp. 178–191). Boston, MA: Heinle.

Maxim, H. H. (2009). Developing advanced formal language abilities along a genre-based continuum. In S. L. Katz & J. Watzinger-Tharp (Eds.), *Conceptions of L2 grammar: Theoretical approaches and their application in the L2 classroom* (pp. 172–188). Boston, MA: Heinle Cengage Learning.

Michelson, K., & Dupuy, B. (2014). Multi-storied lives: Global Simulation as an approach to developing multiliteracies in an intermediate French course. *L2 Journal, 6*(1), 21–49.

Mills, N. (2011). Situated learning through social networking communities: The development of joint enterprise, mutual engagement, and a shared repertoire. *CALICO Journal, 28*(2), 1–24.
Mills, N. A., & Péron, M. (2009). Global Simulation and writing self-beliefs of college intermediate French students. *International Journal of Applied Linguistics, 156*, 239–273.
Musée de l'Histoire de l'Immigration. (2013). *Histoires singulières*. Retrieved from http://www.histoire-immigration.fr/histoire-de-l-immigration/histoires-singulieres
New London Group. (1996). A pedagogy of multiliteracies: Designing social futures. *Harvard Educational Review, 66*(1), 60–92.
Paesani, K. (2005). Literary texts and grammar instruction: Revisiting the inductive presentation. *Foreign Language Annals, 38*(1), 15–24.
Péron, M. (2010). Writing history in the voice of an other: Debyser's *Immeuble* at the advanced level. *Foreign Language Annals, 43*(2), 190–215.
Rasplus, J. (2013, October 19). *L'affaire Leonarda si vous avez raté un* épisode. France Info. Retrieved from http://www.francetvinfo.fr/societe/roms/expulsion-de-leonarda/l-affaire-leonarda-si-vous-avez-rate-un-episode_439152.html
Schulz, R. A. (2006). Reevaluating communicative competence as a major goal in postsecondary language requirement courses. *The Modern Language Journal, 90*(2), 252–255.
Sercu, L. (2002). Autonomous learning and the acquisition of intercultural communicative competence: Some implications for course development. *Language, Culture and Curriculum, 15*(1), 61–74.
Svilpe, L. (2014). Les simulations globales comme outil pour le développement de la compétence communicative dans des situations de communication de la vie quotidienne et professionnelle. In T. Guseva and L. Locmele (Eds.), (pp. 111–120). Proceedings from *Language Environment in University: Accessibility, Quality, Sustainability*. Riga, Latvia: University of Latvia.

Appendices

Appendix A: Sample modules in the ML-GS: (See Dupuy, Michelson, & Petit, 2013)

	Week 2	Week 4	Week 6	Week 11
Discourse Continuum	Introduction and Foundations	Primary Discourses	The Self with Others	Secondary Discourses
GS Focus	Foundations	The Self at Home	The Self with Others	The Self in the World
Pedagogical Unit	GS: Module 2	GS: Module 4	GS: Module 6	GS: Module LL
GS Module	Stereotypes and identities	The building and its apartments	Work life and liesure tinte	Immigration
Cultural Goals	Introduction to France's mull cultural population; understanding stereotypes and prejudices	Understand features, history, and cultural implications of l'Immeuble Haussrriarinieri; compare and contrast typical US and French apartments and reflect on differences	Understand job classifications; understand the law of the 35 hour work-week; compare and contrast leisure activities in France and US	Reflect on similarities and differences between salient issues regarding immigration in France and the US understand how activism is conventionally expressed/practicod in France
Communication functions	Describing others	Expressing self through one's apartment; describing one's apartment	Describing hobbies. professions, lifestyles, daily/weekly routines and activities; Expressing opinions	Expressing and supporting opinions; Asking clarifying questions, Comparing arid contrasting viewpoints; Expressing cause and effect; Drawing conclusions

Language forms	Adjectives; Comparatives; Past tenses	Present tense; there is/there are; it is; posessive pronouns; interrogatives	Expressions with avoir; pronominal verbs; past time tense and expressions (passé composé, plus que parfait, imparfait; temporal adverbs)	Discourse markers; spatio-temporal expressions
Primary Genres	Website: Histoires singulières	Video: Comment choisir les couleurs Video: Marie a du mal à enregistrer son répondeur	Vidéo: Les 35 heures et les loisirs des français	Newpaper article; Frgncptvinfo L'affaire Léo nard a
Secondary Genres	Photograph: French national soccer team "Black, Blanc, Beur' Advertisements: Pub Sanogyi Websi e: Stéréotypés and Préjugés	Image: Pcroc Coupe d'immeuble Images: various features of an immeuble Haussmannien Website: Les immeubles Haussmanniens à Paris	Graphs and charts: Professional sectors Graphs and charts: leisure activities Text: Metronews: 35 heures: ce que vous en pensez	Video; Hollands's public address Video: High school students p rote sting

Appendix B: Considerations for the development of future class-based simulations

1. Determining Goals and Objectives
   - What are your goals and objectives for the course?
   - In what specific ways will a simulation help you achieve these objective(s)?
2. Determining Length and Extent
   - Will the simulation extend for the length of the semester? If so, will there be moments when learners interact as themselves (i.e., reflections on learning, metacognitive reflections on meaning design choices) and how will you signal these?
   - Will the simulation take place during a shorter module within the course? How much time will you need in order to carry out the simulation's objectives?
3. Choosing a Setting
   - Is the setting constrained to a small enough community in which it is reasonable that characters would likely know and interact with each other?
   - Does the setting allow for a variety of specific and identifiable roles?
   - Is the setting familiar enough to learners to allow them to interact within the simulated context? If not, how will your materials and instructional activities help familiarize them with the social and cultural conventions of the setting?
4. Selecting Characters
   - Are the character roles specific and realistic enough to yield a simulated community that will help you achieve the learning objectives, yet general enough to allow learners to create and develop their identities?
   - How much specificity will you provide in creating character roles? Will you specify age *ranges* or precise ages? Will you specify characters' educational and professional backgrounds or allow students to choose?
   - Will you assign character roles or allow learners to choose?
   - What resources will you provide learners to help them develop their characters?
5. Animating the Simulation
   - What is the overarching goal/project or story line for this community?
   - Does the overarching goal/project or story line allow for clearly articulated tasks along the way?
   - Is the goal/project or story line general enough to allow for spontaneity and creativity in advancing the story line or the project?
   - What events and/or incidents will you introduce, and at what frequency, in order to create a dynamic, goal-oriented story line?

6. Selecting Texts and Activities
    - What genres will you use to introduce students to specific LC2 discourses? What will you use as primary texts? Secondary texts?
    - Does the ensemble of your texts include a diversity of genres and texts?
    - What kinds of tasks are best suited to each text in order to draw out various meanings in the text and to call students' attention to linguistic and other semiotic design resources used by texts' authors?
    - Do your weekly and daily lesson plans include a broad-enough range of tasks in order to exploit different meanings and yet a constrained-enough range in order to ensure task familiarity and routine?
7. Assessing Student Learning
    - What tools will you use to assess what your students have learned, and how will you map these onto specific learning tasks? (Rubrics? Portfolios? Paper and pencil exams? Writing and speaking tasks? Peer review?)
    - How will you balance assessment of accurate acquisition of grammatical forms with appropriate application of language in context (genre, relationship between interlocutors, etc.)?
    - How will you incorporate students' own assessment of their learning? (Self-evaluations? Portfolios? Reflections in their L1?)

Chapter 7
Networked Learning: Students as Producers, Curators, and Consumers of Authentic Resources on Campus and Abroad

Jessica Greenfield, Oberlin College
Vivian M. Finch, Stacey Margarita Johnson, Vanderbilt University

Introduction

In this chapter, we explore how authentic language and culture resources are collected, curated, and presented by and for students, and how that process might be improved through a networked learning model rooted in social pedagogies (Bass & Elmendorf, 2012). Generally, in language classrooms, teachers collect and curate resources and present them to students for consumption. Students process the materials and knowledge gained from interaction with authentic resources stays in that classroom. We see two problems with the existing model of authentic resource production. One, students in our language classes need a wider variety of easily available resources to open windows into authentic varieties of target language (L2) and representations of target culture (C2). Two, the existing model does not leverage the great numbers of students who study abroad each year as collectors and curators of authentic representations of L2 and C2. Students in study abroad settings need purposeful learning and assessment activities that foster genuine engagement with C2 in order to become producers of knowledge instead of simply being consumers. While there is a growing body of literature on using tools (e.g., blogs) to centrally collect resources produced by students during study abroad, what happens to these blogs once the travel is over? We wonder if there is any way for these records of experience to be useful. We argue that making student work available on the web is not the end of study abroad blogging, but rather one of the first steps in creating new learning experiences.

How can instructors or entire language programs envision, create, and implement a model that incorporates authentic resources collected by study abroad participants to create a networked learning experience that directly benefits both students abroad and those taking lower-level language courses on campus? After reviewing existing literature on study abroad resource collection and classroom application of authentic resources, we expanded to models using a digital space to create a stable site for collection and curation. The purpose of this research is to evaluate the effectiveness of the first iteration of this networked model, which took place during a short-term study abroad course in Italy. We conclude by proposing ways to expand and improve the project.

Social Pedagogies and Networked Learning

Social pedagogies (Bass & Elmendorf, 2012) stress the importance of student interaction with authentic audiences, in which the process of communicating and representing knowledge is critical to the construction of knowledge. Thus, there is a central emphasis on constituting the classroom as a community of learners connected to an authentic audience. In this chapter, we begin with the premise that technology allows students to engage in this sort of authentic communication with other students across space and time. Knowledge can be generated by one group of students and preserved in an online tool such as a blog, which would subsequently serve as a repository from which other students may draw. This learning repository serves as the central hub for both the students producing knowledge and the students accessing this knowledge.

Central to the concept of social pedagogies is networked learning, in which participants' learning is characterized by online and real-world connections, or paths, among participants and knowledge. In this approach, information and communications technology is used to promote learning connections by providing nodes or hubs of interaction: between one learner and other learners, between learners and instructors, and between a learning community and its learning resources (Siemens, 2008). The implications of networked learning in a Web 2.0 environment are vast for L2 learners, especially when online tools are leveraged in both classroom and study abroad settings. These mediums provide opportunities for students to process new information both synchronously and asynchronously, connect new information with already acquired information in evolving mental models, and connect with other students and the instructors during the process. When implementing a model for networked learning in an L2 learning context, multiple variations are possible, but fruitful possibilities may lie in understanding networked learning as social pedagogy.

One iteration of networked learning as social pedagogy has developed through studies leveraging social media platforms (Blattner & Fiori, 2012; Lomicka & Lord, 2012; Mills, 2011). Alm (2014) examined how students in L2 study abroad contexts used Facebook to form relationships with native speakers and continued to cultivate those after returning home. Those relationships were then further leveraged for instructed language learning through structured online writing assignments on Facebook. Interestingly, students viewed the experience as an informal learning opportunity that supported classroom interactions, rather than an integral part of the classroom learning experience.

How do we move networked, social learning to the center of a student's learning experience abroad? Blogs or other online platforms made available to wider audiences can serve not only as places to publicly post student writing but also as an excellent medium for students to share work such as video or audio recordings, images, and creative pieces. Students can also engage with each other's ideas and experiences abroad. Online platforms can also utilize technology and mediated communication environments that may already be familiar to students (Thorne & Reinhardt, 2008), therefore decreasing the technological learning curve. Structured online writing activities can help students tap into integrative motivation to form and maintain social learning networks that extend through the entire study abroad experience and beyond (Davidson, 2007; Isabelli-Garcia, 2006; Leonard, 2012). Lastly, students' interaction with their generation of L2 blogs can have a substantial impact on their identity as part of a community of language speakers and increase students' intercultural competence (Deardorff, 2006; Isabelli-Garcia, 2006; Jackson, 2005, 2008; Kinginger & Belz, 2005; Lee, 2009; Williams, 2005).

Authentic Resources

Central to the networked learning model is the concept of *authentic resources*, which has several implications in L2 pedagogy. Sometimes, texts (written, audio, video) are described as authentic when created by members of the L2 language group for use by members of that group for authentic purposes (COERLL, 2010). Examples of authentic texts might be advertisements on television or in print, literary texts, or magazine articles. Authentic texts stand in contrast to texts constructed by educators for the purpose of teaching language. Constructed texts intended for language learners emphasize language (Moeller & Fatlin Osborn, 2014), often prioritizing comprehensible language over authentic language and culture. If language education is about real-world access to L2/C2, then authentic texts provide essential opportunities for that kind of learning.

By authentic, we also mean giving students access to authentic language samples that provide glimpses into authentic varieties of language and culture (Menacker, 2001). While authentic language is readily available through strictly defined authentic texts, resources created specifically for language learners can also be useful windows into authentic L2/C2. If students take their own recording device and document how 10 different L2 speakers all answer the question, "How are you doing?" with the purpose of sharing those recordings with other students in a first semester L2 class, the ten recorded answers could not be considered authentic texts by conventional definitions because the recordings were made specifically for the benefit of language learners. However, the samples do represent authentic speech and give students a glimpse into the variety of accents, pragmatics, and cultural contexts represented in language.

Within a networked learning model a third use of the term "authentic" emerges whereby learning objects are produced, curated, and consumed by students. We no longer think of resources as authentic only because of what they convey to the recipient. Rather, learning resources can be authentic because they represent a student's authentic communication to an authentic audience. One example is to use blogging to connect study abroad and on-campus students (Elola & Oskoz, 2008; Thorne & Payne 2005). Another approach is to leverage blogging to help students actively envision themselves as part of a community of language speakers and a community of bloggers (Ducate & Lomicka, 2008).

In sum, for the purpose of this chapter, we are expanding the notion of authentic texts to include any resource that provides learners with authentic uses of language and culture with an authentic audience, be it created or curated by native speaker-members of the L2 community, by the instructor, or by other students.

Collecting Authentic Resources

If an instructor imagines study abroad students as anthropologists learning firsthand about the people who live in the target culture, then it is important for these students to have some skills in anthropological and more broadly sociological research methods. This will allow students to confidently and appropriately gather the kinds of usable data and useful authentic resources for future groups of students or other audiences. For example, learners who study abroad should engage in participant observation, ethnographic interview, and literature analyses in a way that lends itself to constructing knowledge for themselves not only during the experience but also for future access by on-campus L2 learners, who in turn reconstruct knowledge for themselves using the blog posts as authentic resources.

Ethnographic interviews can also have additional learning benefits for students during and immediately following the collection process (Bateman, 2002). In addition to actively connecting language and culture as an independent assignment (Allen, 2000), ethnographic interviews can also be used in the promotion of intercultural communicative competence (ICC) through reflective activities (O'Dowd, 2006; Roberts, 2003; Su, 2008; Thorne, 2003). Students participating in a semester study abroad program conducted ethnographic interviews with L2 speakers and used weekly blog posts to develop their intercultural competence (Lee, 2012). The findings showed that students not only benefitted greatly from the opportunity to interact with native speakers, which created space for cross-cultural exchanges, but also allowed students to critically reflect on those experiences through their weekly blogging. Furthermore, students reported high levels of satisfaction with the learning experience.

Scholars advocate for online writing as part of the language curriculum through tools such as blogs (Armstrong & Retterer, 2008; Bloch, 2007; Elola & Oskoz, 2008). Writing online for authentic audiences has multiple benefits (Purcell, Buchanan, & Friedrich, 2013). Students are more likely to think beyond grade motivations and other extrinsic motivational factors and focus on the quality of the product because they know the audience extends beyond the instructor alone (Bass & Elmendorf, 2012), in this case native speakers or a future cohort of students. Especially effective are blogging opportunities that require students to reflect on their experiences either in class or during study abroad. Reflective writing is tied to benefits such as reflective learning strategies (Hourigan & Murray, 2010), critical reflection (Yang, 2009), and learner independence (Pinkman, 2005). A blog can provide such benefits to students as it simultaneously builds a collection of authentic L2/C2 resources and showcases student work.

In this chapter, we propose to expand Lee and others' work by using the benefits of study abroad blogging to engineer a self-perpetuating cycle of learning and authentic materials enrichment and transmission between cohorts of students on campus and abroad. The blog becomes a platform for the co-creation of knowledge across time and space, the dynamic instrument of a social pedagogy that connects students in different countries, different semesters, and potentially even different institutions.

A Networked Model

The network model assumes that student products created during study abroad are shared through a public-facing digital platform, and then transformed into instructional activities for and/or by L2 learners on campus (see Figure 7.1 conceptual framework).

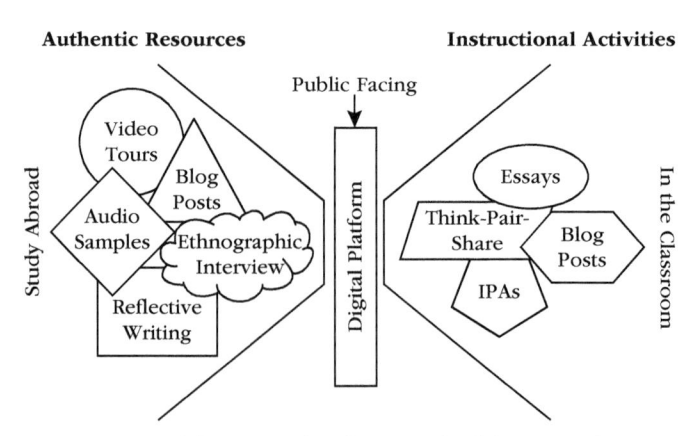

Figure 7.1. Conceptual framework of networked learning between study abroad and on-campus experiences with sample activities

This model requires the instructor to decide what kinds of authentic resources meet the pedagogical needs of both learning contexts. While different kinds of materials can be collected by students in study abroad contexts in order to demonstrate active engagement with the learning objectives, only a subset of those resources would later be useful in a first- or second-year L2 classroom as authentic resources. Study abroad course design should consider thoughtfully the needs of future cohorts of students who will also engage with the materials.

In designing the study abroad experience, several questions need attention before an effective model can be put into place, including the kinds of resources/data student can collect, the modality of the collection (including technology needs), and the format for future display. All these facets must be considered in advance in order to create a system in which the appropriate materials are collected and curated, stored in a safe and stable environment, and then made available for use with future cohorts.

We will focus on the use of blogs in this chapter because of its prevalence in the literature and its selection as the online tool for this particular study, although many interactive web technologies would provide similar benefits (Ducate, Lomicka, & Lord, 2012). As technology advances, new tools may emerge that we have not yet imagined as part of this kind of networked learning (Thorne, 2003), but the model described here is applicable to a variety of technology tools and student experiences.

Methodology

This case study aims to explore how individual instructors or entire language programs can create structured opportunities for networked learning through the creation of a sustainable, stable, and useful space for the collection and curation of authentic L2/C2 resources. We describe how one study abroad course made use of blog-based assignments to collect authentic L2/C2 resources that would then be used as objects of study in on-campus L2 courses. In this section, we will detail the courses involved in this study, the types of assignments required of students, and the case study methods used to collect and analyze the data.

Problems and Research Questions

The first problem we identified is the vetting, contextualization, and perhaps even glossing needed for the plethora of readily available authentic L2 resources to be useful in a novice or Intermediate classroom. Additionally, in order to make L2/C2 contact meaningful, students need purposeful activities, both abroad and on campus, that allow them to engage with C2 and become producers of knowledge, rather than simply consumers. As instructors, we wanted to shape the collection of authentic resources through meaningful study abroad assignments in terms of both their level of engagement with the C2 community and their usability in the language program. Specifically, we wanted to answer the following questions:

1. What kinds of assignments will prove most beneficial to study abroad students while also providing useful resources for subsequent on-campus students?
2. How can this model be made more feasible, and therefore more sustainable, for instructors and students?

As described in the previous section, networked learning is characterized by paths and nodes. Students create learning paths among themselves and among the sites of learning. However, a strong node is important in order to create a site of shared experiences. The shared online space for collecting and curating resources becomes the central hub of activity for students across physical locations, across semesters, and across language proficiency levels.

Additionally, student collectors must find the kind of authentic resources that will be useful to other cohorts of students, or the network will become stagnant and eventually fail. In our model, an administrator is needed to maintain the node serving as the central hub. This initial case study takes place in a setting in which the lead researcher is the instructor of the study abroad and the future on-campus courses, simplifying the network. The instructor is also the administrator of the blog where the resources are collected and curated.

This Case Study

As part of our ongoing research into the viability of a networked pedagogy of authentic resource collection and use (see Finch & Johnson, 2016), and using Creswell's (2007) conception of case study design, the authors intended this study as an exploration of the potential of networked learning. A case study is characterized by relying on a single bounded system, in this case bounded by the course constraints including enrollments, location, and time. A case study also relies on multiple data collection methods to achieve a more holistic view of the case.

The case selected for study was a four-week May term course focused on Mediterranean history and culture, located in Cefalù, Sicily, and taught by one of the authors and lead researcher (Greenfield). The course was not a language-focused course, meaning that students came with varying levels of prior knowledge of Italian, and no particular proficiency level was required.

Once the instructor decided on and designed the data/resource collection tasks, the next challenge was to present the study abroad course activities in a way that was clearly aligned with student and course learning objectives. Structured, aligned activities/assessments (see Appendix A) and detailed rubrics (see Appendix B) provided the context, requirements, and assessment methods to help students contribute in meaningful ways during the study abroad course and to build a varied and rich repository of authentic resources for their on-campus peers. A study was designed to evaluate the course and the potential of the model.

Participants

Fourteen students participated in this study. The group consisted of eight women and six men. There were five seniors, eight juniors, and one sophomore. One student had completed four semesters of Italian language and culture, one had previously completed three semesters, and three had completed two semesters. The remaining nine students had not studied any Italian prior to the trip. As mentioned earlier, there was not a language component to the program, although it counts toward the degree in Italian studies. It also includes core curriculum credit and, therefore, is attractive to students looking to satisfy some of their general education requirements.

As part of a redesign of the Elementary Italian series, this short-term study abroad experience was tasked with collecting authentic cultural materials for potential use in Elementary and Intermediate Italian courses. The participating students were asked to think about what kinds of artifacts, recordings, and samples might prove helpful to language learners, and to collect resources that would be helpful to other learners.

Resource Collection

For resource collection, we anticipated that students would use a mix of their personal digital devices (cellular phones, tablets, and digital cameras) in addition to the three action cameras that were purchased for the program as the result of a grant from the Vanderbilt Institute for Digital Learning. Each student was also provided with an external microphone to capture higher quality audio more easily to enhance their videos and interviews.

The technology associated with this project involved several levels of engagement. While the primary level of technology is accessible to the students, there are additional levels of technological literacy necessary for success. After raw footage is collected by students, it must be edited using programs such as iMovie or Photoshop. These two programs were specifically recommended because of their ubiquity, familiarity to students, and reasonable learning curve. Other programs could also be used. Editing such footage toward subsequent use by others also necessitates adding voiceover and music with additional software such as QuickTime or Garageband. Finally, the students were required to share their final, edited products either on a designated course website or another site (e.g., a YouTube channel). Long-term storage constituted an additional technological issue, which included finding space on the institution's server or storage on flash drives. Student products, in the form of video and narrative blog posts, were to be placed on the course site (http://my.vanderbilt.edu/maymesterinsicily) that is open and accessible by the public (including, of course, future cohorts of Italian students), who can add and respond.

Following are the activities that students undertook: activities intended to result in products that would meet criteria of being both useful for meeting learning objects during study abroad and useful as learning resources for future audiences. Students had the entirety of the one-month program to complete these activities and were required to post at least one for each category on the course website prior to the end of the program. Students were introduced to the assignments in person about six weeks before the course began and had access to the digital explanations of these required elements from one month before the program.

Cultural Observation

The observational activity required students to comment on a particular place or aspect of their experience in a new and foreign culture. Some students opted to observe a specific place (e.g., sitting for 90 minutes in a specific part of town), while others preferred a cultural tradition (e.g., pragmatics of greetings, extrapolating interpersonal relationships based on visual cues). The most important elements of the observational blog post are visualization and commentary. Consequently, detailed instructions are necessary to provide students a thorough understanding of the task requirements (see Appendix C). Observations were expected to include either photographic or video evidence and thick, detailed descriptions that would allow the reader to visualize the scene described. Students were also tasked with including commentary based on their own observational experience, making comparisons to their own culture. This activity is meant to put students in the position of a qualitative researcher, gathering and analyzing data about the culture in which they find themselves.

Guided Tour

The guided video tour required working alone or in pairs to create a video tour of one particular historic site, or of an experience (e.g., historical evidence of human sacrifice or the prevalence of Arab architecture across Sicily) in which students collected footage and information from different site visits. Video tours were expected to provide robust footage of important cultural and historical sites for on-campus students who would not have the opportunity to visit themselves.

Ethnographic Interview

Finally, students abroad were asked to conduct an interview with a local conversation partner that they invited to talk with them about a specific element of the host culture. In order for these interviews to be high enough quality to be used as authentic resources, study abroad participants needed to be familiar with interview techniques and best practices. The requirements were developed to be as clear as possible (see Appendix D), and opportunities were given to practice interviewing skills and receive feedback on those skills prior to the event. There was no restriction on the language of the interview, and it was expected that most students, given their L2 level, would feel more comfortable using English for the interview.

Anticipated Use of Resources

The goal of this project was to create the initial iteration of a digital repository of student-collected and -curated authentic materials for use in on-campus L2 classes. Students in Italian 1101, 1102, and 1103 Elementary Italian language courses would make use of the collected resources as part of their courses. Italian 1101 and 1102 are sequential, semester-long Elementary Italian courses. Italian 1103 is a one-semester intensive Elementary Italian course offered each spring. As indicated in the instructor's field notes, "The interviews and observational blogs will be incorporated into ITA 1101/1102/1103: Elementary Italian to help bolster the cultural element with realia and student-presented and student-accessible materials." Additionally, "There are video tours of many interesting sites that will be utilized in ITA 2203: Italian Journeys." Italian 2203 is Vanderbilt's Intermediate Italian course and is the prerequisite course for our upper division and Minor in Italian Studies specific courses.

Data Collection

Three primary data sources were used in this study. First, the lead researcher and instructor of the study abroad course, Greenfield, kept a detailed field journal in which she recorded her observations and analyses before, during, and after the study abroad course. Second, at various points throughout the course, most notably in the "Exit Survey," students were asked to give feedback as to the success of the course as a whole and the individual activities specifically. Finally, a third source of data was the student work itself. The various blog posts consisting of cultural observations, guided video tours, and ethnographic interviews were analyzed first by the instructor as learning assessments and later by the researchers as a source of data on the effectiveness of the project. All three data sources described here were included in the analysis.

Data Analysis

All three authors contributed to the design and framework of the project, although the lead researcher (Greenfield) led the study abroad, created the resource materials, and collected data during the study abroad experience. Upon the lead researcher's return from Italy, the three authors began meeting weekly to analyze the data. We began by reading and annotating the data individually, and then came together during meetings to compare ideas and analyses, creating three embedded analyses within the case study. By comparing our three separate analyses of each of the three data sources, we aimed to discuss how themes emerged, sort the data accordingly, and establish reliability in our coding and interpretation.

Field Notes

For the analysis of the field notes, the instructor created a summary document, akin to a reflection on lessons learned (Creswell, 2007). The entire set of field notes and the summary document were provided in their entirety to all three authors for individual reading and annotation, followed by the group analysis described earlier.

Exit Survey

The results of the exit survey were compiled into two sets of student feedback: quantitative responses describing satisfaction with their learning experiences and qualitative responses responding to open-ended questions about which learning activities and assessments had been the most beneficial.

Student Work/Blog Posts

In addition to examining the student blog posts and the completed rubrics that the instructor used to provide feedback to students, the researchers used a simplified rubric to evaluate the potential of each of the student blog contributions as an authentic resource for future L2/C2 learners. Each blog post was evaluated according to this rubric (see Appendix E) to determine the most successful blog posts for each category. Then, the most successful blog posts were compared to the least successful blog posts to determine what elements made for engaging, informative, useful contributions to future L2 and/or C2 audiences. The results of this second scoring of blog posts were compiled in a simple table to look for patterns in student work. This not only provided data for this report but also will help to inform how the blog assignments will be reformulated and the rubrics recalibrated for the following year's program. The authors then discussed the elements that contributed to the success of each type of blog post using the analysis procedures described previously.

Findings

Based on our analysis of the first iteration of our networked learning model, we were able to organize the collected data to address the research questions.

Research Question 1

What kinds of assignments will prove most beneficial to study abroad students while also providing useful resources for subsequent on-campus students?

Cultural Observation

The observational blog post asked students to use ethnographic participant observational skills to observe language and culture, compare their observations to what they had learned in class and through readings, and then analyze the experience. Overall, students reported liking the observational blog but expressed some dismay over the timing of their post. "They liked the observational blog, but wished they'd have done it during the first week as a basis for their final project reflections" (Greenfield's field journal). In the exit interview, students who waited until the end of the trip reported that they felt they got less out of it than those who completed it during the first week of the trip.

According to the instructor feedback provided to students, more than half of the observational blog posts demonstrated mastery of the learning objectives. In the secondary analysis (Appendix E) intended to predict the products' usefulness for future cohorts of students, the observational posts were rated by the instructor as the most likely of the three kinds of blog posts to prove helpful for future cohorts of students studying culture with an average rating of 38.9 out of 45 possible points. The observational blog posts were rated highly in all categories but one. They scored particularly high in the categories of "makes a cultural observation of the target culture" and "makes/asks insightful comments/questions about the target culture." Only one category scored low: "includes abundant, relevant and appropriate photographic and/or video evidence" with 10 out of 14 posts scoring only 1 out of 5 on that item.

The most successful observational blog posts—those that scored 90% or above on the evaluation rubric—included photographic or video evidence to provide more context for the narrative. Additionally, highly rated observational blog posts explicitly compared and contrasted C1 and C2, made thoughtful hypotheses based on information from class discussions and readings, and drew attention to misinterpretations, misunderstandings, and expectations that were incorrect. Highlights from the highest rated observational blogs include a student discussing the similarities and differences in how the elderly are treated and regarded in society:

> They take care of themselves, walking up the steep hills around here that have even me as a moderately fit college student huffing and puffing. They smoke when they want (and often), drink what they want, and eat what they want. Maybe instead of Boca Raton we should start sending our senior citizens here. It would be like Spring Break in Cancun for them.

Another student commented on the same phenomenon:

> It is so refreshing to see here that everyone has such love and passion for life instilled in them at a very young age, and that

they carry it with them for the rest of their lives. I can only hope that when I get to their age I am still that excited to wake up every morning when I start living the calm and humble life they all have. To have as much fun as these old men, I had to travel across the world and literally climb mountains. What?! I definitely could learn from these *nonni*, in simply that *La Vita è Bella* (Life is Beautiful), and it should be lived how you want it to be regardless of your age.

Another example concerns a student's preconceptions of how the Italian automotive industry would be represented in everyday life:

Before traveling to Sicily I assumed that Cefalu would be the holy grail of Italian sports cars. Although its [sic] public knowledge that the Italian economy has seen better days, my preliminary research described Cefalu as a relatively wealthy and upscale town with a plethora of Palermitani beach homes and European vacationers. My research apparently was incomplete or at the very least built up unrealistic expectations.

What is most impressive here is that the student recognizes not only that he was operating under inaccurate assumptions but that there are nuances to consider—he does not simply reject his research but expresses that perhaps it was incomplete or too focused to provide an accurate picture of what he might experience.

Consistent with previous research on student blogs in study abroad contexts (Elola & Oskoz, 2008; Jackson, 2005, 2008; Lee, 2012; Williams, 2005), these cultural observations prompted not only self-reflection but also reflection on one's own culture. Furthermore, several students considered higher order consequences and endeavored to consider how the two different governments handle unemployment and social programming. Through introspection and consideration, students were able to more closely examine similarities and differences between American and Italian cultures, and also make well-informed hypotheses and statements about their own traditions and social norms.

Guided Tour

Since students worked in groups instead of alone on the guided tour videos, there were only five submissions in this category. Students reported enjoying the site visits ("I enjoyed the sites which had a physical hike involved.") and accompanying video production. Several students reported enjoying the active and engaging nature of the learning created by a combination of site visits and related blog posts. The level of engagement by the student producers of the videos seemed to be related to reports that this was students' favorite assignment because it allowed them to show what they had learned and attach it to what they found most interesting.

The amount of required information for a four- to seven-minute video is significantly more demanding than a one-page written summary or reaction paper, though students seemed unbothered by the extra work and synthesis required of them. Not only did students analyze and present interesting summaries of assigned readings, as well as reiterate poignant information presented by tour guides and brochures at the sites, but they also conducted additional research to draw important conclusions about the cultural implications of sites or historical events. In informal conversation with the instructor, which was recorded in the field notes, many students reported their preference of the video tour over a traditional written assignment.

The videos generally demonstrated clearly that students were meeting the learning objectives, but in the secondary scoring according to the rubric in Appendix E, the videos received just 32.4 out of a possible 45 points, the lowest scores of the three kinds of blog posts. This suggests that the videos would be the least useful as authentic resources for future L2 students. This category of blog posts as a group received its highest ratings in the category of "includes abundant, relevant and appropriate photographic and/or video evidence," which is to be expected given the medium. However, in most categories on the secondary scoring rubric, the video posts as a group scored especially low leading the authors to predict that these resources would be the least useful for on-campus students. The lowest scoring rubric category was "considers cultural elements respectfully and carefully" in which only one of five guided tour blog posts scored a five out of five. The other four scored one, two, or three points out of five, not because they were disrespectful but because there was no consideration of the cultural elements presented.

As noted in the field journal, "[s]tudents preferred to work in pairs and small groups, but they actually presented MORE info and reaction and opinion in the video projects. I was really pleasantly surprised in how they synthesized the readings and class materials into their video projects." These outcomes exceeded the instructor's expectations, and this was deemed a result of the designated length of the assignment. Similarly, students' desire to include all relevant photo and video footage encouraged them to create voiceovers that lasted the entirety of the short film. It was clear that some students were making important connections between various visited sites, historical events, and architectural evidence, and were drawing informed, insightful conclusions where history had left holes. One group stated:

> We both started to think about how history is such a question mark. Our education system teaches us history as facts, but in reality, we believe that it is not. As seen throughout this video, there are many times in Agrigento's history where historians were guessing. . . . It is easy for the new rulers to come in and destroy the old history or taint what has happened. History is told by the

victors. History is all perspective. History is just opinions of what has happened.

Another group presented the visit to the Valley of the Temples as an episode of *MTV Cribs*, which was a unique and captivating way to draw students into a historical site by likening it to something they already know.

The instructor noted that, "I mentioned the idea of a tutorial (prior to departure) on making the videos and they agreed—many wished they'd started earlier and said that it was more work, but more fun to complete their work in that manner." Students reported in conversation that they wished they had begun earlier in the video making, and so the instructor made plans to build confidence in participants in this area by providing pre-departure training.

> I will run a video making tutorial in a pre-departure meeting so that students are more comfortable and outgoing with their video projects. ALL students were able to create these videos and nearly all commented on how much easier it was than they realized. Several also expressed regret that they hadn't played around with it earlier and that they might have been more adventurous with it if they'd begun earlier. I will also combine the responses and video projects into fewer, but more in depth assignments that will build our blog.

In addition, prior to arriving in the host country, the description and rubric will make clear the need for cross-cultural consideration and commentary so that future guided tours can be effectively used in on-campus classrooms.

Ethnographic Interview

The field notes and grading reveal that the interviews were the least successful blog posts as far as assessing student learning abroad. However, in the secondary scoring rubric (Appendix E) that assessed the usefulness of the blog posts for future students, they rated nearly as high as the observational blog posts with an average score of 38 out of 45. The interviews scored highest in the category of "makes a cultural observation of the target culture" with 12 out of 14 students scoring a five out of five in this area, and the other two students scoring four out of five.

The instructor's impressions from the field journal tell a different story, however. "I was less impressed by the interviews—I felt many lacked direction or were superficial. About half of the interviews included poignant questions and thoughtful feedback, the other half merely reiterated the info discovered in the interview discussion." Most students were quite interested in the similarities and differences in approaches to education and family, while a few were interested in sports, family, and entrepreneurship. Immigration and other social issues were frequently cited in the exit interview as topics of interest, although this did not come up in the ethnographic interviews.

Students reported that they felt insecure about phrasing their questions and staying on task during the interviews, and therefore did not want to submit raw, unedited video footage of the interviews for future students to use as authentic texts. They thought the instructor might be disappointed in them—accurately predicting the instructor's response as noted in the field journal. Many students were able to find something that interested them (e.g., education, business, family relations) and ask pointed questions about Sicilian traditions and approaches to these factors; they were also able to create a culturally sensitive comparison between Sicilian and American culture. Others, however, only regurgitated a series of questions that were mostly non-sequential without exploring answers provided by the interviewee.

The exit interviews showed that students liked conducting the interviews and learning about locals' opinions on different subjects. However, about one-third of the class had to ask for help to find an interview partner. Additionally, an Italian architecture student asked to practice his English with a native speaker, and one of the students in the study abroad group was able to do so through the interviews. Interview participant recruitment is another area where planning could alleviate some of the challenges in future courses.

Interviews took place in English and Italian, depending on the student's language proficiency and confidence in L2. The most successful interview, according to the evaluation rubric used to grade student work for the course, was conducted in Italian and was accompanied by a translation also provided by the student interviewer. This successful student intermixed the authentic audio from the interview with her own commentary. Additionally, the student drew clear comparisons to similar phenomena in America, included visual aids, and said things like, "I can't help but wonder if the job market was better in Sicily, would as many people want to attend college?" when discussing the similarities and differences between C1 and C2.

Another successful interviewer wrapped up her interview by pointing out the importance of realizing that although one person might highlight flaws in a specific interview, this should not overshadow the bigger picture of what she learned during her visit.

> The main thought that I was left with at the end of the interview was that as much as he focused on the flaws of Italy, he still gave me a book about Cefalù at the end of the interview. He prides himself on being Sicilian. He gave me this book because he wants me to understand and appreciate the culture here in Cefalù. I left having a lot of respect for Sicilian culture because despite people feeling the need to leave to enhance their lives, the community in Cefalù keeps pulling them back. Most Americans do not feel this same connection to the community they grew up in.

In those successful interviews, students were able to provide comparisons and contrasts with their own culture and acknowledge the nuances of culture. Interviews in L2 provided not only cultural insight but also authentic speech samples (an aspect that could be improved). Finally, student commentary post-interview incorporated points of views that allowed for engaging discussions and debates for those students viewing or reading the interview.

Research Question 2

How can this model be made more feasible, and therefore more sustainable, for instructors and students?

The challenges and opportunities encountered by students and faculty in this project revealed important findings about how to create a more stable, useful, and sustainable space for the collection and curation of authentic L2 resources. This turned out to involve both technical and pedagogical considerations. In addition to choosing the right tools to collect, edit, store, and disseminate the resources, students also required specific, scaffolded assignments that provided a balance of freedom and clarity.

Technical Considerations

Teaching with technology entails unforeseen roadblocks. Using institutional resources to store and share student work meant using readily available university infrastructure, but it also presented restrictions. For example, exceeding allowable file size was the most common technological barrier, which repeatedly prevented students from uploading their videos to the class blog. The solution was to upload videos to YouTube and hyperlink to the page—"Our video was too big to upload, so here is a link [to YouTube]" was a common notation that accompanied video submissions. In future iterations of this course, using institutional media streaming service (Kaltura) or creating a YouTube channel that is linked to the website might be a feasible solution. One potential problem, however, is that instructors neither maintain ownership of the file nor can they edit them when students upload videos to Kaltura or YouTube. Consequently, instructors would also need a digital repository (like an external hard drive) where they can keep copies of the work for future student use.

Web access during the in-country phase of study abroad was also a problem, particularly student access to the designated blog or course page (in the case study, all 14 students were added as website builders to the institutional WordPress site for the duration of the course) and the platform hosting the page. Free and publicly available sites may pose problems such as malware or viruses, whereas privately hosted servers may impose restrictions on the types of materials that can be posted, the number of site builders or limit access to the students. Investigating as many of these possible roadblocks prior to the start of the project would help to alleviate trouble during the course and allow for potential alternatives should a problem arise.

Despite available technological devices with more storage, students preferred using their own smartphones (mostly iPhones) for photos and video recording, and only one group made use of the available action camera. Because of the short-term nature of the program, familiarity with the new digital technology might have been a factor in the decision to use familiar and personal devices. One student added photos from his digital camera to a video submission. Contrary to the authors' pre-travel hypothesis, the external microphones were rarely utilized. In the few cases in which students did opt to use the external microphone, the quality in the final product was not markedly improved. As for editing, the students in this particular program were somewhat familiar with iMovie and QuickTime and some were comfortable manipulating their footage, adding effects, voiceovers, subtitles, and music. Other students who had never utilized these programs found them user-friendly after a one to two day adjustment period.

Pedagogical Considerations

Creating a framework for a study abroad course that engages students, supports their learning experience, and invites them into the process of generating and collecting authentic resources requires intentional design, a scaffolded approach, and time. One of the first pedagogical considerations is how to structure multiple course access points that meet students where they are at the start of a study abroad experience. This involves thinking about initial assignments that have clear prompts and expectations, are highly structured, and serve as an introduction to the types of thinking, engagement, and perhaps technologies students will be asked to use as the course progresses. The better aligned early assignments are with later assignments and the better they build up to them, the better these later assignments will support a successful learning experience and lead to student collecting useable authentic resources.

Students also ought to have a realistic understanding of the time commitment and efforts involved in the task. Students were not aware of how much time they should dedicate to the blog posts in this particular case study. Additionally, if assignments require students to engage with the local community, then students will need to understand how to engage that community and be mentally prepared for issues that may arise during an assignment. In fact, many students were intimidated by the assignments and postponed submitting them. Consequently, many student expressed regret at waiting and even a desire for the instructor to manage the due dates for them. One student commented in the exit interview, "Could you maybe stagger the blog post due dates? I know we are adults and should be able to choose, but I feel like most of us thought the posts were some intimidating thing when, they really were doable."

Students reacted most favorably to the video tour assignment and also provided the most material with that particular blog post. "Students liked making the videos once they started. They were often hesitant, and often left the video to the last week, but then expressed that they wished they'd have started earlier as they thought it was easier to complete reaction/response HW in this manner" (Greenfield's field notes). The least effective element, in this first iteration of the project, was the one-on-one interview. Students were hesitant to engage in the L2 and often were not confident in their ethnographic interview skills to carry out a thorough interview (though the end results were satisfactory). Instructors will have to make every effort to manage the risk aversion and confidence level by facilitating how students deal with early obstacles in the program (e.g., culture shock, jet lag, work associated with short-term programs), ideally prior to departure.

Next Steps

The logistical obstacles to creating the networked spaces for students to both produce resources as well as draw on previously collected resources could be overwhelming for a single instructor. This networked model could be undertaken collaboratively by a language program, department, or perhaps a language center, which could prove more feasible and sustainable. Additional steps and types of data collection could take place with additional planning, resources, and a solid plan for storage, cataloging, and access.

Collection of L2 Samples

Of particular interest to L2 instructors is the additional collection of authentic speech samples. One of the elements of the Italian curriculum redesign at Vanderbilt was a set of benchmark questions that encompass the conversational skills students should acquire after successfully completing each unit. We propose that future students abroad could ask those predetermined questions from the first-year curriculum to an array of native speakers as they collect their speech samples and donate those recorded responses to a repository accessible by all language instructors in the program. While the cataloging and metadata process would require an investment of time on the part of the language program (or language center), these resources could prove valuable to instructors who are looking for authentic audio samples anchored in C2 contexts for their classes. These samples would present an array of dialects and accents, as well as an array of cultural perspectives elementary-level L2 students could use as models to ask and answer questions.

Creation of a Resource Hub

In the future, the results of this research could be used to expand the learning network to include more instructors and students or to include departmental infrastructure or language centers for the administration of the authentic resources hub. We envision instructors from across several language programs coming together to agree upon a framework for the collection of resources, the creation of a central storage hub for those resources, and an appropriate cataloging system to organize those resources in an effective and efficient way for pedagogical use. The intricacies of this sort of collaboration may be unique, but we envision this resource hub as a cooperative space between undergraduate student collectors, graduate student cataloguers and metadata labelers, and a language center administrator who oversees and maintains the digital hub.

Conclusion

This chapter sought to evaluate the potential of networked learning as a social pedagogy that connects students across different learning contexts, in this case, through a hub of authentic resource collection, curation, and application. We examined the impact of a study abroad course design in which students produce authentic resources to be made available to other L2 students through an asynchronous collection, distribution, and usage cycle. Our findings demonstrate the potential to design study abroad assignments and assessments that include the production of language and culture resources that would be useful to elementary-level L2 students in future courses. In this study, observational blog posts and interviews with locals, which required ethnographic research skills, were the resources produced by students abroad that seemed to have the most potential for on-campus language learners. In future iterations of this model, we intend to make changes based on our research results. First, we plan to include another kind of resource-generating activity, collecting speech samples determined by our programmatic needs, and, second, we will improve the guidelines for the guided tour blog assignment to ensure that the products are more useful for L2/C2 learners. Third, attention will be paid to the technology infrastructure used for the collection and maintenance of the resources, as well as the technological training needed by students in order to carry out these tasks successfully. The networked learning project will also continue to grow as we explore the impact of this repository of authentic resources in lower-level L2/C2 courses as its use expands in a variety of courses within the Italian language program. This research proves instrumental in furthering the goal of developing a student-driven, networked approach that puts social pedagogy in action by turning L2 learners into social agent who have an impact on their environment (in this case their language program by connecting students across time, space, and proficiency level) and bridging students' classroom experience with the world and a real audience (their peers).

References

Allen, L. Q. (2000). Culture and the ethnographic interview in foreign language teacher development. *Foreign Language Annals, 33*, 51–57.

Alm, A. (2014). The socially networked language learner: Implications for tertiary language education. In B. Hegarty, J. McDonald, & S.-K. Loke (Eds.), *Rhetoric and reality: Critical perspectives on educational technology. Proceedings Ascilite Dunedin 2014* (pp. 693–697). Retrieved from http://ascilite.org/conferences/dunedin2014/files/concisepapers/268-Alm.pdf

Armstrong, K., & Retterer, O. (2008). Blogging as L2 writing: A case study. *AACE Journal, 16*, 233–251.

Bass, R., & Elmendorf, H. (2012). *Designing for difficulty: Social pedagogies as a framework for course design in undergraduate education.* Unpublished White Paper for the Teagle Foundation. Retrieved from https://blogs.commons.georgetown.edu/bassr/social-pedagogies/

Bateman, B. (2002). Promoting openness toward culture learning: Ethnographic interviews for students of Spanish. *Modern Language Journal, 86*, 318–331.

Blattner, G., & Fiori, M. (2012). Virtual social network communities: An investigation of language learners' development of sociopragmatic awareness and multiliteracy skills. *CALICO Journal, 29*(1), 24–43.

Bloch, J. (2007). Abdullah's blogging: A generation 1.5 student enters the blogosphere. *Language Learning & Technology, 11*, 128–141.

Center for Open Educational Resources and Language Learning (COERLL). (2010). *Foreign language teaching methods: Culture, lesson 2: Proficiency and cultural literacy, types of texts.* Retrieved from https://coerll.utexas.edu/methods/modules/culture/02/texts.php

Creswell, J. W. (2007). *Qualitative inquiry and research design: Choosing among five approaches* (2nd ed.). Thousand Oaks, CA: Sage.

Davidson, D. E. (2007). Study abroad and outcomes measurements: The case of Russian. *Modern Language Journal, 91*, 276–280.

Deardorff, K. (2006). Identification and assessment of intercultural competence as a student outcome of internationalization. *Journal of Studies in International Education, 10*, 241–266.

Ducate, L., & Lomicka, L. (2008). Adventures in the blogosphere: From blog readers to blog writers. *Computer Assisted Language Learning, 21*, 9–28.

Ducate, L., Lomicka, L., and Lord, G. (2012). Hybrid learning spaces: Re-envisioning language learning. In F. Rubio & J. Thoms (Eds.), 2012 AAUSC Volume, *Hybrid language teaching and learning: Exploring theoretical, pedagogical, and curricular issues* (pp. 67–91). Boston, MA: Heinle.

Elola, I., & Oskoz, A. (2008). Blogging: Fostering intercultural competence development in foreign language and study abroad contexts. *Foreign Language Annals, 41*, 454–478.

Finch, V., & Johnson, S. M. (2016). *Leveraging travel abroad: Collecting and teaching with authentic resources.* Vanderbilt University Center for Teaching. Retrieved from https://cft.vanderbilt.edu/authentic-resources/

Hourigan, T., & Murray, L. (2010). Using blogs to help language students to develop reflective learning strategies: Towards a pedagogical framework. *Australasian Journal of Educational Technology, 26*, 209–225.

Isabelli-Garcia, C. (2006). Study abroad social networks, motivation, and attitudes: Implications for SLA. In M. A. DuFon & E. Churchill (Eds.), *Language learners in study abroad contexts* (pp. 231–258). Clevedon, UK: Multilingual Matters.

Jackson, J. (2005). Assessing intercultural learning through introspective accounts. *Frontiers: The Interdisciplinary Journal of Study Abroad, 11*, 165–186.

Jackson, J. (2008). *Language, identity, and study abroad: Sociocultural perspectives.* London, UK: Equinox.

Kinginger, C., & Belz, J. (2005). Socio-cultural perspectives on pragmatic development in foreign language learning: Microgenetic and ontogenetic case studies from telecollaboration and study abroad. *Intercultural Pragmatics, 2*, 369–422.

Lee, L. (2009). Promoting intercultural exchanges with blogs and podcasting: A study of Spanish-American telecollaboration. *Computer Assisted Language Learning, 22*, 425–443.

Lee, L. (2012). Engaging study abroad students in intercultural learning through blogging and ethnographic interviews. *Foreign Language Annals, 45*(1), 7–21.

Leonard, J. B. (2012). Integrative learning: A grounded theory. *Issues in Integrative Studies, 30*, 48–74.

Lomicka, L., & Lord, G. (2012). A tale of tweets: Analyzing microblogging among language learners. *System, 40*(1), 48–63.

Menacker, T. (2001). *Community language resources: A handbook for teachers* (NFLRC Net Work #22). Honolulu: University of Hawai'i, Second Language Teaching & Curriculum Center. Retrieved from http://www.nflrc.hawaii.edu/networks/NW22.pdf

Mills, N. (2011). Situated learning through social networking communities: The development of joint enterprise, mutual engagement, and a shared repertoire. *CALICO Journal, 28*(2), 345–368.

Moeller, A., & Fatlin Osborn, S. R. (2014). A pragmatist perspective on building intercultural communicative competency: From theory to classroom practice. *Foreign Language Annals, 47*(4), 669–683.

O'Dowd, R. (2006). Combining networked communication tools for students' ethnographic research. In J. Belz & S. Thorne (Eds.), *Internet-mediated intercultural foreign language education* (pp. 147–176). Boston, MA: Thomsen & Heinle.

Pinkman, K. (2005). Using blogs in the foreign language classroom: Encouraging learner independence. *The JALT CALL Journal, 1*, 12–24.

Purcell, K., Buchanan, J., & Friedrich, L. (2013). *The impact of digital tools on student writing and how writing is taught in schools*. Washington, DC: Pew Research Center's Internet & American Life Project. Retrieved from http://www.pewinternet.org/files/old-media/Files/Reports/2013/PIP_NWP%20Writing%20and%20Tech.pdf

Roberts, C. (2003). Ethnography and cultural practice: Ways of learning during residence abroad. In G Alred, M. Byram, & M. Fleming (Eds.), *Intercultural experience and education* (pp. 114–130). Clevedon, UK: Multilingual Matters.

Siemens, G. (2008). Learning and knowing in networks: Changing roles for educators and designers. Presented to ITFORUM for Discussion, January 27, pp. 1–26. Retrieved from http://www.ingedewaard.net/papers/connectivism/2008_siemens_Learning_Knowing_in_Networks_changingRolesForEducatorsAndDesigners.pdf

Su, Y. C. (2008). Promoting cross-cultural awareness and understanding: Incorporating ethnographic interviews in college EFL classes in Taiwan. *Educational Studies, 34*, 377–398.

Thorne, S., & Reinhardt, J. (2008). "Bridging activities," New media literacies, and advanced foreign language proficiency. *CALICO Journal, 25*(3), 558–572.

Thorne, S. L. (2003). Artifacts and cultures-of-use in intercultural communication. *Language Learning & Technology, 7*, 38–67.

Thorne, S. L., & Payne, J. S. (2005). Evolutionary trajectories, Internet-mediated expression, and language education. *CALICO Journal, 22*, 371–397.

Williams, T. R. (2005). Exploring the impact of study abroad on students' intercultural communications skills: Adaptability and sensitivity. *Journal of Studies in International Education, 9*, 356–371.

Yang, S. H. (2009). Using blogs to enhance critical reflection and community of practice. *Educational Technology & Society, 12*, 11–21.

Appendices

Appendix A: Blog Requirements

As part of this course, you are asked to make <u>at least</u> three blog contributions, one in each of the following categories. You may, however, submit additional blog entries if you so choose. In some cases, your blog entries and your responses may overlap. It is your choice how many of your response will be posted on the course blog and you can also choose which entries count toward your grade and which you would like to contribute without grading.

You must submit <u>one of each</u> of the following categories to count toward your grade. Please adhere to guidelines here and feel free to consult with your instructor on any aspect of your work.

1. WRITTEN OBSERVATION (based on observation form)

This written blog entry should be completed on your own. Based on the observation form found on BlackBoard, summarize an observational experience in Sicily. You should feel free to enhance your blog with photos of audio clips but I am most interested in what you can articulate about what you observed. Be sure to use the observation form to help you formulate your thoughts.

2. VIDEO TOUR (may also be completed in pairs or a group of three with special permission)

Your video should encapsulate either a site or a specific experience in an edited 3-7 minute video. Your video should include live footage (you have access to action cams for the course), voice overs, and may also include photos, captions, and subtitles as well. You should consider using iMovie (or a similar program) to edit your short video appropriately.

If you opt for a <u>site</u>, the informational aspects should address the site as a whole (for example the importance of the Valley of the Temples rather than just Temple C). You should draw the audience's attention to elements from the reading, things noted by the tour guide, and your own opinions, reactions, and conclusions.

If you opt for an <u>experience</u>. I'm looking for you to address a specific element that may be addressed at several different sites. For example, you might be interested sacrifice to the gods and choose to include video and photo clips from Agrigento, Siracusa, and Solunto. You might find Arab architecture interesting and include footage from Monreale and Palermo. Again, provide voice over or captioned information from the readings, the guided tours, and your own opinions, reactions, and conclusions.

If you work in pairs or a small group, each person must appear in the video and must contribute to the project.

3. ONE-ON-ONE INTERVIEW (BASED ON INTERVIEW QUESTIONNAIRE)

This blog entry should be a combination of written response and video/audio clips of an interview you conduct with a Sicilian inhabitant (you will have an external microphone that you can attach to a smartphone or other digital device). Your interview may address several different topics, but this blog should focus on a specific element of Sicilian culture (education, religion, sports, etc.). You may bring in differing perspectives from several interviewees, or information you have learned from conversations with new friends and acquaintances around town. Be thorough, specific, and conclusive in your blog post.

Appendix B: Networked Learning Blog Assessment Rubric

	EXCEEDS EXPECTATIONS	MEETS EXPECTATIONS	DOES NOT MEET EXPECTATIONS
Cultural consideration and research (40%)	• Blog post addresses cultural elements as outlined in the assignment explanation using deductive reasoning and evidence based hypotheses to extrapolate meaning and commentary • Considers cultural elements respectfully and carefully, comparing and contrasting in a meaningful way to the student's own culture or another with which they are familiar • Clear evidence of cultural research, drawing from course readings, lectures, discussion, but also incorporating additional research conducted by the student	• Blog post addresses cultural elements as outlined in the assignment explanation • Considers cultural elements respectfully and carefully • Clear evidence of cultural research, drawing from course readings, lectures, discussions	• Blog post addresses some, few, or no cultural elements as outlined in the assignment explanation • Considers cultural elements but is lacking in care and/or respect • Little to no evidence of cultural research • Little or no reference to course readings, lectures, discussions
Organization, Editing (25%)	• Blog post is well organized and edited appropriately • Easy to read / watch / listen • Well organized, engaging, and coherent with relevant commentary and reference to course materials or course learning objectives • Relevant details are abundant and integrated seamlessly into the blog post	• Blog post is well organized and edited appropriately • Easy to read / watch / listen • Well organized, engaging, and coherent • Relevant details are organized and integrated well into the blog post	• Blog post is not well organized and/or is not edited appropriately • Difficult to read/listen/watch • Not engaging and/or coherent • Lack of relevant details integrated into the blog post

(Continued)

	EXCEEDS EXPECTATIONS	**MEETS EXPECTATIONS**	**DOES NOT MEET EXPECTATIONS**
Final Product Professionalism (25%)	• Blog post is polished, well edited, and professional looking with details that go above and beyond the minimum requirements • Blog post includes abundant, relevant and appropriate photographic and/or video evidence to accompany written and/or spoken commentary • Spelling, punctuation, and grammar are appropriate and correct, exhibiting a high level of reflective and intelligent discourse	• Blog post is polished, well edited, and professional looking • Blog post includes relevant and appropriate photographic or video evidence to accompany written or spoken commentary • Spelling, punctuation, and grammar are appropriate and correct	• Blog post is not well polished, edited, and/or is not professional looking • Blog post lacks relevant and/or appropriate photographic of video evidence • Errors in spelling, punctuation, and/or grammar
Follows Specifications (10%)	• Blog post adheres to the specifications outlined the project explanation • Meets and stays within standards of length and content • Efficiently and effectively manages time so that repetition is avoided and poignant, meaningful material is presented in a time sensitive and time conscientious manner	• Blog post adheres to the specifications outlined the project explanation • Meets and stays within standards of length and content	• Blog post does not adhere to the specifications outlined in the project explanation • Does not meet or stay within standards of length and/or content

COMMENTS _____

_____

_____

_____

_____

_____

_____

_____

Appendix C: Observation Form - Basis For Observational Blog Entries

Complete the form with the data requested in the table. You should also utilize the "additional notes" section for observations you make that don't have a place in the chart. Be sure to follow all the steps outlined in the form to ensure success.

PREPARATION:

1. Determine the location of your observation and the type of interaction you will observe
2. Set aside at least 30 minutes for your observation so that you can take in consistencies, inconsistencies, and appropriate details
3. Decide if you will make this a group or individual observation. If working in a group, be sure to decide how you will divide the work - Will each team member observe an area (several piazzas/churches/bars around town) / one gender / etc? Be sure to also plan ahead on how you will take notes so you can spend your time observing and not looking down.

Date and time: _____ **Population observed:** _____

Place and type of event: _____

OBSERVATION:

Fill out the chart and the additional notes section as thoroughly as possible. No detail is too small to be left out The more information you can collect during your observation, the more you have to work with when you synthesize your findings.

OBSERVATION AREA	EXTRAPOLATION, COMMENTS
Appearance (clothing, age, gender, physical appearance) Are there any indicators of profession, socioeconomic class, race, ethnicity, religion, etc?	
Verbal behavior/ interaction (volume of voice, greetings, language/dialect, tone) Do you notice distinctions between age, gender, profession, etc? What dynamics do you notice?	
Physical behavior/gestures (greetings, social distance, physical contact) What do you notice about body language, how speakers use their bodies? How are feelings expressed? Do you notice differences between age, gender, profession, etc?	

(Continued)

OBSERVATION AREA	EXTRAPOLATION, COMMENTS
Traffic (location of entrance, exit, time spent at site)	
How are people entering and exiting? How long are they staying? What differneces do you notice between age, gender, socioeconomic status, etc?	
People who stand out (stature, clothing, other forms of identification)	
What characteristics do you notice that differentiate people from others? Are they approaching others or others approach them? Do they seem to be well-known?	

ADDITIONAL NOTES:

_____
_____
_____
_____
_____

SYNTHESIS:

Create a 1 -2 paragraph wrap up of your observation. Create 2-3 follow up questions that you can use for follow up observations and that can help create meaningful discussion.

WRAP-UP

_____
_____
_____
_____
_____

FOLLOW UP QUESTIONS:

1. _____
2. _____
3. _____

Appendix D

INTERVIEW QUESTIONNAIRE

This form contains some sample questions for you to conduct your one-on-one interview(s). You should feel free to add follow up questions that do not appear on the list if they follow the natural course of your conversation. Be sure to consult the steps to ensure success.

PREPARATION:

1. Determine the subject of your interview [you must interview at least one native Sicilian, but you can conduct additional interviews if you choose, which may be conducted with immigrants)
2. Set aside at least 20 minutes for your interview so that you will not be rushed and can allow your interview to follow a natural path
3. Be empathetic, engaged, and invested in the conversation, allowing your interview subject to speak freely and openly

Date and time: _____   **Profession of interviewee:** _____

Interview participant: _____

SAMPLE QUESTIONS:

Use this list of questions to help you develop a trajectory for your interview. Take note of things you'd like to follow up on and topics that are of particular interest to you. The more information you can gather, the more you will have to work with.

USEFUL PHRASES

Can you be more specific?

Can you give me an example?

When you say _____, what do you mean?

GENERAL QUESTIONS

1. Where are you from and where do you live now?
2. What is a typical day like for you?
3. Could you describe your family?
4. _____
5. _____
6. _____

EDUCATION

1. How does the school system work in Sicily?
2. What kinds of schools did you attend?
3. Is there anything you would change about how the school system is organized?
4. _____
5. _____
6. _____

HEALTH CARE

1. How is healthcare managed in Sicily?
2. How much do you have to pay when you need to visit a doctor for an illness?
3. How do you schedule an appointment with a doctor and how long to you generally have to wait to see a physician?
4. _____
5. _____
6. _____

SPORTS AND RECREATION

1. What sports are popular in Italy?
2. How important are sports to Sicilian society?
3. Do you play a sport? Can you tell me about that?
4. _____
5. _____
6. _____

ADDITIONAL NOTES:

_____
_____
_____
_____
_____
_____

Appendix E

	STRONGLY AGREE (5)	AGREE (4)	NEUTRAL (3)	DISAGREE (2)	STRONGLY DISAGREE (1)	TOTAL
This blog post makes a cultural observation of the target culture						
This blog post makes / asks insightful comments / questions about the target culture						
Blog post includes abundant, relevant and appropriate photographic and/or video evidence to accompany written and/or spoken commentary						
Blog post is polished, well edited, and professional looking with details that go above and beyond the minimum requirements						
Relevant details are abundant and integrated seamlessly into the blog post						
Clear evidence of cultural research, drawing from course readings, lectures, discussion, but also incorporating additional research conducted by the student						

(Continued)

	STRONGLY AGREE (5)	AGREE (4)	NEUTRAL (3)	DISAGREE (2)	STRONGLY DISAGREE (1)	TOTAL
Considers cultural elements respectfully and carefully, comparing and contrasting in a meaningful way to the student's own culture or another with which they are familiar						
Blog post addresses cultural elements as outlined in the assignment explanation using deductive reasoning and evidence based hypotheses to extrapolate meaning and commentary						
Observation - Does the blog include anecdotes and follow up questions?						
Video - Does the video last 3-7 minutes and address either a specific site or a specific experience?						
Interview - Does the write up focus on a specific topic						

Chapter 8
Beyond Participation: Symbolic Struggles with(in) Digital Social Media in the L2 Classroom

Chantelle Warner, University of Arizona

Diane F. Richardson, U.S. Military Academy

Introduction

Participation—that long-standing assessment category on proficiency-oriented language syllabi—has found a new conceptual life over the last few decades through the influence of socioculturally oriented applied linguistic and pedagogical frameworks. Recent studies emerging from these fields have urged educators to encourage students to engage with the social world more broadly and to expand beyond the foreign language classroom. As linguistic anthropologist William Hanks reminds us, "[t]o speak is inevitably to situate one's self in the world, to take up a position, to engage with others in a process of production and exchange, to occupy a social space" (1993, p. 139). A pressing concern for L2 educators is thus which social spaces we inspire learners to enter through our pedagogies and which positions, that is, what forms of participation, we enable them to assume within those spaces. This paper contributes to discussions of social pedagogies in L2 teaching by considering digital social media as not only an opportunity for language educators to access authentic communicative contexts but also a means of enabling learners to expand the scope of positions, which they occupy as users of a new language.

The focus of this article is two instructional studies implemented in different semesters of an intermediate/advanced collegiate German course. The overarching curriculum of the course was inspired by multiliteracies frameworks, which conceptualize language, literacy, and learning as situated in social systems of meaning (e.g., Byrnes & Sprang, 2004; Kern, 2000; Maxim, 2008; Paesani, Allen, & Dupuy, 2016). The creation of a digital media unit was motivated by a desire on the part of the Language Program Director (the first author) and the instructors (one of whom is the second author) to continue to develop learners' awareness of linguistic designs and their effects, while also introducing the potential for increased and less predictable social interaction between students in the class and between students and other German speakers. The first unit, involving networked digital gaming, laid the foundation for the second, a multi-week project engaging with online discussion forums. While many of the students reported that they enjoyed the opportunity to engage with more vernacular genres and with language use outside of the classroom context, others experienced moments of misalignment and contested participation (see also Reinhardt, Warner, & Lange, 2014). At the center of this article is a contrastive analysis of the classroom contributions and reflections of two students, one from each variation of the unit. These case studies offer quite different examples of the kinds of symbolic struggles students face as they try to position themselves within the layered social spaces that form when digital media are integrated into classroom practice.

In what follows, we first outline some of the key ways in which participation has been conceptualized in the more recent history of L2 teaching and argue that these different conceptualizations also entail different positions that learners can take up during in- and out-of-class activities. We then examine how the students in the two case studies positioned themselves at different moments during the course, specifically in relation to the digital media unit. Finally, we conclude by identifying some potential implications for curriculum coordinators and instructors.

From Communities to Contact Zones: Positioning Participation in L2 Teaching

Since the proficiency turn in the early 1980s, *participation* in the sense of "the ability to function in real-life contexts" (Higgs & American Council on the Teaching of Foreign Languages, 1984, p. 12) has remained a stalwart beacon toward which all other language learning objectives can orientate. Proficiency-oriented language teaching was a clear shift away from methods and models in which participation was primarily considered to be a mental activity (see Kern & Liddicoat, 2011) and toward social models of language teaching and learning. However, the matter of what particular forms and contexts of participation classroom-based language teaching ought to integrate has been an ongoing and manifold discussion in post-proficiency L2 educational research and teaching practices over the last few decades.

Communicative language teaching (CLT), which began to dominate methods books and textbooks in step with the proficiency movement, has tended to locate participation in an unspecified group of speakers, a "particular sociocultural group" (Breen & Candlin, 1980, p. 90), by and for whom certain ways of speaking might be deemed *appropriate*, read: "native-like" (Canale & Swain, 1980, p. 16). CLT was heavily influenced by sociolinguist Dell Hymes's concept of *communicative competence*, the ability of a given speech community "to accomplish a repertoire of speech acts, to take part in speech events, and to evaluate their accomplishment by others" (Hymes, 1972, p. 277). When operationalized in language curricula, however, the notion of *speech community* often poses analytical problems for L2 teachers and curriculum designers, who have been left to fill the empty signifier "community"—often with an idealized *imagined community* (to borrow a phrase from Benedict Anderson [1983/2006]; see also Kramsch, 2003, p. xii; Thorne, 2009).

Beginning in the mid-1990s, the American Council for Teachers of Foreign Languages (ACTFL)—the primary standardizing body for foreign language study in the United States—proposed a view of "communities" that diverges from the idea of the classroom as a simulacrum of an imagined native speech community. The 1996 *Standards for Foreign Language Learning* published by ACTFL located participation both very broadly in "Multilingual Communities at Home & Around the World" and as manifested by "using language in and outside of instructional settings" and by engaging in activities for "personal enjoyment and enrichment" (National Standards Collaborative Board, 1996). On the one hand, this definition parallels educational frameworks developing since the mid-1990s, which posit a more global, multilingual, and multicultural body of possible speakers (see also New London Group, 1996). At the same time, it acknowledges the importance of a much more local "community"—fellow language learners and classmates. The layered model of community conceptualized in the *Standards* points to an interesting potential point of tension between the classroom, the imagined national community, and the more geographically distant speech communities within which learners might engage.

Writing two decades ago, the authors of the original *Standards* could not have fully anticipated the ways in which social participation would come unmoored from geographically located social spaces as digitally mediated communication became a predominant form of interaction. The implications of this shift for language and literacy learning have been the focus of a number of studies, including notably Eva Lam's (2000; see also Kramsch, A'Ness, & Lam, 2000) research on the destabilization of cultural identity through participation in online communities, Rebecca Black's (2005) work on affiliation practices in online fanfiction sites, and Steve Thorne's work on networked digital gaming environments (2008, 2011).

The study of digital social spaces has brought critical attention to the ways in which participation and community have been operationalized within fields of education and literacy studies and second language teaching—an intellectual trend that is captured by James Gee's concept of *affinity spaces*. The notion of affinity spaces shifts attention from membership to the space—virtual or physical—in which participation occurs. Affiliation in affinity spaces arises from shared interests, endeavors, or goals. Participation is also less regulated and more varied—the same individual can participate more centrally in some respects or moments and more peripherally in others (Gee, 2005, p. 228). Knowledge and authority are more distributed across participants and more dispersed (across other sites or sources). Gee (2005) contrasts this with a typical classroom space in which participants are segregated by the level of skill, knowledge is evaluated but not shared, participation is restricted, and leadership is concentrated in an individual—the teacher (pp. 230–231). The porousness of affinity spaces means both that individuals can participate without being members, that is, without being perceived by themselves or others as belonging, and that non-participation does not necessarily equate with a sense of not belonging.

Perhaps because *speech community* and *space* are more difficult to situate in the case of digital encounters, work in digital literacies tends to treat language as a complex, relational, and contingent form of human activity (e.g., Kern, 2015; Thorne, 2013) in ways that resonate with poststructuralist and sociocultural approaches to language, literacy, and interculturality. A common thread across these discussions is that participation is an ever-evolving performance of self within socially constituted activity frameworks. It follows that a fundamental mission of language and literacy education—whether in a first, second, or additional language—is to develop learners' capacity for reflective, linguistic practice, as is also emphasized within multiliteracies (or multiple literacies) frameworks for language and literacy teaching (Kern, 2000, 2015; Kramsch, 1993; Swaffar, Arens, & Byrnes, 1991). Through a wide palette of linguistic and other modes of meaning-making—for example, visual, audio, gestural, and spatial modes—social actors *design*, that is, actively transform, the social world around them and their position within it (see Cope & Kalantzis, 2009, p. 184).

A parallel concept appears in Claire Kramsch's more recent work on *symbolic competence*, defined as "the ability to shape the multilingual game in which one invests—the ability to manipulate the conventional categories and societal norms of truthfulness, legitimacy, seriousness, originality—and to reframe human thought and action" (Kramsch & Whiteside, 2008, p. 667). Symbolic competence, as a desideratum of language education, entails developing a sense of which social worlds emergent multilingual language users want to take up space within and how they might re-shape these spaces with their presence and contributions.

As pedagogical principles, the concepts of *design* and *symbolic competence* remind educators and curriculum designers that the goal of L2 education is ideally not only to enable participation in the sense of granting access but also to foster reflective language users "who engage with the world-in-action" (Crosbie, 2005, citing Phipps & Gonzalez, p. 295). The challenge—as literacy scholars Kevin Leander and Gail Boldt have suggested—is that the teacher "make space for fluidity and indeterminacy as the nature of things [. . .] that he or she recognize difference, surprise, and unfolding that follow along paths that are not rational or linear or obviously critical or political" (2012, p. 44). This is of particular importance when that engagement is embedded within the participation structures of the classroom, which carry their own logics, affordances, and constraints. When participation in online spaces outside of the classroom converges with educational practices, as it often does in social pedagogies, the site of participation becomes a kind of *contact zone*, in Marie-Louise Pratt's sense of "social spaces where cultures meet, clash, and grapple with each other, often in contexts of highly asymmetrical relations of power" (1991, p. 34). Pratt suggests contact zone as an alternative to what is viewed as "utopian" ideas of community, whereas the notion of community assumes "that all participants are engaged in the same game and that the game is the same for all players" (1991, p. 38). The concept of contact zones reminds us to pay attention to the kinds of symbolic struggles that are particularly salient in multilingual and multicultural L2 learning contexts, as learners negotiate not only different language capacities but also the systems of power, knowledge, and value within which they take up subject positions in relation to a new language (see Kramsch, 2011, p. 356).

The focus has thus far been on participation in the sense of sociable activity—whether more local or more global and whether conceptualized as communities, affinity spaces, or social worlds. However, before we turn to the case studies, a final way of thinking about participation bears mentioning. The updated version of the ACTFL *Standards* released with the title *World-Readiness Standards for Learning Languages* (National Standards Collaborative Board, 2015) redefines the "Communities Standard" by emphasizing the role of language as a point of access to a "global society" of "global economies and consumers" (p. 100). Within the body text, the more evocative term "community" is more or less replaced by "economy," which results in a set of pedagogical recommendations for enriching the local space of the classroom with consumable products and practices, for example, games, sports, literature, films, and television programs of the "foreign" culture. This promotion of foreign languages as entertainment value bears some resemblance to Ryuko Kubota's research on English language learning as a leisure activity in Japan (2011). Kubota distinguishes between serious leisure, which is oriented toward self-actualization, and casual leisure, which is more hedonic and self-gratifying (p. 475). Kubota notes that while language learning as leisure tends to focus on an imagined community of speakers, the appeal lies in the experience of an "imagined exotic space removed from daily life" (p. 475), rather than on any immediate or envisioned pragmatic intentions for using the language. The learner is then positioned as a consumer who partakes in a new linguistic economy rather than as a participant in social activity.

How we frame participation has implications for which social positions are available and accessible for students in instructional activities. If the native German-speaking community is the primary frame and native-like competence is the goal of language instruction, most U.S.-based learners will only ever be afforded an outsider position. Shifting the scope to the broad body of multilingual speakers who use German opens up a range of possible social roles but does not offer a manageable set of contexts for framing classroom discourse or principles for making curricular choices. Focusing on shared interests across cultures makes the range of contexts more manageable and allows for a multitude of possible position-takings. However, it also potentially limits the linguistic repertoires of learners by restricting their interactions to particular discourse domains. Moreover, while being a fan of a certain cultural practice (e.g., digital games, soccer, and a particular literary genre) can be framed as affiliation and affinity, it can also be a form of consumption. Whereas affinity allows for fluidity of positions (Gee, 2005), consumption seems to encourage a position of cultural consumer that is external to the field of cultural production itself, that is, the learner as cultural tourist rather than as participant.

In the following sections, we describe two pedagogical projects, which were designed to straddle the tensions between unpredictability and principled attention to language awareness. In our analysis of the data we pose the following questions in order to better understand how contact zones are created when classrooms and digitally mediated social spaces collide, enable, or restrict certain kinds of participation: What types of participation are contested by the students and why? What new positions are afforded through the learners' engagement with digital social media? What happens when symbolic systems are in tension, that is, when particular configurations of meaning seem to shift or are incommensurable—for example, different expectations of what participation in the L2 classroom should look like? By analyzing key examples, we address these guiding questions and posit a final one: What potential might different types of participation hold for the activation of symbolic competence in instructed language contexts?

Cases from the Digital Media-Enhanced Classroom

Course Context

The basis of this article is two classroom-based case studies from different instantiations of a digital media unit included in a fifth-semester German course at a large state university in the southwestern United States. The course, officially titled "Encounters in Language and Culture," is a 6-credit unit intermediate/advanced language course and is the first in the curricular sequence in which majors and minors outnumber the students who are taking German for their language requirement. For this reason, a core learning objective is to enable students to understand, analyze, and respond to increasingly complex and more abstract instances of language use, of the sort needed in the advanced-level content courses and for advanced proficiency more generally (see Maxim, 2008). The syllabus is organized around three key genre families—description (here: of people and places), narrative, and position-taking—each of which is paired with a thematic focus (see Table 8.1). In both case studies, digital media units were

Table 8.1. Curricular Organization

Special Topics	Featured Genre Families
The Individual in Society (*Das Individuum in der Gesellschaft*)	Description/Portrayal/Vignette
Stories from German History (*Geschichten aus der deutschen Geschichte*)	Narrative
Ex 1. Gaming and Game Culture (*Gaming und Spielkulturen*) Ex 2. Digital Communities (*Digitale Gemeinschaften*)	Position paper/Opinion piece

implemented in order to expand the space of the classroom and augment what the instructors and course coordinator perceived as the potential two-dimensionality of the text-centric pedagogies that dominated the curriculum (see Lotherington & Ronda, 2014). A primary pedagogical motivation behind these units was to expand the range of social roles students were able to imagine themselves beyond the classroom, by introducing digital social spaces in which participation would be qualitatively different (see also Hanna & De Nooy, 2003, p. 73). Engagement with and within the digital spaces was integrated with more familiar genre-based tasks, which were designed to foster learners' awareness of how particular design choices (grammatical style, word choice, color, font, etc.) can impact meaning—including the kinds of participation and interaction that are favored and legitimized.

Students were guided to observe how they and others used the digital media, to collect examples as they explored either the games and related websites or online forums, and to analyze the linguistic and multimodal designs of these spaces and interactions within them.[1] Students were given some agency in the choice of game or online forum, but they were strongly encouraged to select from a set of options already identified by the instructors and the Language Program Director. This was a practical decision based both on the relatively short span of time and the desire to have the students work in groups with the same game or same discussion forums. Whether to participate directly in the online forums or chat spaces outside of the classroom community was a choice left largely up to the students.

Although the specific assignments varied in both units, there was an emphasis on contemporary discourses (in contrast to the earlier units of the courses which consisted primarily of literary and historical texts) and a focus on position-taking (in the sense of expressing an opinion) through engagement with articles in the

---

[1] The cycle of tasks was loosely based on the "bridging activities" framework proposed by Steve Thorne and Jonathon Reinhardt (2008, p. 556).

gaming unit and forum discussions in the digital communities unit. The culminating assignments for this portion of the course were a group presentation and a position paper, which was written individually and required learners to incorporate personal experiences and critical perspectives. A more detailed description of the tasks, the course context, and the participants is provided in each of the subsequent case studies from the two digital media units in turn.

Data and Analysis

In order to look more closely at the kinds of social positions potentially taken up by students as they negotiated interactions in and around the digital media, we have chosen to focus on two students—Jamie and Jaden.[2] The particular cases of these students provide not only interesting examples of the kinds of positioning different digital media and pedagogical wrap-around activities can afford but also a contrastive sense of how different students negotiate the range of positions available to them. Jamie represents students who are able to position themselves in new and arguably more empowering ways through gaming than are otherwise perceived as available in the classroom; contrastingly, Jaden represents students who excel academically, feel comfortable in their identity as "good" students, but who might still struggle with a digital media unit.

The data collected for this study consist of the classroom artifacts, written and recorded assignments, interactions between students in the Wikispaces, and observations by the researchers, who were also instructors assigned to the courses—the second author in the first case study and the first author in the second case study.[3] These sources provide a partial but compelling view of how the students positioned themselves within and vis-à-vis the media, the tasks, other students, and other German speakers.

Positioning, as an analytical construct, was first introduced in social science research as a means of describing subjectivities as a "history of positioning in discourses" (Holloway, 1984, p. 228). Positioning theory has been developed most notably by Bronwyn Davies and Rom Harré (1990) as well as Harré and Luk van Langenhove (1999), in order to describe "the discursive process whereby people are located in conversations as observably and subjectively coherent participants in jointly produced storylines" (Davies & Harré, 1990, p. 37). In their interactions, participants use "storylines," recurring narratives, to make their contributions and actions meaningful. Positions are then the parts being performed—sometimes fleetingly, sometimes contentiously—by participants. These positions are "jointly produced" in that mutual engagement and a common commitment to the performance of a particular part are involved in sustaining a position taken up

---

[2] These names have been changed to protect the identities of the students.
[3] The first author was also the Language Program Director and curriculum coordinator in both semesters.

by a social actor. This is an element that becomes complicated in *contact zones* because of the ways in which multiple frames are often made salient (see also Kramsch & Whiteside, 2008).

Positioning theory has been used productively as a framework for analyzing classroom discourse—including in L2 learning contexts. Julia Menard-Warwick (2008), for example, analyzed interactions in an adult English as a second language class that primarily served Latina immigrants in the United States and described the tensions between the teachers' assumptions about their identities and the students' perceptions of themselves. While it falls outside of language education, Kate Anderson's (2009) examination of what comes to count as learning relative to teacher formulations of tasks in a fifth-grade math class is also of relevance to this study, in that it points to the important distinction between task and activity—what the teacher would like the learners to do and what the learners actually do (see also Thorne, 2005). Anderson's study also highlights the relationship between participation frameworks and the relative *stickiness* of particular labels, for example, *successful student* and *failed student* (2009, p. 306).

Case Study 1: Killer, Guild Founder, Critic: Finding New Positions through L2 Gaming

The first case study comes from fall 2014—during the third semester of implementation for the gaming unit discussed here. During the 2 ½-week unit, the 27 students in the course engaged in a variety of different practices, including playing digital games and keeping a log of their play in the Wikispaces within which all classmates could read and comment; reading and responding to articles about gaming and gaming cultures; writing a position paper in response to one of the articles; reflecting on various experiences in writing and in audio recordings in German (see Appendix A for more details). Modifications had been made each semester to encourage engagement with other users outside of the classroom, as well as to provide more opportunities for sharing feedback between in-class peers.

Both of these aspects were critical for Jamie, the focus of the first case study. Jamie was a non-traditional student who had learned German at a local community college three years prior to beginning at the university. At the start of the semester, Jamie struggled to complete and submit assignments fully, on time, or at all. In discussions with the instructors and reflective tasks, Jamie voiced general concerns about fitting in at the university and specific concerns about not being linguistically strong enough for the course. For example, when Jamie submitted the first writing assignment of the semester to the online dropbox, there was a message included for the instructors (in English): "It's way too short, but I'm struggling. I'd like to come see you guys in office hours at some point." For that assignment, students were supposed to write circa one page in German about their prior language learning experience, and Jamie was only able to write the following (63 words total):

> *Meine erste Sprache, Englisch, ist auch meine beste. Ich habe Deutsch 202 in [name of community college] Fertiggestellt aber das war in 2010. Meine Deutsch ist sehr rostig. Ich habe Angst und bin besorgt uber dieses Kurs. Ich will mein Bestes zugeben. Ich glaube Deutsch ist wichtig fur mich weil Deutschland ist mein Geburtsland. Ich möchte am Deutshcland zuruck. Ich hoffe ich besser Deutsch dann kann.*
>
> My first language, English, is also my best. I completed German 202 in community college but that was in 2010. My German is very rusty. I am afraid and worried about this class. I want to do my best. I believe German is important for me because Germany is my birth country. I would like to go back to Germany. I hope that I will be better at German then.

While Jamie was immediately upfront and proactive about having fears and concerns and began meeting with the instructors of the course on a regular basis, it was not until the gaming unit that there was a noticeable change in Jamie's classroom participation and demeanor. At the beginning of the gaming unit, students completed an online gamer psychology test (Bartle test) to determine their "gamer DNA" and reflected on the results in an audio recording. In the recording, Jamie, who had prior gaming experience, grappled with the results:

> *Ach so! Ich bin ein Killer mit 80% im Killer und 60% im Entdecker. Killer scheint angstlich. „Hallo, ich bin [Jamie]. Ich heiße [Jamie] und ich bin ein Killer." Das ist vielleicht nicht gut für Partys. Aber nach der Namen, ich mag das, die Idee. Unter Killer sagt es die ist ich strebe nach Wettbewerb, Wettkampf und kämpfen mit anderen Spielern. [. . .]. Es ist ok. Ich fuhle mich es ist gut, weil ohne Wettbewerb und ohne Kampfe mit andere Leute, ich werde nicht alles besser als ich kann sein. So das ist zutreffend. Ich freue mich am besten, wenn ich kampfe mit anderen.* (Our transcription of audio recording—missing Umlauts denote Jamie's pronunciation)
>
> Well! I am a killer, with 80% killer and 60% discoverer. Killer seems scary. "Hello, I'm Jamie. My name is Jamie and I am a killer". That is maybe not good for parties. But except the name, I like the idea. Under "Killer" it says that I strive for challenge, competition and battling with other players. [. . .] It is ok. I feel that it is good because without competition and without competing with other people, I won't be better than I can be. So that is accurate. I am the happiest when I compete with others.

Jamie is ostensibly talking about computer games here—first mentioning the categories that were identified through the Bartle test and then creating an imagined scenario, playing on the seeming scariness of being labeled a "killer" and the related lack of acceptance or belonging that someone who has been labeled as such, as an extreme outsider, may encounter in real-life scenarios or in the gaming world. Throughout the three semesters of implementation, killer was a category that only rarely populated, indicating the uniqueness of participants and learners who identified with it. Jamie, however, reflects on the fact that it is just a label and that when one looks beyond that, at the description and characteristics of the so-called killer, it becomes less scary and a role in which someone who enjoys competition can revel. This reflects a general disposition or tendency to thrive in the face of (symbolic) struggle when taking on a more contested role or position.

After determining their gamer DNA, students were provided a list of free online browser games (see Appendix B), with brief descriptions, and they tested three of their choices in class, taking notes on their reactions. They then formed groups based on their game preferences. Jamie selected the game *Shakes and Fidget* (S&F)[4] and expressed explicitly in a Wikispaces post that he chose this game because of the options for personalization:

> *Man konnte den Avatar in diese Spiel viel personalisiern. [. . .] Personalisierung ist ein Grund ich hatte diesen Spiel wählt. Mehr zu personalisieren gibt mir mehr Interesse in Spiel.*
> You could personalize the Avatar in this game a lot. [. . .] Personalization is a reason why I chose this game. More to personalize gives me more interest in the game.

Jamie's interest in the possibilities of personalization positioned him in this early reflection as an experienced gamer who has clear preferences and knowledge of the affordances of different games.

Jamie ended up in a gaming group with five other students who chose to play S&F, four of whom consented to be included in the current study; they were Adrian, one of the linguistically weakest learners in the class, and Dakota, Bailey, and Tracey—three of the most linguistically proficient students in the class (who also had the three highest grades). Dakota had completed the full four-semester progression of the basic language program at the same university as well as a four-week intensive study abroad program in Germany the summer prior to the course; Bailey was a freshman with six years of high school German experience and had spent four weeks one summer in Germany living with a host family; and Tracey had completed two years of German in high school and three semesters at the university, had been to Germany multiple times in the past, had family in Germany, and her mother spoke German. This group is representative of the varying language learning backgrounds, interests, and motivations of the learners.

---

[4] Shakes and Fidget is a browser game inspired by a comic. Players can create their own character, choose from eight nations, and complete quests. http://www.sfgame.de/

Although Jamie expressed enthusiasm throughout the gaming unit, his participation was somewhat selective in that he only completed four of the seven required gaming logs. However, those posts indicate Jamie's developing sense of belonging, purpose, expertise, as well as his tendency to seek out contact zones beyond the unit requirements. As he described in the first gaming log entry, Jamie took the initiative of creating a guild and inviting the other S&F members to join:

> *Ich hatte eine Gilde gegruenden!! [. . .] Bailey ist jetzt in die Gilde und wir haben der anderen Spieleren eingeladen. Hoffenlich sie werden in der Gilde teilnehmen.*
> I founded a guild! [. . .] Bailey is in the guild now and we invited the other players. Hopefully they will participate in the guild.

While Jamie was initially concerned about whether or not the other members would join and participate in the guild, it was through this act that Jamie became the leader for the S&F gamers. In the responses to this post, five other students expressed excitement and gratitude about participating in the guild. The first reply was from Dakota, who was in general not a fan of digital games and quite vocal in the gaming log about lacking interest in S&F specifically. Dakota joined the guild and wrote:

> *Danke für die Einladung! Ihr seid so nett. Ich habe keine Ahnung, was ich im Spiel tun, aber mindestens bin ich in einer Gilde.*
> Thanks for the invitation! You all are so nice. I have no idea what I'm doing in the game but at least I am in a guild.

Dakota's admitted lack of gaming experience and interest provided Jamie, who struggled linguistically and academically, an opportunity to assume an expert role that had otherwise not been available in class. The other students recognized this role, as demonstrated in a later exchange, in which members suggested designing a coat of arms for their group. It was quickly agreed that Jamie, as their guild founder and leader, would need to approve it, as shown below in the exchange between Tracey and Bailey, which were comments on Jamie's first post on the Wikispaces:

> Tracey: *Haben wir ein Offizielles Wappen? Es ist anders jede Zeit ich sehe es. Ich wird eine gute Wappen machen.*
> Do we have an official coat of arms? It is different every time I see it. I will make a good coat of arms.
>
> Bailey: *Ja [Tracey], ich will ein anderes Wappen haben, aber wie? Ich glaube, dass man ein Gildenwappen nur vorschlagen kann. Vielleicht musst [Jamie] das Guldenwappen akzeptieren.*

> Yes Tracey, I want to have another coat of arms, but how? I believe that you can only suggest a guild coat of arms. Maybe Jamie has to accept the guild coat of arms.

Jamie did not ever respond to this exchange, so there must have been either an in-game chat or in-person conversation regarding the coat of arms, because in the gaming log from day five Jamie wrote:

> *In andern Nachrichten, meine Gilde hat jetzt eine neue Wappe. Die Gildemitglieder entworfen die Wappe und ich, als Gildechef, hatte es genehmigen.*
> In other news, my guild now has a new coat of arms. The guild members designed the coat of arms and I, as guild boss, approved it.

In addition to acknowledging his position as guild boss, Jamie integrated the identity, which had been revealed by—or perhaps assigned by—the gamer DNA test taken at the start of the unit. Jamie's fourth and final game log entry reported an unfortunate in-game battle event:

> *Heute musste ich mit einem Babyelefant gekämpft. Das war zu mich traurig. Der Babyelefant sieht so truarig und süß. Ich bin ein Tier, warum hat das passiert? Muss ich in endlos Gewalt für immer legen? Wie mehr muss ich toten um OK zu sein? Wie viel ist genug?*
> Today I had to fight a baby elephant. That was sad for me. The baby elephant looks so sad and cute. I am an animal, why did that happen? Must I lie in eternal violence forever? How much more must I kill to be OK? How much is enough?

Here Jamie seems to take on the storyline of killer quite literally, by projecting a persona in the game who is doomed to eternal violence yet plagued with remorse. In addition to the gaming log, students were asked to identify key vocabulary words or phrases from the game that they would like to remember. Jamie deviated from the task slightly by choosing two words that were not directly from the game but that were personally relevant to the event described in the log above. They were (1) *Tierqüalerei* (animal cruelty), which Jamie defined as "Wenn man ist grausam gegen tieren" ("When one is cruel to animals"), and (2) *endlos Traurigkeit* (eternal sadness), which was defined as "Wie ich fuhl jetzt" ("How I feel now"). One of only two screenshots that Jamie posted to the class discussion forum was of the battle with the baby elephant and included the comment "sadness without end." Through the context provided by the game, Jamie converted a vocabulary task into an opportunity to extend the storyline initiated by the gamer DNA test, subordinating the task to the imagined world.

During some of the tasks, students were deliberately pointed toward functions of the game and spaces affiliated with the game that would enable them to interact with other players outside of the classroom. Based on the second game log from the fourth day of the unit, it is clear that Jamie had taken initiative to explore these spaces without being asked to do so. In a post titled "Cell phone app," he wrote:

> *Gab es in Spiel ein App fuer Handy! Jetzt kann ich Stadtwache jeden Stunden machen. Das App notifiziert mich wann Stadtwache ist Fertig und ich kann nocheinmal Stadwache machen. Mehr Geld fuer mich meint mehr Geld fuer der Gilde! In Play Store gab es eine Kritik auf Deutsch. Der Kritiker ist nicht Satt mit den App. Schreibt er:* . . .
> There was an app for cell phones in the game! Now I can do city watch every hour. The app notifies me when the city watch is ready and I can do the city watch again. More money for me means more money for the guild! In the Play Store there was a critique in German. The critic was not content with the app. He writes: . . .

Jamie first continued the storyline in which he as the guild boss was responsible for the success of the group, but in the final sentence, he shifted position to game user. Jamie then included the 93-word critique of the S&F app, concluding with his assessment:

> *Naturlich Ich stimme nicht zu. Das App ist nicht als gut als PC Spiel aber man kann benutzt das App wenn man hat keiner Computer.*
> Of course I do not agree. The app is not as good as the PC game but you can use the app when you don't have a computer.

By seeking out the public forum, Jamie revealed a sense of belonging to the larger gaming community. While Jamie did not actively participate in the public game forum—for example, by posting a comment, where the critic and others could have read it—by venturing out of the familiarity of the game and group's Wikispaces, Jamie took a step further into the broader digital world. This tendency to participate beyond the class community was unique. Although Jamie's group was the most active in the class, with a total of 192 posts and comments to the class Wikispaces forums from all members, the other students seemed to prefer the sense of security within their own created community. Shakes and Fidget included not only a chat function for guild members but also the option of sending letters to other guilds; however, in an instructor-prompted discussion about opportunities for interaction within the game, the group members were resistant to this idea, as seen in the following exchange from the group's Wikispaces:

> Tracey: *Wir haben eine Gilde und koennen miteinander chatten in der gilde. Es gibt keine Weltchat, aber wir koennen ein andere Leute in der Ehrenhalle finden und Briefe miteinander schreiben, aber das ist zu viel arbeit.*

We have a guild and can chat with one another in the guild. There is no global chat but we can find other people in the hall of honor and write letters to each other, but that is too much work.

Bailey: *Wir können nur mit anderen Mitgliedern von der Gilde chatten. Es gibt kein globales Chatbox aber wir können Briefe an andere Leute schicken. Ich habe nicht mit einer anderen Person sprechen, ausser meiner Gilde.*

We can only chat with other members of the guild. There is no global chat box but we can send letters to other people. I haven't spoken to another person outside of my guild.

In response to this, two of the other group members discussed the awkwardness of sending a letter to a stranger, concluding that they would not want to do so. This exchange among Jamie's group members demonstrates that while students were enthusiastic about the possibility to interact more with their classmates (the local community), this group of learners did not interact with the larger group of German speakers playing the game. In Jamie's case, the incorporation of digital games and gaming spaces enabled a transformation from "newbie" at the university and in the German language to expert gamer. Jamie's struggle to reposition himself was seemingly alleviated by the ways in which the gaming unit encouraged exploration and playfulness, validated prior experiences and knowledge as an avid gamer, and allowed for sociability within the comfortable space of in-class discussion forums. Jamie thus exemplifies a learner who was able to "develop a sense of voice and purpose specific to a domain or community" (Bass & Elmendorf, n.d.). The community was largely defined as the guild, while interactions with the broader community of German-speaking gamers remained limited. In an interesting coda to the story, Jamie continued in the German program, becoming one of the strongest students and has since decided to pursue graduate work in German studies.

Case Study 2: "I Would Rather Read an Entire Book": Resistant Positioning vis-à-vis Online Discussion Spaces

The digital communities (*digitale Gemeinschaften*) project was piloted in the fall of 2015. Instead of a self-contained unit, the project was designed to be completed in steps across the first 12 weeks of class. The five-day per week class met once every week in the computer lab, where students worked on tasks designed to connect their forays into digital communities with other course readings, discussions, and writing tasks. One of the key objectives was to give students regular opportunities to compare and apply what they were learning about particular genres and linguistic styles within an active community of users. By focusing more on an active forum and shifting the engagement away from a singular type of activity (gaming), the instructors and Language Program Director hoped that more students would take advantage of the interactive affordances of digital media than they had in prior semesters.

On the first day of the digital communities unit, students were asked what they associated with the word "community." They then brainstormed as a class general types of digital communities or platforms for social interaction in which they or their peers participate.

Based on that list, students self-selected a topic of interest to them and were grouped off accordingly. The class of 22 students was thus divided into four groups—one focusing on music, one on literature and film, and one on politics (which was later divided into two groups, because of the size). The students were then given time in class on this same day to find online communities devoted to these interests, which they would be interested in getting to know and potentially participating within. At the end of class, the students compiled a list of potential online spaces. Each of the groups included Reddit discussion threads as a potential forum and listed a specific website: the online version of the magazine *Der Spiegel* for the politics group, a site called DJ Forum for the music group, and Fanfiction.de for the literature and film group.

In these small groups, students met in and out of class over the following 11 weeks to complete a series of tasks designed to move their attention from description and observation to the narration of critical moments experienced while observing the digital community and, finally, to the analysis of the forms of interaction and discourse practices of that community. These mini-ethnographic and sociolinguistic tasks were intended to scaffold the group presentations, which they delivered in the 12th week of the project. The final assignment related to the digital communities was a position paper written in the form of an editorial in a magazine targeting German language learners, such as the publication *Deutsch perfekt!* Students were instructed to consider whether, why, and how learners should participate in online communities. Each of these assignments is described in greater detail in Appendix C.

In order to analyze some of the key symbolic struggles that arose during this project, we will focus on one student, Jaden, who was a member of one of the politics groups. In terms of linguistic proficiency and academic acumen, Jaden was one of the strongest students in the class, a fact recognized by other students who would playfully maneuver to work with her during in-class group work. Jaden had started German at the university and, in the semester prior to our course, had participated in a short-term study abroad program in Germany together with nearly half of the students in the class. This also created a shared history among some students in the class, creating in- and out-group positions during some moments of in-class discussion and group work. Based on in-class comments made by students there is also some indication that Jaden's position as a "strong student" had already become salient during that four-week study abroad course.

In a survey distributed to all students enrolled in German language classes at the start of the term, Jaden indicated "love of German" and "love of languages" as primary reasons for wanting to learn German.⁵ This affective relationship with the language contrasts with how Jaden positioned herself in a linguistic autobiography written in the first week of our course. The one-page account opens with a summary of the courses Jaden had taken and a list of the study abroad scholarships she had received. In a lengthier paragraph spanning about one-third of the page, Jaden then discusses the friends she made while in Germany. Referencing interactions with a tandem conversation partner, Jaden states:

> Wir haben manchmal Deutsch zusammen gesprochen. Sie sprecht auch Englisch. Ihr Englisch war besser als mein Deutsch. Also haben wir mehr Englisch gesprochen. Viele deutsche Leute sprechen Englisch. Ich möchte in einem Laboratorium in Deutschland arbeiten also müss ich besser Deutsch sprechen.
>   We sometimes spoke German together. She also speaks English. Her English was better than my German. So, we spoke more English. Many German people speak English. I want to work in a laboratory in Germany so I have to learn to speak better German.

In this autobiography, the choice of German seemed to be more practically oriented rather than simply out of love for the language. Later in the same autobiography, however, Jaden returned to a focus on German as a leisure activity, devoting an entire paragraph to the books she had purchased while in Germany and committed to read. In this way, Jaden positioned herself as a learner who instrumentalized her personal enjoyment of German for practical gain.

When it came time to choose groups, Jaden did not work with the students who were focusing on literature and film but instead opted for politics.⁶ It became clear early in the project that Jaden felt uneasy about being asked to engage with digital communities. In the group forum discussions and in individual journal reflections written over the course of the unit, Jaden expressed two intersecting reasons for this. In reply to a group mate's post in the Wikispaces forum about the relative civility of discussion in the forum *Politik sind wir* (We Are Politics), Jaden wrote:

> *Ja manchmal vergesse ich, dass ich bei dem Internet bin und ich frage mich selbst "Ist jede deutsche Person total verrueckkt oder . . .?" und dann ich atme tief durch und erinnere mich, dass*

---

⁵ This survey was designed by the previous Language Program Director in order to evaluate the experiences and motivations of students taking German. A detailed discussion of the survey and the results prior to 2014 were discussed in Ecke & Ganz (2014).
⁶ Although it is not possible to ascertain this from the data, both instructors speculated that this might have been because of existing friendships—most of Jaden's closest friends in the class who had also been in Germany for the study abroad course were also in this group. The most academically successful students also dominated this group, so the decision may have also been strategic on Jaden's part.

das Internet die Schuld hat. Das Internet ist nicht einen guten Volksvertreter.

Yeah, sometimes I forget that I am in the Internet and I ask myself "Is every German person completely crazy. . .?" And then I breathe deep and remind myself, that the Internet is to blame. The Internet is a not a good representation of people.

Jaden characterizes the Internet not as a set of social spaces or communities of shared interests but as an agent with the ability to misrepresent a collective culture of people. Later, in a post-midterm reflection in which students were asked to reflect on what they had learned in the course thus far, Jaden took the opportunity to express her dissatisfaction with the digital unit:

Ja ich mag Deutsch und ja ich mag digitale Gemeinschaften aber wenn ich Interessen in Weltpolitik habe, dann werde ich bei internationellen Zeitungen stellen. Ich fürchtete mich vor diesem Kurs, als wir die digitale Gemeinschaften forschten.

Yes I like German and yes I like digital communities but if I were interested in world politics then I would go to international newspapers. I feared this course, when we were doing the digital communities.

Jaden's group was in fact working with online discussion forums associated with German news sites, in particular the highly reputable magazine *Der Spiegel*—many of the posts in their Wikispaces forum came directly from news sites. Later in the same reflection she noted:

Ich hätte lieber ein ganzes deutsches Büch gelesen haben—wie in kleinen literarischen Gruppe. Dann hätte ich mich freuen—und auch mehr gelernt.

I would have rather read an entire German book—like in a little literary group. Then I would have been happier—and have learned more.

This comment echoes her reflection from the beginning of the semester in her autobiography when she had described one of her many learning objectives as being able to read more in German, in particular literary texts related to key moments in German history. This is something Jaden reiterated in the final course reflection, when she noted that a short story depicting the crimes of the Holocaust was her favorite text from the class. For Jaden, more traditional literacy objects, such as newspapers and literary texts, are more appropriate representations of a culture and more desirable materials to engage with in the L2 classroom.

In spite of her dislike of the project, Jaden completed all of the related assignments in full. She posted more in the Wikispaces than almost any other student in the class with a total of five original posts and eight replies. It is also worth noting that all of Jaden's posts in the group's Wikispaces forum focused on German responses to the refugee crisis and in particular on comments she viewed as "extremist" or "racist." In their presentation, Jaden's group was particularly attuned to the differences in register between the sites they observed: *Politik sind wir*, a platform for "critical discussions on political topics," and threads devoted to German politics on the social news aggregator Reddit. One of the other group members presented examples from a discussion of Israel in *Politik sind wir* and commented how surprised they were to see such a civil discussion about such a controversial topic, citing examples of polite speech from the excerpt. Jaden and a fellow student co-presented on Reddit discussion forums during their part of the presentation, noting that German users were generally polite and only seemed to get mean (*schlecht*) when someone said something racist or made jokes about "the ugly part of German history," that is, the Holocaust and Nazi Germany. In fulfilling these assignments, Jenna maintained her position as a successful student even as she remained resistant to the idea of participating in the online forums. In other words, even as Jaden was academically succeeding in tasks that asked her to "attend to forum participation as a genre of communicative behaviour" (Hanna & De Nooy, 2003, p. 80), this seemed to decrease rather than increase her desire to participate in these spaces. This was further evidenced during class discussion immediately following the presentations, when Jaden stated if the students wanted to learn about these topics, they could simply read about them in English. Jaden at this point still did not seem to recognize the elements of discourse, perspective, and ways of speaking, which she and her group had analyzed so thoroughly for the in-class presentation, as important for developing literacy in German.

In the final writing assignment, a magazine publication for German language learners on using social media to learn about the language and culture, Jaden departed from what she had posted in the Wikispaces forum and had presented in terms of both thematic focus and stance. Instead of recounting her own experiences in the discussion forums devoted to contemporary German political discourses, Jaden focused on an event in American history, the terrorist attacks of September 11, 2001. In Jaden's article, "Internationalen Außenperspektive von 9/11: Wie die Deutsche Leute diskutieren 9/11 in der Kontexte der Amerikanischen Politik und Krise" ("International Outside Perspectives from 9/11: How the German People Discuss 9/11 in the Contexts of American Politics and Crisis"), she makes a case for intercultural perspectives on historical events, writing:

> *Diese Thema ist so heikel in den USA, dass sie sehr schlecht diskutiert ist—manchmal scheitert die ganze Diskussion wegen starken Emotionen und Perspektiven. Also ist es leichter, wenn Leute von anderen Länder diese Ereignis diskutieren, weil sie ein emotionelle Distanz—und auch so einen größeren und kläreren Ausblick—haben können.*

> This topic is so controversial in the USA, that it is difficult to discuss—sometimes the entire discussion fails due to strong emotions and perspectives. Thus it is easier, when people from other countries discuss this event, because they can have an emotional distance—and thus also a larger and clearer view.

While there is no reference to the discussion forums she engaged with or the Wikispaces forum, through this reflective observation, Jaden implicitly provided an explanation and perhaps even a defense for the vitriol that she had noted between participants in the German forum discussions related to the refugee crisis. Just as German users had not remained composed when discussing those topics, Jaden claimed U.S. Americans are not able to do so when discussing 9/11. In the conclusion of her article, Jaden emphasized the differences in register and ways of speaking about topics when there is more emotional distance:

> Jede Person soll an diesen Foren kommen, um die Deutschen besser zu verstehen. Man wird doch sehen, dass Deutschen bei dem Internet höflich sich betragen.
> Every person should come to these forums, in order to understand the Germans better. One will then see that Germans behave politely in the Internet.

This statement contradicts the opinions Jaden had expressed while doing the digital media unit regarding reading forums. Jaden seems to have had a change of perspective here, in that she has recognized that the discursive indiscretions she had earlier noted in the German discussion forums were in part a consequence of the topic at hand. While the position she took up for herself remained much the same—the external observer soberly looking in on social activity—this is also linked to the ways in which she preferred to participate in German, for example, reading newspapers and literary texts. However, in her final reflection for the course, Jaden was able to understand the position of other learners and what they might have gained from the digital communities unit, commenting that the unit had not been so good for her, but perhaps had been for other students in the class.

Discussion and Implications

In this chapter we have argued that digital media are a means of exploring the complexities of speech as it manifests in social spaces beyond the classroom and of enabling students to position themselves in alternative ways. We also used the two case studies of Jamie and Jaden to highlight some of the symbolic struggles that can emerge when instructors and curriculum designers change the language game, by bringing together instructed contexts and digitally mediated social spaces. Some of the tensions in the classroom and extracurricular social world that arose within Jamie's gaming group, and in particular in Jaden's initial frustrations with the digital communities project, are quite similar to earlier findings from Hanna and De Nooy's (2003, 2009) accounts of learner experiences in online discussion forums, Ware's (2005) research on intercultural email exchanges, and Reinhardt et al.'s (2014) study on digital gaming in instructed language contexts. Each of these studies found that even when given opportunities to interact in social worlds, learners tended to orient toward the participation frameworks of the classroom, often at the expense of meaningful social interaction. These and other studies have established some of the pedagogical principles that undergird the tasks designed for these two units: the Wikispaces forums and in-class collaboration provided opportunities for support from classmates and the instructors while the literacy-oriented tasks facilitated learners' awareness of elements of style and genre. But the cases of Jamie and Jaden pose a different question to curriculum designers who might want to implement digital social media in their language classes—what do we do when students reject or at the very least seem disinterested in (actively) participating? Since active participation in the online forums and other interactional spaces was encouraged but optional, we were able to see how many students were resistant to communicating with interlocutors outside of the class. Requiring students to communicate in online forums seems to us to pose questions of ethics and expertise that Language Program Directors may not want to take on, but does this mean that engaging with these digitally mediated social spaces is not worthwhile? Based on the case studies we have discussed, we argue that the answer is no.

Jamie's case reminds us (thinking again of Gee's theorization of affinity spaces) that non-participation and non-belonging are not equivalent. The imperative to communicate, that is, the legacy of communicative language teaching, is in some ways at odds with the participation structures of many digital spaces, which afford users the ability to lurk or observe in comfortable silence. While Jamie's decision not to post a review online might be viewed as a missed opportunity to engage in the online community, actions such as taking an informed oppositional position vis-à-vis the published game critic and establishing a leadership role in the S&F gaming group enabled Jamie to position himself as a legitimate contributing member of the classroom community—a position that had previously been difficult for him, perhaps because of the self-described "struggling student" comment that emerged in the first several weeks of the semester.

Jaden's case poses questions about what counts as success in a curriculum that connects a multiliteracies focus on design and discourse awareness—abilities in which she excelled—and social pedagogical principles of relevance, which she resisted. Social pedagogies almost inevitably make assumptions about which communicative contexts and communities are relevant to students. Jaden's stated motivations to learn German echo some of what Kubota described in her discussion of language learning as serious leisure activity. This also resonates with the "global economy" model of community found in the *World-Readiness Standards*, in which languages are a source of cultural capital and enrichment to be consumed by learners. Perhaps this helps to explain why studying literature was more compatible with Jaden's view of appropriate texts for classroom-based language learning, which did not extend to digital social spaces. This seemed to result in a disconnect between the symbolic awareness she exhibited in her academic work and her initial perception of the relevance of the digital spaces for her language learning; however, she was later able to expand her understanding of what counts as appropriate and to see the potential for other learners.

One of the advantages of social pedagogies visible in our case study analyses is that it encourages students to entertain, and sometimes create, alternative positions for themselves. For curriculum developers, this has implications for how we measure the successes and failures of activities involving digital social spaces. Echoing Kubota's (2011) answer to a question posed at the end of her essay on language learning as a leisure activity—how could this "contribute to critical reflection and action for social transformation?"—we might consider the "personal benefits [...] which might be vital to [students] at a certain point of their life trajectory" (p. 487). This means making space in our curricula for paths that are not immediately obvious as transformative (see also Leander & Boldt, 2012). In some senses, the units we designed did exactly this by introducing the possibility of new positionings into a curriculum in which students were most often put in the roles of discourse analysts and language learners. At the same time, the literacy-oriented objectives provided a frame that made it easy for a student like Jaden to resist—but not fully deny—other possible positions.

Unpredictability is by definition hard to plan for. One of the most difficult things that social pedagogies ask instructors to do is to let go—to surrender control of carefully designed tasks and curricula. For Language Program Directors who supervise groups of typically novice instructors, working with digital social media can provide a chance to guide teachers in how to develop responsiveness rather than control. Perhaps we should have pushed Jamie more to post a response to the game reviewer online? Perhaps we could have found a way for Jaden to participate in an online reading group instead? While instructors may not always get things right, opening up the walls of the classroom pushes us as educators to let students negotiate our pre-established notions of success, failure, participation, and relevance as they position themselves in ways we may not have imagined.

References

Anderson, B. (1983/2006). *Imagined communities: Reflections on the origin and spread of nationalism* (Revised ed.). London, UK: Verso.

Anderson, K. T. (2009). Applying positioning theory to the analysis of classroom interactions: Mediating micro-identities, macro-kinds, and ideologies of knowing. *Linguistics and Education, 20*(4), 291–310.

Bass, R., & Elmendorf, H. (n.d.). Designing for difficulty: Social pedagogies as a framework for course design. Retrieved from https://blogs.commons.georgetown.edu/bassr/social-pedagogies/#_ftn1

Black, R. W. (2005). Access and affiliation: The literacy and composition practices of English language learners in an online fanfiction community. *Journal of Adolescent & Adult Literacy, 49*(2), 118–128.

Breen, M., & Candlin, C. (1980). The essentials of a communicative curriculum in language teaching. *Applied Linguistics, 1*(2), 89–112.

Byrnes, H., & Sprang, K. (2004). Fostering advanced L2 literacy: A genre-based, cognitive approach. In H. Byrnes & H. H. Maxim (Eds.), *Advanced foreign language learning: A challenge to college programs* (pp. 47–85). Boston, MA: Heinle Thomson.

Canale, M., & Swain, M. (1980). Theoretical bases of communicative approaches to second language teaching and testing. *Applied Linguistics, 1*(1), 1–47.

Cope, B., & Kalantzis, M. (2009). "Multiliteracies": New literacies, new learning. *Pedagogies: An International Journal, 4*(3), 164–195.

Crosbie, V. (2005). Future directions for modern languages in the higher education landscape: An interview with Alison Phipps and Mike Gonzalez. *Intercultural Communication, 5*(3–4), 294–303.

Davies, B., & Harré, R. (1990). Positioning: The discursive production of selves. *Journal for the Theory of Social Behaviour, 20*, 43–63.

Ecke, P., & Ganz, A. (2014). Student analytics and the longitudinal evaluation of language programs. In J. Norris and N. Mills (Eds.), *Innovation and accountability in language program direction* (pp. 62–82). Boston, MA: Cengage Learning.

Gee, J. P. (2005). Semiotic social spaces and affinity spaces: From the age of mythology to today's schools. In D. Barton & K. Tusting (Eds.), *Beyond communities of practice: Language, power and social context* (pp. 214–232). Cambridge, UK: Cambridge University Press.

Hanks, W. (1993). Notes on semantics in linguistic practice. In C. Calhoun & M. Postone (Eds.), *Towards a reflexive sociology: The social theory of Pierre Bourdieu* (pp. 139–155). Oxford, UK: Basil Blackwell.

Hanna, B., & De Nooy, J. (2003). A funny thing happened on the way to the forum. Electronic discussion and language learning. *Language Learning and Technology, 7*(1), 71–85.

Hanna, B., & De Nooy, J. (2009). *Learning language and culture via public Internet discussion forums*. New York, NY: Palgrave Macmillan.

Harré, R., & van Langenhove, L. (1999). *Positioning theory: Moral contexts of intentional action*. Oxford, UK: Blackwell.

Higgs, T. V., & American Council on the Teaching of Foreign Languages. (1984). *Teaching for proficiency, the organizing principle*. Lincolnwood, IL: National Textbook Co.

Holloway, W. (1984). Gender difference and the production of subjectivity. In J. Henriques, W. Hollway, C. Urwin, C. Venn, & V. Walkerdine (Eds.), *Changing the subject: Psychology, social regulation and subjectivity* (pp. 27–263). London, UK: Methuen.

Hymes, D. (1972). Models of the interaction of language and social life. In J. J. Gumperz & D. Hymes (Eds.), *Directions in sociolinguistics: The ethnography of communication* (pp. 35–71). New York, NY: Holt, Rinehart & Winston.

Kern, R. (2000). *Literacy and language teaching*. New York, NY: Oxford University Press.

Kern, R. (2015). *Language, technology, and literacy*. Cambridge, UK: Cambridge University Press.

Kern, R., & Liddicoat, A. J. (2011). Introduction: From the learner to the speaker/social actor. In C. Kramsch, D. Levy, & G. Zarate (Eds.), *Handbook of multilingualism and multiculturalism* (pp. 77–80). Paris, France: Editions des Archives Contemporaines.

Kramsch, C. (1993). *Context and culture in language teaching*. Oxford, UK: Oxford University Press.

Kramsch, C. (2003). *Language acquisition and language socialization: Ecological perspectives*. New York, NY: Bloomsbury.

Kramsch, C. (2011). The symbolic dimensions of the intercultural. *Language Teaching*, *44*(3), 354–367.

Kramsch, C., A'Ness, F., & Lam, E. (2000). Authenticity and authorship in the computer-mediated acquisition of second language literacy. *Language Learning and Technology*, *4*(2), 78–104.

Kramsch, C., & Whiteside, A. (2008). Language ecology in multilingual settings. Towards a theory of symbolic competence. *Applied Linguistics*, *29*(4), 645–671.

Kubota, R. (2011). Learning a foreign language as leisure and consumption: Enjoyment, desire, and the business of eikaiwa. *International Journal of Bilingual Education and Bilingualism*, *14*(4), 473–488.

Lam, E. (2000). Second language literacy and the design of the self: A case study of a teenager writing on the internet. *TESOL Quarterly*, *34*(3), 457–483.

Leander, K., & Boldt, G. (2012). Rereading "A pedagogy of multiliteracies": Bodies, texts, and emergence. *Journal of Literacy Research*, *45*(1), 22–46.

Lotherington, H., & Ronda, N. S. (2014). 2B or not 2B: From pencil to multimodal programming: New frontiers in communicative competencies. In J. P. Guikema & L. Williams (Eds.), *Digital literacies in foreign and second language education* (pp. 9–28). San Marcos, TX: Calico Monograph Series, 12.

Maxim, H. H. (2008). Developing advanced formal language abilities along a genre-based continuum. In S. L. Katz & J. Watzinger-Tharp (Eds.), *Conceptions of L2 grammar: Theoretical approaches and their application in the L2 classroom* (pp. 172–188). Boston, MA: Cengage Learning.

Menard-Warwick, J. (2008). "Because she made beds. Every day." Social positioning, classroom discourse, and language learning. *Applied Linguistics*, *29*(2), 267–289.

National Standards Collaborative Board. (1996). *Standards for foreign language learning: Preparing for the 21st century*. Alexandria, VA: Author.

National Standards Collaborative Board. (2015). *World-readiness standards for learning languages* (4th ed.). Alexandria, VA: Author.

New London Group. (1996). A pedagogy of multiliteracies: Designing social futures. *Harvard Educational Review*, *66*(1), 60–92.

Paesani, K., Allen, H. W., & Dupuy, B. (2016). *A multiliteracies framework for collegiate foreign language teaching*. Upper Saddle River, NJ: Pearson.

Pratt, M. L. (1991). Arts of the contact zone. *Profession*, 33–40.

Reinhardt, J., Warner, C., & Lange, K. (2014). Digital games as practices and texts: New literacies and genres in an L2 German classroom. In J. P. Guikema & L. Williams (Eds.), *Digital literacies in foreign language education: Research, perspectives, and best practices* (pp. 159–177). San Marcos, TX: Calico Monograph Series, 12.

Swaffar, J., Arens, K. M., & Byrnes, H. (1991). *Reading for meaning: An integrated approach to language learning*. Englewood Cliffs, NJ: Prentice-Hall.

Thorne, S. L. (2005). Epistemology, politics, and ethics in sociocultural theory. *Modern Language Journal*, *89*(3), 393–409.

Thorne, S. L. (2008). Transcultural communication in open internet environments and massively multiplayer online games. In S. Magnan (Ed.), *Mediated discourse online* (pp. 305–327). Amsterdam, Netherlands: Benjamins.

Thorne, S. L. (2009). "Community", semiotic flows, and mediated contribution to activity. *Language Teaching*, *42*(1), 81–94.

Thorne, S. L. (2011). Massively semiotic ecologies and L2 development: Gaming cases and issues. In S. Vandercruysse, G. Clarebout, & S. De Wannemacker (Eds.), *Serious games: The challenge* (pp. 18–31). Berlin, Germany: Springer.
Thorne, S. L. (2013). Digital literacies. In M. R. Hawkins (Ed.), *Framing languages and literacies: Socially situated views and perspectives* (pp. 192–218). New York, NY: Routledge.
Thorne, S. L., & Reinhardt, J. (2008). "Bridging activities," new media literacies, and advanced foreign language proficiency. *CALICO Journal, 25*(3), 558–572.
Ware, P. (2005). "Missed communication" in online communication: Tensions in a German-American telecollaboration. *Language Learning and Technology, 9*(2), 64–89.

Appendices

Appendix A: Gaming unit overview

Day	Topic	Related Task(s)
1	Introduction to Gaming	In class: Brainstorm topics related to gaming and choose one for group project
2	Gamer Types & Game Genres	Out of class: Gamer DNA Bartles test and audio reflection
		In class: Test games
3	Games & Identity	Gaming pre-survey
		Out of class: Create an avatar and written reflection
		In class: Form gaming groups; introduce Wikispaces
		Ongoing out of class throughout remainder of unit: Gaming log, vocabulary list, group project, and individual position paper
4	Avatars & Sexism	Out of class: Read article
		In class: Avatars in our games
5	Gaming & Sexism	Out of class: Read one of five articles
		In class: Mini-presentation in small groups on articles; sexism in our games
6	Gaming & Violence	Out of class: Read one of two online articles
		In class: Violence in our games
7	Gaming as community	Out of class: Read article
		In class: Collaboration in our games
8	Language Use in Computer Game Chats	Out of class: Read article
		In class: Chatting in our games
		Bonus: Create German versions of English chatspeak
9	Group Project Work Day	Out of class: Work on project

(Continued)

Day	Topic	Related Task(s)
10	Language Use in Computer Game Forums	Out of class: Read article on the denigration of the German language
		In class: Denigration of the German language in our games
11	Game Genres & Language Use (*Sprechakte*)	In class: Analyzing language use in our games
12	Gaming & Learning	Out of class: Read online article/interview
		In class: Vocabulary quiz (based on gaming group's collaborative vocab list)
13–15	Group Project Presentations	Out of class: Written group project reflection
	Position Paper	Out of class (throughout and after the unit): Three drafts of a position paper pertaining to one of the gaming topics

Appendix B: List of computer games

Participants were provided the following list of games with brief German descriptions and asked to choose three of the games that they found the most interesting:

- Siedler Online: http://www.diesiedleronline.de/de
- Goal United: http://browsergame.goalunited.org/de
- Grepolis: http://de.grepolis.com
- Farmerama: http://www.farmarama.de
- Shakes and Fidget: http://www.sfgame.de/
- Forge of Empires: http://de.forgeofempires.com/

Appendix C: Digital communities project

The following tasks were originally in German and were shared individually on the course management website as they were assigned. Unless otherwise indicated, these activities were conducted in class, which gave students a chance to collaborate in their groups and gave the instructors opportunities to check in with students.

1. WIKISPACES POSTS

Each of these Wikispaces posts was assigned as homework prior to class in the computer lab. During class time, students would work in their groups to share and elaborate on their posts. This was typically supported by questions or metalanguage introduced by the instructor to help them describe and analyze what they saw in the digital communities. At the end of each class, students would briefly share some of their thoughts and findings. These tasks worked to scaffold the formal presentation, which was one of the culminating projects of the unit. Students were asked to write in German as much as possible, but code-switching was allowed and considered appropriate. They were told to aim for around 100 words, but that a clear and coherent contribution was of most value.

Post 1: What are your first impressions?

Post 2: Getting to know your site (description). Who participates in this community? What does participation look like? How do they behave and interact?

Post 3: Which norms, beliefs, values, and interests are represented in your online communities? Do the participants belong to identifiable social groups? How do you know? To what extent are the site and the discussions targeted at a particular audience?

Post 4: Recount a critical moment from the interactions in your digital community, for example, an argument or a misunderstanding or a heated discussion. What happened? What was said? How did other participants react?

Post 5: Copy an interesting dialogue or discussion from your community. (It can be one you took part in or one you observed.) Analyze the interaction. How do people speak? Is the tone formal or informal, friendly or aggressive? What languages are used?

2. GROUP PRESENTATION

You will work with your group to prepare and deliver a presentation about your digital communities. Report on your own experiences and observations and consult additional resources, such as news articles, research reports, and studies.

Consider the following points in your presentation:
- Design of the website: What does it look like? Which function does it offer?
- Participants/Target audience: Which beliefs/values/interests/attitudes are represented and how? Is it to speak of a particular social milieu? Why, for example, is that stated directly on an "About Us" page? In the user profiles? Is the audience indirectly conveyed through choice of topics, word choice, or ways of speaking?
- Critical and exemplary moments: Choose two to three typical or interesting interactions or contributions from the digital community. Analyze these interactions. What do these moments say about the community, the participants, and the topic?
- Your impressions: What do you like about this community? What don't you like?

3. PAPER

In your group, you have explored digital communities in online spaces. In the third and final paper you will report on these communities. Now imagine that you are writing an article for a publication for German learners, for example, *Deutsch*

Perfekt (http://www.deutsch-perfekt.com). It is your task to show what learners could learn from this space about the topic you chose.

Consider the following aspects:
- Which communities did you explore and why did you choose these spaces?
- What were your reactions to the discussions you encountered?
- Which topics were discussed in these online spaces?
- Would you encourage these communities to other German learners who want to learn about this topic and interact with German speakers?

Chapter 9
"What Makes This So Complicated?" On the Value of Disorienting Dilemmas in Language Instruction

Cori Crane, Duke University
Matthias Fingerhuth, University of Vienna
David Huenlich, Institut für Deutsche Sprache

Introduction

On a late Sunday night in November 2015, a student enrolled in an intermediate German course contacted her instructor to express concerns about a game that was to take place in class the following day. In the previous class on Friday, her instructor had introduced *The Unbroken Treaty*, a type of "Reacting to the Past" (RTTP) pedagogy (Carnes, 2014), in which over three two-hour class periods students would take on historical roles in order to learn about German–Comanche relations from 1847 Texas. In her e-mail, the student voiced serious reservations about the role-playing dimension of the game, which included adopting the position of Comanche characters, an activity she saw as inappropriate for non-native students. Further, the student feared that the game would not be taken seriously by her fellow students, some of whom, she noted, had made offensive jokes in response to the game in Friday's class. Over the weekend, the student had researched on her own the history of Texas German settlement in the Comanche territories, contacted a former student from the class who had participated in the game the previous semester to find out more about the activity, and sought counsel from and issued a formal complaint about the game with the university's Campus Climate Response Team. It was clear from the student's e-mail that she had spent a considerable amount of time thinking and talking with others about the content, pedagogy, and implications of the game, even before it had officially begun.

Upon receiving the e-mail, the student's teacher, a graduate student instructor (GSI), forwarded the message[1] on to the Language Program Director (LPD), another instructor of the course, and one of the developers of the game who was not

---
[1] With the student name redacted.

teaching the class at the time, and asked for guidance on how to respond to the student's concerns. Suddenly, this game, which had been played successfully over three previous semesters in multiple class sections, was raised to a new level, one, the LPD reasoned, that the teachers had neither anticipated nor were likely prepared to adequately deal with. After considering the situation—including the issue of time—the LPD wrote to the German instructors and game developers to announce that *The Unbroken Treaty* would be canceled, and in its place, teachers would discuss the content material with their students during the week. The following morning, the LPD consulted with the university's Division of Diversity and Community Engagement (DDCE), and an emergency meeting facilitated by two representatives from this unit was scheduled for the instructors and game developers later that afternoon to talk about the issues raised with the role-play activity and to develop strategies for handling sensitive topics, such as this one, in the classroom. At the meeting, the group agreed to center instruction around one key question: "What makes the game so complicated?" This question would allow students and teachers to develop deeper understanding about the content material by making space for different positions related to the historical event and the role-play itself.

This chapter chronicles the experiences of four participant groups (pedagogical designer, LPD, teacher, and student) involved in this unexpected event to show the multifaceted, interconnected learning opportunities that emanated from a crisis moment. The study draws on transformative learning theory (Johnson, 2015; Mezirow, 1994, 1997), which sees "disorienting dilemmas" as catalysts for reflection and changes in viewpoint and considers how this theoretical framework can contribute to our understanding of social pedagogies (Bass & Elmendorf, 2011). Following a short description of this framework, four perspectives on the events are presented. First, the game designer outlines the learning goals of RTTP (Carnes, 2014) and *The Unbroken Treaty*, including further game development in light of student objections. Second, the LPD explains the programmatic response to the student concerns and reflects on the professional development needs of GSIs who teach integrated language-content courses. Third, the teacher describes how an alternative lesson plan turned the game cancellation into a rich teachable moment. Finally, analysis of audio-recorded interviews conducted with students from the course reveals how guided class discussions allowed certain learners to question their assumptions and consider other viewpoints. Given this multi-perspectival approach, the contribution should be of interest to LPDs and foreign language (FL) teacher educators interested in supporting teachers in handling difficult topics in the classroom.

Transformative Learning in FL Education

Transformative learning is an ideal framework for investigating the type of learning that takes place in social pedagogies where a major outcome pertains to "the cultivation of certain attitudes or dispositions characteristic of adaptive experts, including the ability to work with uncertainty, adapt to ambiguity or even failure, and to feel increasingly comfortable working at the edges of one's competence" (Bass & Elmendorf, 2011, p. 3). As an adult learning theory concerned with changes in perspective, transformative learning sees in moments of discord potential for individual growth. First developed by Jack Mezirow in the 1970s, the model refers to a:

> process by which we transform our taken-for-granted frames of reference [. . .] to make them more inclusive, discriminating, open, emotionally capable of change, and reflective so that they may generate beliefs and opinions that will prove more true or justified to guide action. (Mezirow, 2012, p. 76)

Perspective-shifting thus connotes more than developing deeper understanding (Brookfield, 2000; Cranton & Taylor, 2012). Rather, it involves reflective engagement with new understandings that do not fit into one's established frames of reference. Over the years, Mezirow's model has undergone significant revision, with 10 non-sequential learning processes identified as contributing to perspective transformation:

1. A disorienting dilemma
2. Self-examination with feelings of guilt or shame
3. A critical assessment of epistemic, sociocultural, or psychic assumptions
4. Recognition that one's discontent and the process of transformation are shared and that others have negotiated a similar change
5. Exploration of options for new roles, relationships, and actions
6. Planning a course of action
7. Acquisition of knowledge and skills for implementing one's plans
8. Provisional trying of new roles
9. Building of competence and self-confidence in new roles and relationships
10. A reintegration into one's life on the basis of conditions dictated by one's new perspective (Mezirow, 1991, pp. 168–169).

At the center of the model is the *disorienting dilemma*, a difficult, often discordant encounter that challenges individuals to question their current values and worldviews. In transformative learning pedagogy, dilemmas are viewed as opportunities for growth and transformation, and while difficult to stage—and some might argue they can never be planned—when they do occur, they are often powerful and emotional, leaving a profound effect on the individual.

For transformative learning to occur, an individual must be willing to engage with unfamiliar viewpoints. This can be difficult in practice, as our own *meaning structures* invite in familiar meanings of experience and encourage us to "resist learning anything that does not comfortably fit" our worldview

(Mezirow, 1994, p. 223).[2] Johnson (2015, p. 19), who studied perspective transformation in FL learners, describes a range of options available to adult learners when they encounter views different from their own, including rejecting, adapting, and adopting new understandings:

> New knowledge that is not consistent with [a student's] meaning perspective will suffer one of several fates: (a) It may be discarded, dismissed as an aberration or impossibility and filtered out by the lens of her meaning perspective, (b) the new input may be modified to better fit into the preexisting worldview of the student, interpreted according to the existing meaning perspective or (c) it may cause a conflict between the previous frame of reference and the new information. If this conflict is explored, it can lead to a transformation of the student's perspective.

For instructed learners, experiences both in- and outside the classroom can trigger a disorienting dilemma, with the intensity level of the disorientation itself varying greatly depending on the nature of the situation. Kiely's (2005) distinction between high- and low-intensity cognitive dissonance is useful in understanding how individuals may process incongruent frames of reference differently, leading to different learning outcomes. With low-intensity dissonance, individuals are confronted with new perspectives that, while new and possibly even strange to them, do not fundamentally alter the individuals' frame of reference. With high-intensity dissonance, in contrast, an individual's meaning structures do not work in the situation, and one has to fundamentally rethink one's values and viewpoints. Disorienting dilemmas are not the only source for perspective transformation, however; changes in view can also develop accumulatively over time through a series of related, nondiscordant experiences (Mezirow, 1994).

Critical reflection proves an essential component in transforming meaning structures, as experience alone is not sufficient. Reflection here denotes thinking about experience in relationship to one's assumptions and belief systems, which often involves dialogue with others, especially with those who hold perspectives different from our own. This constructivist approach to learning emphasizes the individual's ability to make meaning out of experience (Cranton & Taylor, 2012) and further suggests that students must be developmentally ready, maybe even have a predisposition toward change and risk-taking, and have a well of prior life experiences to draw on and react to (Taylor, 2009). It can take time for transformative learning to happen—if it does at all—with age and life experience serving as important factors (Baxter Magolda, 2008). Activities that involve extended

---

[2] *Meaning structures* (Mezirow, 1994 p. 223) consist of both *meaning perspectives* ("broad sets of predispositions resulting from psychocultural assumptions which determine the horizons of our expectations") and *meaning schemes* ("constellation[s] of concept, belief, judgment, and feeling which shape a particular interpretation").

dialogue and reflective time to examine one's assumptions in light of new viewpoints have been shown to contribute most to perspective transformation (King, 2000). Teachers can play an important role in holding space for learners in this process, especially in providing students with *"high* challenge and *high* support" as they learn to interrogate and reframe their positions (Taylor & Elias, 2012, p. 155, italics in original). FL instruction can be a particularly productive site for learners to explore complex content matter from multiple perspectives (e.g., Kearney, 2016; Knutson, 2012; Kramsch, 2009, 2011), with the language teacher in a key position to guide students' reflection on disorienting dilemmas as they arise in instruction (Johnson, 2015). Indeed, transformative pedagogies are compatible with leading intercultural language learning models that see the complexities and ambiguities of intercultural communication as a resource to be exploited in the classroom (compare especially Kramsch's [2009] construct of *symbolic competence*, further elaborated in Liddicoat and Scarino's (2013) discussion of dissonance and consonance and Kearney's (2016) notion of *perspective taking*).

How to support teachers and learners in handling difficult topics that represent diverse viewpoints is explored in the following analysis, as different participant responses to a disorienting dilemma across a collegiate FL program are recounted. Each of the four perspectives addresses two central questions: (1) How did the participants (game designer, LPD, teacher, and students) make sense of the game cancellation? and (2) To what extent did participants undergo a shift in perspective through their experience?

Method

With the unplanned cancellation of the game, a unique opportunity to study disorienting dilemmas in FL instruction presented itself. Student data in the form of structured reflections, written surveys, and focus groups were already in the process of being collected as part of a larger research project on perspective-shifting by one of the authors (also LPD). As it became clear that multiple stakeholders (teachers, administrators, and game designers) had been affected by this event, the decision was made to expand the study's scope to include these additional voices. Teachers and game designers were invited to participate, with two participants (Fingerhuth and Huenlich) self-selecting. The first three accounts presented (game designer, LPD, and instructor) were written over the year following the incident, offering first-hand retrospective reports of each role and providing relevant background information on the game's development, its placement within the curriculum, and its instantiation in the course, respectively.

At the end of the fall 2015 semester, following the week-long instruction devoted to Texas German history, written surveys were administered across the four intermediate German classes to capture the extent to which students perceived their views, values, or behavior to have changed through the course. Of the

51 students who completed the questionnaire, five agreed to take part in follow-up focus group interviews conducted by the LPD. Shortly after classes concluded, these five students participated in hour-long interviews that probed changes in the students' perspectives, including those surrounding the role-play game. Three of the interviewed students were in the same section taught by the instructor profiled in this chapter. To provide a complementary student view of the instructor's account, the analysis focuses primarily on the experiences of these three students. Students' survey responses and interview transcripts were analyzed to determine the extent to which the three learners experienced changes in viewpoint. This section employs direct quotes from the interviews to render the students' individual voices as authentically as possible. Following presentation of these four perspectives, a concluding discussion considers how the individual experiences reflect different developmental processes found in Mezirow's (1991) transformative learning framework.

Four Perspectives
A Game Developer's Perspective (Huenlich)

The Unbroken Treaty is a series of intermediate German language lessons designed as a fully contextualized role-playing game set in 19th-century Texas. The game was tested in a week-long version at the University of Texas at Austin between fall 2014 and summer 2015 in several sessions and is currently being revised as a course module for intermediate/advanced classes that can be played over several weeks. The plot underlying the game is based on a historic event. In 1847, the destinies of two peoples intersected at the Texas frontier: German settlers made a peace agreement with the Penateka Comanche tribe in order to found the settlement of Fredericksburg. The agreement continues to attract attention today as it developed despite years of bloodshed between Anglo settlers and the greater Comanche tribe in the 1840s, and as the main signing parties on the German and Comanche side never violated the treaty—making it an unbroken agreement to this day, at least in theory. The point of departure of the game deals with the difficulties of keeping peace under the terms of the contract: Would it be possible for the Germans and the Comanche to live side by side in peace as the document suggests?

The authors of the game included Adams LaBorde and Devon Donohue-Bergeler and myself who all taught German at the University of Texas at Austin until 2015 and had, prior to the development of the game, little to no knowledge of the history behind Fredericksburg.[3] Coming from different gaming communities

---

[3] The department's expert on Texas German history, Jim Kearney, introduced our team to the topic. He had translated the novel *Friedrichsburg* (Strubberg, 2012), an eyewitness account of the events surrounding the treaty and pointed us to non-fictional literature (e.g., Penninger, 1896).

(e.g., board gaming, drama-based instruction, and live-action role-play), we enjoyed playing games in our classes. Recognizing the immense energies our students funneled into video, online, and board games, we set out to create a role-playing game with an engaging plot, fascinating characters, and thought-provoking rules and hoped it would not only provide suspense and captivating challenges but also offer a context for transformative experiences. Because this was our departure point, we borrowed techniques from RTTP pedagogy that have proven successful in engaging students with serious topics through role-playing. FL teachers have made use of similar techniques in the form of global simulations (GSs) (e.g., Dupuy, 2006; Levine, 2004; Magnin, 2002; Mills & Péron, 2008), where students' adoption of characters can act as a gateway to meaningful engagement with multiple genres and discourses in different sociocultural settings (Michelson & Dupuy, 2014). Engagement with reality, however, differs in that RTTP games spell out victory conditions and playful mechanics for their characters (see later in the chapter), while simulations tend to engage more realistically with a specific task.[4]

Reacting to the past

In 1996, Marc Carnes decided to replace his conventional history lectures with student-led debating sessions in which students assume specific roles and debate historical situations (e.g., Socrates's execution) from their character's intellectual position. Over time, Carnes developed elaborate game sessions with roles and rules eventually arriving at the present shape of RTTP games, that is, full-immersion role-play classes conducted over four to six weeks in which students take the lead, embody historic characters (real or contrived), and—by actively engaging with classical texts—redefine the course of history in the classroom. The built-in game mechanics (e.g., assassination attempts, incarcerations, or temporary abductions of characters) can further alter the outcome of a class. Post-hoc sessions then serve to contrast the classroom with the actual events in history. While one may criticize the partially ahistorical events that are bound to unfold in these classes, Carnes (2014) summarizes the evidence for the pedagogy's positive effects as shown in several studies (e.g., Gorton & Havercroft, 2012; Kelly, 2009; Lightcap, 2009; Stroessner, Beckerman, & Whittaker, 2009); RTTP classes are taken more seriously by students than other courses, and they foster a strong sense of classroom community. Importantly, students leave these courses with a higher capability to take on another person's perspective and show empathy toward others.

For these reasons, we thought presenting the treaty between German settlers and the Penateka Comanche in 1847 as an RTTP-style game offered a crucial social learning experience: by stepping into the shoes of people whom they did not

---

[4] In defining the "reality of function" parameter found in GSs, Levine (2004, p. 27) cites Jones (1984, p. 4): "[t]here is no play—either in a theatrical or in a gaming sense—in a simulation, and if there were, then it would stop being a simulation."

immediately understand, students could try out new behaviors and make mistakes in these situations without serious consequences. Reality, however, presented a different challenge.

Including the Comanche experience

During our first trials of the game, the topic of the Native American characters did not arise as a problem. To my own surprise, several students identified themselves as of Native American descent and expressed great interest in the idea of a game that lent a voice to their own ancestors. One student even reported she had grandparents of Comanche and German descent. This feedback led us to see the presence of Comanche characters in the game as even more important. We subsequently rejected a suggestion by an experienced RTTP teacher to simplify our game by taking out the Native American roles.

While we were aware that the Comanche voices in the game would not be original, we saw it as our job to provide good context and not to write a tight script on what Comanche tribe members in the game would or would not be allowed to say or do. Our hope was that the more students engaged with the materials, the better able they would be in moving past superficial representations. Intriguingly, one of the last free Comanche warriors was an ethnic German from close to Fredericksburg who had been abducted as a young boy. Providing German interviews with a family member of his and with family of other abductees was one of the highlights of the contextualized game materials.

A deeper problem arose as we learned that Texas K-12 curricula are largely silent about the dark chapters of ethnic cleansing in the Lone Star State: by the beginning of the 20th century the Comanche had been practically eliminated from all parts of the state and their forced resettlement in Lawton, Oklahoma, had been completed. These circumstances made our game not only innovative in the way it treated history in a language-teaching context but also made the matter more sensitive than initially anticipated. Having been raised in Germany where the remembrance of the Holocaust is institutionalized and the Shoah is frequently revisited, I was not aware of the lack of reappraisal of the Comanche experience in Texas until late in my engagement with the available materials.

Difficult dialogues and the cancellation of The Unbroken Treaty

The complaints that led to the game's cancellation illuminated new challenges. A student reported that after certain students in a German class had made disturbing racial comments following the game's introduction, other students shared her view that "playing Indian" would be inappropriate.

Carnes (2014) reports similar situations in RTTP games where students deal with roles they deem uncomfortable (e.g., Israeli students embodying Palestinian resistance leaders and Palestinian students taking on the role of Zionists). In one particular instance, an African American student shocked his friends by choosing the character of John Calhoun to figure out "what made Calhoun tick" in order to "move closer to the eye of the hurricane of this nation's legacy of troubled race relations" (Carnes, 2014, p. 220). These dialogues all take place at extreme levels of discomfort. While students may be aware of such conversations, many seem far less aware of the traumatic history they share with Native Americans.

Our group was deeply disappointed when the game was cancelled in response to the elaborate argument the initial student wrote against our work. It appeared to us that our intentions, namely, bringing to life an exceptional counter-narrative to current views of the 19th-century Comanche, were being interpreted in exactly the opposite way. It took time for me to gain distance from this criticism and see its benefits. Today, over a year after the event, we understand two important problems.

First, Native American genocide has not attained the attention it deserves from the society our game addresses. Consequently, of all stakeholders involved, we had spent the most time reading and studying about Comanche history in Texas, and it would have been our job to properly embed the game in a historical framework before it was called off. Structured preparation of all players is now a mandatory part of the game, which ends with a classroom contract in which students acknowledge the difficulties involved in the game.

Games represent different things for different people, the second issue addressed in the contract. For most people the word *game* evokes associations (e.g., diversion, fun) that can be hard to reconcile with serious engagement with a historical topic—let alone with deeply problematic parts of the past. This understanding of games might have contributed to the feeling that cancellation was the safest route when discord appeared. Making students think about their own understanding of games raises the level of awareness for inappropriate behavior in class and strengthens a commitment to the actual historical situation students are engaging with. We hope this will lead to moments of more intense perspective shifts for players of the game.

An LPD's Perspective (Crane)

A year prior to this incident, I had observed David Huenlich stage *The Unbroken Treaty* with his intermediate German class and saw firsthand the unique learning opportunities that this game afforded as learners engaged actively with local history from a German cultural viewpoint while practicing their German meaningfully across different communicative modes. Earlier that semester, David had pitched the game idea to me, and we agreed it would fit well as a final activity in the course situated within the textbook's final chapter on Germans abroad (see Augustyn & Euba, 2015). When I received the e-mail from the concerned student a year later—after three successful runs of the game—I was surprised and uneasy. The student's arguments had given me much to ponder as I found myself now questioning our own pedagogy (e.g., how could I not have seen the obvious complexities inherent in the simulation?) and wondering how the game might be interpreted by different stakeholders, including by those not officially participating in the role-play. As I played out different scenarios and responses in my mind, two major courses of action appeared: to move forward with the game as planned or to cancel it altogether. To drop the game could send a confusing, mixed message about our own stance toward RTTP pedagogy. After all, the students had not actually played the game, and I knew the game developers' intention was to broaden—not limit—cultural understanding about German–Comanche relations. Indeed, this represented my original frame of reference vis-à-vis the game. Yet, to continue *The Unbroken Treaty* would likely mean additional, time-consuming work for the teachers, who were not the game's original authors. Moreover, the serious student concerns could not be ignored.

The seriousness of the situation and the timing of the student's e-mail led me to not move forward with the game as planned. Foremost in my mind was the issue of providing meaningful teacher support at this (literally) eleventh hour. While I felt confident in the instructors' knowledge of the materials, I was concerned they might not have adequate tools to guide what I imagined would be a rather complicated class discussion in which students would have space to express different viewpoints freely and safely. Indeed, the teacher's call for help that accompanied the student's note made me acutely aware that I needed better preparation to support our instructors. Within an hour, I wrote to the four teachers asking them to cancel the game and suggested they adapt the text materials, which students were to have read for homework over the weekend, into a text-based class discussion focused primarily on comprehension and interpretation. I would be in the office at 8 a.m. for anyone who needed help with their lesson plan—well aware all the same that the instructors needed more urgent, hands-on support than simply "being available."

The next morning, I called our university's DDCE office. The director, already informed of the concerns surrounding the game through the formal student complaint filed over the weekend, was ready to help us and offered to facilitate an afternoon meeting with a colleague where the instructors, game developers, and I would try to make sense of the situation and develop strategies for moving forward. In the meantime, I apprised my department chair of the situation and was relieved to receive his support in the decision to cancel the game. We were both on the same page about not putting the GSIs into a classroom situation that they may not be ready to manage given the tremendous sensitivity required in a game whose dynamics had suddenly and quite dramatically shifted.

From my standpoint, this emergency meeting—which lasted two full hours—offered one of the most important learning moments for our group as it gave us space to explore different participant perspectives in the game and see in this crisis situation seeds of a powerful learning experience for our students. During the first hour, we talked about our concerns surrounding the game and its cancellation; all the while, I was aware that my decision made the night before might be disappointing to both designers and teachers, especially given the amount of preparatory work that had already gone into setting up the game. At the meeting, we discussed the difference between intent and impact, as well as the ethics surrounding whose narrative(s) we were telling in the story.[5] Throughout the discussion, we found ourselves repeatedly returning to a central question: "What makes this game so complicated?" Toward the end of the hour, one of the facilitators suggested we use this question, which spoke to both the game's content and its intended pedagogy, as a leitmotif for the remaining lessons. Everyone supported this move, the facilitators and game designers left, and the teachers and I continued to meet for another hour to map out additional discussion questions and strategies to ensure a meaningful experience for all students.

As we got into the intricacies of the lesson plan, the role of English in class discussion became an area of concern. One instructor in particular argued that the new direction of this activity was now detracting from a central goal of the course, learning German. This led to an intense discussion about what we were doing in this intermediate German class, who we were as "language" teachers, and, importantly, what role the target language should play. The consensus we reached was that we could not ignore the urgent issues surrounding the game and needed to provide an environment where students could fully participate. Consequently, we agreed this part of instruction would have to take place in English. That week, I checked in regularly with the teachers and was delighted to hear how well their individual class discussions had gone and to learn of the additional exciting pedagogical work they had produced (see, e.g., Matthias Fingerhuth's contribution in the next section). Far from being a failure, this experience had proved to be a tremendous learning opportunity for many of us.

For me professionally, an important insight gained in the wake of this event was the recognition that as a language teacher educator I needed to better support our instructors, especially GSIs, in handling sensitive and controversial topics in the classroom. The lack of preparation some of the instructors felt—understandably so—in leading and mediating complicated conversations with their students in *The Unbroken Treaty* game underscored for me how my own GSI orientations and teaching methods coursework lacked in this area. Furthermore, I suspected I was not the only LPD who had little experience in training GSIs to manage difficult topics in the classroom and further wondered the extent to which other

---

[5] To help us reflect on the narrator's role in historical storytelling, the facilitators shared the case of Andrea Smith, a controversial scholar of Native American studies, whose misrepresentation as Cherokee prompted public criticism among indigenous female scholars (Various Scholars, 2015).

faculty members felt sufficiently experienced in leading students through highly sensitive, complicated material.[6]

It is worth noting the timing of this incident, which occurred a week before the annual ACTFL conference as I was preparing to present on perspective-shifting within our lower-division curriculum through the lens of transformative learning. The irony of going through a real-life disorienting dilemma in my own program was not lost on me, and throughout the week I found myself thinking about the perspective-shifting in which we (teachers, game developers, students, and administrators) were invited to take part as a result of the student's initial objections. I believe the transformative learning framework enabled me to grasp this sudden and complicated—even uncomfortable—event as an opportunity for further growth. Without that lens, it is quite possible that the situation could have led to feelings of failure and overwhelming stress. While it was certainly not a stress-free situation, the knowledge of disorienting dilemmas as powerful resources for learning about the self helped me gain the perspective I needed to work with and help others around me, as well as understand new aspects to my own program coordination work.

A Teacher's Perspective (Fingerhuth)

The student who had filed the complaint was not in my class and I had not checked my e-mail prior to teaching that Monday morning. Accordingly, I had prepared my German class for what was supposed to happen but never would. The decision to call off the game made sense to me from the perspective of campus politics, though I did not agree with the concerns brought forward. Retrospectively, however, I do believe we could have prepared our students better.

Initially, it was not clear how we would replace the canceled content. One option would have been to just substitute the lesson with content from the book, which addressed German migration in general terms, not specifically related to Texas. Yet, by doing so, we would have missed an opportunity to broaden the students' understanding of German and Texan culture and history. Further, it seemed to me as if such a move might encourage negative speculation on the role-play. Thus, I was pleased when we agreed to center the pedagogy around the incident and the game during the emergency meeting. Much of this meeting was spent explaining the role-play to the DDCE representatives, which yielded for me relevant, though somewhat limited, pedagogical advice for my classroom. Specifically, it was the adoption of ground rules for class discussion that I found most helpful:

---

[6] Such mentorship was all the more important in our specific educational context where the state legislature had recently permitted concealed carry weapons in our classrooms, leading to concerns among faculty and students about the compromised ability to teach sensitive and controversial topics in open dialogue. Viewed from this perspective, the sophisticated skills involved in carefully staging difficult conversations in the classroom can be seen as a core pedagogical survival strategy.

to foster a climate of mutual respect, students were to bring forward their own opinions and perspectives rather than to speak through generalized statements. However, the lessons had to be developed from the ground up with little time, and repurposing the existing materials and exploring new ones was labor-intensive and stressful for me.

After learning about the cancellation, I had communicated the news to my class by e-mail but had not explained the reason for the change of plans or what would happen instead. At the beginning of class, I described the circumstances, avoiding details of the exact concerns the student had voiced against the game, and explained the discussion guidelines mentioned earlier. For our first task, I asked students to consider what aspects of the role-play could have made the game offensive, first individually and then in small group discussions. We then moved to a larger discussion where the entire class could share their ideas. Here, some students found that impersonating a member of a different culture could be indeed problematic. In particular, they argued that resorting to stereotypes or caricaturing when taking on the role of Native Americans could make the game inappropriate or offensive.

As a next step, I directed the students in groups to critically read certain character sheets from the game, briefly introduce their character, and discuss whether the descriptions may potentially be problematic. Among their observations, students found one of the Native American characters portrayed in a negative light, with one particular game mechanic posing a significant potential for conflict: that of Native Americans abducting children from the German settlers, a concern I was able to address in more detail the next class period (see later in the chapter). Following these short presentations, I asked students to compare and contrast the character descriptions with online historical accounts. This yielded different results: they discovered that information on leading figures among the German settlers was readily available, while information on the Comanche figures was sometimes scarce, a discrepancy that revealed uneven research and records in Texas German–Comanche historiography. For individuals who did exist, the class found no strong mismatch between the historical accounts and the game's character descriptions. This research brought up two connected questions at the core of RTTP pedagogy: Can we act as historical figures, and is it appropriate to add fictional elements to a historical setting (Carnes, 2014)? Students seemed to reach the consensus that historical role-playing was not the same as revising history. In this discussion, some students identified their own agency in the game and found that, although the materials seemed appropriate, there was significant potential for portraying the historical events inaccurately or offending through inappropriate behavior.

This brought the first class period to an end. As homework, students would listen to an account of how a child of German settlers was abducted and raised by Comanche and remained strongly influenced by this upbringing until his death after he had integrated back into a non-Native American community. Two days later, we further explored on this basis how appropriate it was to use such events in a game. Some students did not find it problematic, while others felt less at ease about using this mechanic in the game context. In the discussion, we also considered how moral judgments may differ between different cultures: Child abduction from a present-day American perspective is a serious crime; from the perspective of a 19th-century Comanche, however, it could be seen as a legitimate way to grow the community, shedding new light on the question of Native American identity and ethnicity.[7]

This discussion raised students' awareness of different subject positions concerning the treaty and prepared them for further text analysis work in class. Part of the unused preparatory materials for the game consisted of an interview with a historian on the treaty's circumstances and relevance: The treaty was one of integration, not separation, and presented an alternative way of interacting among settlers and Native Americans. Although instances of conflict between the two parties continued, the treaty remained largely respected, showing further that the Comanche were willing to negotiate peace if given a chance. Students additionally listened to a recording of a Comanche Nation member, Charlotte McCurtain, who described how following the 150th anniversary of the treaty in 1996, members of the Comanche Nation celebrated the peace agreement through an annual pow-wow in Fredericksburg till 2011 when the city abruptly ended its support. This suggested that not only academic historiography valued the treaty but it was also remembered as a significant event in the Comanche community.

So what changed for me as a teacher? The incident led me to question the pedagogy we had tried to implement, but ultimately did not alter my view of it. Rather, it changed my experience of American culture as a non-native and of colleges as a part of this culture. I had read and heard much about identity politics in the United States, the case of Rachel Dolezal and others (see Brubaker, 2016), yet I had never been personally affected. Through this incident, American history had suddenly touched my own German class and impacted my understanding of curriculum planning and classroom dynamics. I understand my supervisor's decision to call off the role-play. I wondered how I would have responded and concluded that I would have acted similarly; the threat of public outrage was too real. While remaining sensitive to the potential for offensive content may have always been part of curriculum design and teaching, the events in our program highlighted for me the current importance of this responsibility. Yet to me, the response cannot be to avoid any controversial subject from the start. Instead, teachers and curriculum designers should find ways to make space for students' concerns. The way my

---

[7] The circumstances surrounding Comanche abductions have been explored by Hämäläinen (2008), and in more detail by Rivaya-Martínez (2012). The latter reveals diverse individual patterns ranging from forms of enslavement to far-reaching integration into Comanche society.

class dealt with the incident showed me students are capable of discussing controversial issues and are open to considering different perspectives.

Students' Perspectives

We now explore how students perceived the cancellation of the game and the pedagogies developed in its place through analysis of surveys and interviews, focusing on three students enrolled in the same German class: Katie, Lydia, and John (all pseudonyms).

Students' potential transformative learning moments were first determined using the written surveys. Table 9.1 (Question 11 from the survey) depicts students' responses to 12 possible perspective shifts with which students could

Table 9.1. Changes Reported by Students

Q11: "Here is a list of some changes you may have experienced as a result of learning German this semester. Please check off any that apply to you." (Note: Statements are adapted from King's (1998) Learning Activities Survey.)

	Katie	Lydia	John
1. Something happened that made me question the way I usually act.		x	x
2. Something happened that made me question my ideas about social roles (i.e., how people act/are expected to act).		x	x
3. As I thought about these things, I realized that I did not agree with my previous beliefs or role expectations any more.			
4. Or instead, as I questioned my ideas, I realized I still agreed with my beliefs or role expectations.		x	x
5. I realized that other people also think about their beliefs.		x	x
6. I thought about acting in a different way from my usual beliefs and roles.		x	x
7. I felt uncomfortable with traditional social expectations.			
8. I tried out new roles so that I would become more comfortable or confident in them.			
9. I tried to think of a way to adopt these new ways of acting.			
10. I gathered the information I needed to adopt these new ways of acting.	x		x
11. I began to think about the reactions and feedback I received from my new behavior.			
12. I took action and adopted these new ways of acting.			
13. I do not identify with any of the statements above.			

choose to identify. In the audio-recorded interviews, this question served as a form of stimulated recall to elicit specific examples that would illustrate changes students experienced in or through their German classes.

Changes experienced by two of the three students (Lydia and John) related primarily to questioning and reflecting on one's actions and social roles, as well as others' beliefs. Katie, in contrast, reported only one shift in perspective: that is, seeking out new knowledge. When asked about their thought process as they marked the changes from Question 11, students mentioned cultural topics discussed in class that resonated for them personally: public nudity (Lydia), higher education (Katie), gun control (Lydia), and the Texas German–Comanche game (John, Lydia).

Katie's experience

Katie checked only one item from the list of changes experienced through the course (see Table 9.1), noting in the interview that this change did not relate to the Texas German lesson. While Katie "underst[oo]d why [the game] didn't happen, because someone was offended," she expressed frustration in the class discussions that occurred in its place, particularly in light of assessment issues that surfaced later in a unit test:

> What bothered me was [. . .] what we did in [. . .] the two days we were supposed to do it. [. . .] all we did in class really was discuss if it was really offensive. And we didn't go over the material that much. And so when I took the test, I felt I hadn't been taught it properly. [. . .] I couldn't answer the questions. [. . .] And so I kind of wish that we would have still learned that information in a different way.

The disconnect Katie perceived between her class discussions and the testing on the historical material led her to question the focus of that week's new instructional goals, stating: "I feel like that wasn't what we should have learned."

Lydia's experience

For Lydia, perspective-shifting moments associated with the course referred back to a host of different topics covered (i.e., public nudity, gun control, and the Texas German–Comanche game). In class discussion, Lydia noted how fellow classmates regularly took time to listen to and learn from each other:

> [I]n this class, I've actually had one or two classmates say: "Well, this is what I think and that's what you think, but I don't really understand what you thought. So can you explain it to me?" And then the person explained it and they said: "Oh, okay, well, I don't really believe that still, but can we talk about it a little bit?" And then there was a discussion between the two people. And they were, like: "Okay, I'm not totally convinced yet, but I'll think about it."

This open debate format, which Lydia noted was absent in her other college courses, appears to have been a feature of class discussion cultivated by her instructor throughout the semester, not merely something emerging through the role-play unit. "[W]ith all the information that I had," Lydia reported asking herself after each class discussion, "what was going to be my course of action with swaying to either gun control or no gun control? More modesty or more nudity? Or which way should I sway with the Comanche thing?"

Lydia additionally described how her class analyzed narratives on the game's different historical characters, prompting students to consider how accurately the materials depicted the settler and Comanche roles:

> I think that our class had a really good discussion on it. [. . .] we looked up the characters and then we decided in groups whether or not the character was historically accurate [. . .] we found that there were some parts on it, like the kidnapping of the settlers [. . .] and then the fact that there were some Native American characters that were just completely negatively displayed. And we found that that was a point of contention that could be very, very bad. But then overall we also found that we only looked at five or six characters. And so we didn't know how evenly these positive and negative characters were distributed.

For Lydia, the analysis and discussion provided "a good alternative" to playing the game. At the same time, she suggested such work could have served as strong preparation before participating in the role-play, particularly in communicating a "sense of responsibility with the game" to the students. The class as a whole, Lydia noted, had "all [come] to the agreement that this game [. . .] can go either good or bad because the game is something that is done out of trust."

Lydia not only grasped the concerns surrounding the game ("I understand that someone could be offended by it.") but also expressed disappointment in not playing it ("I was excited to do it, so I was a little bit upset that we ended up not doing it once I ended up learning more about it."). She also reported not experiencing any changes in perspectives on the game, commenting that the social issues were "already really salient in [her] mind right now" through exposure to media.

John's experience

Of the three students, John reported undergoing the most profound perspective shift through the Texas German unit. In explaining his reasons for checking six changes in the survey (see Table 9.1), John noted that the "big role-play game thing" was "at the forefront of [his] mind" for all of them. Indeed, he remarked that the very idea that "this game could be offensive" had "never crossed [his] mind."

John found the alternative instruction in which students discussed "how we felt about [the game], how we thought other people might feel about it, why, and what we could about it" as "very valuable." Through the class discussions surrounding the game's complicated nature, John was able to explore the ethical dimensions of historical role-playing and questioned his own views and actions:

> [A]s a couple of points were kind of brought up from the other side, I started to really try to think about that mindset and think how they might be thinking and why. And so that kind of motivated a lot of this about: If this had continued unchallenged, how would it have gone? And how would *I* have acted in it? How *should* I have acted in it? How *should* I be acting *now*? A lot of those sorts of questions.

Similar to the other interviewed students, John still expressed an interest in wanting to play the game despite understanding the reasons for its cancellation. After weighing different opinions, John returned to the issue of personal responsibility and trust in others as an argument for keeping the role-play, stating that "a lot of us [in the class] would have been respectful and appropriate had we played the game."

Of great interest to John in these class discussions was how Germans might perceive and respond to the role-play situation. "Would it be a big deal?" he asked. "Would it be taken so far, in terms of being cancelled?" For John, such questions were obvious ones to ask, as he reflected on the unique juxtaposition of the two cultures: "because it [the concerns surrounding the game's cancellation] so directly relates to American culture and we're in a German classroom." This self-evident connection, John noted, "really made [him] start to compare how this would be received in a German classroom," and he wondered what his instructor as a native German thought about the series of events, especially in light of current critical issues on race in the United States:

> Because here in America, you know, especially anything racial right now is a really big deal. And it's very curious to me how that is in Germany and how it's been in Germany. Like, has it ever been an issue like it's been here?

Importantly, through this experience John recognized that certain issues might be perceived and felt differently by different groups of people:

> And so then I realized, even though I feel like it's not an offensive game, I should still be mindful of whether or not other people feel it offensive, especially if I go to another country, like say Germany. I'm not going to be 100% aware of what is and what is not offensive. [. . .] It just made me realize that I need to be more conscientious about things as I go into them, in terms of how other people think, especially when it comes to other cultures where it's very different from how *I* was raised. So that was a really big thing, was the discussion prompted by the cancellation of the game.

John's words reveal not only an awareness of diverse culturally based values potentially different from his own but also an ability to see the relevance of this insight for future intercultural contexts that involve interacting with people from the target language culture.

Student learning and perspective-shifting

All three students expressed the desire to have still played the game, despite understanding the complications that led to its cancellation. However, the class discussions appear to have impacted them in different ways. While Katie felt they prevented students from learning the "real" content, ultimately reflected in the testing materials for the unit, Lydia and John found the discussions providing important space for students to exchange differing viewpoints. For Lydia, students' willingness to listen to each other was a regular feature of class discussion in the course throughout the semester. She noted that in the Texas German–Comanche discussion this dialogue was supported by the alternative text analysis activities in which students interrogated the game materials by questioning the depiction and representativeness of certain historical figures. For John, the two class periods allowed students to openly engage in dialogue, "bouncing ideas off of each other and getting somewhere." Overall, both John and Lydia described their class environment in positive, respectful terms, even when "people had pretty firm opinions," as John noted.

The three students responded differently to the game cancellation. Unlike Katie, Lydia and John appear to have experienced shifts in perspective. Both Lydia and John acknowledged the different viewpoints expressed in their class and talked about the importance of maintaining respect and responsibility in playing a game that takes on difficult histories of marginalized communities. For John, in particular, who explicitly stated that the game's offensive potential had never occurred to him before, the events seem to have presented him with a real disorienting dilemma, one that he accepted as an opportunity to question his own beliefs and (possible) actions, as well as those around him.

The classroom experiences described here present a relatively optimistic picture of a highly sensitive situation that despite well-intentioned efforts could have turned out much differently. Amy (a pseudonym) was also interviewed for the study and was in the one German section where the conflict surrounding the game initially erupted. During the interview, she talked at length about the difficult interpersonal dynamics within her German class, leading her to believe that "there [was] a great possibility that it wouldn't be a neutral role-play." In their class discussion, Amy lamented that her classmates held on to their own opinions and "no one really changed their viewpoint." Instead, discussion surrounding the game "got really personal really fast" and "everyone just kind of talked at each other." While this experience represents the view of just one class participant and more information about the instructional context is needed to understand the specific dynamics at play, it raises an important question regarding the level of teacher support needed in successfully facilitating difficult conversations, especially in cases where classroom dynamics might impede an instructor's ability to go deeper on challenging topics (for a similar discussion, see Kramsch's (2015) account of native language instructors who expressed reluctance in presenting certain cultural topics and perspectives with their FL learners).

Discussion

Interconnected Disorienting Dilemmas

Applying a collective lens to these different participant experiences, it becomes clear that the initial disorienting dilemma regarding the ethics surrounding the game ignited multiple, other disorienting dilemmas for the various participants involved: from the LPD's dilemma of how best to support the teachers in this process, to the dilemma surrounding the game cancellation itself, which impacted all connected to the German classes, to the teachers' dilemma in developing sound pedagogy that would thoughtfully respond to the concerns voiced. Additionally, new questions arose in professional dialogues that extended well beyond the program: What does it mean to teach a foreign language and culture? How can we support teachers in handling difficult dialogues? How should we assess deep learning from social pedagogies like RTTP that may not easily map onto traditional testing tools? In this way, the student's voice from the initial e-mail opened the door to a cascade of related dissonant experiences felt by key participants.

Critical Reflection and Perspective-Shifting

As the participant accounts show, these individuals responded to the dissonances in both similar and unique ways that reflect different aspects of Mezirow's processes of perspective transformation. Disappointment at the news of the game's cancellation was felt by all, including the game developers whose frame of reference regarding the game's goals collided with a frame of reference (as represented in the student's e-mail) focused on the positionality of certain participant roles within the game. The very concerns brought up by the student clashed with the game developers' intention to help learners develop understanding for new perspectives on Texas German history—an explicit goal of *The Unbroken Treaty* game and a cornerstone of RTTP pedagogy. This discord, however, spurred the game developers to reassess their own assumptions and integrate awareness of the game's complexity into role-play preparation through a set of concrete actions. In particular, the development of a contract for students and teachers to build understanding of these issues before they enter the game world would raise awareness while expanding the potential for deep perspective-shifting among the game participants.

Critical assessment of assumptions regarding the game happened on many levels, and multiple stakeholders beyond the game developers acknowledged that the situation caused them to see the game's potential to offend. In their reevaluation of the role-play, many individuals tried on new perspectives regarding the game, even if some eventually returned to earlier positions.

The LPD and teachers' assumptions about the game—particularly regarding the responsibility required of its participants—were challenged through this experience, which led to a number of actions that involved not only *responding to* the concerned voices but also *making space for* those voices in moving forward. For the LPD, perspective-shifting centered largely around the expansion of her coordinator role, as she realized that GSIs needed more sophisticated tools in setting up social pedagogies and supporting class discussions. Additionally, she became acutely aware that "participants" involved in the game existed beyond the current classroom walls and that any response to the issues raised against the game would have to be sensitive to that fact. The LPD's series of actions at this time thus represented attempts to acknowledge these different viewpoints and hold space for open dialogue.

Critical reflection for the teacher could be seen in the questions surrounding the ethics of the game and the decision to cancel it. His account, including the pedagogical actions described, showed a new awareness for the high level of responsibility teachers and programs carry in staging social pedagogies and a recognition that, when presented with the task, students can handle this work sensitively in the classroom. To maximize student involvement in the discussion, the teacher introduced ground rules for class discussion and developed lessons in which students would compare different perspectives in Texas German–Comanche history and contextualize these viewpoints in the game. A major theme seen across all participants' narratives is an attempt to empathize with others, including displaying an understanding of decisions made at the programmatic level.

The three student accounts remind us that perspective transformation is highly individualized and cannot happen without certain conditions in place, including the individual's developmental readiness to engage with one's assumptions. Two of the students, John and Lydia, explicitly mentioned actively trying to adopt the point of view of those offended by the role-play during class discussion. John, especially, went so far as to question his own responsibility in the game and to wonder how individuals from his class as well as those from a different culture might have responded had the game been played. Above all, John exhibited not only an understanding that viewpoints and attitudes may clash when individuals do not share the same cultural values but also a sensitivity for what this could mean for future interpersonal dynamics.

While perspective transformation is a well-established goal within FL education (see, for example, Byram, 1997; Kearney, 2016; Liddicoat & Scarino, 2013), FL learners are not always immediately aware of its importance in language study.

Johnson's (2015) qualitative study on the experiences of beginning collegiate FL learners of Spanish revealed a disconnect between what students reported learning ("content and skills that could be reproduced in real-life interactions," p. 94) and what the researcher actually discovered through learning journals and interviews with the students ("grappling with social issues, confronting their own biases or assumptions, or making sense of the world in new ways, " p. 93). This point reflects the situation for Lydia, who reported not experiencing any new viewpoints in her thinking about the game, yet described how critical reading activities in class led her to interrogate the representation of Comanche characters in the game. From a transformative learning perspective, Lydia displayed an ability to critically assess assumptions, although she may not have fully integrated these insights into her meaning perspective. Finally, while Katie reported and displayed no perspective-shifting as a result of the game, it is possible that more critical reflection on the incident may emerge later for her and become part of a series of encounters that contribute to an incremental perspective transformation.

Social Interaction

Many participants noted the role of social interaction in the form of structured and informal conversations as supporting their developing understanding about the different aspects of the game's contents and pedagogy. Kegan's (1994) notion of a "holding environment" in which a teacher, or facilitator, simultaneously supports and challenges individuals as they reframe their position (Taylor & Elias, 2012) reflects in many ways the difficult, yet transformative learning moments that some of the individuals described experiencing in this process. In the classroom, the teacher introduced students to clear discussion guidelines and created tasks that encouraged students to entertain different perspectives on the materials. This echoes King (2000), who found that activities involving sustained dialogue and reflection contributed to English as a Second Language (ESL) learners' perspective transformation. At the program level, the meeting immediately following the game cancellation afforded those involved in administering the pedagogy a crucial safe space to talk about the complexities of the game.

Limitations

Some limitations regarding this study should be acknowledged. First, the analysis presents the experiences of a limited set of individuals whose personal perspectives may not be representative of larger groups. Thus, the study cannot directly account for how other students, instructors, and game developers were impacted by the incident. Similarly, the voices of additional actors involved in this situation—the student who filed the complaint, her teacher, and the university's DDCE office—were not heard in the current study.

While this study takes a multi-perspectival approach from the standpoint of FL pedagogy and teacher education, certain viewpoints are absent in the discussion, including notably the communities represented in the game. Furthermore, discussion of the main participants' positionality in terms of race, class, gender, ethnicity, and other social structures of power goes beyond the scope of the current study. Additional research on how FL teachers and learners can critically reflect on their own power and privilege is, however, urgently needed.

As noted earlier, reflection is a required component of transformative learning. The current study—with its ongoing reflections from the game designer, LPD, and teacher, as well as embedded structured outlets for the participating students in the form of written surveys and interviews—provided participants with extended opportunity to process more deeply their experiences and learning (see also Crane, 2018). Such an acknowledgment reminds us that providing space to reflect on disorienting dilemmas can help support perspective transformation and that critical reflection is often an enduring process.

Social Pedagogies and Language Teacher Education

In describing the learning that resulted from this crisis situation, the study highlights inherent challenges in working with social pedagogies in FL classrooms. Katie's comment about the disconnect in assessment reflects the difficulty in testing students' ability to see and adopt other perspectives. Encouraging students to critically reflect on content and pedagogy requires of teachers' flexibility, openness, and tolerance for the unexpected. As their accounts revealed, all participants' level of responsibility is raised in social pedagogies.

For teacher educators, the study emphasizes the high level of support collegiate instructors require in staging and responding to social pedagogies such as RTTP that involve engagement with multiple perspectives in complex relationships. This holds especially true for pedagogies not originally developed with FL learning in mind. Helping students to process disorienting dilemmas in the classroom is qualitatively different than the traditional "communicative breakdowns" that relate to comprehension or pragmatic failures associated with communicative language teaching. Thus, the type of mentoring needed for GSIs is likely best realized through the concerted work of an active faculty team committed to long-term teacher development. Such a collaborative approach would provide the future professoriate with further perspectives on the value of disorienting dilemmas for FL education.

Acknowledgments

We are grateful to the following individuals for their help with various aspects of this project: Ana Ixchel Rosal, Kristen Hogan, Adams LaBorde, Devon Donohue-Bergeler, Jim Kearney, and, of course, the participating students in this study.

Additionally, this study was generously supported by an ACTFL Research Priorities (Phase III) Grant and a College Research Fellowship with the University of Texas at Austin.

References

Augustyn, P., & Euba, N. (2015). *Stationen: Ein Kursbuch für die Mittelstufe* (3rd ed.). Boston, MA: Cengage Learning.

Bass, R., & Elmendorf, H. (2011). Designing for difficulty: Social pedagogies as a framework for course design. *Teagle Foundation White Paper*. New York, NY: Teagle Foundation. Retrieved from https://blogs.commons.georgetown.edu/bassr/social-pedagogies/#_ftn1/

Baxter Magolda, M. B. (2008). Three elements of self-authorship. *Journal of College Student Development, 49*(4), 269–284.

Brookfield, S. D. (2000). Transformative learning as ideology critique. In J. Mezirow & Associates (Eds.), *Learning as transformation: Critical perspectives on a theory in progress* (pp. 125–148). San Francisco, CA: Jossey-Bass.

Brubaker, R. (2016). The Dolezal affair: Race, gender, and the micropolitics of identity. *Ethnic and Racial Studies, 39*(3), 414–448.

Byram, M. (1997). *Teaching and assessing intercultural communicative competence*. Clevedon, UK: Multilingual Matters.

Carnes, M. C. (2014). *Minds on fire: How role-immersion games transform college*. Cambridge, MA: Harvard University.

Crane, C. (2018). Making connections in beginning language instruction through structured reflection and the World-Readiness Standards for Learning Languages. In P. Urlaub & J. Watzinger-Tharp (Eds.), *The interconnected language curriculum: Critical transitions and interfaces in articulated K-16 contexts* (pp. 51–74). Boston, MA: Heinle.

Cranton, P., & Taylor, E. W. (2012). Transformative learning theory. Seeking a more unified theory. In E. W. Taylor, P. Cranton, & Associates (Eds.), *The handbook of transformative learning. Theory, research, and practice* (pp. 3–20). San Francisco, CA: Jossey-Bass.

Dupuy, B. (2006). *L'Immeuble*: French language and culture teaching and learning through projects in a global simulation. In G. H. Beckett & P. C. Miller (Eds.), *Project-based second and foreign language education: Past, present, and future* (pp. 195–214). Greenwich, CT: Information Age Publishing, Inc.

Gorton, W., & Havercroft, J. (2012). Using historical simulations to teach political theory. *Journal of Political Science Education, 8*(1), 50–68.

Hämäläinen, P. (2008). *The Comanche empire*. New Haven, CT: Yale University.

Johnson, S. M. (2015). *Adult learning in the language classroom*. Buffalo, NY: Multilingual Matters.

Jones, K. (1984). *Simulations in language teaching*. Cambridge, UK: Cambridge University.

Kearney, E. (2016). *Intercultural learning in modern language education. Expanding meaning-making potentials*. Buffalo, NY: Multilingual Matters.

Kegan, R. (1994). *In over our heads. The mental demands of modern life*. Cambridge, MA: Harvard University.

Kelly, K. A. (2009). A yearlong general education course using "Reacting to the Past" pedagogy to explore democratic practice. *International Journal of Learning, 16*(11), 147–156.

Kiely, R. (2005). A transformative learning model for service-learning: A longitudinal case study. *Michigan Journal of Community Service Learning, 12*(1), 5–22.

King, K. P. (1998). *A guide to perspective transformation and learning activities: The Learning Activities Survey*. Philadelphia, PA: Research for Better Schools.

King, K. P. (2000). The adult ESL experience: Facilitating perspective transformation in the classroom. *Adult Basic Education, 10*(2), 69–89.

Knutson, E. (2012). Teaching difficult topics: The example of the Algerian War. *L2 Journal, 4*(1), 83–101.

Kramsch, C. (2009). *The multilingual subject. What foreign language learners say about their experience and why it matters*. Oxford, UK: Oxford University Press.

Kramsch, C. (2011). The symbolic dimensions of the intercultural. *Language Teaching, 44*(3), 354–367.

Kramsch, C. (2015). What can the native language instructor contribute to foreign language education in an era of globalization? *ADFL Bulletin, 43*(2), 88–101.

Levine, G. S. (2004). Global simulation: A student-centered, task-based format for intermediate foreign language courses. *Foreign Language Annals, 37*(1), 26–36.

Liddicoat, A. J., & Scarino, A. (2013). *Intercultural language teaching and learning*. West Sussex, UK: Wiley-Blackwell.

Lightcap, T. (2009). Creating political order: Maintaining student engagement through Reacting to the Past. *PS: Political Science & Politics 42*(1), 175–179.

Magnin, M. C. (2002). An interdisciplinary approach to teaching foreign languages with global and functional simulations. *Simulation & Gaming, 33*(3), 395–399.

Mezirow, J. (1991). *Transformative dimensions of adult learning*. San Francisco, CA: Jossey-Bass.

Mezirow, J. (1994). Understanding transformation theory. *Adult Education Quarterly, 44*(4), 222–232.

Mezirow, J. (1997). Transformative learning: Theory to practice. *New Directions for Adult and Continuing Education, 74*, 5–12.

Mezirow, J. (2012). Learning to think like an adult: Core concepts of transformation theory. In E. W. Taylor, P. Cranton, & Associates (Eds.), *The handbook of transformative learning. Theory, research, and practice* (pp. 73–95). San Francisco, CA: Jossey-Bass.

Michelson, K., & Dupuy, B. (2014). Multi-storied lives: Global simulation as an approach to developing multiliteracies in an intermediate French course. *L2 Journal, 6*(1), 21–49.

Mills, N. A., & Péron, M. (2008). Global simulation and writing self-beliefs of intermediate French students. *ITL-International Journal of Applied Linguistics, 156*, 239–273.

Penninger, R. (1896). *Festausgabe zum 50jährigen Jubiläum der Gründung der Stadt Friedrichsburg* [Commemorative edition on the occasion of the fiftieth anniversary of the founding of Fredericksburg]. Fredericksburg, TX: Robert Penninger.

Rivaya-Martínez, J. (2012). Becoming Comanches: Patterns of captive incorporation into Comanche kinship networks, 1820–1875. In D. W. Adams & C. DeLuzio (Eds.), *On the borders of love and power: Families and kinship in the intercultural American Southwest* (pp. 47–70). Berkeley, CA: University of California.

Stroessner, S. J., Beckerman, L. S., & Whittaker, A. (2009). All the world's a stage? Consequences of a role-playing pedagogy on psychological factors and writing and rhetorical skill in college undergraduates. *Journal of Educational Psychology, 101*(3), 605–620.

Strubberg, F. A. (2012). *Friedrichsburg. Colony of the German Fürstenverein* (J. C. Kearney, trans.). Austin, TX: University of Texas. (Original work published in 1867).

Taylor, E. W. (2009). Fostering transformative learning. In J. Mezirow, E. W. Taylor, & Associates (Eds.), *Transformative learning in practice. Insights from community, workplace, and higher education* (pp. 3–17). San Francisco, CA: Jossey-Bass.

Taylor, K., & Elias, D. (2012). Transformative learning. A developmental perspective. In E. W. Taylor, P. Cranton, & Associates (Eds.), *The handbook of transformative learning. Theory, research, and practice* (pp. 147–161). San Francisco, CA: Jossey-Bass.

Various Scholars. (2015, July 7). Open letter from indigenous women scholars regarding discussions of Andrea Smith. *Indian Country Today*. Retrieved from http://indiancountrytodaymedianetwork.com/2015/07/07/open-letter-indigenous-women-scholars-regarding-discussions-andrea-smith

Part 3
Social Pedagogical Interventions:
A View from the Terrain

Chapter 10
A Socio-Constructivitist Approach to Developing Intercultural Empathy

Isabelle Drewelow, University of Alabama

The field of foreign language learning has increasingly come to emphasize critical awareness of cultural differences to successfully prepare learners for intercultural encounters (M. Byram, 1997; Garrett-Rucks, 2016). Experiencing the complexity and diversity of perspectives engages empathic understanding. As learners come to recognize the situatedness of culture, they can begin to view themselves and others as culturally situated beings (Kearney, 2010). In practice, engaging learners' reflections on the subjective dimension of cultural codes and frames of reference requires moving beyond explicitly comparing differences between cultures (Garrett-Rucks, 2016). To encounter local shared values (Kramsch, 2014), students need to learn to consider the world as it appears to others. This is a necessary first step toward learning to interact respectfully and responsibly across cultures (ACTFL, 2014).

The pedagogical intervention presented in this chapter illustrates an empathy-generating approach articulated around an event that received global exposure: the terrorist attack on the satirical journal *Charlie Hebdo* on January 7, 2015. The learning activities, designed for a third-semester French course (Intermediate level), were guided by the following desired learning outcomes: (1) to recognize that values and frames of reference are culture-bound; (2) to demonstrate awareness of multiple perspectives; (3) to identify historical, social, political, and cultural references tied to the concept of freedom of speech; (4) to appraise and compare perspectives in French and native cultures; and (5) to construct their own viewpoints and interpretations.

I begin the chapter by discussing what motivated the choice of this specific event as the basis for a classroom-based intervention where frames of references can be offered, explored, and reflected upon. Next, I draw on socio-constructivism (Gould, 1996; Su, 2011) and geosemiotics theory (Scollon & Scollon, 2003) to frame the instructional learning approach. To facilitate the adaptation to lower or higher level French (or other language) courses, I provide step-by-step instructions for implementation of the research and creative projects. I then describe how to make use of the sequence for the purpose of training graduate teaching assistants in designing learning activities that encourage interpretation and reflection. The chapter concludes with suggestions for using this pedagogical sequence as a template for further curricular development.

A Perspective-Generating Event

The results of a Brulé Ville et Associés (BVA) Orange iTélé survey published on January 7 and 8, 2016, motivated the development of this pedagogical intervention. One year to the day after the terrorist attack on *Charlie Hebdo*, 1,026 French citizens were polled via phone and the Internet. To the question "Consider the events that occurred a year ago in Paris. Which one of these sentences best represents your position?" 76% responded "Je suis Charlie" (I am Charlie) and 22% "Je ne suis pas Charlie" (I am not Charlie). Forcing respondents to choose between one sentence or the other without offering more nuanced choices may give the impression that freedom of speech trumps empathy toward groups targeted by satire and that there are only two acceptable categories. However, the way in which the dichotomy suggested by the question is perceived, interpreted, and processed will vary based on the point of view from which it is considered. Creating a space in the instructional setting to directly encounter differing "referential and symbolic networks of meaning" (Kearney, 2010, p. 334) can help students grasp the emotional and intellectual dimension of *Charlie Hebdo's* symbolism in the French collective consciousness and the significance of the terrorist attack from differing French perspectives.

Subjectivities and Cultural Understandings of Freedom

An investigation into variations in reactions to the January 2015 attack should begin with a consideration of differences regarding cultural frames of reference related to the conception of freedom. While some rendering of freedom is universal and present across cultures, its mental and physical representations differ, reflecting a culturally situated understanding of the concept. The opportunity to examine and contrast what freedom means for learners and for members of the target culture can generate a new appraisal of a familiar (if perhaps mono-culturally centered) concept. Awareness that freedom may be construed differently can help learners grasp the influence of culture(s) on their own and interlocutors' subjectivity, which "is locked into the historical experience of groups" (Freadman, 2014, p. 368).

Identifying frames of reference that fuel differences can make visible symbolic meanings and myths within a group's collective cultural imagination but may not reveal "power differentials and conflict within and between cultures" (Kramsch, 2009, p. 244). Frames of reference used within a discursive context expose differing interpretations, perceptions, and feelings tied to an individual's subjectivity.

The juxtaposition of multiple points of view, however, is not sufficient to learn to cope with the complexity of constantly shifting reactions and opinions "subject to the continuous 'play' of history, culture and power" (Hall & Hall, 1990, p. 225). K. A. Byram (2011) remarked that "in the absence of targeted consciousness-raising, students may not be aware of, let alone appreciate, the differing perceptions and modes of thought with which the L2 operates" (p. 528). Thus, learners need the opportunity to address their own cultural subjectivity through personal and emotional engagement with (or interactions within) the learning experience. As they move beyond interpretation of others' intentions, learners reenvision their own selves (Kearney, 2010) and are empowered to derive their own meaningful understanding of the contextual use of frames of reference.

Empathy-Building Activities in a Classroom-Based Environment

Fostering the possibility of gaining an emic engagement in the target culture (Knutson, 2006) requires an approach that lets learners both directly observe and share how values, judgments, and mental constructs condition products, practices, and interactions (Freadman, 2014). Kearney (2010) advocates for the conceptualization of the instructional environment as a cultural immersive experience because it creates a space to recognize the self and members of the target culture as "cultural subject rather than cultural object" (Brière, 1986, p. 204). In a classroom-based experiential context learners are social actors, emotionally and intellectually involved in the learning process (Kohonen, 2001). They actively examine and analyze variations in meaning making and as a result are empowered to communicate their own informed interpretation (M. Byram, 2010).

The pedagogical intervention presented in this chapter combines a socio-constructivist approach and geosemiotics theory to create a multisensory classroom-based immersive experience. Investigating how language and signs make meaning in relation to where and when they are physically appearing (Scollon & Scollon, 2003) can transform learners into researchers and discourse analysts. As active participants in the learning process, they activate previous knowledge and experiences to guide themselves in discovering answers through observation, research, and evaluation of cultural frames of reference appearing in signs. Through interpretation, reflection, and expression of points of view, they co-construct new knowledge and gain new insights (Gould, 1996; Su, 2011). With this type of approach to learning, instructors can "learn along with students, relieving them of the role of expert in the culture learning process" (Knutson, 2006, p. 601). This consideration is especially relevant for language program direction because graduate teaching assistants might feel nervous or ill-equipped to engage in teaching culture in this manner (Schulz, 2007).

Digital Mediation Used in the Pedagogical Intervention

A classroom-based cultural immersive experience framed within a socio-constructivist approach suggests the efficacy of collaborative engagement inside and outside the classroom. LinoIt, a visual and text-based digital and interactive bulletin board, creates a multidimensional and multimodal assemblage environment in which learners can decide what information to share and how to find the information (Mitchell, 2016). They give each other access to multiple voices and images to undertake their evaluation of what may be shared, what may be different, and rely on each other's choices and reflections to uncover influences on differences and similarities. Thus, with this tool both learners and instructors co-research and coproduce content. As a result, the learning experience becomes more personally engaging since learners are in charge of choosing the signs and by extension the frames of references to be investigated and analyzed. No LinoIt account is necessary for students, but instructors must create one. It is recommended to keep the canvas private so only students and their instructor can see it.

The Pedagogical Intervention

The pedagogical sequence consists of a series of research-based and interactive activities divided in three phases for a course meeting three times a week during 50 minutes. Project-based assignments ensure continuous student engagement. For the purposes of this chapter, the sequence is presented in English; however, it should be noted that all the material used is in French and the activities are conducted in French.

Phase 1: Recognizing That Values and Frames of Reference Are Culture-Bound

The sequence begins with two main activities. During the first 50-minute session, learners and their instructor consider alternate viewpoints and develop a critical reflection on symbolic meaning making. The first activity invites students to analyze, contrast, and reflect upon the embodiment of freedom in the United States and in France.

Step 1. Organize students in groups of two or three and ask them to list three elements that embody freedom for an American (a prompt projected on the board can offer guidance, showing, for example, an object, monument, person, name, or adjective). Once the lists are complete, each group is invited to share while a student records results on the board.

Step 2. Invite students to observe which elements are the most cited, to give an opportunity to form an awareness of the ideological mapping of the concept.

Step 3. Ask students to do an image search on the Internet using their cell phones, tablets, or computers for "Les symboles de la liberté en France" (Symbols of freedom in France). One of the images that appears is Delacroix's painting of "Liberty leading the people" (La Liberté guidant le peuple). Other images may refer to trees; display Marianne, who embodies the French Republic; or refer to pencils or doves. Have students consider the images resulting from their Internet search and list three possible elements that embody freedom for the French. The lists will most likely produce a reference to the French Republic.

The second activity builds on the first, providing the opportunity for learners to consider the association between freedom and republic.

Step 4. At the end of the first activity discussion, invite students to search the Internet for images of symbols associated with the French Republic and post them to the LinoIt board (prior to the class meeting, instructors will need to create a LinoIt canvas and share the link with students). The board can be projected in the classroom.

Step 5. Once the corpus of images is created, organize students in groups of two or three, and ask them to discuss the following questions based on the images posted:
1. What symbols can you identify across the pictures?
2. How is freedom represented and characterized in these images?
3. How does *liberté* relate to *république*?

Once the groups have finished preparing their answers, a general discussion can ensue with the whole class.

Phase 2: Encountering Multiple Reifications of Freedom of Speech

The next class session focuses on an exploration of French perspectives on freedom of speech. Students and their instructor engage in direct observations and reflections through analysis of photos and signage during the Marche Républicaine (Republican Walk) organized on January 11, 2015. On that day, four million people across France took to the streets to pay tribute to the 17 victims of the January 7 terrorist attack.

Step 1. Start by projecting side by side the Delacroix painting "Liberty leading the people" and two photos that the media have titled "The pencil leading the people" (Le crayon guidant le peuple) taken by the independent photographer Martin Argyroglo and by Reuters Agency photographer Christophe Mahé during the Marche Républicaine.

Both photos echo Delacroix's painting showing a young man brandishing a pencil, the statue "The Triumph of the Republic" depicting the symbolic Marianne, a French flag, and a crowd amassed at the foot of the statue. Ask students to consider the symbols appearing in both photos and to give their opinions of how they see the images connecting.

Step 2. Invite students inside the Marche Républicaine. Ask them to search on the Internet for photos of the demonstration and post on a common LinoIt board three photos where signage (other than the ubiquitous "Je suis Charlie") created by the demonstrators is clearly visible and readable. Students may write under their photo one or two sentences explaining their choices.

Step 3. Once the corpus is assembled, divide students into groups of two or three so they can proceed to analyze the data. To guide the process, the instructor can display the following prompts:
- Identify common elements across the different signage appearing on the LinoIt board. Possibilities:
  – Words
  – Images
  – Symbols
  – Quotes
  – Famous names
- Create categories to classify recurrent appearances
- Look for emerging patterns
- Create themes, based on the ideas expressed

Step 4. Once finished, pair each group with another to compare and refine analysis. Each group is then asked to present a theme and explain how the data support it.

Step 5. End the session with the projection of the following blurb, which summarizes the French conceptualization of freedom of speech:

The right to say, write or print what you want is rooted in the declaration of rights that came with the 1789 French Revolution. However, that freedom of speech ends at defaming, slandering, or inciting to hate others based on their, religion or sex.

Ask students to discuss in their research group the following two questions:

- For many, the journal *Charlie Hebdo* embodies freedom of speech. How?
- Can you really laugh and poke fun at everything?

At the conclusion of this session, invite students to imagine that they participated in the Marche Républicaine and that they decided to make their own sign. What would their sign say?

Phase 3: Constructing Learners' Own Viewpoints

The final class session is designed to prompt students to develop their own informed insights on the topic. By exploring why one-fifth of the population does not feel they are Charlie (results of the BVA Orange iTélé survey poll), students can start unraveling the complexity and diversity of the conceptualization of freedom of speech in contemporary France.

Step 1. Start with a display of students' signs and ask them to identify in groups of two or three choices of words, symbols, and references. Are there patterns emerging from the signs? Invite students to consider the themes appearing in their own signs and to explain their decisions.

Step 2. Project the results of the BVA Orange iTélé survey poll and show a video that France 2 (one of the main French television channels) aired on the evening news on January 12, 2015, the day after the Marche Républicaine. The story reports on some primary school and high school students who did not respect the government mandated minute of silence to pay tribute to the victims. Ask the following questions:
- Based on the news report, how did the students justify their reaction?
- The teacher interviewed states that children in his school have the impression that 50% of the French population is against everything that embodies Muslims.
  – How do they form their impression?
  – Does this impression reflect reality?
  – What is your reaction to this attitude?

This last question connects back to the students' home culture, the United States, offering an additional opportunity to consider and reflect on the similitudes of the issue and how certain issues or concepts, despite apparent cross-cultural applicability, may conceal deep cultural differences. Students may relate the varying opinions expressed in France about the *Charlie Hebdo* attack to, for example, diverse opinions in the United States regarding the Black Lives Matter movement.

Activating Reflections through Assessments

This pedagogical intervention incorporates three assignments introduced at the end of each class session. The objective is to engage personal reflections on the subjectivity of cultural differences throughout the sequence. They can be assembled in a learning portfolio as suggested by Schulz (2007) to document students' journey of discovery. Each component provides an opportunity for personal expression and for reflection on the diversity of symbolic meanings. Engaging their own subjective interpretations encourages students to recognize their own and others' emotional attachment to the meaning of freedom, laying out the foundation for new appreciations to emerge and intercultural empathy to develop.

Assignment 1. At the end of the first class session (Phase 1), students are asked to reflect in a paragraph on how their conception of freedom compares to the French point of view. The objective of this first assignment is to prompt students to make sense of what has been discussed during that first session and to connect these ideas back to their own life.

Assignment 2. Asking students to make their own sign for the Marche Républicaine at the end of the second session (Phase 2) lets them connect directly with the topic by investing more personally. It compels them to voice their own conceptualization of freedom of speech and to encounter alternate understanding informed by differing frames of reference.

Assignment 3. The final assignment asks students to adopt the "identity" of an editorial journalist working for a media outlet and in that role to present opinions, viewpoints, or new insights gained during the explorative classroom activities. In this project, students can further explore potential connections to their own lives initiated in the first assignment. They can develop a multimodal BuzzFeed article with captioned animated .gif pictures (they can use the website giphy.com to find .gifs in several languages or make their own) and commentaries (one to three sentences per image) or a digital presentation with a recording of their own commentaries. The instructor can provide several options to students so they can pursue their own interests. Topics, for example, can include (1) Contrast French and American points of view on freedom, (2) What is l'esprit Charlie? (3) What does freedom of speech mean for the French and for Americans? and (4) To be or not to be Charlie?

The three components should be assigned different weight; the BuzzFeed article (or digital presentation) requiring much more time investment than the paragraph and the demonstration sign. To establish clear expectations for student performance and consistent grading criteria, it is recommended that instructors develop three rubrics (one for each component). The following categories were used in developing the rubric for this pedagogical intervention: content (relevant, elaborate, clear, logical organized); creativity (original, inventive, reflective); visual support (engaging, illustrates content); word choices (vocabulary); language control (grammar); and spelling and punctuation.

Considerations for Language Program Direction

With this pedagogical intervention, Language Program Directors (LPDs) can address both their responsibilities for curriculum design for courses under their supervision (in this case intermediate level) and graduate teaching assistants' professional training. The suggestions provided next demonstrate a potential avenue for preparing graduate teaching assistants to design their own classroom-based cultural immersive experience.

Engaging Graduate Teaching Assistants in Developing the Activities for the Pedagogical Intervention

From the practical standpoint of sequence implementation, scalability, and cross-sectional comparability, it might be tempting for the LPD to deliver the pedagogical intervention as a ready-to-use packet. However, giving teaching assistants the opportunity to collaborate on the design of the teaching material transforms them from consumers/executors to producers of curricular activities. The involvement of all graduate teaching assistants (and not solely the ones who are teaching the third-semester course) in the process establishes a community focused on curriculum building, in which competencies and experiential knowledge of the various members are engaged and valued.

To manage the development of the pedagogical material, I suggest creating four teams. Each team receives an instructor guide presenting the pedagogical sequence, learning outcomes, the steps in each phase, and detailed instructions on how to create a LinoIt account. Three teams are responsible for developing the material necessary to implement each phase. Team 1 creates a student worksheet for Phase 1, a PowerPoint presentation with prompts for teaching, a handout for assignment 1, and the grading rubric. Team 2 develops the PowerPoint for the lesson, a handout for assignment 2, and the rubric. Team 3 is in charge of the teaching PowerPoint, the student handout for assignment 3, and its rubric. The fourth team's task is to review all the material for consistency and accuracy. To encourage an interactive process facilitating collaboration, peer mentoring, and reflections, all the documents can be stored in a Dropbox folder. Graduate teaching assistants can use the comment function in each document to make edits and offer suggestions.

Involving Graduate Teaching Assistants in Program Articulation and Curricular Expansion

This pedagogical intervention can be used as model and template to develop additional sequences based on other cultural and sociological constructs or major events. Using LinoIt, graduate teaching assistants can submit ideas and indicate the appropriate level (introductory or intermediate) and explain why. Face-to-face brainstorming sessions provide the opportunity to discuss how the suggested constructs and events might fit within the existing curriculum, stimulating reflections on program articulation. Once a selection is agreed upon, graduate teaching assistants can start the process of developing learning outcomes, material, teaching tools, and assessments. Using this type of approach establishes a sense of community within a program, provides firsthand experience in curriculum development, and assists the LPD in creating an intercultural language learning environment.

References

American Council on the Teaching of Foreign Languages (ACTFL). (2014). *Reaching global competence.* Retrieved from https://www.actfl.org/sites/default/files/news/GlobalCompetencePositionStatement0814.pdf

Brière, J.-F. (1986). Cultural understanding through cross-cultural analysis. *The French Review, 60*(2), 203–208.

Byram, K. A. (2011). Using the concept of perspective to integrate cultural, communicative, and form-focused language instruction. *Foreign Language Annals, 44*(3), 525–543.

Byram, M. (1997). *Teaching and assessing intercultural communicative competence.* Clevedon, UK: Multilingual Matters.

Byram, M. (2010). Linguistic and cultural education for bildung and citizenship. *The Modern Language Journal, 94*(2), 317–321.

Freadman, A. (2014). Fragmented memory in the global age: The place of storytelling in modern language curricula. *The Modern Language Journal, 98*(1), 373–385.

Garrett-Rucks, P. (2016). *Intercultural competence in instructed language learning: Bridging theory and practice.* Charlotte, NC: Information Age Publishing.

Gould, J. S. (1996). A constructivist perspective on teaching and learning in the language arts. In C. T. Fosnot (Ed.), *Constructivism: Theory, perspectives, and practice* (pp. 92–102). New York, NY: Teachers College.

Hall, E. T., & Hall, M. R. (1990). *Understanding cultural differences: Keys to success in West Germany, France, and the United States.* Yarmouth, ME: Intercultural Press.

Kearney, E. (2010). Cultural immersion in the foreign language classroom: Some narrative possibilities. *The Modern Language Journal, 94*(2), 332–336.

Knutson, E. M. (2006). Cross cultural awareness for second/foreign language learners. *The Canadian Modern Language Review, 62*(4), 591–610.

Kohonen, V. (2001). Towards experiential foreign language education. In V. Kohonen, R. Jaatinen, P. Kaikkonen, & J. Lehtovaara (Eds.), *Experiential learning in foreign language education* (pp. 8–60). Harlow, UK: Pearson Education.

Kramsch, C. (2009). Third culture and language education. In V. Cook & L. Wei (Eds.), *Contemporary applied linguistics* (Vol. 1, pp. 233–254). London, UK: Continuum.

Kramsch, C. (2014). Teaching foreign languages in an era of globalization: Introduction. *The Modern Language Journal, 98*(1), 296–311.

Mitchell, C. (2016). *Culture, L2 self, and emotion in the digital realm: Developing learners' interest in continuing to study Spanish* (Unpublished doctoral dissertation). University of Alabama, Tuscaloosa, AL.

Schulz, R. (2007). The challenge of assessing cultural understanding in the context of foreign language instruction. *Foreign Language Annals, 40*(1), 9–26.
Scollon, R., & Scollon, S. W. (2003). *Discourses in place: Language in the material world*. New York, NY: Routledge.
Su, Y.-C. (2011). Promoting intercultural understanding and reducing stereotypes: Incorporating the cultural portfolio project into Taiwan's EFL college classes. *Educational Studies, 37*(1), 73–88.

Chapter 11
Of Cookies and Saints: Deconstructing L2 Learners' Myths of the Target Culture

Vincent L. VanderHeijden, University of Texas at Austin

Introduction

Instructors of less commonly taught languages (LCTLs) often face two related challenges concerning the types of students who study their languages. First, some learners, who have little knowledge about the target-language culture (TLC), begin their language learning experience with a certain mythology about what the TLC is. For second language (L2) learners of Dutch, this naiveté may manifest itself in students who imagine the Netherlands as the apotheosis of a progressive society. The second challenge concerns heritage learners, who comprise a significantly high proportion of language classes among LCTLs (Brown, 2009) and who often have a highly idiosyncratic understanding of the TLC as filtered through particular familial relations. Devising a curriculum for this range of experience presents LCTL instructors, in particular, with great opportunities for exploring approaches to cultural learning that focus on developing students' understanding of both their home culture (C1) and the TLC.

This chapter describes how explorations of the relationship between past practices and contemporary products promote deeper understanding among low-Intermediate L2 learners of Dutch. The activities are written for students as intercultural learners (Byram, 1997) for whom integrating cultural newness can be a disorienting experience. To that end, structured reflection (Crane, 2016) stimulates integrative, connection-making work necessary for students to make sense of confounding contemporary issues in the TLC. By directly confronting—with guidance—complex cultural factors, students develop both a more accurate awareness of the TLC and effective tools to later use as independent L2 speakers. I conclude with a discussion of implications for language teacher development and language programs in general.

Conceptual Frameworks

Approaches to learning culture have moved decisively in the past 25 years toward a notion of competency and interaction (Byram, 1997; Deardorff, 2006; MLA Ad Hoc Committee on Foreign Languages, 2007; Rathje, 2007; Risager, 1998), where learners are asked to become more aware of themselves as people with culture. Deep cultural learning of another's cultural perspectives and practices is arguably incomplete without an awareness of one's own cultural positions and prejudices. Byram (2010) speaks of critical reflection as an exercise in becoming aware of one's own cultural filters. Sosulski (2013) proposes transformational learning as a process, similarly reliant on structured reflection that helps students come to terms with dissonances they experience in their learning process: "Long after they have forgotten the verb for 'to interpret,'[...], if they can look back upon their second language learning experiences as a series of transformative moments in which they learned to see the world —and themselves—in different and more nuanced ways, then we will have done well indeed" (p. 91). This dovetails in meaningful ways with the very definition of Bass and Elmendorf's notion of "traits of adaptive expertise" (2012, p. 3), which are flexible, and emphasize interaction and creative learning with application beyond specific courses and contents.

This chapter addresses complex intercultural encounters and my approach is informed on the one hand by Byram's (1997) understanding of Critical Cultural Awareness (*Savoir s'engager*), which reflects an ability to take a critical stance based on products, practices, and perspectives (Byram, 1997) from both the TLC *as well as* one's home culture. It is fundamental to the notion of the intercultural speaker as someone who can mediate cultures to respective audiences. Additionally, it stipulates a thorough understanding of the self as a culturally constructed individual (Byram, Gribkova, & Starkey, 2002).

On the other hand, the approach is also indebted to Sosulski's (2013) work on transformative learning as learning that helps students develop tools and habits of mind to help them negotiate experiences that engender "bewildering difference" (p. 92). Indeed, transformative learning is complementary to critical cultural awareness as it is predicated on the ability to take "a critical stance toward one's own set of assumptions . . . [coupled] . . . with deepened understanding of the structured nature of cultural frames of reference" (p. 93). Both Byram (2010) and Sosulski (2013) encourage reflective practice—structured, critical engagement with one's questions and dissonances—to help students begin to open their perspectives and question their assumptions.

Instructional Context

The Dutch program is located at a large public university in the Southwest. Only two intensive language courses are offered each year: introductory and advanced Dutch. The learning sequences described here occur after approximately 70–90 contact hours, about mid-way through the sequence. Each year 15–20 students complete this program. The most successful students have placed at the B1 level of the Common European Framework of Reference (CEFR) when evaluated in the Netherlands for summer study. Upper-division language study is possible only as independent study. The author, the sole instructor of the language courses, was trained in applied linguistics and German. Students study Dutch for various reasons, with four standing out in particular: personal relationships with Dutch speakers, vocational interests, travel interests, or rapid fulfillment of the university's language requirement.

Pedagogical Focus: Traditional Products with Contemporary Import

The two cultural products examined here serve as touchstones to uniquely difficult aspects of Dutch culture and history: colonialism and race. The lessons presented model strategies of analysis and reflection while maintaining a complementary focus on language learning. Next I provide cursory background on these matters before explicating the learning activities.

Speculaas is a well-known Dutch cookie and provides L2 learners of Dutch with an accessible lesson on contemporary cultural products that connect to particular histories. *Speculaas* has been associated with the winter feast of St. Nicholas since before the 18th century (Kruijswijk & Nesse, 2006), and its mix of spices (i.e., nutmeg, cinnamon, allspice, mace, and ginger) has been featured in *speculaas* recipes for at least four centuries. This time depth is the touchstone into the Netherlands' colonial past: What did it take to procure these ingredients on the other side of the globe in the 17th century? What were the monetary and human costs of 10 grams of nutmeg in the Dutch Golden Age? Or of pepper? Even a cursory reflection on such questions reveals a violent and destructive legacy of the *Verenigde Oostindische Compagnie* (VOC), the corporation with the authority to produce and transport spices among and from what became the Dutch Southeast Asian colonies. To this day, the Dutch "Golden Age" remains a potent cultural trope that glosses over the human and environmental cost of the 17th century's "embarrassment of riches" (Schama, 1987).

The figure of *Zwarte Piet* (Black Pete), the attendant of St. Nicholas, is an even more sensitive flashpoint. The feast of St. Nicholas (*St. Niklaas* or *Sinterklaas*) on December 5 and 6 is arguably the second-most "Dutch" holiday on the calendar just behind King's Day. Indeed, participation in *Sinterklaas* is a performance of nationhood (Jordan, 2014). St. Nicholas's arrival by steamboat in November is a nationally televised event and a daily newscast for children (scripted and highly produced) apprises them of his progress and travails as he wends his way through the country. Stores are flooded with sweets and baked goods, *Sinterklaas* himself visits schools, attended by his many ever helpful *Zwarte Pieten*, songs are sung, presents are bought, and poems are written. *Sinterklaas* season seems to penetrate nearly every corner of the Netherlands.

Zwarte Piet figures with the saint since well before the mid-19th century, when the now-canonical book *Sinterklaas en zijn Knecht* (Schenkman, 1850) was first published (Brienen, 2014). In Schenkman's (1850) tale, *Piet* is an attendant, who makes sure his master has taken note of all good and bad children, rewarding the good with sweets and small gifts and punishing the bad by packing them in sacks to take back to Spain. *Zwarte Piet* is also the "muscle," moving heavy crates of gold and gifts, reminiscent of a valet or footman. This class-based relationship aside, allegations of racist characterizations arise when one is confronted with *Piet's* visual representation. Throughout the 19th century and indeed well into the 20th, *Piet's* depictions came to feature ever more exaggerated features (full, over-red lips, a broad nose, unruly hair, and gold hoop earrings), and his page's costume stabilized (multicolored garments, frilled collar and tam). Because slavery was not dismantled in the Dutch colonies until 1863, 13 years after Schenkman's book, contemporary audiences would have understood *Piet* as St. Nicholas's slave (Brienen, 2014). Even in the 21st century, *Piet* is played by actors in blackface: white actors with black shoe-polish make-up, wigs of curly black hair, reddest-red lipstick, and dressed in stylized pages' costumes.[1]

Despite this challenging imagery, teachers of Dutch cannot ignore the centrality of the *Sinterklaas* holiday (Jordan, 2014) in their courses. To do so would be akin to teachers of American English ignoring the fourth of July. Moreover, heritage speakers in the class will already have their own experiences with these holiday figures, some with more critical distance than others. Yet, teaching the holiday will consistently evoke strong reactions based on America's own violent and contested history of slavery, Jim Crow, minstrelsy, and blackface. Thus, *Sinterklaas* and *Zwarte Piet* become an opportunity to teach students to negotiate simultaneously their personal reactions to such imagery and their learning of the cultural practice in the practitioners' words (Byram, 1997).

Pedagogical Interventions

Each of the two learning sequences has two main instructional goals that situate culture learning as applying to both the TLC and home culture. The first uses authentic materials to build language skills, such as *identify*, *describe*, and *compare*, as appropriate to the level taught. The second goal addresses strategy and skill development on a more intrapersonal level.

---

[1] In the final weeks of the 2017 parliamentary election campaign, the anti-immigrant Dutch Freedom Party proposed national legislation codifying these features of dress and countenance as official *Zwarte Piet* costuming.

Speculaas, the Dutch Golden Age in a Cookie

This unit has two goals and one primary outcome. First, it functions as a demonstration of how the historical past features in contemporary cultural products. It also models one possible way to inquire into the subsurface aspects of such cultural products (though the model's applicability for practices and perspectives is not excluded). The learning outcome is that students acquire an ability to begin making similar inquiries into both the TLC and the C1.

For the purposes of this project, students are presented with a recipe in Dutch and are assigned three tasks to complete at home: (1) identify the English names of the spices; (2) research where these spices grew in the 15th or 16th century; and (3) identify what these spices cost today at both a Dutch supermarket (available online) and a local American one. Such tasks are well within students' language abilities at this point in their studies. Finally, students write a short reflection in English in which they hypothesize what it may have taken to bring these spices from the Southeast Indies to the Netherlands in a preindustrial age of tall ships.

The following class meeting centers on the case of nutmeg, which has a particularly problematic history. Nutmeg grew on only one island in Indonesia, Run Island, which the Dutch acquired from the English in 1667. To maintain its monopoly, the VOC repressed a population uprising, reducing a population of 15,000 people to only 600 (Thring, 2010). The Dutch were not able to hold on to the monopoly in the long term, but their tenure on Run Island serves as an example of the lengths to which the VOC was willing to go in order to control the global trade of just one tropical spice in holiday cookies (though nutmeg's use extended beyond baking).

During class, students collaboratively read two alternate accounts of nutmeg's history. The first includes the effective "depopulation" of Run Island (adapted from a website heavily reliant on primary sources). The second account appeared on the Dutch language *National Geographic* website (Veld, 2014). Scanning activities prompted students to work together to extract factual information first (who, what, where, when), which they organized into a table to facilitate a comparison of the two texts: What information do both texts present? What aspects does only one address? The groups presented their ideas in the large group. Further discussion of such techniques can be found in Swaffar and Arens' (2006) work on the précis. This analysis not only reinforced students' learning but also crucially revealed that the *National Geographic* text omitted any discussion of atrocities. Once students articulated this difference, the instructor prompted them to consider the kinds of texts and their audiences, consistent with multiple literacies approaches to language learning (Kern, 2000; Paesani, Allen, & Dupuy, 2016). Thus, the social space of the classroom is used to allow students to collaboratively extract information, which then informs their emergent understanding.

Finally, students reflected on their original hypotheses. The goal of this reflection—first done individually as written homework—was for learners to consider their ideas about the Netherlands and hold those against an aspect of history unknown to most Americans. They were asked to simply "record" their thinking: What did they know about Dutch colonial history? What did they know about the Dutch spice trade (or the acquisition of Manhattan, for that matter)? How were they reacting to this learning? How should we interpret the author's omission of atrocities in the *National Geographic* article? Finally, students were asked to consider possibly analogous moments of dissonance in U.S. history. The subsequent class session provided the social space for students to engage each other on these reflections.

Reacting to *Zwarte Piet*: Do We See What We Understand?

Whereas engaging with *speculaas* focused students' inquiry on the cultural object external to themselves, an exploration of *Zwarte Piet*, for the reasons elaborated earlier, is a much more personal endeavor. The ability to engage with *Zwarte Piet*'s complexity in a critical way requires that learners begin developing an understanding of themselves as members of a culture. Likewise, critical reflection is a skill that develops over time. To that end, students were assigned three structured reflective writing assignments throughout the semester, which prompt them to think about how they understand culture and how it manifests in their lives. Students were assessed on their ability to tie their thinking to their lived experience, practices, products, and perspectives they have encountered both inside and outside the classroom. They received feedback on the precision with which they engaged the topic in the prompt. As beginning language learners, they answered these prompts in English.

Students were introduced to *Sinterklaas* and *Zwarte Piet* in three stages spanning four lesson hours. These stages were sequenced to familiarize learners with the figures and the holiday as well as to provide them with new language resources to engage in description and narration. Only in the third stage did students begin working with the contentious contemporary representation.

1. Vocabulary building. Using full-color images, students described clothing and colors, activities, seasons, and so on. They then compared additional images of Santa Claus. In addition to introducing new vocabulary, these activities were rich in opportunities for recycling learned material in a new context.

2. Narrative text. Students read an adapted version of *Sinterklaas en zijn knecht* in modern Dutch. Activities expanded on who the figures are and what they do, allowing learners to practice past narration and description.

3. Video analysis. Students viewed a segment of the highpoint of the *Sinterklaasjournaal*'s season, the grand arrival in the Netherlands (Prickaerts, 2001–2015), where thousands of Dutch families line canals singing carols of the season and "journalists" interview prominent

figures including the city's mayor. The occasion has all the trappings of the red carpet transplanted to a gray December day at a small harbor and features myriad Black Petes in blackface parading through a Dutch city of the 21st century.

In order to help students critically process this material, they completed two tasks while watching. First, they recorded their personal reactions in English. The prompt acknowledged that they would likely have unexpected and complicated reactions, which might include emotions from shock to anger to wonderment. Students also recorded any questions they had.

Second, students addressed content questions in Dutch that helped them to describe what they saw and to separate these descriptions from their evaluative, affective responses. This activity, borrowing from Bennett and Bennett's "Describe, Interpret, Evaluate" (D.I.E.) framework (cited in Nam, 2012), encourages learners to practice a suspension of judgment pending careful observation and collection of information (e.g., "Does that comment describe, seek meaning, or judge?"). The questions to guide students' observation were:

- Whom do you see in the video?
- What do they look like (clothing, emotions on their faces, etc.)?
- What are the people doing in the video?
- What else do you see in the video, aside from the people?
- Finally, what is the event that you see?

The subsequent in-class discussion provided learners with an opportunity to consider the reasons for their reactions (always tied to American history and taboos, and seldom informed by Dutch perspectives) and how they can be better informed by Dutch perspectives. Using the at-home observation questions further helped distinguish description from judgment. Students further refined sorting their reactions using the D.I.E. framework. Ultimately, students articulated the role their American culture played when encountering something culturally new.

Such engagement with the *Sinterklaas* holiday addressed several goals. First, students learn to acknowledge the experience of dissonance, such as when *Sinterklaas* and *Zwarte Piet* intersect with American students' cultural histories and perspectives on race relations and the taboo on blackface. This intersection leads to a second goal: students and instructor alike explore ways to understand an individual's reactions to cultural difference. Finally, the focus on students' reactions to difference as well as the process of informed, critical reflection, emphasizes skills to improve understanding (of the self as well as of outside cultural perspectives). Additionally, though this activity occurred among Novice-High/ Intermediate Low students, the intense contemporary debate in the Netherlands over charges of racism attached to the depiction of *Zwarte Piet* could be used with advanced students to develop more sophisticated language skills such as argumentation.

Implications and Conclusions

The above discussion describes instructional interventions in which beginning language students explored and considered contentious sites of Dutch history and cultural practices. The activities were staged to stimulate reflection on students' own cultures and culturally inflected reaction to difference. They highlighted cognitively dissonant moments, which clash with U.S. students' undifferentiated stereotypes of Dutch tolerance and progressivity and offered practices that are applicable to intercultural encounters even after students leave the classroom.

The design of such activities unfolded only in part from a sensitivity to the complications of real life in the TLC. Yes, instructors must have the requisite content knowledge to design lessons on the conflicts and discomforts of the studied community. However, equally important is an approach that asks what learners need in order to come to terms with such tensions. Structured, reflective activities have the potential to be the space in which students can take time to listen to themselves as they process and puzzle through difficult ideas. Such reflections also provide an added benefit to the instructor, as they become spaces in which we can better listen to and understand our students and their needs. The activities described earlier allow for integrated language and culture learning; exploration of contemporary, complicated issues in the TLC; they promote development of transferrable skills that foster a better understanding of the self and others.

As with any new instructional unit, the development of these learning activities requires time. Instructors need to thoughtfully consider the myriad intersections of the cultural artifact in question with the (mis)perceptions their students can bring to the encounter. Gradual design of these activities, in collaboration with instructional teams, can provide valuable professional development opportunities, especially for graduate instructors.

Instructors also need a certain amount of curricular freedom to incorporate these moments into the syllabus, particularly in programs that must "cover" a fixed number of chapters in a textbook. Conventionally published textbooks will not address the content and perspectives considered here. Nor will they provide the flexibility and customization required to improve the lessons over time. Instructors must be provided the space to develop these lessons to their potential. LCTLs especially need this space, because appropriate instructional resources can be difficult to find. Blyth (2013) suggested that open educational resources (OERs) are especially well-suited to help LCTL instructors overcome this shortage of learning materials. This possible solution presents both a challenge and a benefit to the field: instructors become designers, reviewers, publishers, distributors, and adapters of their materials. The creation and distribution of instructional materials move out of the control of publishers and into the purview of instructors.

References

Bass, R., & Elmendorf, H. (2012). Excerpt from *Designing for difficulty: Social pedagogies as a framework for course design in undergraduate education*. Retrieved August 8, 2017, from https://mville.digication.com/alison_s_carsons_eportfolio/ePortfolio_and_Teaching_and_Learning (bottom of the page)

Blyth, C. (2013). Special issue commentary LCTLs and technology: The promise of open education. *Language Learning & Technology, 17*(1), 1–6.

Brienen, R. (2014). Types and stereotypes: Zwarte Piet and his early modern sources. In P. Essed & I. Hoving (Eds.), *Dutch racism* (pp. 179–200). New York, NY: Rodopi.

Brown, A. V. (2009). Less commonly taught language and commonly taught language students: A demographic and academic comparison. *Foreign Language Annals, 42*(3), 405–423.

Byram, M. (1997). *Teaching and assessing intercultural communicative competence*. Clevedon, UK: Multilingual Matters.

Byram, M. (2010). Linguistic and cultural education for bildung and citizenship. *The Modern Language Journal, 94*(2), 317–321.

Byram, M., Gribkova, B., & Starkey, H. (2002). *Developing the intercultural dimension in language teaching*. Strasbourg: Council of Europe.

Crane, C. (2016). Making connections in beginning language instruction through structured reflection and the World-Readiness Standards for Learning Languages. In P. Urlaub & J. Watzinger-Tharp (Eds.), *The interconnected language curriculum: Critical transitions and interfaces in articulated K-16 contexts* (pp. 51–74). Boston, MA: Cengage Learning.

Jordan, J. (2014). The enunciation of the nation: Notes on Colonial Refractions in the Netherlands. In P. Essed & I. Hoving (Eds.), *Dutch racism* (pp. 201–218). New York, NY: Rodopi B.V.

Kern, R. (2000). *Literacy and language teaching*. Oxford: Oxford University Press.

Kruijswijk, M., & Nesse, M. (2006). *Nederlandse jaarfeesten en hun liederen door de eeuwen heen*. Hilversum, The Netherlands: Uitgeverij Verloren.

MLA Ad Hoc Committee on Foreign Languages. (2007). *Foreign languages and higher education: New structures for a changed world*. New York, NY: Modern Language Association of America.

Nam, K. A. (2012). Framework: Describe-analyze-evaluate (DAE). In K. Berardo & D. K. Deardorff (Eds.), *Building cultural competence: Innovative activities and models* (pp. 53–57). Sterling, VA: Stylus Publishing, LLC.

Paesani, K. A., Allen, H. W., & Dupuy, B. (2016). *A multiliteracies framework for collegiate foreign language teaching. Theory and practice in second language classroom instruction series*. Upper Saddle River, NJ: Pearson Prentice Hall.

Prickaerts, A. (Producer). *Het Sinterklaasjournaal*. (2001–2015). [Television Series]. Hilversum, The Netherlands: NTR.

Rathje, S. (2007). Intercultural competence: The status and future of a controversial concept. *Language & Intercultural Communication, 7*(4), 254–266.

Risager, K. (1998). Language teaching and the process of European integration. In M. Byram & M. Fleming (Eds.), *Language learning in intercultural perspective: Approaches through drama and ethnography* (pp. 242–254). Cambridge: Cambridge University Press.

Schama, S. (1987). *The embarrassment of riches: An interpretation of Dutch culture in the Golden Age*. New York, NY: Knopf.

Schenkman, J. (1850). *Sinterklaas en zijn Knecht* (G. Theod, trans.). Amsterdam, The Netherlands: Bom.

Sosulski, M. (2013). From Broadway to Berlin: Transformative learning through German Hip-Hop. *Unterrichtspraxis, 46*(1), 91–105.

Swaffar, J., & Arens, K. (2006). *Remapping the foreign language curriculum: An approach through multiple lteracies.* New York, NY: Modern Language Association of America.

Thring, O. (2010). Consider nutmeg. *The Guardian.* Retrieved from https://www.theguardian.com/lifeandstyle/wordofmouth/2010/sep/14/consider-nutmeg

Veld, A. (2014). Vechten voor nootmuskaat. *National Geographic.* Retrieved August 28, 2016, from http://www.nationalgeographic.nl/artikel/vechten-voor-nootmuskaat

Chapter 12
Engaging Students in Intentional Cultural Learning during Study Abroad

Lara Ducate and Lara Lomicka, University of South Carolina

Introduction

As the number of undergraduates studying abroad steadily rises to 1 in 10 undergraduates in 2016 (see Open Doors Report by the Institute for International Education, 2016), students need to be equipped to navigate living in another country and a different culture. In a recent column, Godwin-Jones (2016) describes how study abroad has changed, including the availability of technology, increased travel options, and the duration of study abroad. For example, last year 63% of students participating in study abroad programs went abroad for eight weeks or less (Godwin-Jones, 2016; Open Door Report, 2016). While the benefits of short-term study abroad include increased cultural awareness and target language (TL) use (Schmidt-Rinehart & Knight, 2004), small gains in oral proficiency, attitude and motivation (Martinsen, 2010), and improvements in cultural and pragmatic competence (Brubaker, 2007; Reynolds-Case, 2013), short-term study abroad also proves to be challenging. Rourke and Kanuka (2012) claim that students in shorter programs often circumvent opportunities for immersion in the local language and culture. They suggest that "avoiding any real need to grapple with intercultural issues, [participants] were in continual contact with their friends and family back home via Facebook, email, and text messaging" (p. 8). Specifically, during short-term stays, research also reports that students indicated that they had little interaction with locals, even in situations where they lived with host families (Knight & Schmidt-Rinehart, 2002, 2010; Schmidt-Rinehart & Knight, 2004).

Given the reported lack of interaction with locals and even with host families, it is crucial that we find ways to engage students in the culture in which they are studying. When students travel overseas, some are equipped with a checklist of things to do or not to do in the target country. While lists may be beneficial in some ways, an alternative (or complementary) approach is to engage students with the target country and culture by encouraging them to intentionally notice their surroundings and environment. The LESCANT model

(Victor, 1992) is a pedagogical framework that equips students to ask questions, notice their surroundings, and become actively engaged observers of their environments. While student blogs, Instagram, and other social media outlets continue to serve as exciting tools for students to document travel and experiences chronologically, as they occur, they do not necessarily ensure that students will delve deeper into critical and reflective thinking. Providing structures and tasks to help students accomplish meaningful engagement with their local milieu can help move them toward the development of situated cultural knowledge and appreciation. This chapter outlines a project in which students were encouraged to engage with and reflect on the local culture using the LESCANT model during their five-week, short-term study abroad program and then reports on the findings based on the online photo collages they maintained during their trip, their final presentations, and surveys completed at the end of the study abroad experience.

Context of Project: Thematic Documentation

In this action research project, students documented their experiences thematically rather than chronologically during their five weeks in Wittenberg, Germany. Ten students chose an instructor-provided topic, such as transport, graffiti, openings, or healthy living, and then identified elements of these themes found in signs and visual representations in the target country. Next, they prepared a digital representation of their theme using Padlet, an online virtual bulletin board (https://padlet.com), and discussed interpretations of these digital images with their host families, who served as intercultural informants to help them make sense of their experiences and sociocultural context (Bakhtin, 1984). Host family informants confirmed or supplemented students' findings and shared culturally relevant information with them.

During their participation in this project, we asked students to actively engage in their environment—to notice what might go unseen, to document what might not appear as obvious, and to identify cultural elements that might not be immediately apparent. As teachers, it is important that we help learners "make culturally-encoded connections between forms, contexts, and meaning in a variety of mediums" (Chun, 2016, pp. 106–107). To ensure the success of this project, contributions from all users were essential to generate content or help with the development process. As Chun (2008) points out, "user-generated content, [. . .] looking for ways to get users involved and feeling like co-developers is what is known as the 'architecture of participation'" (p. 38). By having different topics and serving as co-creators, the students were able to gain a more holistic view of the products, practices, and perspectives within a culture (Cutshall, 2012).

Study Abroad, Noticing, and the LESCANT Model

As students negotiate a new sociocultural and historical context during study abroad and engage in dialogue with new ideas, values, and worldviews, they have the opportunity to grow in their understandings of the world and themselves. As participants examine their own worldview, they are sometimes forced to reassess their beliefs as they learn more about the target culture and seek to integrate their new understandings of the target culture with their previous experiences (Jackson, 2008; Kinginger, 2004; Pavlenko & Lantolf, 2000). The research literature, however, shows variable results regarding what students gain from study abroad experiences: language learning (e.g., in proficiency—Isabelli, 2004; Segalowitz & Freed, 2004; motivation—Allen, 2010), or cultural development (e.g., Brubaker, 2007; Watson, Siska, & Wofel, 2013). And of course, mere participation in study abroad does not necessarily result in learning more about the host country's culture or language (Kinginger, 2009). The LESCANT model helps draw students' attention to the goals of the study abroad experience by encouraging them to notice and document cultural elements and practices in order to augment, and potentially shift, their understanding of the world.

The noticing hypothesis (Schmidt, 1990, 1994, 2001) claims that input does not become intake for language learning unless it is noticed or consciously registered. The premise is that noticing linguistic features induces higher amounts of intake from the available input. To encourage students to become more aware of their surroundings, this study facilitated intentional noticing of elements of the target culture. We focused students' attention on various themes in the target culture by means of the LESCANT model (Victor, 1992). "LESCANT" is an acronym for language, environment, social organization, context, authority, non-verbal, and time. Informed by this model, students were asked to group cultural observations around a particular theme to digitally document those observations and then to reflect, classify, and record their experiences. Students' work, therefore, was both deliberate and intentional in their interaction with culture during the study abroad. As Drewelow (2013) claims, "What learners will acquire, and how they will respond to it, are shaped by a dialogic process between their own representations about the target language, the target culture, and beliefs about the language learning process and students' interactions with peers, their instructors, the media, and other sources of information" (p. 160). Our students were pushed to examine their own ideas about culture as well as their beliefs and to make sense of what they observed as they navigated new sociocultural contexts.

The LESCANT model provides a structured way for students to discuss and reflect on their cultural encounters and experiences (see Table 12.1). Originally designed for international business, Kelm (2011) first implemented this model in L2/international business contexts (http://laits.utexas.edu/lescant/), where he created and maintained a digital database for students and faculty to submit image files and reflect by way of short commentaries on cultural observations while

Table 12.1. The LESCANT Model

LESCANT Model	Definition (from Kelm, 2011; Victor, 1992)
Language	At times, cultures differ due to language differences, which may include attitudes about your own language, insider relationships for those who speak a foreign language, decisions related to which language is used, and how to speak in ways that others will understand you.
Environment	The physical reality such as size, surroundings, population density, climate, food, topography, and so forth.
Social organization	Divisions in society such as kinship and family, education, class, religion, occupation, and gender.
Context	How directly people communicate ideas and words versus how important it is to build a "context" within that communication.
Authority	The role of authority figures and how power and decision making is accomplished. Authority also looks at leadership style and the relationship between bosses and their subordinates.
Non-verbal	Dress and adornment, colors, touch, smell, and the quality of one's voice.
Time	How we organize our calendar and schedule, but it focuses on cultures that follow monochronic time (those that handle one task at a time) and those that follow polychronic time (those that engage in many tasks at the same time).

studying abroad or traveling. Kelm (2011) noted that his students traveling to China experienced "a sense of empowerment in being able to make [. . .] connections, noticing cultural behaviors that students might have otherwise not appreciated" (p. 518). The LESCANT model provides a lens through which students can purposefully notice cultural elements and, as a result, justify why these elements align with a particular category, thus utilizing both reflective and critical skills. Key elements of the LESCANT model are described in Table 12.1.

Due to the documented successes with the LESCANT model (see also Ducate & Lomicka, 2016), it was deemed a promising framework to encourage noticing among the students in our project. Having explored ideas related to cultural interaction, study abroad, and noticing, the next section presents the project, research questions, and preliminary results and provides ideas for implementing similar projects during a short-term study abroad experience.

Methods

Research Questions

During this project, students were encouraged to notice the unfamiliar and to make sense of the cultural images they documented in the L2 setting. Additionally, it was our hope that students would engage in translingual and transcultural experiences (MLA Ad Hoc Committee on Foreign Languages, 2007). Based on these goals, we identified the following research questions:

1. What do students notice as they intentionally pay attention to a particular theme in the host country?
2. How do students' understanding of German or their own cultures change over the five-week program?

Participants

Ten students who were studying abroad for five weeks in Wittenberg, Germany, participated in the project. While in Wittenberg, they lived with German host families and participated in language and culture classes for five to six hours each week day at a language institute and engaged in several planned excursions to Dresden, Berlin, and Halle. Most afternoons were open for free-time activities and exploring. Students ranged in age from 19 to 21 years; there were nine males and one female. All of them had taken courses through Intermediate German. Eight of the 10 students had never been to Germany before, and 2 had briefly visited one other time. Nine of the students were German minors with eight of those majoring in international business or another business-related major. The other German minor was a public relations major and the 10th student was a marine science major. Their goals for this study abroad trip were to learn and experience more about German culture and to improve their German language proficiency. All of the eight business students were planning on spending a semester abroad the following spring, so they viewed this shorter summer trip as preparation for their upcoming longer sojourn away from home.

Pedagogical Intervention

As part of the assigned project, students were instructed to choose a topic from a list of themes identified and provided by the instructor (openings, transportation, home life, free time, cityscape, food/restaurants, graffiti/street art, street signs, healthy living, environmentalism) and to take pictures of images depicting their theme during their five-week sojourn in Germany. During their five weeks abroad, they chose at least 15 culturally salient pictures to post to their personalized Padlet site (see Appendix A for a list of the Padlet URLs, listed by theme). Students focused their projects and thematic discussions on digital images they took from the different cities they visited, including Wittenberg, Berlin, Dresden, and Halle. Due dates for the collection of pictures were spread out over the five weeks to ensure that students posted continuously throughout the program. Students met all together once or twice each week with the supervising teacher from their home institution to discuss their findings. Their teacher served as a mediator to help draw attention to what may have initially been superficial stereotypes to help students reflect more deeply on what they were noticing and to lead guided discussion with the class to help them think about the various perspectives within the sociocultural context they were exploring (Lantolf & Thorne, 2006). In addition to pictures, students were required to describe how the images related to LESCANT categories. Students were introduced to the LESCANT categories in a predeparture meeting where they viewed example photos and practiced categorizing them. They were made aware that there are not necessarily correct answers, but that they should support why they would classify a picture in a certain category. Toward the end of the program, students chose five digital representations (and their corresponding interpretations, which were posted to their Padlets) to discuss with their host family informants. To gain additional perspectives on each digital representation, students worked through interpretations with their host families and revised their initial understandings if necessary. While the host families could have had access to the Padlets since they were available online, students only shared them during their scheduled conversation in which they focused only on their personal Padlet. The purpose of including the host family informants in the tasks was not only to engage students in cultural discussions with their families but also to confirm interpretations or dispel misunderstandings about what was noticed about culture, which they also noted on their Padlets with their initial interpretations in order to help them grow in their intercultural understandings (Bakhtin, 1984; Rourke & Kanuka, 2012). Finally, on the last day of class, students chose three compelling and meaningful images to present to the class, including their interpretations and what they learned from their host family informants, during 10-minute presentations conducted in English. Students also discussed what they gleaned from the project about German culture, culture in general, and about themselves. At the end of the presentations, students completed a short survey on their reactions to the project and what they learned from their pictures and their classmates' presentations.

    The data analyzed in this project included (1) students' 10 Padlets including 15 pictures each and the corresponding captions/descriptions, (2) transcriptions of the final presentations, and (3) post-project surveys (see Appendix B). As an action research project, the researchers performed a qualitative analysis on each of the data sets in order to identify salient themes in students' responses to the project and in their products. The researchers also focused on themes within aspects of German culture that students noticed and how their ideas about culture evolved over the five-week program. The pictures and the comments in the Padlets were analyzed for the types of photos that were posted and commonalities between what students noticed. Excerpts from student writing are not corrected and are presented in the original form. Presentations and discussion occurred in English. After the presentations were transcribed, themes within the presentations were identified and similar findings were grouped together. Surveys were examined for emerging themes in each of the questions. This emic approach to qualitative analysis (Creswell, 2013; Denzin & Lincoln, 2013; Maxwell, 2012; Yin, 2009) employed the students' data as a starting point. Rather than beginning with preconceived notions or hypotheses, the inductive analysis was driven by the themes discovered in the data to better understand the perspective of the students (Brubaker, 2007; Du, 2015; Kinginger, 2011, 2013) and to document their perspectives on culture throughout the five-week program.

Results and Discussion

Results will be presented from three areas: Padlet themes, presentation themes, and survey data. As mentioned earlier, data sets were analyzed for shared themes; examples within each type of data and theme will be discussed.

Padlets

The analysis of students' Padlets led to the identification of several themes that spanned the instructor-provided topics. Although students were assigned topics, they interpreted them flexibly and were able to include a variety of pictures within the larger theme they were assigned. For example, in the openings category, a student included pictures of opened windows and interpreted these as a way to save energy and to have fresh air circulating through rooms. He also posted pictures of gates, front doors, a well, the Brandenburg gate, a train station, a harbor, and the door to which Martin Luther hung the 95 Theses. By including so many different types of openings, the student was able to focus on the historical impact and context of some of these openings as well as how they fit into the LESCANT categories, which helped him to grasp the larger implications of some of these sites. For example, when describing the Brandenburg gate, he traced the history of the gate to what it currently represents, "a symbol of peace after the fall of the Berlin Wall, but in its original construction, it was a sign of separation and distinction among the German people," and cross-categorized it as social organization because of the role it has played in German society.

While some topics lent themselves to more superficial interpretations such as signs, graffiti, and transportation, the LESCANT categorization compelled the students to think about the larger context of the image even if it did not seem to have particular significance in German history or culture at first glance. Linking LESCANT to their assigned categories provided a framework to encourage deeper analysis than if they had only thought about the picture in regard to their themes. The student assigned to transportation, for example, linked the different languages on the subway ticket machine to language, the shops in the train station to environment, a cyclist waiting to cross the street as authority (because he was waiting until the light changed), and the fast train to the category of time since one can travel between cities so quickly and the German rail has a reputation for being punctual. The student who was assigned graffiti found examples of language in the writing on graffiti images, social organization in the graffiti with social commentary, and authority regarding a painting of Anne Frank: "This painting is the embodiment of (Authority) theme and how too much power can become a real evil such as what happened to Anne Frank." The student who focused on street signs was also able to link his signs to larger topics within German culture with the help of the LESCANT framework. For example, he found examples of low and high context signs based on their clarity, authority since many signs are there to mandate certain behavior, and environment for bus and bike signs since they benefit the environment. Rather than simply posting a collection of types of transportation, graffiti, or signs in Germany, LESCANT helped each of these students to analyze different topics within the context of German society and culture.

Delineating Differences

In some cases, students used the Padlet project to delineate differences they found between what they are familiar with in American culture and what they experienced in German culture. While it is not within the scope of this chapter to consider in detail how each student's previous individual experiences determined what he/she noticed in German culture, the role of students' previous sociocultural experiences must be noted as influencing what they discerned and commented on during their five-week sojourn (Byrd Clark & Dervin, 2014). In the German home life Padlet, for example, the author noted aspects that he found interesting about a German home, most of which fell into the categories of social organization and environment. He especially noticed not wearing outside shoes inside, drying clothes on clotheslines, and recycling. He came to various conclusions from this project, including that Germans like to keep their homes "neat and clean" since they do not wear shoes inside. He then confirmed some of these assertions during his interview with his host mother, when she explained, for example, why their bathrooms are small. Additional topics that differed from the U.S. students' prior experiences included healthy living and environmentalism. These topics were further analyzed through the LESCANT categories of social organization, environment, and time. Two authors commented on the propensity of bicycles, home and community gardens, and green spaces, which they felt were more common in Germany than in their home communities in the United States. Images of antismoking campaign ads, home remedies, and free health care were also topics in healthy living, as were pictures of solar panels and wind turbines, separated trash cans for recycling, and depots to which to return bottles in the environment category. From these pictures, students made interpretations about the importance of the environment, health, and nature in the German society they experienced, which also have to do with how people live (social organization), what they surround themselves with (environment), and how they spend time (time). While it is possible to find some of these "differences" in students' home culture, students may now be more open to noticing similar features when they return home now that their worldview has been shifted and broadened (Jackson, 2008).

Forging Similarities

There were also categories that acknowledged or delineated similarities between the German life students experienced and their lives in the United States, such as free time, where the author noticed that Germans engage in many free-time activities that are similar to those practiced by Americans, such as listening to live music, attending festivals, being in nature, attending church events, watching sports, and sightseeing. Social organization, environment, and time were also common categories within free time because of the descriptions of spending time with friends and family and where they spent that time. The student who chose restaurants pointed out different types of restaurants and thereby noticed the diversity within Wittenberg but categorized most of his pictures as either social organization, because that was where people congregated to eat, or language, because of how the items were listed on the menu or the name of the restaurant. The diversity of restaurants seemed to correspond to the diversity one might find in an American city, he noted. The student responsible for cityscapes also noticed the diversity of buildings and architectural features one might find in a German city, from new to old and traditional to modern. He classified many of his pictures as environment, which fits with the theme of cityscapes, non-verbal for the feelings evoked by some of the structures he photographed, such as the Holocaust memorial in Berlin and the Buchenwald concentration camp, and time for the history contained in and represented by the buildings: "Our tour guide in Berlin said to us, 'we don't forget our history, but we do move on.' This picture displays that well." Many of these themes found in the Padlets reoccurred when students contributed their final presentations at the end of their study abroad program.

Presentations

Even though there were 10 different categories for which students came up with varying analyses about German culture, participants converged on several collective interpretations of German culture based on the products, practices, and perspectives they had seen in their own and their classmates' presentations. The main comments centered on time, environment, and social organization, which are categories in the LESCANT framework. Whether students were focusing on healthy living, food, free-time activities, or openings, the LESCANT themes occurred in most of the categories. The assigned topics spanned numerous dimensions of culture and students tended to agree in their conclusions about what they learned about German culture, showing specific instances of a heightening of cultural awareness and a reflective reassessment of some of their earlier beliefs (Jackson, 2008; Pavlenko & Lantolf, 2000).

Time

Germany has traditionally been viewed as a culture that holds a monochronic approach to time, emphasizing schedules and promptness. The LESCANT model prompts students to draw attention to how schedules and time are viewed in other places. Students noticed that Germans seem to take time to enjoy themselves and to really engage in activities, rather than doing something for the sake of completing it. For example, several students remarked on meal times: "Our experience has been we go to dinner and it's an event. You sit down, you eat, you drink, you eat, you drink more. And you're there for quite some time, it's not you scarf down some food and then do something." Another commented, "They really do care about that family time to sit down and discuss politics, what you're doing in school, why you can really get beyond that surface level stuff." A student who focused on transportation noticed a similar phenomenon in trains: "I feel like as their traveling around with family on the trains, the trains are kind of set up where you're able to have family time on the train because you're looking at each other. Whereas when we're traveling, we're in cars, everyone kind of zoned into themselves. I thought that was really interesting and probably goes more into German life and their actual culture when they're able to actually sit there and talk to the family, communicate with each other as their traveling and moving around." Another issue that resonated was the volume of time people seemed to engage in leisure activities, such as going to concerts or festivals, eating out, and working on their homes, cars, and gardens. While a stereotype of Germans is that they are hard workers, students noticed, for example, "We hear about this hard working German mentality but they also like to celebrate everything that they can and find an excuse to. It's really cool. Work hard, play hard." To these students, reflecting on the use of time during conversation, activities, and dinner was striking and challenged them to compare how they value time in their own families.

Environment

A theme that overlapped with time is what students titled Germans' connection to nature, which intersects with the LESCANT category of environment. Many students were surprised at the lengths to which Germans would go to protect the environment, such as recycling, returning used bottles for a deposit, riding bikes, hanging laundry to dry, and traveling by train. As one student pointed out, "I don't think many American citizens would go that far out of their way to actually keep bottles and bring them with them to the supermarket (. . .) So I think it's really telling for the culture and how they're more willing to go out of their way to, not only get their money back, but also help the environment."

Other evidence of Germans' connection to nature were demonstrated by a thermometer on the terrace of a host family's house, how often their families ate outside, rode bikes, and efficiently utilized green spaces in cities and their own yards, such as planting gardens and erecting wind turbines in large fields. A student noted that even the Parliament building (Reichstag) had solar panels and efficient ways to bring in light and heat as a model to the rest of the country. The healthy living student also remarked on nature's influence on mental health, helping people stay centered, and providing home remedies for various illnesses. One presentation concluded with the following quote, which nicely summarizes what he learned about Germans' connection to nature and what it meant to him and his view of American culture:

> Overall the thing I learned is Germans are a lot more environmentally friendly. They're much more conscious about it overall but also I was actually surprised because it seems like, in this case actually, they are much less concerned about time then we are in the states. Because when we do things, we are very much concerned about how long it will take us to do them. How far out of my own way do I have to go to do this thing. Whereas they're much more willing to go out of their way to take public transportation, put their clothes out on a drying line as opposed to a dryer, and stuff like that. They're more willing to sacrifice that time if they think it benefits them more in the long run. Whereas we are more focused on overall convenience and time saved. So that was probably one of the most poignant things I found from my project.

Social Organization

The final topic that came up in most presentations was an aspect of social organization, which seemed to help students understand why things were organized as they were. One student commented, "I think I learned that mostly (. . .) they operate their lives in their households significantly different than the way we do in the United States. But it's not necessarily the wrong way of doing it. Everybody has their way of doing it. And most importantly, if they came to our country they would find what we do odd. So it's kind of interesting, just kind of open your mind and see other possibilities with your own household." Wearing slippers at home, having common courtyards, and spending time in one's garden were topics raised in several projects and students made sense of them by explaining them as part of social organization. They realized that denser living quarters affect how people act and live so that they are more aware of others. The healthy living student even extrapolated this idea to universal health care and explained it as a social responsibility to take care of everyone, "but here they kind of understand it more of a social responsibility for everybody to take care of everybody. [. . .] It's just a very interesting topic to me because I don't think a system like that would ever work in the U.S. But it's cool that it works for them."

Within social organization, diversity and openness to other cultures were also common themes. Students noticed diversity in architecture, food, art, and graffiti, and found there to be a general openness to other cultures through the open boarders, ease of travelling between countries, and transport of goods and people throughout Europe. Openness also came up in regard to conversations with others, "and so I guess the idea of openness, this project has taught me a lot about the people themselves, communicating with them and how open they are to talking about things. Their views on a lot of things that we are too uncomfortable to discuss, they are very blunt, not everybody obviously, but I think I can see the definite trend with a lot of people I've met. A lot of topics that are usually off limits for us are fair game for them. So it's very refreshing to have conversations with people that you would normally have to get to know someone for a long time before you can have them. So it's been a wonderful experience." Many of these student reflections are reiterated in the survey results, discussed in the following section.

Survey

Based on the survey data, it was evident that the project did indeed allow students to notice and interpret aspects of German culture that they likely would have otherwise ignored. When asked what they encountered that they had not expected, one student commented that she was "surprised by how much information you can get out of a simple picture, and the stories that lie behind them that most people wouldn't notice or take the time to think about. I really didn't expect to get as much out of each photo as I did." Two students also noticed similarities to what they might find in the United States: "Many of these pictures could also be in the US. It's good to remember how different we are while being very similar." However, another stated "finding more differences than I expected was the most surprising thing from the photos." Others were surprised by more specific aspects of Germany, such as the "massive and beautiful architecture that is found in almost every German city," solar panels on the Reichstag building, diversity, and how much Germans seem to enjoy their time together. Digital images helped students to discover and attend to their surroundings and to more deeply interpret unique aspects of German culture.

When asked about similarities and differences in German and American cultures, students had varying answers. In terms of similarities, they noticed trends with regard to healthy markets, organic food, and environmentalism. Another student felt that the concept of time was similar among cultures: "We enjoy travel, history, and concerts." Speaking to differences, a student who focused on healthy living noticed that the health-care systems are very different and there are more gardens and bikes in Germany. Students felt that there was a greater emphasis on healthy living in Germany and that Germans take the lead regarding wind and solar power. Several students noticed the trend that Germans are more "willing to recycle or participate in environmental programs." Due to "their love of nature and outdoors," they try to lessen the impact on their surroundings and produce less environmental waste than Americans. These results echo those found in the

Padlet analysis; some students focused on similarities between the two cultures, while others found more differences.

When asked if these projects facilitated conversations with their host families, 7 out of the 10 students said it was helpful to have the questions to stimulate conversation and to facilitate learning while the other three did not feel their hosts engaged in the discussion as much as they would have liked. With the help of a native speaker informant, the majority of the students could delve deeper into their reflections on the photos to affirm or adjust their new understandings about the German culture (Bakhtin, 1984). The final question for students addressed a shifting of their understanding of German/American culture based on their pictures and conversations with their host families. Most students commented that they were now more open to other cultures and had gained a more expansive view of the world. They realized now that the United States is "just one nation among many." One student noticed: "Things about the American culture that I wish were different, but hadn't realized were even an issue before." Other students changed their ideas about German culture: "I have always thought of German culture as being super-efficient and timely, so I would say that my opinion about that shifted. I have now seen them take time out of their day to both recycle and spend time in the garden, which was surprising to me, because we would not do that kind of thing very often." Another student appreciated having to pay attention to his surroundings: "It's too easy to focus on the task at hand or get caught up in your own mind, but the project reinforced the idea that I am here for cultural and linguistic immersion." As noted by Mitchell (2016) and Chun (2015), actively creating their own content through technology increased their interaction with cultural content and ideally their global competence. Through the project, with the help of their teacher and the LESCANT categories, they were pushed to reassess their cultural beliefs as they were confronted with analyzing and interpreting various aspects of German culture (Du, 2015; Kinginger, 2011, 2013; Pavlenko & Lantolf, 2000). In addition, by producing publicly shared projects, they expanded their view regarding the many different themes and student-produced interpretations.

Implementation and Pedagogical Recommendations

Even though this project was initially designed for a short-term study abroad experience, the LESCANT model would also work well domestically. Coordinators and supervisors in first-year language programs could implement projects where students collaborate to complete tasks that allow them to visually and intentionally notice aspects of their own culture and discuss it with native speaker partners or compare domestically documented cultural elements with pictures from the target culture. For example, course schedules and majors/minors are often a common topic in beginning textbooks. Students could compare an image of their daily class schedule to images of class schedules in the target culture and analyze what they have in common. Alternatively, using the context of apartments and houses, students could construct a similar comparison. In language programs with study abroad trips, students overseas could complete a LESCANT Padlet project; their pictures could then serve as input (or be added to a database or Flickr) for beginning-level students in the United States to examine, analyze, and even compare to pictures they find with those in their native culture. In our estimation, such activities would be possible even at lower levels of language study. Cultural discussions and written reflections could take place in the TL or in English depending on students' language proficiency.

Conclusion

As described in the discussion of Padlet descriptions, three themes emerged from the presentations and survey results, and most students converged on a small number of conclusions about German culture. Students attained these reflections through different topics and digital images. This project also allowed students to delve into the target culture, explore a new technological application, and exercise critical thinking as they explored a variety of themes that helped them expand their worldviews and perceptions of themselves and others. Most students commented that they would not have noticed these details had it not been for the project: "It was cool because without this project I probably wouldn't have thought about half these things. (. . .), so it was cool to (. . .) look deeper into their lives here."

By drawing attention to these products, practices, and perspectives, students were able to grapple with German culture and have access to perhaps otherwise unconsidered perspectives of their own culture. Through their work ". . . students can be guided to reflect on their conception of culture by elaborating their own definitions" in a way "that incorporates facts, products, figures, practices and perspectives (big C and little c culture)" (Drewelow, 2012, p. 299). As is evident from the quotes shared, students tended not to judge German culture, but compared it to what they were familiar with. Although students were only in Germany for five weeks, they concentrated on different aspects of German culture as they engaged in meaningful interaction with various informants and peers. Students were able to move beyond a focus on various intercultural issues, as identified in other study abroad contexts (Reynolds-Case, 2013; Rourke & Kanuka, 2012; Schmidt-Rinehart & Knight, 2004), and showed a move toward a more agentive stance that included analyzing their findings guided by the LESCANT model. Their personal and collective analyses pushed them to reflect, negotiate, and examine their observations in different ways, leading to a heightened sense of intercultural competence and encouraging them to be more open other cultures.

As demonstrated through previous research and this project, the act of noticing can have a significant impact on students' linguistic (Schmidt, 1990, 1994, 2001) and cultural awareness (Ducate & Lomicka, 2016). Participants were encouraged to interact with locals and delve into the target culture by examining different themes. Observation of these themes led them to develop curiosity, awareness, knowledge, and sensitivity to the German culture. Since all of the students were engaged in the project, they often found themselves comparing LESCANT categories and themes outside of class. In some cases, students were actively driving their own cultural discussions, another way to engage students in cultural discovery (Drewelow, 2012). While technology can keep study abroad students connected to their friends, family, language, and culture back home (Rourke & Kanuka, 2012), it can also be utilized as a way to intentionally cultivate meaningful interaction within the target culture. These daily confrontations with difference can potentially help increase their capacity for intercultural and global competence (Jackson, 2008; Mitchell, 2016) and expand their understanding of the world and themselves (Jackson, 2008; Kinginger, 2004). Based on these findings, it is our hope that future studies will further investigate cultural noticing in longer study abroad programs, among students with varying language proficiencies, and domestically at all levels of language instruction.

References

Allen, H. (2010). Language-learning motivation during short-term study abroad: An activity theory perspective. *Foreign Language Annals, 43*(1), 27–49.

Bakhtin, M. (1984). *Problems of Dostoevsky's poetics* (C. Emerson, ed., and trans.). Minneapolis, MN: University of Minnesota Press.

Brubaker, K. (2007). Six weeks in the Eifel: A case for culture learning during short-term study abroad." *Die Unterrichtspraxis/Teaching German, 40*(2), 118–123.

Byrd Clark, J. S., & Dervin, F. (2014). Introduction. In J. S. Byrd Clark & F. Dervin (Eds.), *Reflexivity in language and intercultural education: Rethinking multilingualism and interculturality* (pp. 1–42). New York, NY: Routledge.

Chun, D. (2008). Computer-mediated discourse in instructed environments. In S. Magnan (Ed.), *Mediating discourse online* (pp. 15–45). Amsterdam, The Netherlands: John Benjamins.

Chun, D. M. (2015). Language and culture learning in higher education via telecollaboration. Pedagogies. *An International Journal, 10*(1), 5–21. doi: http://doi.org/10.1080/1554480X.2014.999775

Chun, D. M. (2016). The role of technology in SLA research. *Language Learning & Technology, 20*(2), 98–115.

Creswell, J. W. (2013). *Qualitative inquiry & research design: Choosing among five approaches* (3rd ed.). Thousand Oaks, CA: Sage.

Cutshall, S. (2012). More than a decade of Standards: Integrating "cultures" in your language instruction. *The Language Educator*, April, 32–37.

Denzin, N. K., & Lincoln, Y. S. (Eds.). (2013). *The landscape of qualitative research* (4th ed.). Los Angeles, CA: Sage.

Drewelow, I. (2012). Learners' perceptions of culture in a first-semester foreign language course. *L2 Journal, 4*(2). Retrieved from https://escholarship.org/uc/item/73m1p5dx

Drewelow, I. (2013). Impact of instruction on shaping or reshaping stereotypical cultural representations in an introductory French course. *Foreign Language Annals, 46*(2), 157–174.

Du, H. (2015). American college students studying abroad in China: Language, identity, and self-presentation. *Foreign Language Annals, 48*(2), 250–266.

Ducate, L., & Lomicka, L. (2016). Using mobile devices and the LESCANT model to promote cultural awareness. In A. Palalas & M. Ally (Eds.), *The international handbook of mobile assisted language learning* (pp. 222–259). Beijing: China Central Radio & TV University Press Co.

Godwin-Jones, R. (2016). Integrating technology into study abroad. *Language Learning & Technology, 20*(1), 1–20. Retrieved from http://llt.msu.edu/issues/february2016/emerging.pdf

Institute for International Education. (2016). *Open Doors Report on International Education Exchange*. Retrieved from http://www.iie.org/Research-and-Publications/Open-Doors#.WL28lRIrKHp

Isabelli, C. (2004). Study abroad for advanced foreign language majors: Optimal duration for developing complex structures. In H. Byrnes & H. Maxim (Eds.), *Advanced foreign language learning: A challenge to college programs* (pp. 114–130). Boston, MA: Heinle.

Jackson, J. (2008). *Language, identity, and study abroad: Sociocultural perspectives*. London, UK: Equinox.

Kelm, O. R. (2011). Social media: It's what students do. *Business Communication Quarterly, 74*(4), 505–520. doi:10.1177/1080569911423960

Kinginger, C. (2004). Alice doesn't live here anymore: Foreign language learning as identity (re)constructions. In A. Pavlenko & A. Blackledge (Eds.), *Negotiation of identities in multilingual contexts* (pp. 219–242). Clevedon, UK: Multilingual Matters.

Kinginger, C. (2009). *Language learning and study abroad: A critical reading of research*. Basingstoke, UK: Palgrave Macmillan.

Kinginger, C. (2011). Enhancing language learning in study abroad. *Annual Review of Applied Linguistics, 31*, 58–73.

Kinginger, C. (2013). Identity and language learning in study abroad. *Foreign Language Annals, 46*(3), 339–358.

Knight, S. M., & Schmidt-Rinehart, B. C. (2002). Enhancing the homestay: Study abroad from the host family perspective. *Foreign Language Annals, 35*, 190–201.

Knight, S. M., & Schmidt-Rinehart, B. C. (2010). Exploring conditions to enhance student/host family interaction abroad. *Foreign Language Annals, 43*(1), 64–79. doi:10.1111/j.1944-9720.2010.01060.x

Lantolf, J. P., & Thorne, S. L. (2006). *Sociocultural theory and the genesis of second language development*. Oxford, UK: Oxford University Press.

Martinsen, R. (2010). Short-term study abroad: Predicting changes in oral skills. *Foreign Language Annals, 43*, 504–530.

Maxwell, J. A. (2012). *Qualitative research design: An interactive approach* (3rd ed.). Thousand Oaks, CA: Sage.

Mitchell, C. (2016). Web 2.0 use to foster learners' intercultural sensitivity: An exploratory study. In P. Rucks & A. E. Fantini (Eds.), *Dimension special issue: Focus on intercultural competence*. Atlanta, GA: SCOLT Publications.

MLA Ad Hoc Committee on Foreign Languages. (2007). Foreign languages and higher education: New structures for a changed world. Retrieved from http://www.mla.org/pdf/forlang_news_pdf.pdf

Pavlenko, A., & Lantolf, J. P. (2000). Second language learning as participation and the (re)construction of selves. In J. P. Lantolf (Ed.), *Sociocultural theory and second language learning* (pp. 155–177). Oxford, UK: Oxford University Press.

Reynolds-Case, A. (2013). The value of short-term study abroad: An increase in students' cultural and pragmatic competency. *Foreign Language Annals, 46*, 311–322. doi:10.1111/flan.12034

Rourke, L., & Kanuka, H. (2012). Student engagement and study abroad. *Canadian Journal of University Continuing Education, 38*(1), 1–12.

Schmidt, R. (1990). The role of consciousness in second language learning. *Applied Linguistics, 11,* 129–158.

Schmidt, R. (1994). Implicit learning and the cognitive unconscious: Of artificial grammars and SLA. In N. Ellis (Ed.), *Implicit and explicit learning of languages* (pp. 165–209). London, UK: Academic Press.

Schmidt, R. (2001). Attention. In P. Robinson (Ed.), *Cognition and second language instruction* (pp. 3–32). New York, NY: Cambridge University Press.

Schmidt-Rinehart, B., & Knight, S. (2004). The homestay component of study abroad: Three perspectives. *Foreign Language Annals, 37*(2), 254–262.

Segalowitz, N., & Freed, B. (2004). Context, contact, and cognition in oral fluency acquisition: Learning Spanish in at home and study abroad contexts. *Studies in Second Language Acquisition, 26,* 173–199.

Victor, D. (1992). *International business communication.* New York, NY: HarperCollins Publishers Inc.

Watson, J. R., Siska, P., & Wofel, R. (2013). Assessing gains in language proficiency, cross-cultural competence, and regional awareness during study abroad: A preliminary study. *Foreign Language Annals, 46*(1), 62–79.

Yin, R. K. (2009). *Case study research,* 4th ed. Thousand Oaks, CA: Sage. Sage.

Appendices

Appendix A: Padlet topics and URLs

Padlet Topics	URLs
Openings	https://padlet.com/laraducate/38zsfvo15xxh
Transportation	https://padlet.com/laraducate/k0ucnadzzfx0
German home life	https://padlet.com/laraducate/izwrpvc9t3gx
Free-time/recreational activities	https://padlet.com/laraducate/64vv5d30uvxf
Cityscape	https://padlet.com/laraducate/dr17jxwce3j6
Restaurants	https://padlet.com/laraducate/i1mf9ei5v6bl
Graffiti/street art	https://padlet.com/laraducate/hirb35uyc2j2
Street signs	https://padlet.com/laraducate/e0akxidp8776
Healthy living	https://padlet.com/laraducate/d2ec9rn69xdz
Environmentalism	https://padlet.com/laraducate/o5zxlxqlcl6w

Appendix B: Post-survey

POST-WITTENBERG SURVEY—SUMMER 2016

We are conducting a research study about using the LESCANT model to learn about German culture. As part of the study, we will be analyzing the Padlet posts and final presentations completed by all members of class this semester and audio recording the final presentations. Additionally, I would like to invite you to participate in the study by filling out this survey about your experiences with the project this semester. Completion of the survey is entirely voluntary and will have no impact on your course grades. The audio recordings will be kept on a locked computer. The results of the study may be published or presented at professional meetings, but the identity of students will not be revealed. If you do not want me to analyze your course work as part of the study, please let me know. Should you choose to decline participation, it will in no way affect your grades in the course or the work required of you in the course. Thank you, The Researchers.

1. Name
2. Program
3. Length of time in host country
4. Last German class taken
5. Previous experience in Germany
6. Year/Age
7. Major/minor
8. What was your theme?
9. Describe two to three of the pictures you included in the Padlet and comment on why you chose them?
10. What surprised you most from the pictures you took?
11. Describe your most interesting picture. Why did you find it to be interesting?
12. What similarities did you see in how the theme is represented in American and German cultures?
13. What differences did you see in how the theme is represented in American and German cultures?
14. How did the theme facilitate conversation between you and your host family? What kinds of topics did you discuss?
15. Based on the pictures you took and your conversations with the native speaker host family, how did your understanding of German/American culture shift?

Chapter 13
L'incubateur: Increasing Student Engagement through Global Simulation and Gaming Pedagogy in the L2 Classroom

Jeanne M. Johnson, El Dorado Middle School

Introduction

Students in my French class often appear to be more interested in grades than acquiring the target language (L2) and developing their understanding of French-speaking cultures. This led me to reflect on ways in which I could better frame learning opportunities to remedy this situation. The nascent body of research on gaming (e.g., Gee, 2005; Steinkuehler, 2007, 2008; Sykes & Reinhardt, 2012) and social pedagogies (e.g., Bass & Elmendorf, 2012) offers evidence that games could be a means to increase engagement and social interaction centered around the L2. Indeed, games offer an opportunity for contextualized, situated, goal-driven language use in a culturally relevant environment. Additionally, learning through games has been shown to lower the consequences of failure (Gee, 2005), to potentially trigger interest-driven learning, and to foster literacy practices (Steinkuehler, 2007, 2008).

This project describes action research I conducted in which I created a gaming environment in my French classroom. Anchored in the overarching concept of Global Simulation (GS), this learning environment also incorporated an element of competition. My background in project-based learning inspired me to use competition as a means of developing engagement among the students. The students involved in the project were from a French III class in a high-performing suburban high school outside of San Francisco, California.

Pedagogical and Theoretical Frameworks
What Is Global Simulation?
Global Simulation (GS) was developed in France as a pedagogical framework for teaching French and was more widely introduced by Debyser (1996, 1999) and researched by Caré (1993) and Yaiche (1998) within the framework of

L'immeuble, where they simulated a Paris apartment building setting wherein the learners assumed imaginary character roles (in L2 education, see Dupuy, 2006; Mills & Péron, 2009). GS is a communicative approach on one level and on another, an immersion activity that encourages students to act out scenarios that are related to the curriculum based on characters that they have developed themselves (Levine, 2004; Mills, 2009). For example, Mills (2009) had her students develop a *Guide du routard* entry. Students were playing the exploratory traveler going to France to find information about a specific region, which they had to write up in that genre. In a related study with Intermediate-level college French students, Mills and Péron (2009) explored the influence of GS on the writing self-efficacy on 148 students. These students reported higher writing self-concept in French and increased confidence in their writing tasks as a result of their relationships to the characters they had developed.

Educators have used GS in the L2 classroom to reach various pedagogical goals. Levine (2004) orchestrated three different GSs in his Intermediate German classes and found that GS, when carefully scaffolded, affords students the opportunity to engage with a nonlinear, culturally rich learning environment that provides "varied opportunities for meaningful, task-oriented interaction" (p. 34). The simulations ranged from the public to the private spheres. One involved organizing a film festival, and another involved setting up a cultural museum that reflected the target culture. Levine's insights and recommendations on how to structure a GS curriculum proved to be a very useful source as I developed my own methodology.

GS can also focus more in the interpersonal sphere where learners interact with one another in social interactions, such as virtually meeting up with friends and other social activities. Engaging third-year college students on a semester-long GS, Dupuy (2006) used the original idea of *L'immeuble* but with some interesting twists. She successfully simulated life in an apartment building in Paris and used a novel to move the action of the simulation. In addition to the novels, the participants were exposed to authentic video resources in the target language and used social media as they interacted as neighbors in the building. Participants responded positively, and their feedback and the results of the study suggest that the GS increased engagement.

A similar GS study was conducted by Michelson and Dupuy (2014) in a fourth-semester French course. This study was also based on *L'immeuble* (Debyser, 1996) and involved an apartment building scenario in the 14th district in Paris. The 12 participants, all native English speakers, took on francophone identities with the goal developing meaning by taking on a new personality and "re-examin[ing] their views on language, culture, and communication" (p. 33). The results of the study showed that although several of the students still viewed language as a code, by the end of the simulation, they focused more on culture and meaning.

Pedagogical Influences

In addition to the influence of GS, four main areas of research informed the design of my curriculum with the purpose of strengthening student engagement: James Gee's (2005) video game design principles, particularly the concept of agency in design and just-in-time information access; Mihayli Csikszentmihalyi's (1997) Flow theory and more specifically the notion of high engagement and motivation; Henry Jenkins's (2009) participatory culture and its potential for creative expression; and Hazel Markus and Paula Nurius's (1986) possible self theory and how students could be guided to envision themselves as being or acting differently in various contexts and for various purposes. Thus, the GS model used was a blend of many other previously studied GS models, from which ideas were integrated into La Halle Freyssinet simulation. The following is a description of the tools used in collecting data to measure student engagement.

Objectives

This research sought to evaluate whether (1) GS would increase engagement in my high school French III course, (2) participants react positively to GS, and (3) students develop a deeper understanding of culture as they learn language skills while focusing less on grades and more on the tasks devoted to GS. To answer these questions about the impact of GS on student engagement, I used a variety of qualitative and quantitative data sources that I collected from both the instructor and the participants.

Methodology

Participants

At the time of the study, approximately 2,700 students were enrolled at the high school, with that number projected to reach 3,700 over the next five years. The ethnic breakdown of students at my school was 59% Asian, 19% Caucasian, 6% Hispanic/Latino, 5% Filipino, and 4% African American. Most of the students were enrolled in Advanced Placement (AP) courses and were earning university credits while still in high school as a result of AP exam scores and attending night classes at the local community college.

Fifty-two students (34 females, 18 males), between the ages of 14 and 17, participated in this study. About 40 of the participants were Asian, 7 White, 2 Hispanic, 2 Filipino, and 1 African American. Only 7 of the participants reported French as their second language; the remaining participants spoke another language at home other than English. A few students reported French as their fourth language. In addition, over 85% of the participants were enrolled in at least one AP course, with 50% taking more than two AP courses.

Of the 94% of the parents who completed a survey, 52% have earned graduate degrees. Many of these parents work for locally based multinational companies or work in various professions that require high levels of education. This contributed to making the high school an environment where educational attainment was highly valued. In fact, in my own experience, the ever-increasing attention put on earning advanced college units, building a competitive college application through extracurricular activities and SAT scores, and having a grade point average beyond a 4.0 seemed to be focusing students' attention on grades instead of enjoying the learning process. Engagement and empowerment in learning appeared to be taking a back seat to the need to have the "right answer." Consequently, at the start of the course (pre-GS), students seemed less engaged and were only focused on doing just enough to earn an A.

Data Sources

Before starting the simulation, I administered a survey on participants' demographics to be able to correlate these data to the measurement of engagement. Additionally, demographic data gave some richer insights into the participants, including information about prior language learning experiences and engagement. Data were also collected specifically on students' prior and current engagement in French class. In order to evaluate how students' engagement evolved over time (on a rating scale of 1–4), the participants completed this survey three different times throughout the simulation: before the start of the GS, after the third task, *Je me déplace*, and then again after the fourth phase called *On en profite*. The questions in the survey were written specifically to measure the enjoyment of studying French, specifically how certain aspects of choice and relevance impacted students' engagement. As such, it was a useful tool for me to reflect and possibly adjust the simulation according to the participant feedback.

Participants also wrote a final reflection after the final marketing presentation (described later in the chapter). This final reflection aimed at getting overall feedback that would contribute to collecting data about whether the simulation increased their engagement in French class. This final paper was a means of probing for deeper reflection on engagement and was used to supplement the other engagement measures. In this final reflection, I coded comments to attempt to quantify students' engagement.

Pedagogical Procedures

In this project, the objectives for students were to imagine themselves as creators of start-up companies in La Halle Freyssinet and envision specific scenarios in which they had to interact in French. For example, students might create a product and market it to an audience or develop a business plan and compete for investors.

Introducing the Start-Up Incubator

La Halle Freyssinet is an actual start-up incubator located in the 13th Arrondissement in Paris. At the onset of this research, the construction of La Halle Freyssinet was not complete. The nearly 370,000-square foot former train station is being built to house 1,000 start-ups and recently opened in June 2017 under the name Station F (https://stationf.co). At the time of the kick-off of the student project, there was a website with videos of what the space would look like upon completion. I used this website to introduce participants to the idea of a start-up incubator. This initial explanation of the project was done in the L1 to ensure that students understood what their roles in the experiment would be.

Once the participants were clear on the concept of converting the classroom into a virtual setting, they began developing their roles in the start-up incubator by creating their future selves in the L2. They were given specific guidelines about geographical location, including their virtual proximity to La Halle Freyssinet in the 13th arrondissement of Paris. They were also required to create their résumé as if it were 10 years in the future. This allowed them to explore their future identities in the target language. The appropriate vocabulary and grammar structures were provided to the students when needed, according to the task in question. Students presented their future selves to their peers, which provided valuable information for myself and for other students who would be searching for colleagues for their start-up enterprise teams. Participants were encouraged to room together in Paris, selecting just the right apartment, including furniture and other decorations. Students also presented their living spaces to the class, an opportunity to recycle previous vocabulary from their first two years of French.

From then on, when students arrived for French class, they were given a detailed task in the L2. Some of the tasks, which were designed to encourage exploration of their virtual neighborhoods, included planning an evening out with friends, seeing a movie on a Saturday night, and other outings involving finding activities and transportation to them. These outings were assigned to the participants using a web-based classroom where they could share their experiences through blogging, which usually required students to produce new vocabulary and specific grammar structures that were supported by short, focused grammar reviews and the occasional introduction of a new grammar structure.

After their virtual future selves were established, participants were introduced to La Halle Freyssinet as the venue for start-ups in the 13th arrondissement in Paris. They explored the website for the venture, which is now called Station F. They were encouraged to imagine themselves in this workspace, developing an enterprise based on their personal interests, prior background knowledge, future aspirations, and a vision of a marketable niche to be filled. Students were encouraged to choose colleagues that would reflect their own work ethics and about what start-up ideas would interest them. Despite my anxiety about these groups forming organically on the basis of participants' interests, teams materialized without problems.

Start-Ups in Paris as Authentic Texts

In the preliminary stages of the virtual start-up incubator, participants worked on authentic texts in the form of news articles, websites, and videos, most of which focused on existing start-up enterprises in Paris and environs. In some instances, students would be assigned to interact with the start-ups as virtual consumers in response to a task. For example, students looked at a text on a rideshare start-up. They were provided with materials to facilitate their comprehension of the article and related website, including grammar structures that were targeted and that would be included in their responses in the task.

Participants were exposed to enterprises in different sectors such as medical services, fashion, and food-related businesses, to name a few. They were also encouraged to investigate sectors in which they were interested on mystarup.paris.fr, which proved to be a valuable resource. This independent exploration of current start-ups located in Paris was engaging for the students because they were researching what interested them rather than being assigned texts.

Our research on the start-up scene in Paris brought us into a partnership with an actual start-up called Meludia, a web-based music instruction program. The founder of this company became interested in our project. Since this company was in its founding stage and looking for feedback from potential subscribers, we agreed to use the site and provide feedback to the developer. This led to an exciting exchange between the founder of the company and the participants. We arranged a video conference call so the students could ask advice about their own companies that they were developing in their teams. They prepared questions in advance in the target language. On the morning of the video conference, participants met with the founder of Meludia at an elegant hotel in Paris as he had just finished a meeting with a potential investor. Students attempted to ask their questions in the L2, but the dialogue quickly transitioned to English, in which our colleague in France was fluent. He gave us a lesson on how start-ups are funded and encouraged our students in their own virtual start-ups. So the pedagogical merits were not the L2 conversation, as initially planned. However, student engagement was high during that call, which was one of the objectives. There was also a valuable cultural exchange during the call, as students learned about business practices that in turn informed their start-up projects. In short, the benefits far outweighed the lack of L2 production during the call itself and made it a useful building block to the course.

The GS Units

The length of the study was from August to January, an entire academic semester. The project progresses in five phases presented in the following table:

Phase 1	*Je me présente...*	September

1. Students are introduced to models on how to introduce themselves. They recycle the vocabulary needed to talk about themselves, their families and their daily routine, and their work life that they learned in the previous year.
2. Students begin to produce a profile on Haiku Learning and interact with others that live in their neighborhood. Business and business networking vocabulary and grammar are essential and are introduced and reinforced through formative and summative assessments.
3. Students are assigned correspondents from our partner school in Narbonne, France, with the goal of the French students becoming business consultants.

Phase 2	*La start-up*	October

1. Students continue to experience business vocabulary in contexts of actual use.
2. A series of start-ups are presented to the participants through articles and media such as commercials and YouTube videos.
3. Students share out, in the L2, their interests and what sort of product or service they would like to create.
4. Students begin to take on their roles and begin to design and create the marketing plan.
5. Students continue to create entries on a daily basis.
6. An emphasis is put on the subjunctive tense.
7. Students are presented with appropriate vocabulary and grammar structures that enable them to increase their ability to express themselves.
8. Students are evaluated on a weekly basis, formatively and summatively. Students, now working on a team, also have one assessment as a team where they all receive one grade.

Phase 3	*Je me déplace...*	November–December

1. Students explore the realm of transportation. Vocabulary and grammar conventions that support the discussion of "getting around" Paris are presented, including giving directions, finding the best restaurants, and traveling outside of Paris and beyond for possible business opportunities.
2. Students present, as part of an assessment, a tour of their neighborhood and workspace.

Phase 4	*On en profite!*	December

1. As the holiday season begins, students explore the various winter holidays that are celebrated. Culturally related texts are presented. Students express how they spend the holiday season according to what is presented to them during their analysis of texts.
2. Since students have been working hard, they must decide on how to take some time to honor their efforts so far. Students plan and execute a holiday party to celebrate their ongoing efforts.
3. Party planning: vocabulary, grammar, and etiquette are presented; students are evaluated as a team on their efforts.
4. Students make their first formal presentation of an actual start-up in Paris they have researched.
5. Participants are encouraged to contact the founders of these companies.

Phase 5	*Le marketing!*	January

1. After the winter break, it is time to finalize the marketing plan and begin planning the final presentation.
2. Students are presented with presentational skill-building activities.
3. Students are in production mode on their websites.
4. Students present their final marketing plan to the class.
5. Participants who do not present the plan form a question panel and are assessed on the quality and depth of their questions to the presenters.
6. Students write a final reflection in their L1, which serves as a data source to include in findings.

Findings

Did GS increase student engagement in my French III classes? The results of this study of GS and student engagement were overall positive in the narratives but less revealing in the quantitative surveys. This may be due in part to the limitations of accurately measuring engagement. Quantifying engagement and differentiating it from motivation also becomes a factor. On the one hand, motivation refers to learners and the way in which they approach the material when there is a reward, such as a positive grade or evaluation. On the other hand, engagement happens when learners are deeply involved in the L2 material, but the reward is the enjoyment and intrinsically valuable learning that they experience from the tasks.

Getting Started

The student feedback narratives in November indicated a slight decrease in engagement. It is important to mention that when asked whether they preferred the simulation to using the textbook, 38% of the participants said they preferred the use of the textbook. They used words such as "structure," "worksheets," and "easier to understand." Other participants who preferred the simulation used comments, including the words "freedom to choose," "more relevant to real life," and, my favorite, "it connects to my radical side." Instructor journal entries during this time were also consistent with the decline in engagement. I noted on five occasions during the month of November when I perceived the students to be off-task and six times when they seemed less engaged than usual.

In contrast to the aforementioned data, in November, participants were also asked to finish the sentence: "I feel truly engaged in learning when. . ." A pattern emerged out of the participant responses. Out of 46 participant responses, 41.5% cited something having to do with working with a group of peers as true engagement. For example, "I feel truly engaged when you give us a group assignment and we all work on it together." Another participant said, "I feel truly engaged when I can collaborate with my peers." However, 19.5% of participants offered more teacher-centered completions to this sentence, such as, "I feel truly engaged when the information is clear and concise" or ". . . when I have been given clear directions and explanations." Others offered responses more related to learning modes and how they process or demonstrate what they learned as a completion to the sentence like "I feel truly engaged when I am up and doing an activity like speaking. . ." Another 11% offered a response that was more related to choice. One participant stated, "I feel truly engaged when there is designing involved and I am given a very vast amount of options." An equal 6.5% said either something related to project learning or just having fun. One student said, "I feel truly engaged when I am allowed to enjoy what I do instead of following a strict standard."

Adding Structure

In light of these data, I decided to "tighten" up the curriculum. I also took students' age into consideration. Many of the students were responding favorably to the simulation and actually showed characteristics of flow and engagement, that is to say intense motivation for and absorption in the task at hand at a time when the challenge level and the skill level are simultaneously high. A small portion of the students, however, were using the simulation as a way to avoid tasks to the dismay of their partners. I addressed this situation by bringing back classroom procedures that I had previously been neglecting and that students had been used to in previous years. I reinstated a *verbe du jour* activity, regular conversation activities in the L2, and consented to include some activities from the textbook. The simulation did not lose momentum, and simultaneously the students were given what they perceived to be structure. More regular assessments were also given to increase accountability (e.g., quizzes).

GS and Engagement

The first question on the survey addressed how much they enjoyed French class, in general. Before the GS began, about 55% of the participants agreed that French class was one of their favorite places to be during the day, while another 11% strongly agreed to French class being their favorite. This could be indicative of a rather high level of initial engagement. However, about 33% did not agree with the statement. Not one student strongly disagreed. The student interviews and narratives showed that a very small percentage of students did not respond to the GS.

From the surveys, there seemed to be a dip in engagement midway through the study, which could be partly due to the semester-length duration of the study. While doing the simulation for the first time, an instructor must create materials from day to day, which is a tall order. When students were asked if they wished they could continue working in French class when the class period ended because they were enjoying what they were doing, 10% of participants reported "often" in August. This number dipped slightly in November and then climbed back up to 11% in January. While only a small percentage of participants reported this, I find it to be compelling evidence for this pedagogical approach.

Overall, student engagement increased slightly from the previous years as a result of GS. The start-up activity challenged them just enough without being too difficult. This was primarily a result of adding an element of choice, as well. Although the data show that those who did not previously enjoy French class rose by 2%, the overall amount of participants who disagreed with the statement that French class was one of their favorite places decreased by 10%. Overall, by the end of the simulation, 75% of the participants reported French class as being one of their favorite places to be during the day, up from 67% from the beginning of the year. In other words, the data show that student engagement increased during the GS.

In interviews, students were asked about the challenges they faced during the GS that were an obstacle to their engagement in the material. About 28% of the students indicated that the nature of the GS at least one time or more throughout the semester was an obstacle to their engagement. One student said, "Generally, this start-up didn't teach me anything. I don't learn anything compared to just using the traditional teaching with the textbooks." Another student said, "The thing that bothered me is the more focus on building a company than on learning French." On the other hand, 43% of the students stated that there was no challenge to their engagement during the GS. One student replied, "I actually didn't experience any challenges in the start-up activity that affected my engagement. Our group is always on task, we are kind, open-minded, responsible, and we know that we must win the start-up competition, which motivates us to work harder." Many students said that they didn't face any challenges that hindered their engagement. Another 13% focused on the challenges that group work put on their engagement, while 15% offered various responses not related to the nature of GS but more issues such as technological difficulties or personal issues related to the organization. Finally, one student offered up a fear of public speaking as a challenge to engagement.

Finally, an additional insight that emerged from the data concerns the notion of future selves. When participants were asked whether or not this simulation inspired them to reflect on their future educational and career goals, 57% of the participants reported that the start-up simulation inspired a career pathway for them. When participants were asked whether the simulation should be repeated the following year, only two participants reported that it should not be repeated.

Students showed evidence of language learning in the elaboration of their final projects and during their final presentations. Students had been instructed not to memorize their lines. Most students delivered genuine presentations, whether about Parisian life, their future selves, or even the final funding pitch, which was judged by community members. There was very little reading from slides, and no cue cards were allowed. The projects students chose to pursue indicated their creativity, their agility with language, and their mindset as a connected generation: a social network for foodies (foodbook.com), a blog reporting impartial news (intheloop.com), a car fueled by sea water (dri3ve.com), or a smart contact lens (eyecomp.com).

Conclusion

This study arose out of my frustration and my perception of a preoccupation with grades on the part of my students. As an instructor, it is frustrating when students are focused more on the grade than being engaged in the content. This experience was rewarding for me as an educator because the students were frequently immersed in problem-solving activities, and the collaboration between students and with me as the instructor were also engaging.

My first observation regarding the findings of this study is that a focus on grades and high engagement in learning French are not mutually exclusive. There are cultural reasons that explain students' preoccupation with grades, and while prioritizing their GPAs didn't change, qualitative and quantitative measures of engagement did increase as a result of GS. There remained not only frequent questions about grades but also abundant conversations relating to French language, culture, and other content areas. I also recognized and, in a way, came to terms with the cultural background and daily pressures for academic success that these students faced. Most importantly, this action research project helped me understand how to structure a pedagogical intervention that placed meaning at its center. In turn, it helped students envision not only their engagement in French class but also their future selves in and with French.

References

Bass, R., & Elmendorf, H. (2012). Designing for difficulty: Social pedagogies as a framework for course design. Retrieved from https://blogs.commons.georgetown.edu/bassr/social-pedagogies/

Caré, J.-M. (1993). Le village: une simulation globale pour débutants. *Le Français dans le monde, 34*(261), 48–57.

Csikszentmihalyi, M. (1997). *Finding flow: The psychology of engagement with everyday life. The masterminds series.* New York, NY: Basic Books.

Debyser, F. (1996). *L'immeuble.* Paris, France: Hachette.

Debyser, F. (1999). L'art pédagogique de la simulation. Retrieved April 19, 2007, from http://www.missionlaique.asso.fr/pedagogie/pdf/franc36/cf36p63.pdf

Dupuy, B. (2006). "L'Immeuble": French language and culture teaching and learning through projects in a global simulation. In G. H. Beckett & P. Chamness Miller (Eds.), *Project-based learning in second language education: Past, present and future, research in second language learning* (pp. 195–214). Greenwich, CT: Information Age Publishing, Inc.

Gee, J. P. (2005). Pleasure, learning, video games, and life: The projective stance. *E-Learning, 2*(3), 211. doi:10.2304/elea.2005.2.3.2

Jenkins, H. (2009). *Confronting the challenges of participatory culture: Media education for the 21st century.* Cambridge, MA: The MIT Press.

Levine, G. S. (2004). Global simulation: A student-centered, task-based format for Intermediate foreign language courses. *Foreign Language Annals, 37*(1), 26–36. doi:10.1111/j.1944-9720.2004.tb02170.x

Markus, H., & Nurius, P. (1986). Possible selves. *American Psychologist, 41*(9), 954–969. doi:10.1037/0003-066x.41.9.954

Michelson, K., & Dupuy, B. (2014). Multi-storied lives: Global simulation as an approach to developing multiliteracies in an Intermediate French course. *L2 Journal, 6*(1), 21–49.

Mills, N. (2009) Task-based course development: A guide du Routard simulation. In L. Stone & C. Wilson-Duffy (Eds.), *Task-based III: Expanding the range of tasks with online resources.* Publication of the International Association for Language Learning Technology.

Mills, N., & Péron, M. (2009). Global simulation and writing self-beliefs of Intermediate french students. *International Journal of Applied Linguistics, 156*, 239–273.
Steinkuehler, C. A. (2007). Massively multiplayer online gaming as a constellation of literacy practices. *eLearning, 4*(3), 297–318.
Steinkuehler, C. A. (2008). Cognition and literacy in massively multiplayer online games. In J. Coiro, M. Knobel, C. Lankshear, & D. Leu (Eds.), *Handbook of research on new literacies* (pp. 611–634). Mahwah, NJ: Erlbaum.
Sykes, J., & Reinhardt, J. (2012). *Language at play: Digital games in second and foreign language teaching and learning*. Upper Saddle River, NJ: Pearson-Prentice Hall.
Yaiche, F. (1998). Construire et simuler avec les apprenants (Constructing and simulating with students). *NeusprachlicheMitteilungen aus Wissenschaft und Praxis, 51*(4), 227–235.

Editors

Sébastien Dubreil (Ph.D., Emory University) is Teaching Professor of French and Francophone Studies, Second Language Acquisition, and Technology-Enhanced Learning at Carnegie Mellon University. Specializing in CALL, he focuses on the use of technology in fostering transcultural learning. His most recent research examines the notions of social pedagogies, linguistic landscapes, and game-based language and culture learning.

Steven L. Thorne (Ph.D., University of California-Berkeley) is Professor of Second Language Acquisition in the Department of World Languages and Literatures at Portland State University (USA), with a secondary appointment in the Department of Applied Linguistics at the University of Groningen (the Netherlands). His interests include new media, mobile technologies, contextual traditions of language analysis, and usage-based and distributed approaches to language development.

Contributors

Misla Barco (M.A., San Jose State University; M.A., The National Hispanic University) is an educator, community activist, and cultural ambassador. She teaches Spanish for heritage learners and heads the Spanish Department at East Palo Alto Academy, where she co-developed and co-teaches a Spanish community engagement course. In 2012, Misla was a National Teacher honoree and received the Stanford Community Award.

Vivian Brates, (M.A., Georgetown University, Latin American Studies/Economic Development, and M.A., UC Santa Barbara, Spanish/Latin American Literature), is a native of Argentina has worked as a human rights observer (UN International Civilian Mission in Haiti), an international consultant and an election monitor (Haiti, Dominican Republic, Venezuela, and Guatemala). Since 2005, she has served as Lecturer in Spanish at Stanford University.

Alberto Bruzos (Ph.D. in Linguistics, Universidad de León) is Director of the Spanish Language Program at Princeton University. He has published on linguistic relativity and the pragmatics of irony. Currently, his research interest lies in language ideologies, the role of language in the critique of neoliberalism, and the commercialization of language in L2 education.

Irene Carvajal (M.F.A., San Francisco Art Institute) is a multidisciplinary Costa Rican American artist whose practice includes printmaking, collage, sculpture, and installation. She is the recipient of the Bronze Roller Award. She currently lectures at San Jose State University and Stanford University.

Stéphane Charitos (Ph.D. University of North Carolina-Chapel Hill) is Director of the Language Resource Center at Columbia University. He has given papers and published in areas as diverse as 16th- and 20th-century French and Francophone literature, cultural and film studies, modern Greek studies, critical theory, and on issues related to technology, globalization, and language education.

Cori Crane (Ph.D., Georgetown University) is Associate Professor of the Practice and German Language Program Director at Duke University. Her research focuses on curriculum development, systemic functional linguistics, language teacher education, and reflective teaching and learning. Her publications have appeared in *L2 Journal, Die Unterrichtspraxis/Teaching German, Profession*, and previous AAUSC volumes.

Citlalli Del Carpio, (M.A. in Spanish Language and Culture, Arizona State University) is a native of Mexico City, a lecturer in Spanish at Stanford University. She is a certified oral and writing proficiency tester for the American Council on the Teaching of Foreign Languages (ACTFL).

Isabelle Drewelow (Ph.D. in Second Language Acquisition, University of Wisconsin-Madison) is Associate Professor of French and Applied Linguistics and Language Program Director for elementary-and intermediate-level French language instruction at the University of Alabama. Since 2010, she has supervised graduate student assistants there.

Lara Ducate (Ph.D., University of Texas at Austin) is Professor of German and Applied Linguistics at the University of South Carolina, where she serves as the Director of Basic Courses for the German Program. Her research interests include teacher education, intercultural learning, mobile learning, study abroad, service learning, integrative learning, and incorporating sustainability into the curriculum.

Vivian Finch (Ph.D., Vanderbilt University) is an Assistant Director at the Vanderbilt University Center for Teaching, with a primary focus on graduate student and postdoctoral professional development. She is also affiliated faculty in the Department of German, Russian, and East European Studies, where she teaches German language courses.

Matthias Fingerhuth (Ph.D., University of Texas at Austin) holds a postdoctoral position at the Special Research Program (SFB) "German in Austria" at the University of Vienna. His research focuses on linguistic variation in German.

Jessica Greenfield (Ph.D., University of North Carolina-Chapel Hill) is the Director of the Cooper International Learning Center and Lecturer in Italian language, literature, and culture at Oberlin College. Her research interests include the Scholarship of Teaching and Learning, building intercultural competency, and Mediterranean history and culture.

Paitra Houts (M.A. in Education, Stanford University) spent six years working with the Boys & Girls Clubs of the Peninsula, supporting community partnerships and student growth. She currently serves as the Director of Community Engaged Learning focused on Education at Stanford.

David Huenlich (Ph.D., University of Texas at Austin) is a junior researcher at the Institut für Deutsche Sprache (Institute for the German Language) in Mannheim, Germany, and is currently studying the linguistic integration of refugees. Apart from his research in migration linguistics, he develops teaching tools for language and content courses.

Jeanne M. Johnson (M.A. in French Instruction, Southern Oregon University) is a secondary French teacher at El Dorado Middle School in Concord, California. She received her B.A. in History from the University of California, Berkeley. She has a strong interest in technology-enhanced project-based learning with a focus on increasing learner engagement, transcultural learning, and language acquisition.

Stacey Margarita Johnson (Ph.D., University of Memphis) is an Assistant Director at Vanderbilt University's Center for Teaching and Senior Lecturer in the Department of Spanish and Portuguese. Her work on critical pedagogy and technology includes the podcast "We Teach Languages" as well as books on adult learning in language classrooms and hybrid language instruction.

Lara Lomicka (Ph.D., Penn State University) is Professor of French at the University of South Carolina, where she works as Faculty Principal of Preston Residential College. Previously she served as Graduate Director for Languages and Basic Courses Director for French. Her research focuses on intercultural learning, social media, and CALL.

Alice A. Miano (Ph.D. in education in language, literacy, society, and culture from the University of California, Berkeley) is Coordinator of the Spanish Language Program and Lecturer in Spanish at Stanford University and is a certified ACTFL trainer and tester in oral and writing proficiency.

Kristen Michelson (Ph.D., University of Arizona) is Assistant Professor (French and Applied Linguistics) and French Language Program Director at Texas Tech University. Her research focuses on learner-centered multiliteracies-oriented pedagogies in teaching and learning foreign languages, including global simulation and digital social reading, teacher professional development, and the role of discourse in shaping learner beliefs.

Lindsy Myers (Ph.D. in French Linguistics, University of Texas at Austin) is Associate Teaching Professor of French and Director of the beginning language program at the University of Missouri–Kansas City. Her research interests include the study of spoken French and its application to the classroom.

Stéphanie Pellet (Ph.D. in French Linguistics, University of Texas at Austin) is Associate Professor of French and Coordinator of French Lower-Division at Wake Forest University. Her research interests include French pragmatics, L2 literacy, and Web 2.0 for language learning.

Elyse Petit (Ph.D., University of Arizona) is Senior Lecturer of French at Vanderbilt University. Her interests focus on the fusion of new and critical media literacies approaches to foster language learning and social justice awareness and to enhance learners' voice and agency. Her recent projects include digital storytelling, digital social reading, and global simulation.

Diane F. Richardson (binational Ph.D. program, Trans-cultural German Studies, at Universität Leipzig and University of Arizona) is Assistant Professor of German at the U.S. Military Academy, West Point. Her research focusses on language and literacy learning, with particular interest in ambiguity, multilingualism, and linguistic landscapes.

Diana Ruggiero (Ph.D. in Spanish, the Ohio State University) is an Assistant Professor of Spanish at the University of Memphis. She specializes in Spanish for Specific Purposes (SSP) and Community Service Learning (CSL). Her current research concerns SSP and CSL pedagogy, design, assessment, and issues.

Vincent L. VanderHeijden (Ph.D., University of Texas at Austin) is Lecturer of German and Dutch at the University of Texas at Austin where he directs the Dutch Language Program and teaches early-advanced German courses. His research interests focus on the intersection of culture and language learning in instructional contexts.

Nelleke VanDeusen Scholl (Ph.D, University of California-Berkeley) is Associate Dean of Yale College, Director of the Center for Language Study, and Professor

(Adjunct) of Linguistics at Yale University. Her research focuses on applied linguistics, technology, and heritage language education. With Nina Spada, she is Series Editor of *Language Learning and Language Teaching* (John Benjamins).

Chantelle Warner (Ph.D, University of California-Berkeley) is Associate Professor of German Studies, faculty member of the interdisciplinary program in Second Language Acquisition and Teaching, and Co-Director of CERCLL at the University of Arizona, where she also directs the German Language Program. Her research focuses on affective, experiential and aesthetic dimensions of language use and learning.